Rosenauer & Weathersby

TEXAS

Real Estate Promulgated Contracts

OnCourse Learning

Texas Real Estate Promulgated Contracts, First Edition

Johnnie Rosenauer and Melissa Weathersby

Executive Editor: Sara Glassmeyer

Project Manager: Arlin Kauffman, LEAP Publishing Services

Print and Digital Project Manager: Abby Franklin

Art and Cover Composition: Chris Dailey

Cover Image: © David Hughes

The credit lines are as follows:

Chapter 1 - Shutterstock_168857699 - © Shutterstock / Pressmaster

Chapter 2 - Shutterstock_154987517 - © Shutterstock / wavebreakstudio

Chapter 3 - Shutterstock_189588863 - © Shutterstock / Stuart Jenner

Chapter 4 - Shutterstock_174543086 - © Shutterstock / Monkey Business Images

Chapter 5 - Shutterstock_154681310 - © Shutterstock / Minerva Studio

Chapter 6 - Shutterstock 156241634 - © Shutterstock / pressmaster

Chapter 7 - Shutterstock_193501406 - © Shutterstock / pressmaster

Chapter 8 - Shutterstock_166727513 - © Shutterstock / g-stockstudio

Chapter 9 - Shutterstock_154985321 - © Shutterstock / Bartek Zyczynski

For product information and technology assistance, contact us at **OnCourse Learning and Sales Support, 1-855-733-7239.**

For permission to use material from this text or product.

Library of Congress Control Number: 2015943826

ISBN-13: 978-1-62980-004-2

ISBN-10: 1-62980-004-X

OnCourse Learning
3100 Cumberland Blvd., Suite 1450
Atlanta, GA 30339
USA

Visit us at **www.oncoursepublishing.com**

Printed in the United States of America
2 3 4 5 6 7 20 19

BRIEF CONTENTS

CONTENTS

Contents

CHAPTER 4   COVENANTS, COMMITMENTS, AND NOTICES   145

CHAPTER 5   CLOSING, POSSESSION, AND MORE   163

CHAPTER 8   OTHER REAL ESTATE MATTERS   221

TABLE OF TREC PROMULGATED CONTRACTS, ADDENDA, NOTICES, AND FORMS

TITLE	FORM NUMBER
PROMULGATED CONTRACTS	
Unimproved Property Contract	9-12 (11/02/2015) (Effective January 1, 2016 for required use)
One to Four Family Residential Contract (Resale)	20-13 (11/02/2015) (Effective January 1, 2016 for required use)
New Home Contract (Completed Construction)	24-14 (11/02/2015) (Effective January 1, 2016 for required use)
New Home Contract (Incomplete Construction)	23-14 (11/02/2015) (Effective January 1, 2016 for required use)
Farm and Ranch Contract	25-11 (11/02/2015) (Effective January 1, 2016 for required use)
Residential Condominium Contract (Resale)	30-12 (11/02/2015) (Effective January 1, 2016 for required use)
PROMULGATED ADDENDA	
Addendum for Sale of Other Property by Buyer	10-6 (as of 12/05/2011)
Addendum for Back-up Contract	11-7 (as of 12/05/2011)
Addendum for Release of Liability on Assumed Loan and/or Restoration of Seller's VA Entitlement	12-3 (as of 12/05/2011)
Seller's Temporary Residential Lease	15-5 (as of 12/05/2011)
Buyer's Temporary Residential Lease	16-5 (as of 12/05/2011)
Seller Financing Addendum	26-7 (11/02/2015) (Effective January 1, 2016 for required use)
Environmental Assessment, Threatened or Endangered Species, and Wetlands Addendum	28-2 (as of 12/05/2011)
Addendum for Coastal Area Property	33-2 (as of 12/05/2011)
Addendum for Property Located Seaward of the Gulf Intracoastal Waterway	34-4 (as of 12/05/2011)
Addendum for Property Subject to Mandatory Membership in an Owner's Association	36-8 (as of 12/05/2011)

Third Party Financing Addendum for Credit Approval	40-7 (11/02/2015) (Effective January 1, 2016 for required use)
Loan Assumption Addendum	41-2 (as of 12/05/2011)
Addendum for Reservation of Oil, Gas, and Other Minerals	44-2 (as of 11/18/2014)
Short Sale Addendum	45-1 (as of 12/05/2011)
Addendum for Property in a Propane Gas System Service Area	47-0 (as of 2-01-2014)
PROMULGATED AMENDMENT	
Amendment to Contract	39-8 (11/02/2015) (Effective January 1, 2016 for required use)
PROMULGATED RESALE CERTIFICATES	
Condominium Resale Certificate	32-4 (11/02/2015) (Effective January 1, 2016 for required use)
Subdivision Information, Including Resale Certificate for Property Subject to Membership in a Property Owner's Association	37-5 (as of 2-10-2014)
PROMULGATED NOTICE	
Notice of Buyer's Termination of Contract	38-5 (11/02/2015) (Effective January 1, 2016 for required use)
PROMULGATED CONSUMER DISCLOSURES	
Consumer Information Form	CN 1-2 (11/02/2015) (Effective February 1, 2016 for required use)
Disclosure of Relationship with Residential Service Company	RSC 2 (11/02/2015) (Effective January 1, 2016 for required use)
APPROVED OPTIONAL/VOLUNTARY USE FORMS	
Notice to Prospective Buyer	OP-C (as of 12/5/2011)
Seller's Disclosure of Property Condition	OP-H (08/17/2015) (Effective January 1, 2016 for required use)
Texas Real Estate Consumer Notice Concerning Hazards or Deficiencies	OP-I (as of 05/04/2015)
Information about Brokerage Services	IABS 1-0 (11/02/2015) (Effective February 1, 2016 for required use)
Lead Based Paint Addendum	OP-L (as of 12/5/2011)
Non-Realty Items Addendum	OP-M (as of 12/5/2011)
Reverse Mortgage Financing Addendum	OP-N (as of 4/28/2014) **BEING REPEALED PER TREC; EFFECTIVE JAN 1, 2016**

**ALWAYS check the TREC website PRIOR to using any of these forms to be sure you are using the most up-to-date and current form!**

PREFACE

The concept of proper documentation associated with real estate transactions in Texas is of huge importance. The Texas Real Estate Commission (TREC) confirms this by making contracts and promulgated forms the *ONLY required* topics in pre-licensing coursework that have two different classes assigned to address these issues.

The strategy employed in this book is to *familiarize* the reader with the various forms that are often attached to TREC promulgated sales contracts. Not all of the various documents will be used in every transaction. In truth, some forms will rarely, if ever, be used by a licensee, depending upon their respective marketplaces. However, that does not eliminate the need for a licensee to be aware of them.

More than just becoming aware, we feel it is important for the reader to have some practice time in completing the various forms, in order to help insure comfort and competence with the documentation. So there are numerous scenarios throughout the book that require completion of the relevant contracts and supporting documents.

This approach has worked well in other publications and classes we have been involved with over a long period of time with a diverse selection of students. It is our hope it will work effectively for you as well.

JOHNNIE ROSENAUER is Professor and Program Coordinator of Real Estate for San Antonio College (SAC). He joined the faculty at SAC in 1974, two years after the Real Estate Program was created, and has served as Coordinator almost continuously since 1980.

Johnnie holds a B.B.A. in Real Estate and Marketing from Texas State University and was in the first graduating class from the University of Texas at San Antonio (UTSA), receiving his M.A. in Higher Education and Management. He earned an Ed.D. in Adult Education from Texas A&M University in 1984, where his research focused on testing anxiety among real estate license test takers.

Dr. Rosenauer has authored or co-authored numerous Texas-specific and national texts. He has also authored or co-authored over 50 professional articles dealing with real estate, land management, testing, and effective teaching.

He served for over eight years as Director of the Raul S. Murguia Learning Institute, a professional development effort for San Antonio College which gained national attention for its successful endeavors. He has served as an adjunct faculty member in the Graduate Colleges at Texas A&M University, UTSA, and Texas A&M San Antonio. Johnnie was recently awarded the Life Time Achievement Award from the Texas Real Estate Teachers Association. This is the 10th time the award has been offered in TRETA's 39 year history.

Johnnie has practiced farm and ranch brokerage, land management, and wildlife consulting in south central Texas for over four decades. A fourth-generation land owner in Frio and Atascosa counties, he attempts to practice sound stewardship on his own properties, raising quality native whitetail deer and breeding AQHA horses.

Johnnie is married to Danell, who comes from a multiple-generation, land-owning family from western Oklahoma. They have two children, Jessica and Corban, and live in Spring Branch, Texas.

MELISSA WEATHERSBY grew up at Randolph Air Force Base in San Antonio, Texas. After graduating from Judson High School, she earned her Bachelor of Business Administration degree (Management) from Southwest Texas State University, and her MBA from Webster University. She is currently working on her Doctorate of Education (with a specialization in Higher

Education and Adult Learning) at Walden University. Melissa is a passionate advocate for personal financial literacy in the education system.

Melissa's professional management background began in banking. When the banks merged in 1999, she left the corporate world and began her own mortgage company and real estate company. She ended her banking career as Assistant Vice President/ Banking Center Manager at Bank of America.

Melissa received her real estate license in 1998, and in 2001, she was selected by the San Antonio Business Journal as one of San Antonio's 40 under 40 rising stars out of 270 applicants. She became a real estate broker in 2002. During the unstable industry years of 2005-2007, she even worked as an appraiser for both Dallas County Appraisal District and Bexar Appraisal District in both the residential and commercial departments.

Her academic experience began in 2006 as an adjunct real estate instructor at St. Philips College, one of the five campuses of Alamo Colleges. In 2008, she was hired as Director of Corporate Training and Continuing Education at Northeast Lakeview College, the newest Alamo Colleges campus, in Workforce Development. She spent four years in that position creating, negotiating, and selling certificate and contract training programs to students, school districts, local businesses and military installations. She led several committees, and was certified as a Franklin Covey 7 Habits Facilitator. In 2012, Melissa was a recipient of the National Institute of Staff and Organizational Development Excellence Award which recognizes teaching and leadership excellence in higher education institutions in the United States, Canada, Bermuda, British Virgin Islands, and the United Kingdom.

Melissa is currently an adjunct real estate instructor at San Antonio College and is still an active real estate broker. In 2014, she was recognized in the inaugural edition of Who's Who San Antonio Top 100 Women for her entrepreneurial excellence. She enjoys speaking and teaching at conferences and workshops and is also a life coach for clients needing assistance with business, career development, personal finances, or personal development.

Melissa is an avid equestrian. She began riding at the age of 3 and has enjoyed every spectrum of the sport from Hunter/Jumper Pentathlon horses to Saddle Seat Equitation to rodeo barrel racing. She is a certified horsemanship instructor. Melissa is also a former high school rodeo queen and former member of the Southwest Texas State rodeo team.

A C K N O W L E D G M E N T S

Our thanks extend to Abby Franklin and Sara Glassmeyer from OnCourse for their wonderful guidance and trust in our efforts. They are true professionals and we are grateful for them.

A big thank you and acknowledgment goes out to our reviewers who can help make a book clearer and more effective.

Phyllis Goodrich, Rick Knowles, and Wayne Thorburn provided us some good perspectives we had not considered and we thank them for their efforts.

We would surely be remiss in not acknowledging the experiences our students have allowed us to gain in the classrooms, teaching real estate and other subjects. We believe it is very true that a person never really masters a topic until they can artfully teach it to someone else.

The many practitioners and consumers that we have worked with over the combined 55+ years of our professional practice have had a significant influence on our understanding of the real estate profession.

On a personal level we would like to thank our families for their support, encouragement, confidence, and love. How blessed we are to have them in our lives.

For JR, this book is dedicated to Robert E. Zeigler and wife Dr. Mary Zeigler, retired President of San Antonio College, has been a friend, mentor, and boss for many years and I thank him for his influence and confidence. He surely helped to "raise me" into whatever professional success has come my way in my career within Higher Education. On an entirely different and brand new level, this book is dedicated to our new granddaughter, Stevie Priscilla Rodriguez, born in the summer of 2014. If she is anything like her mother, she will have me twisted around her little finger pretty rapidly. My wonderful wife, Danell says Stevie already has me there! Being a grandparent is a new experience for us and we are surely enjoying it a great deal.

For MW, I thank my Maker for opening doors of opportunity to share my passion of teaching others.

This book is dedicated to my students who keep my teaching gift ignited. It was with you in mind that this book was created.

A special thank you to Dr. Johnnie Rosenauer whose friendship and guidance has been invaluable. I appreciate the opportunity to collaborate on such a great project.

We want to make the book readable. Our view is that it is pretty easy to make complex things harder. But the really good practitioner, author, and pre-licensing related books should make things clearer and more useful to you, the reader.

One of many things that over 55 years combined of practicing and teaching real estate has taught us is the value of transparency/full disclosure. To that extent, prior to beginning the content of this text, there are some things we want to disclose to the readers, as follows:

1. The primary purpose of this book is for Texas Real Estate Pre-Licensing. Therefore, the majority of the audience who will use it will be those studying in order to obtain (maybe re-obtain) their Sales/Broker License. The content found in these chapters is a reflection of the topics that the Texas Real Estate Commission (TREC) has decided are important. The structure is done to help insure the class you take using this book will follow an acceptable curriculum in order to gain credit as part of your Pre-Licensing coursework.

2. This book and the class you are taking are in *no way* a substitution for a solid Post Licensing training program. We are convinced that the single most important aspect of a new person's Broker selection should be a very well defined, orderly training period with adequate support and supervision for at least your first year in the business. Pick the very best Broker/company possible for your needs, and not just the most convenient one. Your particular sponsoring Broker should have policies and procedures in place that will guide you on the way to handle most of the situations you experience in your career.

3. We are not holders of law degrees or licensed to practice law in Texas or any other state. Do not misconstrue any of the material here as designed to offer legal advice. The views here are from experienced and successful real estate educators, as well as practitioners in the field. But that is as far as it goes. Grannie Rosenauer would often say, "Know your place in life." Seems like good advice for both new licensees and authors in the field of real estate!

4. The forms in this book will not always be up to date. At the time of publishing, the documents included were the most current available. *But one or more can change at any time.* Be prudent in searching the TREC website to insure you are using the proper forms and contracts. We highly recommend you get into the habit of routinely checking for the current forms by going to: http://www.trec.state.tx.us/formslawscontracts/forms/forms-contracts.asp

5. There will be some redundancy in this book/class along with the one you take for Law of Contracts. While the focus here is more on the addenda and notices, TREC rules say this course must address the information needed to complete the promulgated One to Four Family Residential Contract and other real estate contracts. Consequently, that documentation is included in the material.

The above statements are not designed to be negative in nature. Rather, the intent is to be upfront on what our goals are for the book and what the limitations are by the nature of the topic.

In writing this text, we have carefully attempted to follow the guidelines below for the benefit of the reader:

1. This book will be as complete and accurate as possible. Every effort will be made to insure what you are studying is "good stuff" in terms of being correct.

2. When opinions are made, we will try to state them as such.

3. We will try to make complex things a bit easier to understand *and* to explain.

4. You will find at the end of each chapter a **Lessons to Learn** section where a scenario is given in order to see how you might handle it. There will be a response from the authors on our ideas found at the back of the book. These types of situational practices are designed to give you an understanding of some of the challenges you will be facing in the industry when "out on the streets." Keep in mind that there may be more than one solution to some of the scenarios.

5. You will be involved with the book. In each chapter, you will discover some questions to think about and respond to. In some chapters, and especially towards the end of the book, you will find we have included a number of cases/situations/scenarios where you will be asked alone and/or in groups to correctly use the documents this book helps you learn about. This kind of hands-on learning is useful and needed when you are called upon to accurately create an offer to include all the appropriate forms/addenda/notices required **FOR REAL** as a professional practitioner. We often reference in our industry the importance of real estate equity-building as part of the investment strategy. Our hope is that you will invest yourself in this material and help create a stronger understanding about these forms. This is an important investment for you to make at this point in time.

6. The final thing that the authors and all those involved with this book desire is to give you some confidence and competence in the use of these very important documents. Real estate is an exciting and fulfilling career when you are adequately prepared. Collectively, we all hope this product will help you in your progress on a successful path in our industry. Our sincere best wishes!

Chapter 1

An Overview of Contracts

LEARNING OBJECTIVES

When you have completed this chapter, you will be able to:

1. List the essential elements of a valid contract.
2. Distinguish between fraud, misrepresentation, and puffing.

KEY TERMS

addendum	fully executed
amendment	mutual agreement
assign	misrepresentation
bilateral	mutual rescission
consideration	statute of limitation
contract	time is of the essence
default	unenforceable
discharged	unilateral
effective date	valid
executed	void
executory	voidable
fraud	

OVERVIEW

Before we begin to explore the various factors involved in the promulgated forms covered in this text, a few words of perspective might be appropriate. Life is full of what might be considered contracts, and we enter into them without even thinking too much about it. Some non-real estate examples would include:

"I will meet you at the mall at 4."

"Sure, you can go out tonight, *if* you have your room clean."

"I will get back to you with the information before I leave work today."

Do any of the examples above sound like something you have said? Without getting too legal, each of those illustrations could be considered a potential contract. For our purposes, in this text, we will be focusing on something a bit more complex—dealing with established (promulgated) documents and not just verbal examples. But in covering the points about the various contracts and forms throughout this book, please keep in mind what the Texas Real Estate Commission (TREC) says over and over again: A licensee *can fill out* a promulgated form, but must refrain from giving what might be construed as legal advice. Doing so will result in what TREC and the courts would refer to as "the unauthorized practice of law." Refer back to the introduction when I said we must know our place.

There are many definitions of what a contract is. For our purposes, the one used in this text will be from Evans/Rosenauer's *Texas Real Estate Contracts 4e*, OnCourse Learning, 2015.

A **contract** is "a promise or a set of promises for the breach of which the law gives a remedy, or the performance of which the law in some way recognizes as a duty." Sometimes the parties agree to *do* something. We generally call that performance. In our industry, we generally only get paid if the deal gets finalized (performed). Sometimes the parties to the contract agree *not to do* something.

In order to help you create a "good contract" (a term often used in real estate circles, but not necessarily an accurate one), we need to understand that there are different levels of a contract in terms of its being considered "good." The most important status a contract can have in terms of performance is that it be **valid**. This means the document meets all the required conditions to be considered legally binding. Those conditions are discussed below.

Another status condition is a contract that is **void**. This means it is essentially dead in the water. The contract does not meet one or more of the essential elements of a valid contract and, as such, there is something missing from it that prevents it from being "good." For example, if Vernell Walker offers Conrad Krueger $250,000 for his property and Conrad accepts all the other terms and conditions, but counters the offering price with a response of $300,000, the original contract is void. Vernell is no longer under obligation to honor her original offer, much less agree to Conrad's counter proposal. There is no "meeting of the minds" on the price of the property, so it is time to offer a benediction on this contract, for it is dead. That does not mean that the transaction cannot progress with further negotiations and be resurrected, but the original offer/contract no longer exits.

Another example is a contract that is **voidable**. This means the contract may be killed/avoided by one of the parties. Sometimes the literature on contracts uses the example of a minor (underage person) to illustrate this concept. My preference is to point out that if one of the parties involved in the contract fails to do what they said they would do, the other party can stay with the deal or bail out. You might consider a voidable contract as a "maybe" kind of agreement, as long as one party has the right to stay in or get out of the agreement.

Unenforceable contracts also need to be considered. It means that for some reason, the contract cannot be enforced. A good example is a contract where the agreement was not fully carried out during a prescribed period of time. The lapse of time could render an agreement unenforceable. A solution to this particular example is to file an extension prior to the lapsed timeline.

ESSENTIAL ELEMENTS OF A VALID CONTRACT

Now to the "good" contract elements. The status of **valid** is where we want our contracts to be. There are lots of tricks of the trade to remember and lists of things a person must keep straight. One of the tools we use is to make up a word from the first letter of each of the words necessary to recall (an acronym).

To help ourselves and our students, we employ the acronym **COCLAD** for the "laundry list" of needed elements to insure a contract meets the test of validity:

C = Competent Parties

O = Offer and Acceptance

C = Consideration

L = Legal Purpose

A = Agreement Signed and In Writing

D = Description (i.e., Legal Description)

On the following pages, we will discuss each of these elements briefly.

COMPETENT PARTIES

Generally speaking, this means a person has *not* been classified as being mentally incompetent. Such a determination can be done only by a legal process. The other issue is the age of a person. Generally, people under the age of 18 are considered minors. Certainly, there are exceptions, but for the most part, these two standards will apply. Keep in mind that some of us have experienced moments when we made real estate (and non-real estate) decisions where later on, we asked the question, "What was I thinking?" But that is not an excuse or reason to try and deny competence!

OFFER AND ACCEPTANCE

As we will see later on in this chapter, most of our real estate contracts are considered **bilateral**. For this part, what we are focusing on is that certain terms and conditions have been tendered to one party, and the other party has agreed to those specified in the offer. It is sometimes stated that the parties have come together with a meeting of the minds, or they are of one accord. Basically, they are on the same page. The key here for the licensees involved is to help people understand what they are agreeing to. Remember: *No legal advice!* We are assuming there is no false information purposely presented by either side of the contract. We will look at this concept closely when Seller's Disclosure of Property Condition is presented in a later chapter.

CONSIDERATION

In certain scenarios, this word could mean thoughtfulness or kindness. In the world of real estate, the term **consideration** means something of value is given for something else of value. While we typically have earnest money (to be discussed in another chapter) associated with our contracts, this is *not* a requirement. There is a clear precedence (at least in my mind) that our courts have held that a promise for a promise is ample consideration without the need for earnest money. However, I doubt many sellers are willing to place their property under contract with simply a pledge to purchase. Keep in mind that consideration can be comprised of other things besides dollars. Other property (an exchange) would suffice. So might professional services, or in the case of a family member, it could be "love and affection."

However, the most common form of consideration used is earnest money. This is designed to show the buyer's real intent (earnestness) and gives the seller some sense of comfort, knowing those funds could be (but are not necessarily guaranteed to be) used as relief if the buyer defaults down the road. A question often arises in terms of *how much* earnest money is required. It is completely and purely a matter of negotiations between the buyer and seller. I have personally been involved in transactions where under $50 of earnest money held the deals together, and on the other end of the spectrum, I was in a ranch deal once where the buyer left $50,000 on the table to cancel the transaction! (My seller said thanks and told me to wait until he spent the $50K, and then we would try to sell it again!) My stock in trade answer to the public and to my students is that if I represent a buyer, I want that party to put down one dollar less than they are willing to walk away from. If the seller is my client, I want one more dollar in escrow than the potential buyer is willing to lose.

LEGAL PURPOSE

Understandably, the concept that a contract does not contemplate an unlawful activity is implicit in our real estate practice. Any prudent licensee would not want to be part of an agreement that cannot stand the light of exposure. A situation where a violation is contemplated, or exists within *any* part of the deal, should cause the licensee to promptly run away from being involved.

This legal purpose aspect needs a bit of further explanation. Suppose a developer is offering to buy a vacant piece of land subject to the ability to get the tract rezoned from Residential Single Family to Commercial. This is not an illegal activity. There is simply a contingency that must be satisfied, or the transaction will not be completed.

AGREEMENT SIGNED AND IN WRITING

We established at the start of this chapter that not all contracts have to be in written format. However, in real estate transactions, for practical purposes it is safe to say that real estate agreements *need* to be in writing. And not only in writing, but approved by signatures from the involved principals and/or their appropriately designated representatives. Some readers may be quick to say that an oral lease under one year in length where no sale is contemplated is okay. My response is yes, but how can you demonstrate the exact agreement that was reached if a misunderstanding arises and there is no documentation? Play it safe and put it in writing, *correctly* spelling out the details of the agreement to avoid confusion and misunderstandings as much as humanly possible regarding the responsibilities and rights of the respective parties.

LEGAL DESCRIPTION

The last component of a valid contract is one of being able to find the property with a high degree of accuracy. I am not sure where you live, but in my area, there are a whole lot of streets that sound remarkably similar. 123 Oak Street can be North or South. Or it can be Oak Lane or Oak Mill or Oak Avenue, or take your pick. The more urban areas will rely on the recorded plat of subdivision, where the developer must offer up a legal description that goes something like, "Lot 7 Block 3 New City Block (or in some cases County Block) 6151 in the Arrowhead Heights Subdivision." This is so important that it is located prominently in paragraph 2 of the earnest money contract—right after the parties are identified. Only after the legal description will the contract have a blank for the "known as" piece (where the physical street address is added). Note that the street address is an extra and not a component of the legal description.

In the more rural settings of Texas, a legal description will be done in the metes and bounds survey method. In this case, there is a POB (Point of Beginning) where the survey will stop and end. In between, with a very detailed citation of distance and direction (if a current survey), will be additional markers called monuments.

Here is an example of what a metes and bounds legal description would look like:

716 acres more or less being

640 acres out of the T.A. & M Survey Number 7, Abstract 31

40 acres out of the J.L. & R Survey Number 3, Abstract 9

And 36 acres more or less out of the E.M. & G Survey Number 4, Abstract 2

As described in a deed dated November 17, 2014, from Greg and Patricia Salyers to Michelle Nover, Trustee for the Joseph and Patricia Nover Trust.

In either case, there are discussions about current vs. new survey requirements found in paragraph 6 of the earnest money contract that will be addressed later in the book.

EXECUTED VS. EXECUTORY CONTRACTS

So you have made an offer, handled the negotiations, and obtained a written and signed agreement on all points. Once the parties are informed of the agreement, you have reached the stage of an **executed** contract. This means you have a contract that becomes immediately effective. Note that this *does not mean all the work is done*. It simply means the terms and conditions have been outlined and agreed upon. Generally speaking, this is the period where loans are applied for, title work is done, and possibly some inspections are made and surveys prepared. The sale is not yet consummated; rather, the parties are fulfilling their agreed-to obligations and activities. In the industry, we often refer to the status as Sale Pending, Under Contract, or In the Title Company.

Once all important tasks are done and a closing actually occurs, the contract will then be **fully executed**. We might call this the Done Deal stage. Closing and funding have occurred and it is time to celebrate. This is a nice stage to be in.

In contrast to being at the finish line with the deal, an **executory** contract is one that has not been fully completed. Think of it as sort of a work in progress. Just below paragraph 24 of the promulgated earnest money contract, we have a space where a broker involved in the transaction will fill in the blanks for the day, month, and year once final acceptance has occurred. This is important not just because it creates an **effective date** for the transaction. All aspects of the contract that have a timeline for certain activities and duties use the effective date to measure the schedule. It is the day when the meter starts running, so to speak.

BILATERAL VS. UNILATERAL

Real estate contracts between buyer and seller are known as **bilateral contracts**. This means there are rights and responsibilities on both sides of the contract. The seller has agreed to convey the property and the buyer has agreed to give some form of consideration (usually money) in return. *Most* of the contracts involved in real estate will be bilateral in nature.

However, there are examples of **unilateral contracts** as well. I tend to think of these as kind of an "IF I do this, THEN you will do that" type of agreement.

Sometimes this is explained as an agreement of action dependent on a definite act. A good example would be the Buyer Representation or Listing Agreement Contract. In the most boiled-down aspect, these agreements say IF the licensee finds a suitable property or a qualified buyer, THEN the principal will pay them for their services. IF the licensee fails to perform, THEN the principal is under no obligation to pay the licensee.

Most of the literature used to research this book point out that an example of unilateral contracts would be the option period within a sales contract agreement. The seller accepts an option payment. Then the buyer has XX days to decide whether to purchase or not. IF the buyer decides to purchase, THEN the seller must sell. IF the purchaser decided to decline, THEN the seller cannot force the sale. Keep in mind, the option payment is different than the earnest money. Both of these will be discussed later on in this text.

REASONABLE TIME VS. TIME IS OF THE ESSENCE

Real estate transactions are complex business agreements. There are any number of terms and conditions that must be met by both parties and additional service providers. Loan arrangements, surveys, inspections, and title commitments are all examples of activities that generally have a timeline to be accomplished. In some transactions, there is a need to execute an extension of time to finalize certain obligations by one or more of the parties involved in the sale. When preparing an offer, the creator (and others who review the contract) must ask if the timelines being outlined are in the proper sequence. For example, if a survey is going to be required to execute a title commitment, the contract cannot call for the commitment BEFORE the survey is completed. Avoid potential major problems by insuring that the dates specified make sense and that appropriate time is allocated for the duties involved. The idea of reasonable time might best be shown with the use of the statement "on or before," found in paragraph 9 of the promulgated earnest money contracts. But note that right after this projected closing date is a statement allowing for an extension of time due to objections found within paragraph 6.

The perspective of time is different when the phrase **time is of the essence** is included in a contract. This term means that the exact dates as outlined in the agreement *must* be honored. There are several of the promulgated documents that include these words. The various addendums using the phrase include:

10-6 Addendum for Sale of Other Property by Buyer

11-7 Addendum for Back-Up Contract

40-7 Third Party Financing Addendum for Credit Approval

45-1 Short Sale Addendum

OP-N Reverse Mortgage Financing Addendum

Conventional wisdom suggests that a licensee *does not* include that phase into a contract or addendum. The Broker-Lawyer Committee, discussed in the next chapter, put those words where they thought them best to go, and left them out for the same set of reasons. If a consumer instructs a licensee to include that wording, it is probably a really good idea to refer the consumer to an attorney who can advise them about the pros and cons of such an inclusion.

ADDENDA VS. AMENDMENT

Continuing with our understanding of key terms within the scope of this book, the term **addendum** means there is certain additional information that is to become a part of the "original" nine-page earnest money contract. At the time of this writing, TREC has posted 13 different Addendums on its website. If you sell ranches in west Texas or homes in central Texas, it is unlikely you will ever need to use Form 33-2, Addendum for Coastal Area Property, or Form 33-4, Addendum for Property Located Seaward of the Gulf Intracoastal Waterway. Likewise, if you are engaged in commercial property sales and leasing in downtown Dallas or Houston, it would be rare for you to be filling out Form 44-2, Addendum for Reservation of Oil, Gas, and Other Minerals.

Certain other addenda would be much more common. Form OP-C, Seller's Disclosure of Property Condition, and Form ABS 1-0, Information About Brokerage Services, for example, are very often used and each licensee needs to be able to correctly and confidently create and explain.

An **amendment** is a change or adjustment to an existing contract. Unlike the large number of addenda on the TREC website, there is only one amendment. It is Form 39-8, Amendment to Contract, and it addresses areas like price changes, closing date adjustments, repairs, and costs of said repairs. It is almost certain you will be required to use this amendment during your career as a licensee and it would be prudent to become very familiar with this relatively simple, but extremely important, document.

In the case of all of the above-referenced documents, the principals involved will need to sign, and an effective date will need to be put in after an agreement has been reached.

PERFORMANCE OR TERMINATION OF A CONTRACT

A successful real estate career is built upon the ability of the licensee to have transactions that are consummated. Our industry is performance-based in terms of honors and rewards (financially and otherwise). So the very best way to finalize a real estate transaction, assuming no harm to the principals involved, is to have the deal **discharged** by performance. Discharged means the transaction is terminated. This means all the details and agreements have been fulfilled and the transaction is officially and formally over.

Performance can take some additional shapes and forms besides the original parties bringing the contract to a close. We sometimes see a contract to purchase **assigned**. Assignment means transferring the rights of a contract to another party. A common example is when Jackie Hernandez and Carmen Garcia agree to purchase a parcel of property and then assign the contract to a Limited Liability Corporation (LLC) that they create. So Ms. Hernandez and Ms. Garcia could assign the contract to C & J Real Estate Ventures, LLC. As long as the original contractual agreement does not disallow such a transfer, the assignment is legal. There should be something in writing where Carmen and Jackie create a document that says they are assigning their rights to the LLC entity. This assignment document should be signed by both of them and shared with other parties to the contract.

Another example of an assignment is when the original purchaser(s) assign the contract to a third party, not of their creation. For example, Val Calvert can assign the contract to Susan Espinoza under the same terms and conditions above. Ms. Calvert may even profit from this transfer, possibly to the chagrin of the seller. But the assignor (Ms. Calvert) has done nothing wrong, unless specifically prohibited under the original agreement.

Keep in mind that assignment of a contract does not automatically release the assigning party from liability of performance.

Default of contract is yet another topic that needs to be addressed in this section, at least preliminarily. Sometimes a party to the contract does not perform as they agreed to. Paragraph 15 of the promulgated earnest money contract speaks to the remedies (solutions) the non-defaulting party(ies) would have in the event of this happening. By mutual agreement, as part of the original agreement, the options of the non-defaulting party can be limited to certain activities or dollar amounts.

Sometimes the best option regarding a contract is to call it quits. Both parties can, by **mutual agreement**, cancel the contract and just forget the whole thing. Returning to the original pre-contract position is known as **mutual**

rescission. In this example, earnest money will be returned and all parties will go their separate ways without further liability or responsibility.

Keep in mind the above examples have both parties agreeing to actions. **Unilateral** (where only one party decides to do something about changing the existing contract) decisions can have some significant consequences.

Any time a licensee is in a property transfer situation and things start to go sideways, the licensee should seek advice and counsel from the sponsoring broker or other appropriate supervisor. The best and safest way a contract can be terminated is by performance or mutual agreement.

TERMINATION CHECKLIST

The following checklist is offered as a consolidated reminder of *some* of the more common ways a contract can be terminated. We hope it proves helpful in reminding you of the "good and bad" ways of contract termination. But please keep in mind that discussions on contract termination with principals should be conducted *only* after seeking guidance from your sponsoring broker or another senior member of the management team.

- Performance: The deal is finalized.
- Mutual Agreement: Let's all go back to zero and try again with someone else.
- Lapse of Time: Things did not get done in a timely manner.
- Breach: One party does not do what they are supposed to do, and the other party walks away from the deal.
- Failure to Perform: Similar to above, someone just did not uphold their end of the bargain.
- Impossibility: Sometimes a person just cannot do what they promised to do, such as clearing a title issue from long ago. It you can't, you can't, so the contract is done.
- Death or Insanity: If one of the parties is no longer competent (or alive), it is pretty hard to finalize the sale. If the seller dies, his or her estate could still sell the property, but not without the selling party being revised to "The Estate Of."
- Property Destruction: In a nutshell, you cannot sell what no longer exists.

Some of the above examples are found internal to the promulgated contracts you will review in this class, as well as in the real estate contracts class required as part of your pre-licensing coursework.

STATUTE OF LIMITATIONS

Unfortunately, sometimes the transaction associated with the various forms and attachments do have problems, even after closing. A frequent question that is asked from consumers is, "How long do I have to try and get some aspect of the transaction corrected if something is wrong?" In lay-person terms, a **statute of limitation** is the timeline established by law that a person has to bring legal action to correct some form of misconduct. Certainly, this topic will require discussion with an attorney if serious pursuit is contemplated by a person who feels they have been wronged. A common example in real estate would be where **fraud** is claimed. Fraud is the intent to deceive. By contrast, **misrepresentation** is a situation where a mistake was made. The key difference is that in fraud, the party/parties conducting the falsehood *knew* they were not telling the truth. In the case of misrepresentation, the error may have been based upon wrong information passed along without prior knowledge of its inaccuracy.

We strongly recommend you avoid discussion about legal options and timeframes with consumers. Let the legal experts speak and advise to these matters.

In summary, it is important to understand the "language" of contracts—i.e., not only knowing what a contract is, but how to *confirm* whether or not it is "good." That is, to know if the contract meets the essential elements of validity. Also, it is of equal importance to be able to *create* a contract correctly. All of the key terms placed at the front of this chapter represent important first steps in becoming proficient in the use of the "tools of the trade" within real estate known as contracts, amendments, and addenda.

REVIEW AND DISCUSSION QUESTIONS

1. How is a valid contract different from a voidable one?

2. What is the difference between an addendum and an amendment?

3. What does the term "bilateral contract" mean?

4. Explain the term "time is of the essence" as it relates to the subject matter in this book.

5. Please list the essential elements of a valid contract as explained in this chapter.

6. What portion of the earnest money contract speaks to options in the event of default?

LESSONS TO LEARN

You represent, as the buyer's agent, Gerry and Cynthia Guerra in the purchase of a home located at 923 Winding Way. The Guerras are under contract to purchase. Some time prior to closing, they come to tell you that they have changed their minds about this house and want to back out of the contract. What they want to know is, can they withdraw from the transaction? How do you respond?

Chapter 2

Laws, Rules, and Regulations

LEARNING OBJECTIVES

When you have completed this chapter, you will be able to:

1. Describe the role of the Broker-Lawyer Committee and the Texas Real Estate Commission in the creation and approval of promulgated forms.
2. Describe the commission rules regarding the use of promulgated forms.
3. Differentiate between when a promulgated form must be used and when a transaction is exempt from that requirement.
4. Explain the importance of presenting offers to a seller in a timely manner.

KEY TERMS

TRELA (Texas Real Estate License Act)

TREC (Texas Real Estate Commission)

Broker-Lawyer Committee

promulgate

offer

counteroffer

unauthorized practice of law

fiduciary

THE TEXAS REAL ESTATE LICENSE ACT

In Texas, real estate candidates who wish to become salespersons or brokers must pass an exam designed to test their competency of real estate principles and Texas law. The most notable of these laws is the **Texas Real Estate License Act (TRELA)**, which establishes operating guidelines for real estate practitioners, real estate inspectors, residential service companies, and those offering timeshare interests.

Initially, real estate agents in Texas were first licensed through the securities division of the Secretary of State's office by the Real Estate Dealer's License Act of 1939 (HB 17, 46th Legislature, Regular Session). The Act's name was changed to the Texas Real Estate License Act (TRELA) in 1955. The purpose of TRELA is to protect the public from dishonest or incompetent brokers or salespeople, prescribe certain minimum standards and qualifications for licensing brokers and salespersons, maintain high standards in the real estate profession, and protect licensed brokers and salespersons from unfair or improper competition.

In 1949, the **Texas Real Estate Commission (TREC)** was created to administer the Act. TREC is a nine-member, policymaking commission appointed by the governor and confirmed by the state senate. Six members must be active in real estate as full-time brokers—including the five years previous to his or her appointment—and three must be members of the public who must have no affiliation with real estate brokerage. Each member must be a qualified voter. The commission has rule-making authority, and the rules of the commission have the full force and effect of law. The TREC website has a "question and answer" section from the Enforcement Division, which can provide interpretations for many questions left unanswered by the license act itself, at www.trec.texas.gov/questions/faq-enf.asp.

Chapter 1101 of the Texas Occupation Code, better known as the Real Estate License Act, will be analyzed in this chapter with respect to contracts, forms, and addenda.

Sec. 1101.155. RULES RELATING TO CONTRACT FORMS.

(a) *The commission may adopt rules in the public's best interest that require license holders to use contract forms prepared by the Texas Real Estate Broker-Lawyer Committee and adopted by the commission.*

(b) *The commission may not prohibit a license holder from using for the sale, exchange, option, or lease of an interest in real property on a contract form that is:*

(1) *prepared by the property owner; or*

(2) *prepared by an attorney and required by the property owner.*

(c) *A listing contract form adopted by the commission that relates to the contractual obligations between a seller of real estate and a license holder acting as an agent for the seller must include:*

(1)   a provision informing the parties to the contract that real estate commissions are negotiable; and

(2)   a provision explaining the availability of Texas coastal natural hazards information important to coastal residents, if that information is appropriate.

Before participating in the business of completing any contract forms that bind the sale, lease, temporary lease, or rental of any real property, the licensee should become completely acquainted with what the law does and does not allow.

UNAUTHORIZED PRACTICE OF LAW

TRELA specifically prohibits licensees from practicing law by giving opinions or counsel regarding the validity or legal sufficiency of an instrument that addresses real property rights, or as to the status of title to real estate. TRELA clearly establishes that it is illegal for the licensee to draw a deed, note, deed of trust, will, or other written instrument that transfers or may transfer an interest in or title to real property. The license act authorizes the Texas Real Estate Commission to suspend or revoke a broker's or salesperson's license for the **unauthorized practice of law**. In order to safeguard valid sales contracts, licensees should always advise sellers and buyers to obtain legal counsel if they do not understand the stipulations of the various contract forms that the Act requires licensees to use.

Completing any of the promulgated forms that TREC provides is not considered practicing law. The licensee is free to explain to the principals the meaning of the factual statements or business details contained in the contracts as long as the licensee does not offer or give legal advice. TRELA gives permission for a licensee to complete a contract form that may bind the sale, exchange, option, lease, or rental of any interest in real estate property as long as forms are used that have been prepared by or are required by the property owner, or have been provided by the real estate commission, prepared by an attorney licensed by Texas, and approved by that attorney for a particular type of transaction.

Sec. 1101.654. SUSPENSION OR REVOCATION OF LICENSE OR CERTIFICATE FOR UNAUTHORIZED PRACTICE OF LAW.

(a)   The commission shall suspend or revoke the license or certificate of registration of a license or certificate holder who is not a licensed attorney in this state and who, for consideration, a reward, or a pecuniary benefit, present or anticipated, direct or indirect, or in connection with the person's employment, agency, or fiduciary relationship as a license or certificate holder:

(1) drafts an instrument, other than a form described by Section 1101.155, that transfers or otherwise affects an interest in real property; or

(2) advises a person regarding the validity or legal sufficiency of an instrument or the validity of title to real property.

(b) Notwithstanding any other law, a license or certificate holder who completes a contract form for the sale, exchange, option, or lease of an interest in real property incidental to acting as a broker is not engaged in the unauthorized or illegal practice of law in this state if the form was:

(1) adopted by the commission for the type of transaction for which the form is used;

(2) prepared by an attorney licensed in this state and approved by the attorney for the type of transaction for which the form is used; or

(3) prepared by the property owner or by an attorney and required by the property owner.

THE BROKER-LAWYER COMMITTEE

One of the advisory committees that exists under TRELA is the **Broker-Lawyer Committee**.

This 13-member committee is composed of six licensed real estate brokers (appointed by TREC), six lawyers who are active members of the Texas State Bar (appointed by the president of the State Bar of Texas), and one public member, appointed by the governor. They serve staggered six-year terms.

The Broker-Lawyer Committee drafts and revises contract forms for use by real estate licensees. Their purpose is to expedite real estate transactions and reduce controversies while protecting the interests of the parties involved.

The Broker-Lawyer Committee does not **promulgate**, or publish, forms for mandatory use by licensees. Only TREC has been given rule-making authority. The Broker-Lawyer Committee develops forms and proposes their adoption, but it is TREC that promulgates the forms for mandatory use. The Act clearly establishes the membership in and responsibilities of the committee.

SUBCHAPTER F. TEXAS REAL ESTATE BROKER-LAWYER COMMITTEE

Sec. 1101.251. DEFINITION OF COMMITTEE. In this subchapter, "committee" means the Texas Real Estate Broker-Lawyer Committee.

Sec. 1101.252. COMMITTEE MEMBERSHIP.

(a) The Texas Real Estate Broker-Lawyer Committee consists of 13 members appointed as follows:

  (1) six members appointed by the commission;

  (2) six members of the State Bar of Texas appointed by the president of the state bar; and

  (3) one public member appointed by the governor.

(b) Appointments to the committee shall be made without regard to the race, creed, sex, religion, or national origin of the appointee.

Sec. 1101.254. POWERS AND DUTIES.

(a) In addition to other delegated powers and duties, the committee shall draft and revise contract forms that are capable of being standardized to expedite real estate transactions and minimize controversy.

(b) The contract forms must contain safeguards adequate to protect the principals in the transaction.

Use of Promulgated Forms

TREC Rule 537.11 addresses the use of standardized forms and lists the forms that are currently promulgated (published) for **mandatory** use by a licensee when the form fits a particular transaction. Although an "approved" TREC form *may* be used by a licensee, a **promulgated** form *must* be used by a licensee for that particular contract situation. Rule 537.11(a) defines the four exceptions to this requirement:

1. *Transactions in which the licensee is functioning solely as a principal, not as an agent;*

2. *Transactions in which an agency of the United States government requires a different form to be used;*

3. *Transactions for which a contract form has been prepared by the property owner or prepared by an attorney and required by the property owner; or*

4. *Transactions for which no standard contract form has been promulgated by the Texas Real Estate Commission, and the licensee uses a form prepared by an attorney at law licensed by this state and approved by the attorney for the particular kind of transactions involved or prepared by the Texas Real Estate Broker-Lawyer Committee and made available for trial use by licensees with the consent of the commission.*

A notice on TREC's website advises non-licensees who obtain the forms for use in a real estate transaction to contact a real estate licensee or an attorney for assistance. Promulgated contract forms are available to any person; however, TREC contract forms are intended for use only by licensed real estate brokers or salespersons who are trained for their correct use. TREC Rule 537.11 (d-h) adds further explanation by stating the following:

(d) *A licensee may not undertake to draw or prepare documents fixing and defining the legal rights of the principals to a real estate transaction.*

(e) *In negotiating real estate transactions, the licensee may fill in forms for such transactions, using exclusively forms which have been approved and promulgated by the commission or such forms as are otherwise permitted by these rules.*

(f) *When filling in a form authorized for use by this section, the licensee may only fill in the blanks provided and may not add to or strike matter from such form, except that licensees shall add factual statements and business details desired by the principals and shall strike only such matter as is desired by the principals and as is necessary to conform the instrument to the intent of the parties.*

(g) *A licensee may not add to a promulgated contract form factual statements or business details for which a contract addendum, lease or other form has been promulgated by the commission for mandatory use.*

(h) *Nothing in this section shall be deemed to prevent the licensee from explaining to the principals the meaning of the factual statements and business details contained in the said instrument so long as the licensee does not offer or give legal advice.*

The Real Estate Commission has promulgated and approved the following forms for the licensee's use:

6 promulgated contracts

15 promulgated addenda (including 2 temporary leases)

1 promulgated amendment

2 promulgated resale certificates

1 promulgated notice

2 promulgated consumer disclosures

6 approved forms

A complete list of each of the above types of forms appears at the end of this section.

Because the forms change regularly, visit TREC's website for information about current forms, including the date the form was promulgated and the current version number of the form. Earlier versions of forms may not be used; to do so could be considered the unauthorized practice of law, an illegal act (www.trec.state.tx.us/formslawscontracts/forms/forms-contracts. asp). The version number (form number) of the form is included on the bottom right corner of each page of the form. Pay attention to the form numbers! While most real estate practitioners refer to the form by its title, it is not uncommon to also hear the form referred to by its number instead of its name (i.e., "One to Four Family Residential Resale Contract" or "Form 20-13").

PROMULGATED CONTRACTS

- Unimproved Property Contract
- One to Four Family Residential Contract (Resale)
- New Home Contract (Incomplete Construction)
- New Home Contract (Completed Construction)
- Farm and Ranch Contract
- Residential Condominium Contract (Resale)

PROMULGATED ADDENDA

- Addendum for Sale of Other Property by Buyer
- Addendum for Back-Up Contract
- Addendum for Release of Liability on Assumed Loans and/or Restoration of
- Seller's VA Entitlement
- Seller's Temporary Residential lease
- Buyer's Temporary Residential Lease
- Seller Financing Addendum
- Environmental Assessment, Threatened or Endangered Species, and Wetlands Addendum
- Addendum for Coastal Area Property
- Addendum for Property Located Seaward of the Gulf Intracoastal Waterway
- Addendum for Property Subject to Mandatory Membership in an Owners' Association

- Third Party Financing Addendum for Credit Approval
- Loan Assumption Addendum
- Addendum for Reservation of Oil, Gas and Other Minerals
- Short Sale Addendum
- Addendum for Property in a Propane Gas System Service Area

PROMULGATED AMENDMENT

- Amendment to Contract

PROMULGATED RESALE CERTIFICATES

- Condominium Resale Certificate
- Subdivision Information, Including Resale Certificate for Property Subject to
- Mandatory Membership in an Owners' Association

PROMULGATED NOTICE

- Notice of Buyer's Termination of Contract

PROMULGATED CONSUMER DISCLOSURES

- Consumer Information Form 1-1
- Disclosure of Relationship with Residential Service Company

APPROVED OPTIONAL/VOLUNTARY USE FORMS

- Notice to Prospective Buyer
- Seller's Disclosure of Property Condition
- Texas Real Estate Consumer Notice Concerning Hazards or Deficiencies
- Information About Brokerage Services
- Lead-Based Paint Addendum
- Non-Realty Items Addendum

PRESENTING OFFERS AND MULTIPLE OFFERS

Because of the **fiduciary** relationship that exists between an agent and the principal, it is imperative that any and all offers are presented to the principal as quickly as reasonably possible. TREC rules require immediate presentation. **Offers** must be in writing and may be hand delivered, transmitted by fax, mailed, or submitted electronically (i.e., via email). Failure to present an offer to a property owner may result in the suspension or revocation of one's license under the provisions of the Texas Real Estate License Act. It may also result in a lawsuit from the property owner. Failure to present an offer is a breach of a licensee's fiduciary duties. Unless instructed otherwise by the owner in writing, all offers must be presented. A seller's instruction not to present backup offers must also be given to the licensee in writing.

When presented with a written offer, the seller may:

- accept it,
- reject it,
- counter it, or
- do nothing—that is, ignore it.

When an offer is not acceptable to the property owner, the owner may invite the offeror to submit another offer. This may be done by using the Texas Association of REALTORS® (TAR) Seller's Invitation to Buyer to Submit New Offer form, available to TAR members at www.TexasREALTORS.com. Licensees who are not members of TAR may just create a letter to convey this message to the offeror. As encouragement to submit another offer, the owner should give the offeror information that will shed some light on what terms would be more acceptable to the offeree.

Until an offer or counteroffer is accepted, rejected, or withdrawn, it is active or "live." For example, if the seller has countered one offer and then a better offer comes in, the seller must be careful to withdraw his counteroffer to the first buyer before making a counteroffer to the second buyer. If the seller agrees to the offer *exactly as it was made* and signs the contract (executes), the offer has been accepted. Any changes by the seller to the terms proposed by the buyer creates a **counteroffer**. The buyer is relieved of his or her original offer because the seller has, in effect, rejected it. The buyer can accept the seller's counteroffer or reject it and, if desired, make another counteroffer. Any change in the last offer made results in a counteroffer until one party finally agrees to the other party's last offer and both parties initial all changes and execute the final contract.

An offer or counteroffer may be withdrawn at any time before it has been accepted (regardless of whether the person making the offer or counteroffer agreed to keep the offer open for a set period of time). Moreover, an offer is not considered to be accepted until the person making the offer has been notified of the other party's acceptance.

MULTIPLE OFFERS

TREC Rule 535.156 addresses the issue of handling multiple offers. TREC Rule 535.156(a) specifically requires a licensee "to convey to the principal all known information which would affect the principal's decision on whether or not to accept or reject offers." Subsection 535.156(c) further provides that "a licensee has an affirmative duty to keep the principal informed at all times of significant information applicable to the transaction or transactions in which the licensee is acting as agent for the principal." Therefore, the rules require the listing agent to submit all written purchase offers to the seller until a buyer and the seller have a fully executed contract.

There are a few exceptions to these rules. These include instances where the seller has specifically instructed the listing broker—in writing—not to bring the seller any offers below a certain price, or situations in which a binding contract has been executed between a seller and buyer. Always have such directives written and signed by the seller and retained in the property file for that particular client. Rule 535.156(a) provides that the licensee shall have no duty to submit offers to the principal after the principal has accepted an offer." Additionally, the listing agent is prohibited from sharing any information about one buyer's offer with another buyer.

All offers should be presented promptly, and no offer has priority over another. The agent representing each potential buyer should be notified that multiple offers have been received; however, the listing agent must keep the terms and conditions of the other offers confidential.

The real estate broker or salesperson should communicate all offers, acceptances, or other responses as soon as possible to avoid questions that might come up regarding whether an acceptance, rejection, or counteroffer has effectively taken place. Notification of contract acceptance can be made verbally, with written confirmation recommended to avoid any future disagreements.

WHEN DOES THE OFFER BECOME THE CONTRACT?

The offer becomes a contract when all parties have agreed to all terms of the offer and have signed the contract. The final day of acceptance is the date on which the contract becomes binding between the parties. In order for a contract to become binding and effective, four things must take place:

1. The contract must be in writing.
2. Buyer and seller must sign a final contract and initial all changes.
3. Acceptance must be complete.
4. The last party to accept must communicate that acceptance back to the other party or to the other party's agent.

The effective date of the contract is the date on which the communication of acceptance was made. The promulgated contract forms instruct the agent acting for the broker to fill in this final date of acceptance as the effective date.

SUMMARY

Texas real estate is governed by state laws. The Texas Real Estate Law Act (TRELA) establishes operating guidelines for real estate practitioners, real estate inspectors, residential service companies, and those offering time-share interests. The Texas Real Estate Commission enforces TRELA. The Broker-Lawyer Committee is an advisory committee who drafts and revises contract forms for use by real estate licensees. The Broker-Lawyer Committee develops forms and proposes their adoption, but it is TREC that promulgates the forms for mandatory use. These forms and contracts may not be altered or re-written by any licensee. Licensees must use the promulgated forms unless their transaction is one which may be exempted from mandatory use.

TREC rules contain provisions regarding the presentation of offers and multiple offers. When presented with multiple written offers, the seller has four choices: accept it, reject it, counter it, or do nothing—that is, ignore it.

The offer becomes a contract when all parties have agreed to all terms of the offer and have signed the contract. The final day of acceptance is the date on which the contract becomes binding between the parties.

REVIEW QUESTIONS

1. What is TRELA?

2. Who is TREC?

3. What does TRELA consider "the unauthorized practice of law"?

4. Who is the Broker-Lawyer Committee?

5. How many promulgated contracts are there? Addenda?

6. What options does the seller have upon receiving a written offer?

LESSONS TO LEARN

Sales agent Melanie is a new REALTOR® and is excited to present her first offer to her client. Melanie agrees to meet Seller Samantha to present the offer and is surprised to find that Samantha has her own contract and insists on using her document and not the TREC promulgated contract that the buyer has made the offer with. What should Melanie do? Is Seller Samantha permitted to use her contract and not the TREC contract? Why or Why not?

EQUAL HOUSING OPPORTUNITY

PROMULGATED BY THE TEXAS REAL ESTATE COMMISSION (TREC)   11-2-2015

UNIMPROVED PROPERTY CONTRACT
NOTICE: Not For Use For Condominium Transactions

1. PARTIES: The parties to this contract are _____(Seller)
and _____(Buyer). Seller agrees
to sell and convey to Buyer and Buyer agrees to buy from Seller the Property defined below.

2. PROPERTY: Lot _____, Block _____,
_____Addition,
City of _____, County of_____,
Texas, known as_____
(address/zip code), or as described on attached exhibit together with all rights, privileges and
appurtenances pertaining thereto, including but not limited to: water rights, claims, permits, strips
and gores, easements, and cooperative or association memberships (the Property).

3. SALES PRICE:
A. Cash portion of Sales Price payable by Buyer at closing ....$_____
B. Sum of all financing described in the attached: ❑ Third Party Financing Addendum,
❑ Loan Assumption Addendum, ❑   Seller Financing Addendum.............$_____
C. Sales Price (Sum of A and B) ....$_____

4. LICENSE HOLDER DISCLOSURE: Texas law requires a real estate license holder who is a party
to a transaction or acting on behalf of a spouse, parent, child, business entity in which the license
holder owns more than 10%, or a trust for which the license holder acts as trustee or of which the
license holder or the license holder's spouse, parent or child is a beneficiary, to notify the other
party in writing before entering into a contract of sale. Disclose if applicable:_____
_____.

5. EARNEST MONEY: Upon execution of contract by all parties, Buyer shall deposit $_____
as earnest money with _____,
as escrow agent, at _____
(address). Buyer shall deposit additional earnest money of $_____ with escrow agent
within _____ days after the effective date of this contract. If Buyer fails to deposit the earnest
money as required by this contract, Buyer will be in default.

6. TITLE POLICY AND SURVEY:
A. TITLE POLICY: Seller shall furnish to Buyer at ❑Seller's ❑Buyer's expense an owner's policy of
title insurance (Title Policy) issued by_____
(Title Company) in the amount of the Sales Price, dated at or after closing, insuring Buyer
against loss under the provisions of the Title Policy, subject to the promulgated exclusions
(including existing building and zoning ordinances) and the following exceptions:
(1) Restrictive covenants common to the platted subdivision in which the Property is located.
(2) The standard printed exception for standby fees, taxes and assessments.
(3) Liens created as part of the financing described in Paragraph 3.
(4) Utility easements created by the dedication deed or plat of the subdivision in which the
Property is located.
(5) Reservations or exceptions otherwise permitted by this contract or as may be approved by
Buyer in writing.
(6) The standard printed exception as to marital rights.
(7) The standard printed exception as to waters, tidelands, beaches, streams, and related
matters.
(8) The standard printed exception as to discrepancies, conflicts, shortages in area or boundary
lines, encroachments or protrusions, or overlapping improvements: ❑ (i) will not be
amended or deleted from the title policy; or ❑(ii) will be amended to read, "shortages in
area" at the expense of ❑Buyer ❑Seller.
B. COMMITMENT: Within 20 days after the Title Company receives a copy of this contract, Seller
shall furnish to Buyer a commitment for title insurance (Commitment) and, at Buyer's expense,
legible copies of restrictive covenants and documents evidencing exceptions in the Commitment
(Exception Documents) other than the standard printed exceptions. Seller authorizes the Title
Company to deliver the Commitment and Exception Documents to Buyer at Buyer's address
shown in Paragraph 21. If the Commitment and Exception Documents are not delivered to
Buyer within the specified time, the time for delivery will be automatically extended up to 15
days or 3 days before the Closing Date, whichever is earlier. If, due to factors beyond Seller's
control, the Commitment and Exception Documents are not delivered within the time required,
Buyer may terminate this contract and the earnest money will be refunded to Buyer.
C. SURVEY: The survey must be made by a registered professional land surveyor acceptable to
the Title Company and Buyer's lender(s). (Check one box only)
❑ (1) Within _____ days after the effective date of this contract, Seller shall furnish to Buyer and
Title Company Seller's existing survey of the Property and a Residential Real Property

Initialed for identification by Buyer_____ _____ and Seller _____ _____   TREC NO. 9–12

Affidavit promulgated by the Texas Department of Insurance (T-47 Affidavit). **If Seller fails to furnish the existing survey or affidavit within the time prescribed, Buyer shall obtain a new survey at Seller's expense no later than 3 days prior to Closing Date.** If the existing survey or affidavit is not acceptable to Title Company or Buyer's lender(s), Buyer shall obtain a new survey at ☐ Seller's ☐Buyer's expense no later than 3 days prior to Closing Date.

☐ (2) Within _____ days after the effective date of this contract, Buyer shall obtain a new survey at Buyer's expense. Buyer is deemed to receive the survey on the date of actual receipt or the date specified in this paragraph, whichever is earlier.

☐ (3) Within _____ days after the effective date of this contract, Seller, at Seller's expense shall furnish a new survey to Buyer.

D. OBJECTIONS: Buyer may object in writing to (i) defects, exceptions, or encumbrances to title: disclosed on the survey other than items 6A(1) through (7) above; or disclosed in the Commitment other than items 6A(1) through (8) above; (ii) any portion of the Property lying in a special flood hazard area (Zone V or A) as shown on the current Federal Emergency Management Agency map; or (iii) any exceptions which prohibit the following use or activity:

_____.
Buyer must object the earlier of (i) the Closing Date or (ii) _____ days after Buyer receives the Commitment, Exception Documents, and the survey. Buyer's failure to object within the time allowed will constitute a waiver of Buyer's right to object; except that the requirements in Schedule C of the Commitment are not waived. Provided Seller is not obligated to incur any expense, Seller shall cure the timely objections of Buyer or any third party lender within 15 days after Seller receives the objections and the Closing Date will be extended as necessary. If objections are not cured within such 15 day period, this contract will terminate and the earnest money will be refunded to Buyer unless Buyer waives the objections.

E. TITLE NOTICES:
  (1) ABSTRACT OR TITLE POLICY: Broker advises Buyer to have an abstract of title covering the Property examined by an attorney of Buyer's selection, or Buyer should be furnished with or obtain a Title Policy. If a Title Policy is furnished, the Commitment should be promptly reviewed by an attorney of Buyer's choice due to the time limitations on Buyer's right to object.
  (2) MEMBERSHIP IN PROPERTY OWNERS ASSOCIATION(S): The Property ☐is ☐is not subject to mandatory membership in a property owners association(s). If the Property is subject to mandatory membership in a property owners association(s), Seller notifies Buyer under §5.012, Texas Property Code, that, as a purchaser of property in the residential community identified in Paragraph 2 in which the Property is located, you are obligated to be a member of the property owners association(s). Restrictive covenants governing the use and occupancy of the Property and all dedicatory instruments governing the establishment, maintenance, and operation of this residential community have been or will be recorded in the Real Property Records of the county in which the Property is located. Copies of the restrictive covenants and dedicatory instruments may be obtained from the county clerk. **You are obligated to pay assessments to the property owners association(s). The amount of the assessments is subject to change. Your failure to pay the assessments could result in enforcement of the association's lien on and the foreclosure of the Property.** Section 207.003, Property Code, entitles an owner to receive copies of any document that governs the establishment, maintenance, or operation of a subdivision, including, but not limited to, restrictions, bylaws, rules and regulations, and a resale certificate from a property owners' association. A resale certificate contains information including, but not limited to, statements specifying the amount and frequency of regular assessments and the style and cause number of lawsuits to which the property owners' association is a party, other than lawsuits relating to unpaid ad valorem taxes of an individual member of the association. These documents must be made available to you by the property owners' association or the association's agent on your request. **If Buyer is concerned about these matters, the TREC promulgated Addendum for Property Subject to Mandatory Membership in a Property Owners Association should be used.**
  (3) STATUTORY TAX DISTRICTS: If the Property is situated in a utility or other statutorily created district providing water, sewer, drainage, or flood control facilities and services, Chapter 49, Texas Water Code, requires Seller to deliver and Buyer to sign the statutory notice relating to the tax rate, bonded indebtedness, or standby fee of the district prior to final execution of this contract.
  (4) TIDE WATERS: If the Property abuts the tidally influenced waters of the state, §33.135, Texas Natural Resources Code, requires a notice regarding coastal area property to be included in the contract. An addendum containing the notice promulgated by TREC or required by the parties must be used.
  (5) ANNEXATION: If the Property is located outside the limits of a municipality, Seller notifies Buyer under §5.011, Texas Property Code, that the Property may now or later be included in

Initialed for identification by Buyer_____ _____ and Seller _____ _____   TREC NO. 9-12

Contract Concerning _____ Page 3 of 8 11-2-2015
(Address of Property)

the extraterritorial jurisdiction of a municipality and may now or later be subject to annexation by the municipality. Each municipality maintains a map that depicts its boundaries and extraterritorial jurisdiction. To determine if the Property is located within a municipality's extraterritorial jurisdiction or is likely to be located within a municipality's extraterritorial jurisdiction, contact all municipalities located in the general proximity of the Property for further information.

(6) PROPERTY LOCATED IN A CERTIFICATED SERVICE AREA OF A UTILITY SERVICE PROVIDER: Notice required by §13.257, Water Code: The real property, described in Paragraph 2, that you are about to purchase may be located in a certificated water or sewer service area, which is authorized by law to provide water or sewer service to the properties in the certificated area. If your property is located in a certificated area there may be special costs or charges that you will be required to pay before you can receive water or sewer service. There may be a period required to construct lines or other facilities necessary to provide water or sewer service to your property. You are advised to determine if the property is in a certificated area and contact the utility service provider to determine the cost that you will be required to pay and the period, if any, that is required to provide water or sewer service to your property. The undersigned Buyer hereby acknowledges receipt of the foregoing notice at or before the execution of a binding contract for the purchase of the real property described in Paragraph 2 or at closing of purchase of the real property.

(7) PUBLIC IMPROVEMENT DISTRICTS: If the Property is in a public improvement district, §5.014, Property Code, requires Seller to notify Buyer as follows: As a purchaser of this parcel of real property you are obligated to pay an assessment to a municipality or county for an improvement project undertaken by a public improvement district under Chapter 372, Local Government Code. The assessment may be due annually or in periodic installments. More information concerning the amount of the assessment and the due dates of that assessment may be obtained from the municipality or county levying the assessment. The amount of the assessments is subject to change. Your failure to pay the assessments could result in a lien on and the foreclosure of your property.

(8) TEXAS AGRICULTURAL DEVELOPMENT DISTRICT: The Property ❑   is ❑   is not located in a Texas Agricultural Development District. For additional information, contact the Texas Department of Agriculture.

(9) TRANSFER FEES: If the Property is subject to a private transfer fee obligation, §5.205, Property Code requires Seller to notify Buyer as follows: The private transfer fee obligation may be governed by Chapter 5, Subchapter G of the Texas Property Code.

(10) PROPANE GAS SYSTEM SERVICE AREA: If the Property is located in a propane gas system service area owned by a distribution system retailer, Seller must give Buyer written notice as required by §141.010, Texas Utilities Code. An addendum containing the notice approved by TREC or required by the parties should be used.

(11) NOTICE OF WATER LEVEL FLUCTUATIONS: If the Property adjoins an impoundment of water, including a reservoir or lake, constructed and maintained under Chapter 11, Water Code, that has a storage capacity of at least 5,000 acre-feet at the impoundment's normal operating level, Seller hereby notifies Buyer: "The water level of the impoundment of water adjoining the Property fluctuates for various reasons, including as a result of: (1) an entity lawfully exercising its right to use the water stored in the impoundment; or (2) drought or flood conditions."

7. PROPERTY CONDITION:

A. ACCESS, INSPECTIONS AND UTILITIES: Seller shall permit Buyer and Buyer's agents access to the Property at reasonable times. Buyer may have the Property inspected by inspectors selected by Buyer and licensed by TREC or otherwise permitted by law to make inspections. Seller at Seller's expense shall immediately cause existing utilities to be turned on and shall keep the utilities on during the time this contract is in effect.
NOTICE: Buyer should determine the availability of utilities to the Property suitable to satisfy Buyer's needs.

B. ACCEPTANCE OF PROPERTY CONDITION: "As Is" means the present condition of the Property with any and all defects and without warranty except for the warranties of title and the warranties in this contract. Buyer's agreement to accept the Property As Is under Paragraph 7B (1) or (2) does not preclude Buyer from inspecting the Property under Paragraph 7A, from negotiating repairs .or treatments in a subsequent amendment, or from terminating this contract during the Option Period, if any.
(Check one box only)
❑ (1) Buyer accepts the Property As Is.
❑ (2) Buyer accepts the Property As Is provided Seller, at Seller's expense, shall complete the following specific repairs and treatments: _____
_____.
(Do not insert general phrases, such as "subject to inspections" that do not identify specific repairs and treatments.)

C. COMPLETION OF REPAIRS: Unless otherwise agreed in writing: (i) Seller shall complete all agreed repairs and treatments prior to the Closing Date; and (ii) all required permits must be obtained, and repairs and treatments must be performed by persons who are licensed to

Initialed for identification by Buyer_____ _____ and Seller _____ _____   TREC NO. 9–12

Contract Concerning _____Page 4 of 8 11-2-2015
(Address of Property)

provide such repairs or treatments or, if no license is required by law, are commercially engaged in the trade of providing such repairs or treatments.   At Buyer's election, any transferable warranties received by Seller with respect to the repairs and treatments will be transferred to Buyer at Buyer's expense. If Seller fails to complete any agreed repairs and treatments prior to the Closing Date, Buyer may exercise remedies under Paragraph 15 or extend the Closing Date up to 5 days, if necessary, for Seller to complete repairs and treatments.

D. ENVIRONMENTAL MATTERS: Buyer is advised that the presence of wetlands, toxic substances, including asbestos and wastes or other environmental hazards, or the presence of a threatened or endangered species or its habitat may affect Buyer's intended use of the Property. If Buyer is concerned about these matters, an addendum promulgated by TREC or required by the parties should be used.

E. SELLER'S DISCLOSURES: Except as otherwise disclosed in this contract, Seller has no knowledge of the following:
(1) any flooding of the Property which has had a material adverse effect on the use of the Property;
(2) any pending or threatened litigation, condemnation, or special assessment affecting the Property;
(3) any environmental hazards that materially and adversely affect the Property;
(4) any dumpsite, landfill, or underground tanks or containers now or previously located on the Property;
(5) any wetlands, as defined by federal or state law or regulation, affecting the Property; or
(6) any threatened or endangered species or their habitat affecting the Property.

8. **BROKERS' FEES:** All obligations of the parties for payment of brokers' fees are contained in separate written agreements.

9. **CLOSING:**
A. The closing of the sale will be on or before _____, 20_____, or within 7 days after objections made under Paragraph 6D have been cured or waived, whichever date is later (Closing Date). If either party fails to close the sale by the Closing Date, the non-defaulting party may exercise the remedies contained in Paragraph 15.
B. At closing:
(1) Seller shall execute and deliver a general warranty deed conveying title to the Property to Buyer and showing no additional exceptions to those permitted in Paragraph 6 and furnish tax statements or certificates showing no delinquent taxes on the Property.
(2) Buyer shall pay the Sales Price in good funds acceptable to the escrow agent.
(3) Seller and Buyer shall execute and deliver any notices, statements, certificates, affidavits, releases, loan documents and other documents reasonably required for the closing of the sale and the issuance of the Title Policy.
(4) There will be no liens, assessments, or security interests against the Property which will not be satisfied out of the sales proceeds unless securing the payment of any loans assumed by Buyer and assumed loans will not be in default.

10. **POSSESSION:**
A. Buyer's Possession: Seller shall deliver to Buyer possession of the Property in its present or required condition upon closing and funding.
B. Leases:
(1) After the Effective Date, Seller may not execute any lease (including but not limited to mineral leases) or convey any interest in the Property without Buyer's written consent.
(2) If the Property is subject to any lease to which Seller is a party, Seller shall deliver to Buyer copies of the lease(s) and any move-in condition form signed by the tenant within 7 days after the Effective Date of the contract.

11. **SPECIAL PROVISIONS:** (Insert only factual statements and business details applicable to the sale. TREC rules prohibit license holders from adding factual statements or business details for which a contract addendum or other form has been promulgated by TREC for mandatory use.)

12. **SETTLEMENT AND OTHER EXPENSES:**
A. The following expenses must be paid at or prior to closing:
(1) Expenses payable by Seller (Seller's Expenses):
(a) Releases of existing liens, including prepayment penalties and recording fees; release of Seller's loan liability; tax statements or certificates; preparation of deed; one-half of escrow fee; and other expenses payable by Seller under this contract.
(b) Seller shall also pay an amount not to exceed $ _____ to be applied in the following order: Buyer's Expenses which Buyer is prohibited from paying by FHA, VA, Texas Veterans Land Board or other governmental loan programs, and then to other Buyer's Expenses as allowed by the lender.

Initialed for identification by Buyer_____ _____ and Seller _____ _____   TREC NO. 9-12

Contract Concerning _____Page 5 of 8 11-2-2015
(Address of Property)

(2) Expenses payable by Buyer (Buyer's Expenses): Appraisal fees; loan application fees; origination charges; credit reports; preparation of loan documents; interest on the notes from date of disbursement to one month prior to dates of first monthly payments; recording fees; copies of easements and restrictions; loan title policy with endorsements required by lender; loan-related inspection fees; photos; amortization schedules; one-half of escrow fee; all prepaid items, including required premiums for flood and hazard insurance, reserve deposits for insurance, ad valorem taxes and special governmental assessments; final compliance inspection; courier fee; repair inspection; underwriting fee; wire transfer fee; expenses incident to any loan; Private Mortgage Insurance Premium (PMI), VA Loan Funding Fee, or FHA Mortgage Insurance Premium (MIP) as required by the lender; and other expenses payable by Buyer under this contract.

B. If any expense exceeds an amount expressly stated in this contract for such expense to be paid by a party, that party may terminate this contract unless the other party agrees to pay such excess. Buyer may not pay charges and fees expressly prohibited by FHA, VA, Texas Veterans Land Board or other governmental loan program regulations.

13. PRORATIONS AND ROLLBACK TAXES:
   A. PRORATIONS: Taxes for the current year, interest, maintenance fees, assessments, dues and rents will be prorated through the Closing Date. The tax proration may be calculated taking into consideration any change in exemptions that will affect the current year's taxes. If taxes for the current year vary from the amount prorated at closing, the parties shall adjust the prorations when tax statements for the current year are available. If taxes are not paid at or prior to closing, Buyer shall pay taxes for the current year.
   B. ROLLBACK TAXES: If this sale or Buyer's use of the Property after closing results in the assessment of additional taxes, penalties or interest (Assessments) for periods prior to closing, the Assessments will be the obligation of Buyer. If Assessments are imposed because of Seller's use or change in use of the Property prior to closing, the Assessments will be the obligation of Seller. Obligations imposed by this paragraph will survive closing.

14. CASUALTY LOSS: If any part of the Property is damaged or destroyed by fire or other casualty after the effective date of this contract, Seller shall restore the Property to its previous condition as soon as reasonably possible, but in any event by the Closing Date. If Seller fails to do so due to factors beyond Seller's control, Buyer may (a) terminate this contract and the earnest money will be refunded to Buyer (b) extend the time for performance up to 15 days and the Closing Date will be extended as necessary or (c) accept the Property in its damaged condition with an assignment of insurance proceeds, if permitted by Seller's insurance carrier, and receive credit from Seller at closing in the amount of the deductible under the insurance policy. Seller's obligations under this paragraph are independent of any other obligations of Seller under this contract.

15. DEFAULT: If Buyer fails to comply with this contract, Buyer will be in default, and Seller may (a) enforce specific performance, seek such other relief as may be provided by law, or both, or (b) terminate this contract and receive the earnest money as liquidated damages, thereby releasing both parties from this contract. If Seller fails to comply with this contract, Seller will be in default and Buyer may (a) enforce specific performance, seek such other relief as may be provided by law, or both, or (b) terminate this contract and receive the earnest money, thereby releasing both parties from this contract.

16. MEDIATION: It is the policy of the State of Texas to encourage resolution of disputes through alternative dispute resolution procedures such as mediation. Any dispute between Seller and Buyer related to this contract which is not resolved through informal discussion will be submitted to a mutually acceptable mediation service or provider. The parties to the mediation shall bear the mediation costs equally. This paragraph does not preclude a party from seeking equitable relief from a court of competent jurisdiction.

17. ATTORNEY'S FEES: A Buyer, Seller, Listing Broker, Other Broker, or escrow agent who prevails in any legal proceeding related to this contract is entitled to recover reasonable attorney's fees and all costs of such proceeding.

18. ESCROW:
   A. ESCROW: The escrow agent is not (i) a party to this contract and does not have liability for the performance or nonperformance of any party to this contract, (ii) liable for interest on the earnest money and (iii) liable for the loss of any earnest money caused by the failure of any financial institution in which the earnest money has been deposited unless the financial institution is acting as escrow agent.
   B. EXPENSES: At closing, the earnest money must be applied first to any cash down payment, then to Buyer's Expenses and any excess refunded to Buyer. If no closing occurs, escrow agent may: (i) require a written release of liability of the escrow agent from all parties, (ii) require payment of unpaid expenses incurred on behalf of a party, and (iii) only deduct from the earnest money the amount of unpaid expenses incurred on behalf of the party receiving the earnest money.
   C. DEMAND: Upon termination of this contract, either party or the escrow agent may send a release of earnest money to each party and the parties shall execute counterparts of the release and deliver same to the escrow agent. If either party fails to execute the release, either party may make a written demand to the escrow agent for the earnest money. If only one party makes written demand for the earnest money, escrow agent shall promptly provide

Initialed for identification by Buyer_____ _____ and Seller _____ _____   TREC NO. 9-12

a copy of the demand to the other party. If escrow agent does not receive written objection to the demand from the other party within 15 days, escrow agent may disburse the earnest money to the party making demand reduced by the amount of unpaid expenses incurred on behalf of the party receiving the earnest money and escrow agent may pay the same to the creditors. If escrow agent complies with the provisions of this paragraph, each party hereby releases escrow agent from all adverse claims related to the disbursal of the earnest money.
  D. **DAMAGES:** Any party who wrongfully fails or refuses to sign a release acceptable to the escrow agent within 7 days of receipt of the request will be liable to the other party for (i) damages; (ii) the earnest money; (iii) reasonable attorney's fees; and (iv) all costs of suit.
  E. **NOTICES:** Escrow agent's notices will be effective when sent in compliance with Paragraph 21. Notice of objection to the demand will be deemed effective upon receipt by escrow agent.

19.**REPRESENTATIONS:** All covenants, representations and warranties in this contract survive closing. If any representation of Seller in this contract is untrue on the Closing Date, Seller will be in default. Unless expressly prohibited by written agreement, Seller may continue to show the Property and receive, negotiate and accept back up offers.

20.**FEDERAL TAX REQUIREMENTS:** If Seller is a "foreign person," as defined by applicable law, or if Seller fails to deliver an affidavit to Buyer that Seller is not a "foreign person," then Buyer shall withhold from the sales proceeds an amount sufficient to comply with applicable tax law and deliver the same to the Internal Revenue Service together with appropriate tax forms. Internal Revenue Service regulations require filing written reports if currency in excess of specified amounts is received in the transaction.

21.**NOTICES:** All notices from one party to the other must be in writing and are effective when mailed to, hand-delivered at, or transmitted by fax or electronic transmission as follows:

To Buyer at: _____

To Seller at: _____

Phone: (___)_____   Phone: (___)_____

Fax: (___)_____   Fax: (___)_____

E-mail: _____   E-mail: _____

22.**AGREEMENT OF PARTIES:** This contract contains the entire agreement of the parties and cannot be changed except by their written agreement. Addenda which are a part of this contract are (check all applicable boxes):

❏ Third Party Financing Addendum

❏ Seller Financing Addendum

❏ Addendum for Property Subject to Mandatory Membership in a Property Owners Association

❏ Buyer's Temporary Residential Lease

❏ Seller's Temporary Residential Lease

❏ Addendum for Reservation of Oil, Gas and Other Minerals

❏ Addendum for "Back-Up" Contract

❏ Addendum for Coastal Area Property

❏ Environmental Assessment, Threatened or Endangered Species and Wetlands Addendum

❏ Addendum for Property Located Seaward of the Gulf Intracoastal Waterway

❏ Addendum for Sale of Other Property by Buyer

❏ Addendum for Property in a Propane Gas System Service Area

❏ Other (list): _____

Contract Concerning _____Page 7 of 8 11-2-2015
(Address of Property)

23. TERMINATION OPTION: For nominal consideration, the receipt of which is hereby acknowledged by Seller, and Buyer's agreement to pay Seller $_____ (Option Fee) within 3 days after the effective date of this contract, Seller grants Buyer the unrestricted right to terminate this contract by giving notice of termination to Seller within _____ days after the effective date of this contract (Option Period). Notices under this paragraph must be given by 5:00 p.m. (local time where the Property is located) by the date specified. If no dollar amount is stated as the Option Fee or if Buyer fails to pay the Option Fee to Seller within the time prescribed, this paragraph will not be a part of this contract and Buyer shall not have the unrestricted right to terminate this contract. If Buyer gives notice of termination within the time prescribed, the Option Fee will not be refunded; however, any earnest money will be refunded to Buyer. The Option Fee ☐will ☐will not be credited to the Sales Price at closing. **Time is of the essence for this paragraph and strict compliance with the time for performance is required.**

24. CONSULT AN ATTORNEY BEFORE SIGNING: TREC rules prohibit real estate license holders from giving legal advice. READ THIS CONTRACT CAREFULLY.

Buyer's
Attorney is: _____   Seller's
Attorney is: _____

_____   _____

Phone: (____) _____   Phone: (____) _____

Fax: (____) _____   Fax: (____) _____

E-mail: _____   E-mail: _____

**EXECUTED the _____day of _____, 20_____ (EFFECTIVE DATE).
(BROKER: FILL IN THE DATE OF FINAL ACCEPTANCE.)**

_____   _____
Buyer   Seller

_____   _____
Buyer   Seller

The form of this contract has been approved by the Texas Real Estate Commission. TREC forms are intended for use only by trained real estate license holders. No representation is made as to the legal validity or adequacy of any provision in any specific transactions. It is not intended for complex transactions. Texas Real Estate Commission, P.O. Box 12188, Austin, TX 78711-2188, (512) 936-3000 (http://www.trec.texas.gov) TREC NO. 9-12. This form replaces TREC NO. 9-11.

| Contract Concerning _____ | Page 8 of 8 11-2-2015 |
| (Address of Property) | |

BROKER INFORMATION
(Print name(s) only. Do not sign)

| Other Broker Firm   License No. | Listing Broker Firm   License No. |

represents ☐ Buyer only as Buyer's agent / ☐ Seller as Listing Broker's subagent

represents ☐ Seller and Buyer as an intermediary / ☐ Seller only as Seller's agent

Associate's Name — License No.

Listing Associate's Name — License No.

Licensed Supervisor of Associate — License No.

Licensed Supervisor of Listing Associate — License No.

Other Broker's Address — Fax

Listing Broker's Office Address — Fax

City — State — Zip

City — State — Zip

Associate's Email Address — Phone

Listing Associate's Email Address — Phone

Selling Associate's Name — License No.

Licensed Supervisor of Selling Associate — License No.

Selling Associate's Office Address — Fax

City — State — Zip

Selling Associate's Email Address — Phone

Listing Broker has agreed to pay Other Broker_____ of the total sales price when the Listing Broker's fee is received. Escrow agent is authorized and directed to pay other Broker from Listing Broker's fee at closing.

OPTION FEE RECEIPT

Receipt of $_____ (Option Fee) in the form of _____ is acknowledged.

Seller or Listing Broker — Date

CONTRACT AND EARNEST MONEY RECEIPT

Receipt of ☐ Contract and ☐ $_____ Earnest Money in the form of _____ is acknowledged.

Escrow Agent: _____ Date: _____

By: _____

Email Address

Phone: (____) _____

Address

Fax: (____) _____

City — State — Zip

TREC NO. 9-12

PROMULGATED BY THE TEXAS REAL ESTATE COMMISSION (TREC)
11-2-2015
ONE TO FOUR FAMILY RESIDENTIAL CONTRACT (RESALE)
NOTICE: Not For Use For Condominium Transactions

1. PARTIES: The parties to this contract are _____
(Seller) and _____(Buyer).
Seller agrees to sell and convey to Buyer and Buyer agrees to buy from Seller the Property defined below.

2. PROPERTY: The land, improvements and accessories are collectively referred to as the "Property".
   A. LAND: Lot _____ Block_____, _____
      Addition, City of _____ , County of _____,
      Texas, known as _____
      (address/zip code), or as described on attached exhibit.
   B. IMPROVEMENTS: The house, garage and all other fixtures and improvements attached to the above-described real property, including without limitation, the following **permanently installed and built-in items,** if any: all equipment and appliances, valances, screens, shutters, awnings, wall-to-wall carpeting, mirrors, ceiling fans, attic fans, mail boxes, television antennas, mounts and brackets for televisions and speakers, heating and air-conditioning units, security and fire detection equipment, wiring, plumbing and lighting fixtures, chandeliers, water softener system, kitchen equipment, garage door openers, cleaning equipment, shrubbery, landscaping, outdoor cooking equipment, and all other property owned by Seller and attached to the above described real property.
   C. ACCESSORIES: The following described related accessories, if any: window air conditioning units, stove, fireplace screens, curtains and rods, blinds, window shades, draperies and rods, door keys, mailbox keys, above ground pool, swimming pool equipment and maintenance accessories, artificial fireplace logs, and controls for: (i) garage doors, (ii) entry gates, and (iii) other improvements and accessories.
   D. EXCLUSIONS: The following improvements and accessories will be retained by Seller and must be removed prior to delivery of possession:_____
      _____.

3. SALES PRICE:
   A. Cash portion of Sales Price payable by Buyer at closing............................. $_____
   B. Sum of all financing described in the attached: ❑ Third Party Financing Addendum,
      ❑ Loan Assumption Addendum, ❑ Seller Financing Addendum .... $_____
   C. Sales Price (Sum of A and B).. $_____
4. LICENSE HOLDER DISCLOSURE: Texas law requires a real estate license holder who is a party to a transaction or acting on behalf of a spouse, parent, child, business entity in which the license holder owns more than 10%, or a trust for which the license holder acts as a trustee or of which the license holder or the license holder's spouse, parent or child is a beneficiary, to notify the other party in writing before entering into a contract of sale. Disclose if applicable:_____
   _____.

5. EARNEST MONEY: Upon execution of this contract by all parties, Buyer shall deposit $_____ as earnest money with _____, as escrow agent, at _____ (address). Buyer shall deposit additional earnest money of $_____ with escrow agent within _____ days after the effective date of this contract. If Buyer fails to deposit the earnest money as required by this contract, Buyer will be in default.
6.TITLE POLICY AND SURVEY:
   A. TITLE POLICY: Seller shall furnish to Buyer at ❑ Seller's ❑ Buyer's expense an owner policy of title insurance (Title Policy) issued by _____ (Title Company) in the amount of the Sales Price, dated at or after closing, insuring Buyer against loss under the provisions of the Title Policy, subject to the promulgated exclusions (including existing building and zoning ordinances) and the following exceptions:
      (1) Restrictive covenants common to the platted subdivision in which the Property is located.
      (2) The standard printed exception for standby fees, taxes and assessments.
      (3) Liens created as part of the financing described in Paragraph 3.
      (4) Utility easements created by the dedication deed or plat of the subdivision in which the Property is located.

Initialed for identification by Buyer_____ _____ and Seller _____ _____   TREC NO. 20-13

Contract Concerning _____ Page 2 of 9   11-2-2015
(Address of Property)

(5) Reservations or exceptions otherwise permitted by this contract or as may be approved by Buyer in writing.
(6) The standard printed exception as to marital rights.
(7) The standard printed exception as to waters, tidelands, beaches, streams, and related matters.
(8) The standard printed exception as to discrepancies, conflicts, shortages in area or boundary lines, encroachments or protrusions, or overlapping improvements: ❑(i) will not be amended or deleted from the title policy; or ❑(ii) will be amended to read, "shortages in area" at the expense of ❑Buyer ❑Seller.

B. COMMITMENT: Within 20 days after the Title Company receives a copy of this contract, Seller shall furnish to Buyer a commitment for title insurance (Commitment) and, at Buyer's expense, legible copies of restrictive covenants and documents evidencing exceptions in the Commitment (Exception Documents) other than the standard printed exceptions. Seller authorizes the Title Company to deliver the Commitment and Exception Documents to Buyer at Buyer's address shown in Paragraph 21. If the Commitment and Exception Documents are not delivered to Buyer within the specified time, the time for delivery will be automatically extended up to 15 days or 3 days before the Closing Date, whichever is earlier. If, due to factors beyond Seller's control, the Commitment and Exception Documents are not delivered within the time required, Buyer may terminate this contract and the earnest money will be refunded to Buyer.

C. SURVEY: The survey must be made by a registered professional land surveyor acceptable to the Title Company and Buyer's lender(s). (Check one box only)
❑(1)Within _____ days after the effective date of this contract, Seller shall furnish to Buyer and Title Company Seller's existing survey of the Property and a Residential Real Property Affidavit promulgated by the Texas Department of Insurance (T-47 Affidavit). **If Seller fails to furnish the existing survey or affidavit within the time prescribed, Buyer shall obtain a new survey at Seller's expense no later than 3 days prior to Closing Date.** If the existing survey or affidavit is not acceptable to Title Company or Buyer's lender(s), Buyer shall obtain a new survey at ❑Seller's ❑Buyer's expense no later than 3 days prior to Closing Date.
❑(2)Within _____ days after the effective date of this contract, Buyer shall obtain a new survey at Buyer's expense. Buyer is deemed to receive the survey on the date of actual receipt or the date specified in this paragraph, whichever is earlier.
❑(3)Within _____ days after the effective date of this contract, Seller, at Seller's expense shall furnish a new survey to Buyer.

D. OBJECTIONS: Buyer may object in writing to defects, exceptions, or encumbrances to title: disclosed on the survey other than items 6A(1) through (7) above; disclosed in the Commitment other than items 6A(1) through (8) above; or which prohibit the following use or activity: _____.
Buyer must object the earlier of (i) the Closing Date or (ii) _____ days after Buyer receives the Commitment, Exception Documents, and the survey. Buyer's failure to object within the time allowed will constitute a waiver of Buyer's right to object; except that the requirements in Schedule C of the Commitment are not waived by Buyer. Provided Seller is not obligated to incur any expense, Seller shall cure the timely objections of Buyer or any third party lender within 15 days after Seller receives the objections and the Closing Date will be extended as necessary. If objections are not cured within such 15 day period, this contract will terminate and the earnest money will be refunded to Buyer unless Buyer waives the objections.

E. TITLE NOTICES:
(1) ABSTRACT OR TITLE POLICY: Broker advises Buyer to have an abstract of title covering the Property examined by an attorney of Buyer's selection, or Buyer should be furnished with or obtain a Title Policy. If a Title Policy is furnished, the Commitment should be promptly reviewed by an attorney of Buyer's choice due to the time limitations on Buyer's right to object.
(2) MEMBERSHIP IN PROPERTY OWNERS ASSOCIATION(S): The Property ❑is ❑is not subject to mandatory membership in a property owners association(s). If the Property is subject to mandatory membership in a property owners association(s), Seller notifies Buyer under §5.012, Texas Property Code, that, as a purchaser of property in the residential community identified in Paragraph 2A in which the Property is located, you are obligated to be a member of the property owners association(s). Restrictive covenants governing the use and occupancy of the Property and all dedicatory instruments governing the establishment, maintenance, or operation of this residential community have been or will be recorded in the Real Property Records of the county in which the Property is located. Copies of the restrictive covenants and dedicatory instruments may be obtained from the county clerk. **You are obligated to pay assessments to the property owners association(s). The amount of the assessments is subject to**

Initialed for identification by Buyer_____ _____ and Seller _____ _____   TREC NO. 20-13

change. Your failure to pay the assessments could result in enforcement of the association's lien on and the foreclosure of the Property.
Section 207.003, Property Code, entitles an owner to receive copies of any document that governs the establishment, maintenance, or operation of a subdivision, including, but not limited to, restrictions, bylaws, rules and regulations, and a resale certificate from a property owners' association. A resale certificate contains information including, but not limited to, statements specifying the amount and frequency of regular assessments and the style and cause number of lawsuits to which the property owners' association is a party, other than lawsuits relating to unpaid ad valorem taxes of an individual member of the association. These documents must be made available to you by the property owners' association or the association's agent on your request.
If Buyer is concerned about these matters, the TREC promulgated Addendum for Property Subject to Mandatory Membership in a Property Owners Association(s) should be used.

(3) STATUTORY TAX DISTRICTS: If the Property is situated in a utility or other statutorily created district providing water, sewer, drainage, or flood control facilities and services, Chapter 49, Texas Water Code, requires Seller to deliver and Buyer to sign the statutory notice relating to the tax rate, bonded indebtedness, or standby fee of the district prior to final execution of this contract.

(4) TIDE WATERS: If the Property abuts the tidally influenced waters of the state, §33.135, Texas Natural Resources Code, requires a notice regarding coastal area property to be included in the contract. An addendum containing the notice promulgated by TREC or required by the parties must be used.

(5) ANNEXATION: If the Property is located outside the limits of a municipality, Seller notifies Buyer under §5.011, Texas Property Code, that the Property may now or later be included in the extraterritorial jurisdiction of a municipality and may now or later be subject to annexation by the municipality. Each municipality maintains a map that depicts its boundaries and extraterritorial jurisdiction. To determine if the Property is located within a municipality's extraterritorial jurisdiction or is likely to be located within a municipality's extraterritorial jurisdiction, contact all municipalities located in the general proximity of the Property for further information.

(6) PROPERTY LOCATED IN A CERTIFICATED SERVICE AREA OF A UTILITY SERVICE PROVIDER: Notice required by §13.257, Water Code: The real property, described in Paragraph 2, that you are about to purchase may be located in a certificated water or sewer service area, which is authorized by law to provide water or sewer service to the properties in the certificated area. If your property is located in a certificated area there may be special costs or charges that you will be required to pay before you can receive water or sewer service. There may be a period required to construct lines or other facilities necessary to provide water or sewer service to your property. You are advised to determine if the property is in a certificated area and contact the utility service provider to determine the cost that you will be required to pay and the period, if any, that is required to provide water or sewer service to your property. The undersigned Buyer hereby acknowledges receipt of the foregoing notice at or before the execution of a binding contract for the purchase of the real property described in Paragraph 2 or at closing of purchase of the real property.

(7) PUBLIC IMPROVEMENT DISTRICTS: If the Property is in a public improvement district, §5.014, Property Code, requires Seller to notify Buyer as follows: As a purchaser of this parcel of real property you are obligated to pay an assessment to a municipality or county for an improvement project undertaken by a public improvement district under Chapter 372, Local Government Code. The assessment may be due annually or in periodic installments. More information concerning the amount of the assessment and the due dates of that assessment may be obtained from the municipality or county levying the assessment. The amount of the assessments is subject to change. Your failure to pay the assessments could result in a lien on and the foreclosure of your property.

(8) TRANSFER FEES: If the Property is subject to a private transfer fee obligation, §5.205, Property Code, requires Seller to notify Buyer as follows: The private transfer fee obligation may be governed by Chapter 5, Subchapter G of the Texas Property Code.

(9) PROPANE GAS SYSTEM SERVICE AREA: If the Property is located in a propane gas system service area owned by a distribution system retailer, Seller must give Buyer written notice as required by §141.010, Texas Utilities Code. An addendum containing the notice approved by TREC or required by the parties should be used.

(10) NOTICE OF WATER LEVEL FLUCTUATIONS: If the Property adjoins an impoundment of water, including a reservoir or lake, constructed and maintained under Chapter 11, Water Code, that has a storage capacity of at least 5,000 acre-feet at the impoundment's normal operating level, Seller hereby notifies Buyer: "The water level of the impoundment of water adjoining the Property fluctuates for various reasons, including as

a result of: (1) an entity lawfully exercising its right to use the water stored in the impoundment; or (2) drought or flood conditions."

7.PROPERTY CONDITION:

A. ACCESS, INSPECTIONS AND UTILITIES: Seller shall permit Buyer and Buyer's agents access to the Property at reasonable times. Buyer may have the Property inspected by inspectors selected by Buyer and licensed by TREC or otherwise permitted by law to make inspections. Any hydrostatic testing must be separately authorized by Seller in writing. Seller at Seller's expense shall immediately cause existing utilities to be turned on and shall keep the utilities on during the time this contract is in effect.

B. SELLER'S DISCLOSURE NOTICE PURSUANT TO §5.008, TEXAS PROPERTY CODE (Notice): (Check one box only)

❑ (1) Buyer has received the Notice.

❑ (2) Buyer has not received the Notice. Within _____ days after the effective date of this contract, Seller shall deliver the Notice to Buyer. If Buyer does not receive the Notice, Buyer may terminate this contract at any time prior to the closing and the earnest money will be refunded to Buyer. If Seller delivers the Notice, Buyer may terminate this contract for any reason within 7 days after Buyer receives the Notice or prior to the closing, whichever first occurs, and the earnest money will be refunded to Buyer.

❑ (3)The Seller is not required to furnish the notice under the Texas Property Code.

C. SELLER'S DISCLOSURE OF LEAD-BASED PAINT AND LEAD-BASED PAINT HAZARDS is required by Federal law for a residential dwelling constructed prior to 1978.

D. ACCEPTANCE OF PROPERTY CONDITION: "As Is" means the present condition of the Property with any and all defects and without warranty except for the warranties of title and the warranties in this contract. Buyer's agreement to accept the Property As Is under Paragraph 7D(1) or (2) does not preclude Buyer from inspecting the Property under Paragraph 7A, from negotiating repairs or treatments in a subsequent amendment, or from terminating this contract during the Option Period, if any.
(Check one box only)

❑ (1) Buyer accepts the Property As Is.

❑ (2) Buyer accepts the Property As Is provided Seller, at Seller's expense, shall complete the following specific repairs and treatments: _____
_____.
(Do not insert general phrases, such as "subject to inspections" that do not identify specific repairs and treatments.)

E. LENDER REQUIRED REPAIRS AND TREATMENTS: Unless otherwise agreed in writing, neither party is obligated to pay for lender required repairs, which includes treatment for wood destroying insects. If the parties do not agree to pay for the lender required repairs or treatments, this contract will terminate and the earnest money will be refunded to Buyer. If the cost of lender required repairs and treatments exceeds 5% of the Sales Price, Buyer may terminate this contract and the earnest money will be refunded to Buyer.

F. COMPLETION OF REPAIRS AND TREATMENTS: Unless otherwise agreed in writing: (i) Seller shall complete all agreed repairs and treatments prior to the Closing Date; and (ii) all required permits must be obtained, and repairs and treatments must be performed by persons who are licensed to provide such repairs or treatments or, if no license is required by law, are commercially engaged in the trade of providing such repairs or treatments. At Buyer's election, any transferable warranties received by Seller with respect to the repairs and treatments will be transferred to Buyer at Buyer's expense. If Seller fails to complete any agreed repairs and treatments prior to the Closing Date, Buyer may exercise remedies under Paragraph 15 or extend the Closing Date up to 5 days if necessary for Seller to complete the repairs and treatments.

G. ENVIRONMENTAL MATTERS: Buyer is advised that the presence of wetlands, toxic substances, including asbestos and wastes or other environmental hazards, or the presence of a threatened or endangered species or its habitat may affect Buyer's intended use of the Property. If Buyer is concerned about these matters, an addendum promulgated by TREC or required by the parties should be used.

H. RESIDENTIAL SERVICE CONTRACTS: Buyer may purchase a residential service contract from a residential service company licensed by TREC. If Buyer purchases a residential service contract, Seller shall reimburse Buyer at closing for the cost of the residential service contract in an amount not exceeding $_____. Buyer should review any residential service contract for the scope of coverage, exclusions and limitations. **The purchase of a residential service contract is optional. Similar coverage may be purchased from various companies authorized to do business in Texas.**

8.BROKERS' FEES: All obligations of the parties for payment of brokers' fees are contained in separate written agreements.

Contract Concerning _____ Page 5 of 9   11-2-2015
(Address of Property)

9. CLOSING:

A. The closing of the sale will be on or before _____, 20_____, or within 7 days after objections made under Paragraph 6D have been cured or waived, whichever date is later (Closing Date). If either party fails to close the sale by the Closing Date, the non-defaulting party may exercise the remedies contained in Paragraph 15.

B. At closing:

    (1) Seller shall execute and deliver a general warranty deed conveying title to the Property to Buyer and showing no additional exceptions to those permitted in Paragraph 6 and furnish tax statements or certificates showing no delinquent taxes on the Property.

    (2) Buyer shall pay the Sales Price in good funds acceptable to the escrow agent.

    (3) Seller and Buyer shall execute and deliver any notices, statements, certificates, affidavits, releases, loan documents and other documents reasonably required for the closing of the sale and the issuance of the Title Policy.

    (4) There will be no liens, assessments, or security interests against the Property which will not be satisfied out of the sales proceeds unless securing the payment of any loans assumed by Buyer and assumed loans will not be in default.

    (5) If the Property is subject to a residential lease, Seller shall transfer security deposits (as defined under §92.102, Property Code), if any, to Buyer. In such an event, Buyer shall deliver to the tenant a signed statement acknowledging that the Buyer has acquired the Property and is responsible for the return of the security deposit, and specifying the exact dollar amount of the security deposit.

10. POSSESSION:

A Buyer's Possession: Seller shall deliver to Buyer possession of the Property in its present or required condition, ordinary wear and tear excepted: ❑upon closing and funding ❑according to a temporary residential lease form promulgated by TREC or other written lease required by the parties. Any possession by Buyer prior to closing or by Seller after closing which is not authorized by a written lease will establish a tenancy at sufferance relationship between the parties. **Consult your insurance agent prior to change of ownership and possession because insurance coverage may be limited or terminated. The absence of a written lease or appropriate insurance coverage may expose the parties to economic loss.**

B. Leases:

    (1) After the Effective Date, Seller may not execute any lease (including but not limited to mineral leases) or convey any interest in the Property without Buyer's written consent.

    (2) If the Property is subject to any lease to which Seller is a party, Seller shall deliver to Buyer copies of the lease(s) and any move-in condition form signed by the tenant within 7 days after the Effective Date of the contract.

11. SPECIAL PROVISIONS: (Insert only factual statements and business details applicable to the sale. TREC rules prohibit license holders from adding factual statements   or   business details for which a contract addendum, lease or other form has been promulgated by TREC for mandatory use.)

12. SETTLEMENT AND OTHER EXPENSES:

A. The following expenses must be paid at or prior to closing:

    (1) Expenses payable by Seller (Seller's Expenses):

        (a) Releases of existing liens, including prepayment penalties and recording fees; release of Seller's loan liability; tax statements or certificates; preparation of deed; one-half of escrow fee; and other expenses payable by Seller under this contract.

        (b) Seller shall also pay an amount not to exceed $_____ to be applied in the following order: Buyer's Expenses which Buyer is prohibited from paying by FHA, VA, Texas Veterans Land Board or other governmental loan programs, and then to other Buyer's Expenses as allowed by the lender.

    (2) Expenses payable by Buyer (Buyer's Expenses): Appraisal fees; loan application fees; origination charges; credit reports; preparation of loan documents; interest on the notes from date of disbursement to one month prior to dates of first monthly payments; recording fees; copies of easements and restrictions; loan title policy with endorsements required by lender; loan-related inspection fees; photos; amortization schedules; one-half of escrow fee; all prepaid items, including required premiums for flood and hazard insurance, reserve deposits for insurance, ad valorem taxes and special governmental assessments; final compliance inspection; courier fee; repair inspection; underwriting fee; wire transfer fee; expenses incident to any loan; Private

Initialed for identification by Buyer_____ _____ and Seller _____ _____   TREC NO. 20-13

Mortgage Insurance Premium (PMI), VA Loan Funding Fee, or FHA Mortgage Insurance Premium (MIP) as required by the lender; and other expenses payable by Buyer under this contract.

B. If any expense exceeds an amount expressly stated in this contract for such expense to be paid by a party, that party may terminate this contract unless the other party agrees to pay such excess. Buyer may not pay charges and fees expressly prohibited by FHA, VA, Texas Veterans Land Board or other governmental loan program regulations.

13. **PRORATIONS:** Taxes for the current year, interest, maintenance fees, assessments, dues and rents will be prorated through the Closing Date. The tax proration may be calculated taking into consideration any change in exemptions that will affect the current year's taxes. If taxes for the current year vary from the amount prorated at closing, the parties shall adjust the prorations when tax statements for the current year are available. If taxes are not paid at or prior to closing, Buyer shall pay taxes for the current year.

14. **CASUALTY LOSS:** If any part of the Property is damaged or destroyed by fire or other casualty after the effective date of this contract, Seller shall restore the Property to its previous condition as soon as reasonably possible, but in any event by the Closing Date. If Seller fails to do so due to factors beyond Seller's control, Buyer may (a) terminate this contract and the earnest money will be refunded to Buyer (b) extend the time for performance up to 15 days and the Closing Date will be extended as necessary or (c) accept the Property in its damaged condition with an assignment of insurance proceeds, if permitted by Seller's insurance carrier, and receive credit from Seller at closing in the amount of the deductible under the insurance policy. Seller's obligations under this paragraph are independent of any other obligations of Seller under this contract.

15. **DEFAULT:** If Buyer fails to comply with this contract, Buyer will be in default, and Seller may (a) enforce specific performance, seek such other relief as may be provided by law, or both, or (b) terminate this contract and receive the earnest money as liquidated damages, thereby releasing both parties from this contract. If Seller fails to comply with this contract, Seller will be in default and Buyer may (a) enforce specific performance, seek such other relief as may be provided by law, or both, or (b) terminate this contract and receive the earnest money, thereby releasing both parties from this contract.

16. **MEDIATION:** It is the policy of the State of Texas to encourage resolution of disputes through alternative dispute resolution procedures such as mediation. Any dispute between Seller and Buyer related to this contract which is not resolved through informal discussion will be submitted to a mutually acceptable mediation service or provider. The parties to the mediation shall bear the mediation costs equally. This paragraph does not preclude a party from seeking equitable relief from a court of competent jurisdiction.

17. **ATTORNEY'S FEES:** A Buyer, Seller, Listing Broker, Other Broker, or escrow agent who prevails in any legal proceeding related to this contract is entitled to recover reasonable attorney's fees and all costs of such proceeding.

18. **ESCROW:**
A. ESCROW: The escrow agent is not (i) a party to this contract and does not have liability for the performance or nonperformance of any party to this contract, (ii) liable for interest on the earnest money and (iii) liable for the loss of any earnest money caused by the failure of any financial institution in which the earnest money has been deposited unless the financial institution is acting as escrow agent.

B. EXPENSES: At closing, the earnest money must be applied first to any cash down payment, then to Buyer's Expenses and any excess refunded to Buyer. If no closing occurs, escrow agent may: (i) require a written release of liability of the escrow agent from all parties, (ii) require payment of unpaid expenses incurred on behalf of a party, and (iii) only deduct from the earnest money the amount of unpaid expenses incurred on behalf of the party receiving the earnest money.

C. DEMAND: Upon termination of this contract, either party or the escrow agent may send a release of earnest money to each party and the parties shall execute counterparts of the release and deliver same to the escrow agent. If either party fails to execute the release, either party may make a written demand to the escrow agent for the earnest money. If only one party makes written demand for the earnest money, escrow agent shall promptly provide a copy of the demand to the other party. If escrow agent does not receive written objection to the demand from the other party within 15 days, escrow agent may disburse the earnest money to the party making demand reduced by the amount of unpaid expenses incurred on behalf of the party receiving the earnest money and escrow agent may pay the same to the creditors. If escrow agent complies with the provisions of this paragraph, each party hereby releases escrow agent from all adverse claims related to the disbursal of the earnest money.

Contract Concerning _____ Page 7 of 9   11-2-2015
(Address of Property)

D. DAMAGES: Any party who wrongfully fails or refuses to sign a release acceptable to the escrow agent within 7 days of receipt of the request will be liable to the other party for (i) damages; (ii) the earnest money; (iii) reasonable attorney's fees; and (iv) all costs of suit.

E. NOTICES: Escrow agent's notices will be effective when sent in compliance with Paragraph 21. Notice of objection to the demand will be deemed effective upon receipt by escrow agent.

19. **REPRESENTATIONS:** All covenants, representations and warranties in this contract survive closing. If any representation of Seller in this contract is untrue on the Closing Date, Seller will be in default. Unless expressly prohibited by written agreement, Seller may continue to show the Property and receive, negotiate and accept back up offers.

20. **FEDERAL TAX REQUIREMENTS:** If Seller is a "foreign person," as defined by applicable law, or if Seller fails to deliver an affidavit to Buyer that Seller is not a "foreign person," then Buyer shall withhold from the sales proceeds an amount sufficient to comply with applicable tax law and deliver the same to the Internal Revenue Service together with appropriate tax forms. Internal Revenue Service regulations require filing written reports if currency in excess of specified amounts is received in the transaction.

21. **NOTICES:** All notices from one party to the other must be in writing and are effective when mailed to, hand-delivered at, or transmitted by fax or electronic transmission as follows:

To Buyer at: _____   **To Seller at:** _____

_____   _____

Phone: (___) _____   Phone: (___) _____

Fax: (___) _____   Fax: (___) _____

E-mail: _____   E-mail: _____

22. **AGREEMENT OF PARTIES:** This contract contains the entire agreement of the parties and cannot be changed except by their written agreement. Addenda which are a part of this contract are (Check all applicable boxes):

☐ Third Party Financing Addendum

☐ Seller Financing Addendum

☐ Addendum for Property Subject to Mandatory Membership in a Property Owners Association

☐ Buyer's Temporary Residential Lease

☐ Loan Assumption Addendum

☐ Addendum for Sale of Other Property by Buyer

☐ Addendum for Reservation of Oil, Gas and Other Minerals

☐ Addendum for "Back-Up" Contract

☐ Addendum for Coastal Area Property

☐ Environmental Assessment, Threatened or Endangered Species and Wetlands Addendum

☐ Seller's Temporary Residential Lease

☐ Short Sale Addendum

☐ Addendum for Property Located Seaward of the Gulf Intracoastal Waterway

☐ Addendum for Seller's Disclosure of Information on Lead-based Paint and Lead-based Paint Hazards as Required by Federal Law

☐ Addendum for Property in a Propane Gas System Service Area

☐ Other (list): _____

_____

Initialed for identification by Buyer_____ _____ and Seller _____ _____   TREC NO. 20-13

(Address of Property)

23. TERMINATION OPTION: For nominal consideration, the receipt of which is hereby acknowledged by Seller, and Buyer's agreement to pay Seller $_____ (Option Fee) within 3 days after the effective date of this contract, Seller grants Buyer the unrestricted right to terminate this contract by giving notice of termination to Seller within _____ days after the effective date of this contract (Option Period). Notices under this paragraph must be given by 5:00 p.m. (local time where the Property is located) by the date specified. If no dollar amount is stated as the Option Fee or if Buyer fails to pay the Option Fee to Seller within the time prescribed, this paragraph will not be a part of this contract and Buyer shall not have the unrestricted right to terminate this contract. If Buyer gives notice of termination within the time prescribed, the Option Fee will not be refunded; however, any earnest money will be refunded to Buyer. The Option Fee ☐will ☐will not be credited to the Sales Price at closing. **Time is of the essence for this paragraph and strict compliance with the time for performance is required.**

24. CONSULT AN ATTORNEY BEFORE SIGNING: TREC rules prohibit real estate license holders from giving legal advice. READ THIS CONTRACT CAREFULLY.

Buyer's Attorney is: _____   Seller's Attorney is: _____

_____   _____

Phone: (   ) _____   Phone: (   ) _____

Fax: (   ) _____   Fax: (   ) _____

E-mail: _____   E-mail: _____

**EXECUTED the _____day of _____, 20____ (EFFECTIVE DATE).
(BROKER: FILL IN THE DATE OF FINAL ACCEPTANCE.)**

_____   _____
Buyer   Seller

_____   _____
Buyer   Seller

TREC NO. 20-13

Contract Concerning _____ Page 9 of 9   11-2-2015
(Address of Property)

BROKER INFORMATION
(Print name(s) only. Do not sign)

Other Broker Firm _____ License No. | Listing Broker Firm _____ License No.

represents ☐ Buyer only as Buyer's agent
☐ Seller as Listing Broker's subagent

represents ☐ Seller and Buyer as an intermediary
☐ Seller only as Seller's agent

Associate's Name _____ License No.

Licensed Supervisor of Associate _____ License No.

Other Broker's Address _____ Fax

City _____ State _____ Zip

Associate's Email Address _____ Phone

Listing Associate's Name _____ License No.

Licensed Supervisor of Listing Associate _____ License No.

Listing Broker's Office Address _____ Fax

City _____ State _____ Zip

Listing Associate's Email Address _____ Phone

Selling Associate's Name _____ License No.

Licensed Supervisor of Selling Associate _____ License No.

Selling Associate's Office Address _____ Fax

City _____ State _____ Zip

Selling Associate's Email Address _____ Phone

Listing Broker has agreed to pay Other Broker_____of the total sales price when the Listing Broker's fee is received. Escrow agent is authorized and directed to pay other Broker from Listing Broker's fee at closing.

OPTION FEE RECEIPT

Receipt of $_____ (Option Fee) in the form of _____ is acknowledged.

_____   _____
Seller or Listing Broker   Date

CONTRACT AND EARNEST MONEY RECEIPT

Receipt of ☐ Contract and ☐ $_____ Earnest Money in the form of _____ is acknowledged.

Escrow Agent: _____   Date: _____

By: _____   _____
                                                            Email Address

_____   Phone: (____)_____
Address

_____   Fax: (____)_____
City   State   Zip

TREC NO. 20-13

44

PROMULGATED BY THE TEXAS REAL ESTATE COMMISSION (TREC)   11-2-2015

NEW HOME CONTRACT

(Completed Construction)

NOTICE: Not For Use For Condominium Transactions or Closings Prior to Completion of Construction

1. PARTIES: The parties to this contract are _____
(Seller) and _____(Buyer). Seller agrees to sell and convey to Buyer and Buyer agrees to buy from Seller the Property defined below.

2. PROPERTY: Lot _____,Block_____,
_____Addition,
City of_____,County of_____,
Texas, known as _____
(address/zip code), or as described on attached exhibit, together with: (i) improvements, fixtures and all other property located thereon; and (ii) all rights, privileges and appurtenances thereto, including but not limited to: permits, easements, and cooperative and association memberships. All property sold by this contract is called the "Property".

3. SALES PRICE:
A. Cash portion of Sales Price payable by Buyer at closing......................$_____
B. Sum of all financing described in the attached: ❏ Third Party Financing Addendum,
 ❏ Loan Assumption Addendum, ❏ Seller Financing Addendum ......$_____
C. Sales Price (Sum of A and B)...$_____

4. LICENSE HOLDER DISCLOSURE: Texas law requires a real estate license holder who is a party to a transaction or acting on behalf of a spouse, parent, child, business entity in which the license holder owns more than 10%, or a trust for which the license holder acts as trustee or of which the license holder or the license holder's spouse parent or child is a beneficiary, to notify the other party in writing before entering into a contract of sale. Disclose if applicable:_____
_____.

5. EARNEST MONEY: Upon execution of this contract by all parties, Buyer shall deposit $_____ as earnest money with _____,
as escrow agent, at _____
(address). Buyer shall deposit additional earnest money of $_____ with escrow agent within _____ days after the effective date of this contract. If Buyer fails to deposit the earnest money as required by this contract, Buyer will be in default.

6. TITLE POLICY AND SURVEY:
A. TITLE POLICY: Seller shall furnish to Buyer at ❏Seller's ❏Buyer's expense an owner policy of title insurance (Title Policy) issued by _____.
 (Title Company) in the amount of the Sales Price, dated at or after closing, insuring Buyer against loss under the provisions of the Title Policy, subject to the promulgated exclusions (including existing building and zoning ordinances) and the following exceptions:
 (1) Restrictive covenants common to the platted subdivision in which the Property is located.
 (2) The standard printed exception for standby fees, taxes and assessments.
 (3) Liens created as part of the financing described in Paragraph 3.
 (4) Utility easements created by the dedication deed or plat of the subdivision in which the Property is located.
 (5) Reservations or exceptions otherwise permitted by this contract or as may be approved by Buyer in writing.
 (6) The standard printed exception as to marital rights.
 (7) The standard printed exception as to waters, tidelands, beaches, streams, and related matters.
 (8) The standard printed exception as to discrepancies, conflicts, shortages in area or boundary lines, encroachments or protrusions, or overlapping improvement: ❏ (i) will not be amended or deleted from the title policy; or ❏(ii) will be amended to read, "shortages in area" at the expense of ❏Buyer ❏Seller.
B. COMMITMENT: Within 20 days after the Title Company receives a copy of this contract, Seller shall furnish to Buyer a commitment for title insurance (Commitment) and, at Buyer's expense, legible copies of restrictive covenants and documents evidencing exceptions in the Commitment (Exception Documents) other than the standard printed exceptions. Seller authorizes the Title Company to deliver the Commitment and Exception Documents to Buyer at Buyer's address shown in Paragraph 21. If the Commitment and Exception Documents are not delivered to Buyer within the specified time, the time for delivery will be automatically extended up to 15 days or 3 days before the Closing Date, whichever is earlier. If, due to factors beyond Seller's control, the Commitment and Exception Documents are not delivered within the time required, Buyer may terminate this contract and the earnest money will be refunded to Buyer.

Initialed for identification by Buyer_____ _____ and Seller _____ _____   TREC NO. 24-14

Contract Concerning _____ Page 2 of 9   11-2-2015
(Address of Property)

C. SURVEY: The survey must be made by a registered professional land surveyor acceptable to the Title Company and Buyer's lender(s). (Check one box only)

❑ (1) Within _____ days after the effective date of this contract, Seller shall furnish to Buyer and Title Company Seller's existing survey of the Property and a Residential Real Property Affidavit promulgated by the Texas Department of Insurance (T-47 Affidavit). **If Seller fails to furnish the existing survey or affidavit within the time prescribed, Buyer shall obtain a new survey at Seller's expense no later than 3 days prior to Closing Date.** If the existing survey or affidavit is not acceptable to Title Company or Buyer's lender(s), Buyer shall obtain a new survey at ❑ Seller's ❑ Buyer's expense no later than 3 days prior to Closing Date.

❑ (2) Within _____ days after the effective date of this contract, Buyer shall obtain a new survey at Buyer's expense. Buyer is deemed to receive the survey on the date of actual receipt or the date specified in this paragraph, whichever is earlier.

❑ (3) Within _____ days after the effective date of this contract, Seller, at Seller's expense shall furnish a new survey to Buyer.

D. OBJECTIONS: Buyer may object in writing to defects, exceptions, or encumbrances to title: disclosed on the survey other than items 6A(1) through (7) above; disclosed in the Commitment other than items 6A(1) through (8) above; or which prohibit the following use or activity: _____.

Buyer must object the earlier of (i) the Closing Date or (ii) _____ days after Buyer receives the Commitment, Exception Documents, and the survey. Buyer's failure to object within the time allowed will constitute a waiver of Buyer's right to object; except that the requirements in Schedule C of the Commitment are not waived by Buyer. Provided Seller is not obligated to incur any expense, Seller shall cure the timely objections of Buyer or any third party lender within 15 days after Seller receives the objections and the Closing Date will be extended as necessary. If objections are not cured within such 15 day period, this contract will terminate and the earnest money will be refunded to Buyer unless Buyer waives the objections.

E. TITLE NOTICES:

(1) ABSTRACT OR TITLE POLICY: Broker advises Buyer to have an abstract of title covering the Property examined by an attorney of Buyer's selection, or Buyer should be furnished with or obtain a Title Policy. If a Title Policy is furnished, the Commitment should be promptly reviewed by an attorney of Buyer's choice due to the time limitations on Buyer's right to object.

(2) MEMBERSHIP IN PROPERTY OWNERS ASSOCIATION(S): The Property ❑is ❑is not subject to mandatory membership in a property owners association(s). If the Property is subject to mandatory membership in a property owners association(s), Seller notifies Buyer under §5.012, Texas Property Code, that, as a purchaser of property in the residential community identified in Paragraph 2A in which the Property is located, you are obligated to be a member of the property owners association(s). Restrictive covenants governing the use and occupancy of the Property and all dedicatory instruments governing the establishment, maintenance, and operation of this residential community have been or will be recorded in the Real Property Records of the county in which the Property is located. Copies of the restrictive covenants and dedicatory instruments may be obtained from the county clerk. **You are obligated to pay assessments to the property owners association(s). The amount of the assessments is subject to change. Your failure to pay the assessments could result in enforcement of the association's lien on and the foreclosure of the Property.** Section 207.003, Property Code, entitles an owner to receive copies of any document that governs the establishment, maintenance, or operation of a subdivision, including, but not limited to, restrictions, bylaws, rules and regulations, and a resale certificate from a property owners' association. A resale certificate contains information including, but not limited to, statements specifying the amount and frequency of regular assessments and the style and cause number of lawsuits to which the property owners' association is a party, other than lawsuits relating to unpaid ad valorem taxes of an individual member of the association. These documents must be made available to you by the property owners' association or the association's agent on your request. **If Buyer is concerned about these matters, the TREC promulgated Addendum for Property Subject to Mandatory Membership in a Property Owners Association should be used.**

(3) STATUTORY TAX DISTRICTS: If the Property is situated in a utility or other statutorily created district providing water, sewer, drainage, or flood control facilities and services, Chapter 49, Texas Water Code, requires Seller to deliver and Buyer to sign the statutory notice relating to the tax rate, bonded indebtedness, or standby fee of the district prior to final execution of this contract.

(4) TIDE WATERS: If the Property abuts the tidally influenced waters of the state, §33.135, Texas Natural Resources Code, requires a notice regarding coastal area property to be included in the contract. An addendum containing the notice promulgated by TREC or required by the parties must be used.

Initialed for identification by Buyer_____ _____ and Seller _____ _____   TREC NO. 24-14

(5) ANNEXATION: If the Property is located outside the limits of a municipality, Seller notifies Buyer under §5.011, Texas Property Code, that the Property may now or later be included in the extraterritorial jurisdiction of a municipality and may now or later be subject to annexation by the municipality. Each municipality maintains a map that depicts its boundaries and extraterritorial jurisdiction. To determine if the Property is located within a municipality's extraterritorial jurisdiction or is likely to be located within a municipality's extraterritorial jurisdiction, contact all municipalities located in the general proximity of the Property for further information.

(6) PROPERTY LOCATED IN A CERTIFICATED SERVICE AREA OF A UTILITY SERVICE PROVIDER: Notice required by §13.257, Water Code: The real property, described in Paragraph 2, that you are about to purchase may be located in a certificated water or sewer service area, which is authorized by law to provide water or sewer service to the properties in the certificated area. If your property is located in a certificated area there may be special costs or charges that you will be required to pay before you can receive water or sewer service. There may be a period required to construct lines or other facilities necessary to provide water or sewer service to your property. You are advised to determine if the property is in a certificated area and contact the utility service provider to determine the cost that you will be required to pay and the period, if any, that is required to provide water or sewer service to your property. The undersigned Buyer hereby acknowledges receipt of the foregoing notice at or before the execution of a binding contract for the purchase of the real property described in Paragraph 2 or at closing of purchase of the real property.

(7) PUBLIC IMPROVEMENT DISTRICTS: If the Property is in a public improvement district, §5.014, Property Code, requires Seller to notify Buyer as follows: As a purchaser of this parcel of real property you are obligated to pay an assessment to a municipality or county for an improvement project undertaken by a public improvement district under Chapter 372, Local Government Code. The assessment may be due annually or in periodic installments. More information concerning the amount of the assessment and the due dates of that assessment may be obtained from the municipality or county levying the assessment. The amount of the assessments is subject to change. Your failure to pay the assessments could result in a lien on and the foreclosure of your property.

(8) TRANSFER FEES: If the Property is subject to a private transfer fee obligation, §5.205, Property Code, requires Seller to notify Buyer as follows: The private transfer fee obligation may be governed by Chapter 5, Subchapter G of the Texas Property Code.

(9) PROPANE GAS SYSTEM SERVICE AREA: If the Property is located in a propane gas system service area owned by a distribution system retailer, Seller must give Buyer written notice as required by §141.010, Texas Utilities Code. An addendum containing the notice approved by TREC or required by the parties should be used.

(10) NOTICE OF WATER LEVEL FLUCTUATIONS: If the Property adjoins an impoundment of water, including a reservoir or lake, constructed and maintained under Chapter 11, Water Code, that has a storage capacity of at least 5,000 acre-feet at the impoundment's normal operating level, Seller hereby notifies Buyer: "The water level of the impoundment of water adjoining the Property fluctuates for various reasons, including as a result of: (1) an entity lawfully exercising its right to use the water stored in the impoundment; or (2) drought or flood conditions."

7. PROPERTY CONDITION:

A. ACCESS, INSPECTIONS AND UTILITIES: Seller shall permit Buyer and Buyer's agents access to the Property at reasonable times. Buyer may have the Property inspected by inspectors selected by Buyer and licensed by TREC or otherwise permitted by law to make inspections. Seller at Seller's expense shall immediately cause existing utilities to be turned on and shall keep the utilities on during the time this contract is in effect.

B. ACCEPTANCE OF PROPERTY CONDITION: "As Is" means the present condition of the Property with any and all defects and without warranty except for the warranties of title and the warranties in this contract. Buyer's agreement to accept the Property As Is under Paragraph 7B(1) or (2) does not preclude Buyer from inspecting the Property under Paragraph 7A, from negotiating repairs or treatments in a subsequent amendment, or from terminating this contract during the Option Period, if any.
(Check one box only)
❏ (1)Buyer accepts the Property As Is.
❏ (2)Buyer accepts the Property As Is provided Seller, at Seller's expense, shall complete the following specific repairs and treatments:_____(Do not insert general phrases, such as "subject to inspections," that do not identify specific repairs and treatments.)

C. WARRANTIES: Except as expressly set forth in this contract, a separate writing, or provided by law, Seller makes no other express warranties. Seller shall assign to Buyer at closing all assignable manufacturer warranties.

Contract Concerning _____Page 4 of 9   11-2-2015
(Address of Property)

D. INSULATION: As required by Federal Trade Commission Regulations, the information relating to the insulation installed or to be installed in the Improvements at the Property is: (check only one box below)
☐ (1) as shown in the attached specifications.
☐ (2) as follows:
    (a) Exterior walls of improved living areas: insulated with_____ insulation to a thickness of _____ inches which yields an R-Value of _____.
    (b) Walls in other areas of the home: insulated with _____ insulation to a thickness of _____ inches which yields an R-Value of _____.
    (c) Ceilings in improved living areas: insulated with_____ insulation to a thickness of _____ inches which yields an R-Value of _____.
    (d) Floors of improved living areas not applied to a slab foundation: insulated with_____ _____ insulation to a thickness of _____ inches which yields an R-Value of _____.
    (e) Other insulated areas: insulated with _____insulation to a thickness of _____ inches which yields an R-Value of _____.
All stated R-Values are based on information provided by the manufacturer of the insulation.

E. LENDER REQUIRED REPAIRS AND TREATMENTS: Unless otherwise agreed in writing, neither party is obligated to pay for lender required repairs, which includes treatment for wood destroying insects. If the parties do not agree to pay for the lender required repairs or treatments, this contract will terminate and the earnest money will be refunded to Buyer. If the cost of lender required repairs and treatments exceeds 5% of the Sales Price, Buyer may terminate this contract and the earnest money will be refunded to Buyer.

F. COMPLETION OF REPAIRS, TREATMENTS, AND IMPROVEMENTS: Unless otherwise agreed in writing: (i) Seller shall complete all agreed repairs, treatments, and improvements (Work) prior to the Closing Date; and (ii) all required permits must be obtained, and Work must be performed by persons who are licensed to provide such Work or, if no license is required by law, are commercially engaged in the trade of providing such Work. At Buyer's election, any transferable warranties received by Seller with respect to the Work will be transferred to Buyer at Buyer's expense. If Seller fails to complete any agreed Work prior to the Closing Date, Buyer may exercise remedies under Paragraph 15 or extend the Closing Date up to 5 days if necessary for Seller to complete Work.

G. ENVIRONMENTAL MATTERS: Buyer is advised that the presence of wetlands, toxic substances, including asbestos and wastes or other environmental hazards or the presence of a threatened or endangered species or its habitat may affect Buyer's intended use of the Property. If Buyer is concerned about these matters, an addendum promulgated by TREC or required by the parties should be used.

H. SELLER'S DISCLOSURE: Except as otherwise disclosed in this contract, Seller has no knowledge of the following:
    (1) any flooding of the Property which has had a material adverse effect on the use of the Property;
    (2) any pending or threatened litigation, condemnation, or special assessment affecting the Property;
    (3) any environmental hazards that materially and adversely affect the Property;
    (4) any dumpsite, landfill, or underground tanks or containers now or previously located on the Property;
    (5) any wetlands, as defined by federal or state law or regulation, affecting the Property; or
    (6) any threatened or endangered species or their habitat affecting the Property.

I. RESIDENTIAL SERVICE CONTRACTS: Buyer may purchase a residential service contract from a residential service company licensed by TREC. If Buyer purchases a residential service contract, Seller shall reimburse Buyer at closing for the cost of the residential service contract in an amount not exceeding $_____ . Buyer should review any residential service contract for the scope of coverage, exclusions and limitations. **The purchase of a residential service contract is optional. Similar coverage may be purchased from various companies authorized to do business in Texas.**

8. BROKERS' FEES: All obligations of the parties for payment of brokers' fees are contained in separate written agreements.

9. CLOSING:
    A. The closing of the sale will be on or before _____, 20_____, or within 7 days after objections made under Paragraph 6D have been cured or waived, whichever date is later (Closing Date). If either party fails to close the sale by the Closing Date, the non-defaulting party may exercise the remedies contained in Paragraph 15.
    B. At closing:
        (1) Seller shall execute and deliver a general warranty deed conveying title to the Property to Buyer and showing no additional exceptions to those permitted in Paragraph 6 and furnish tax statements or certificates showing no delinquent taxes on the Property.
        (2) Buyer shall pay the Sales Price in good funds acceptable to the escrow agent.
        (3) Seller and Buyer shall execute and deliver any notices, statements, certificates, affidavits,

Initialed for identification by Buyer_____ _____ and Seller _____ _____   TREC NO. 24-14

Contract Concerning _____ Page 5 of 9   11-2-2015
                                    (Address of Property)

releases, loan documents and other documents reasonably required for the closing of the sale and the issuance of the Title Policy.
(4) There will be no liens, assessments, or security interests against the Property which will not be satisfied out of the sales proceeds unless securing the payment of any loans assumed by Buyer and assumed loans will not be in default.

10. POSSESSION:
A. Buyer's Possession: Seller shall deliver to Buyer possession of the Property in its present or required condition, ordinary wear and tear excepted: ❑ upon closing and funding ❑ according to a temporary residential lease form promulgated by TREC or other written lease required by the parties. Any possession by Buyer prior to closing or by Seller after closing which is not authorized by a written lease will establish a tenancy at sufferance relationship between the parties. **Consult your insurance agent prior to change of ownership and possession because insurance coverage may be limited or terminated. The absence of a written lease or appropriate insurance coverage may expose the parties to economic loss.**
B. Leases: After the Effective Date, Seller may not execute any lease (including but not limited to mineral leases) or convey any interest in the Property without Buyer's written consent.

11. SPECIAL PROVISIONS: (Insert only factual statements and business details applicable to the sale. TREC rules prohibit license holders from adding factual statements or business details for which a contract addendum, lease or other form has been promulgated by TREC for mandatory use.)

12. SETTLEMENT AND OTHER EXPENSES:
A. The following expenses must be paid at or prior to closing:
(1) Expenses payable by Seller (Seller's Expenses):
(a) Releases of existing liens, including prepayment penalties and recording fees; release of Seller's loan liability; tax statements or certificates; preparation of deed; one-half of escrow fee; and other expenses payable by Seller under this contract.
(b) Seller shall also pay an amount not to exceed $ _____ to be applied in the following order: Buyer's Expenses which Buyer is prohibited from paying by FHA, VA, Texas Veterans Land Board or other governmental loan programs, and then to other Buyer's Expenses as allowed by the lender.
(2) Expenses payable by Buyer (Buyer's Expenses): Appraisal fees; loan application fees; origination charges; credit reports; preparation of loan documents; interest on the notes from date of disbursement to one month prior to dates of first monthly payments; recording fees; copies of easements and restrictions; loan title policy with endorsements required by lender; loan-related inspection fees; photos; amortization schedules; one-half of escrow fee; all prepaid items, including required premiums for flood and hazard insurance, reserve deposits for insurance, ad valorem taxes and special governmental assessments; final compliance inspection; courier fee; repair inspection; underwriting fee; wire transfer fee; expenses incident to any loan; Private Mortgage Insurance Premium (PMI), VA Loan Funding Fee, or FHA Mortgage Insurance Premium (MIP) as required by the lender; and other expenses payable by Buyer under this contract.
B. If any expense exceeds an amount expressly stated in this contract for such expense to be paid by a party, that party may terminate this contract unless the other party agrees to pay such excess. Buyer may not pay charges and fees expressly prohibited by FHA, VA, Texas Veterans Land Board or other governmental loan program regulations.

13. PRORATIONS AND ROLLBACK TAXES:
A. PRORATIONS: Taxes for the current year, maintenance fees, assessments, dues and rents will be prorated through the Closing Date. The tax proration may be calculated taking into consideration any change in exemptions that will affect the current year's taxes. If taxes for the current year vary from the amount prorated at closing, the parties shall adjust the prorations when tax statements for the current year are available. If taxes are not paid at or prior to closing, Buyer will be obligated to pay taxes for the current year.
B. ROLLBACK TAXES: If additional taxes, penalties, or interest (Assessments) are imposed because of Seller's use or change in use of the Property prior to closing, the Assessments will be the obligation of Seller. Obligations imposed by this paragraph will survive closing.

14. CASUALTY LOSS: If any part of the Property is damaged or destroyed by fire or other casualty after the effective date of this contract, Seller shall restore the Property to its previous condition as soon as reasonably possible, but in any event by the Closing Date. If Seller fails to do so due to factors beyond Seller's control, Buyer may (a) terminate this contract and the earnest money will be refunded to Buyer (b) extend the time for performance up to 15 days and the Closing Date will be extended as necessary or (c) accept the Property in its damaged condition with an assignment of insurance proceeds, if permitted by Seller's insurance carrier, and receive credit from Seller at closing in the amount of the deductible under the insurance policy. Seller's obligations under this paragraph are independent of any other obligations of Seller under this contract.

Contract Concerning _____ Page 6 of 9   11-2-2015
(Address of Property)

15. DEFAULT: If Buyer fails to comply with this contract, Buyer will be in default, and Seller may (a) enforce specific performance, seek such other relief as may be provided by law, or both, or (b) terminate this contract and receive the earnest money as liquidated damages, thereby releasing both parties from this contract. If Seller fails to comply with this contract Seller will be in default and Buyer may (a) enforce specific performance, seek such other relief as may be provided by law, or both, or (b) terminate this contract and receive the earnest money, thereby releasing both parties from this contract.

16. MEDIATION: It is the policy of the State of Texas to encourage resolution of disputes through alternative dispute resolution procedures such as mediation. Subject to applicable law, any dispute between Seller and Buyer related to this contract which is not resolved through informal discussion will be submitted to a mutually acceptable mediation service or provider. The parties to the mediation shall bear the mediation costs equally. This paragraph does not preclude a party from seeking equitable relief from a court of competent jurisdiction.

17. ATTORNEY'S FEES: A Buyer, Seller, Listing Broker, Other Broker, or escrow agent who prevails in any legal proceeding related to this contract is entitled to recover reasonable attorney's fees and all costs of such proceeding.

18. ESCROW:
A. ESCROW: The escrow agent is not (i) a party to this contract and does not have liability for the performance or nonperformance of any party to this contract, (ii) liable for interest on the earnest money and (iii) liable for the loss of any earnest money caused by the failure of any financial institution in which the earnest money has been deposited unless the financial institution is acting as escrow agent.
B. EXPENSES: At closing, the earnest money must be applied first to any cash down payment, then to Buyer's Expenses and any excess refunded to Buyer. If no closing occurs, escrow agent may: (i) require a written release of liability of the escrow agent from all parties, (ii) require payment of unpaid expenses incurred on behalf of a party, and (iii) only deduct from the earnest money the amount of unpaid expenses incurred on behalf of the party receiving the earnest money.
C. DEMAND: Upon termination of this contract, either party or the escrow agent may send a release of earnest money to each party and the parties shall execute counterparts of the release and deliver same to the escrow agent. If either party fails to execute the release, either party may make a written demand to the escrow agent for the earnest money. If only one party makes written demand for the earnest money, escrow agent shall promptly provide a copy of the demand to the other party. If escrow agent does not receive written objection to the demand from the other party within 15 days, escrow agent may disburse the earnest money to the party making demand reduced by the amount of unpaid expenses incurred on behalf of the party receiving the earnest money and escrow agent may pay the same to the creditors. If escrow agent complies with the provisions of this paragraph, each party hereby releases escrow agent from all adverse claims related to the disbursal of the earnest money.
D. DAMAGES: Any party who wrongfully fails or refuses to sign a release acceptable to the escrow agent within 7 days of receipt of the request will be liable to the other party for (i) damages; (ii) the earnest money; (iii) reasonable attorney's fees; and (iv) all costs of suit.
E. NOTICES: Escrow agent's notices will be effective when sent in compliance with Paragraph 21. Notice of objection to the demand will be deemed effective upon receipt by escrow agent.

19. REPRESENTATIONS: All covenants, representations and warranties in this contract survive closing. If any representation of Seller in this contract is untrue on the Closing Date, Seller will be in default. Unless expressly prohibited by written agreement, Seller may continue to show the Property and receive, negotiate and accept back up offers.

20. FEDERAL TAX REQUIREMENTS: If Seller is a "foreign person," as defined by applicable law, or if Seller fails to deliver an affidavit to Buyer that Seller is not a "foreign person," then Buyer shall withhold from the sales proceeds an amount sufficient to comply with applicable tax law and deliver the same to the Internal Revenue Service together with appropriate tax forms. Internal Revenue Service regulations require filing written reports if currency in excess of specified amounts is received in the transaction.

21.NOTICES: All notices from one party to the other must be in writing and are effective when mailed to, hand-delivered at, or transmitted by fax or electronic transmission as follows:

To Buyer		**To Seller**	
at:	_____	at:	_____
	_____		_____
Phone:	( )_____	Phone:	( )_____
Fax:	( )_____	Fax:	( )_____
E-mail:	_____	E-mail:	_____

Initialed for identification by Buyer_____ _____ and Seller _____ _____   TREC NO. 24-14

22. AGREEMENT OF PARTIES: This contract contains the entire agreement of the parties and cannot be changed except by their written agreement. Addenda which are a part of this contract are (check all applicable boxes):

❑ Third Party Financing Addendum

❑ Seller Financing Addendum

❑ Addendum for Property Subject to Mandatory Membership in a Property Owners Association

❑ Buyer's Temporary Residential Lease

❑ Loan Assumption Addendum

❑ Addendum for Sale of Other Property by Buyer

❑ Addendum for Reservation of Oil, Gas and Other Minerals

❑ Addendum for "Back-Up" Contract

❑ Addendum for Coastal Area Property

❑ Environmental Assessment, Threatened or Endangered Species and Wetlands Addendum

❑ Seller's Temporary Residential Lease

❑ Short Sale Addendum

❑ Addendum for Property Located Seaward of the Gulf Intracoastal Waterway

❑ Addendum for Property in a Propane Gas System Service Area

❑ Other (list): _____

_____

_____

_____

23. TERMINATION OPTION: For nominal consideration, the receipt of which is hereby acknowledged by Seller, and Buyer's agreement to pay Seller $_____ (Option Fee) within 3 days after the effective date of this contract, Seller grants Buyer the unrestricted right to terminate this contract by giving notice of termination to Seller within _____ days after the effective date of this contract (Option Period). Notices under this paragraph must be given by 5:00 p.m. (local time where the Property is located) by the date specified. If no dollar amount is stated as the Option Fee or if Buyer fails to pay the Option Fee to Seller within the time prescribed, this paragraph will not be a part of this contract and Buyer shall not have the unrestricted right to terminate this contract. If Buyer gives notice of termination within the time prescribed, the Option Fee will not be refunded; however, any earnest money will be refunded to Buyer. The Option Fee ❑will ❑will not be credited to the Sales Price at closing. **Time is of the essence for this paragraph and strict compliance with the time for performance is required.**

24. CONSULT AN ATTORNEY BEFORE SIGNING: TREC rules prohibit real estate license holders from giving legal advice. READ THIS CONTRACT CAREFULLY.

Buyer's
Attorney is: _____

Seller's
Attorney is: _____

_____

_____

Phone: (   ) _____

Phone: (   ) _____

Fax: (   ) _____

Fax: (   ) _____

E-mail: _____

E-mail: _____

Contract Concerning _____ Page 8 of 9   11-2-2015

(Address of Property)

EXECUTED the _____day of _____, 20____ (EFFECTIVE DATE).
(BROKER: FILL IN THE DATE OF FINAL ACCEPTANCE.)

This contract is subject to Chapter 27 of the Texas Property Code. The provisions of that chapter may affect your right to recover damages arising from a construction defect. If you have a complaint concerning a construction defect and that defect has not been corrected as may be required by law or by contract, you must provide the notice required by Chapter 27 of the Texas Property Code to the contractor by certified mail, return receipt requested, not later than the 60th day before the date you file suit to recover damages in a court of law or initiate arbitration. The notice must refer to Chapter 27 of the Texas Property Code and must describe the construction defect. If requested by the contractor, you must provide the contractor an opportunity to inspect and cure the defect as provided by Section 27.004 of the Texas Property Code.

_____
Buyer

_____
Buyer

_____
Seller

_____
Seller

TREC NO. 24-14

Contract Concerning _____ Page 9 of 9   11-2-2015
(Address of Property)

BROKER INFORMATION
(Print name(s) only. Do not sign)

| Other Broker Firm | License No. | Listing Broker Firm | License No. |

represents ☐ Buyer only as Buyer's agent

☐ Seller as Listing Broker's subagent

represents ☐ Seller and Buyer as an intermediary

☐ Seller only as Seller's agent

| Associate's Name | License No. | Associate's Name | License No. |

| Licensed Supervisor of Associate | License No. | Licensed Supervisor of Listing Associate | License No. |

| Other Broker's Address | Fax | Listing Broker's Office Address | Fax |

| City | State | Zip | City | State | Zip |

| Associate's Email Address | Phone | Listing Associate's Email Address | Phone |

| Selling Associate's Name | License No. |

| Licensed Supervisor of Selling Associate | License No. |

| Selling Associate's Office Address | Fax |

| City | State | Zip |

| Selling Associate's Email Address | Phone |

Listing Broker has agreed to pay Other Broker_____of the total sales price when the Listing Broker's fee is received. Escrow agent is authorized and directed to pay other Broker from Listing Broker's fee at closing.

OPTION FEE RECEIPT

Receipt of $_____ (Option Fee) in the form of _____ is acknowledged.

_____   _____
Seller or Listing Broker   Date

CONTRACT AND EARNEST MONEY RECEIPT

Receipt of ☐Contract and ☐$_____ Earnest Money in the form of _____
is acknowledged.

Escrow Agent: _____   Date: _____

By: _____
                                                                                  _____
                                                                                  Email Address

_____   Phone: (_____) _____
Address

_____   Fax: (_____) _____
City   State   Zip

TREC NO. 24-14

PROMULGATED BY THE TEXAS REAL ESTATE COMMISSION (TREC)   11-2-2015
NEW HOME CONTRACT
(Incomplete Construction)
NOTICE: Not For Use For Condominium Transactions or Closings Prior to Completion of Construction

1. PARTIES: The parties to this contract are _____ (Seller) and _____(Buyer). Seller agrees to sell and convey to Buyer and Buyer agrees to buy from Seller the Property defined below.

2. PROPERTY: Lot _____,Block_____,_____ Addition, City of_____,County of _____Texas, known as _____(address/zip code), or as described on attached exhibit, together with: (i) improvements, fixtures and all other property described in the Construction Documents; and (ii) all rights, privileges and appurtenances thereto, including but not limited to: permits, easements, and cooperative and association memberships. All property sold by this contract is called the "Property".

3. SALES PRICE:
   A. Cash portion of Sales Price payable by Buyer at closing ....$_____
   B. Sum of all financing described in the attached: ❑   Third Party Financing Addendum,
        ❑   Loan Assumption Addendum, ❑   Seller Financing Addendum ......$_____
   C. Sales Price (Sum of A and B) ....$_____

4. LICENSE HOLDER DISLCOSURE: Texas law requires a real estate license holder who is a party to a transaction or acting on behalf of a spouse, parent, child, business entity in which the license holder owns more than 10%, or a trust for which the license holder acts as trustee or of which the license holder or the license holder's spouse, parent or child is a beneficiary, to notify the other party in writing before entering into a contract of sale. Disclose if applicable:_____ _____.

5. EARNEST MONEY: Upon execution of this contract by all parties, Buyer shall deposit $_____ as earnest money with _____, as escrow agent, at _____(address). Buyer shall deposit additional earnest money of $_____ with escrow agent within _____days after the effective date of this contract. If Buyer fails to deposit the earnest money as required by this contract, Buyer will be in default.

6. TITLE POLICY AND SURVEY:
   A. TITLE POLICY: Seller shall furnish to Buyer at ❑Seller's ❑Buyer's expense an owner policy of title insurance (Title Policy) issued by _____(Title Company) in the amount of the Sales Price, dated at or after closing, insuring Buyer against loss under the provisions of the Title Policy, subject to the promulgated exclusions (including existing building and zoning ordinances) and the following exceptions:
      (1)Restrictive covenants common to the platted subdivision in which the Property is located.
      (2) The standard printed exception for standby fees, taxes and assessments.
      (3) Liens created as part of the financing described in Paragraph 3.
      (4) Utility easements created by the dedication deed or plat of the subdivision in which the Property is located.
      (5) Reservations or exceptions otherwise permitted by this contract or as may be approved by Buyer in writing.
      (6) The standard printed exception as to marital rights.
      (7) The standard printed exception as to waters, tidelands, beaches, streams, and related matters.
      (8)The standard printed exception as to discrepancies, conflicts, shortages in area or boundary lines, encroachments or protrusions, or overlapping improvements: ❑ (i) will not be amended or deleted from the title policy; or ❑(ii) will be amended to read, "shortages in area" at the expense of ❑Buyer ❑Seller.
   B. COMMITMENT: Within 20 days after the Title Company receives a copy of this contract, Seller shall furnish to Buyer a commitment for title insurance (Commitment) and, at Buyer's expense, legible copies of restrictive covenants and documents evidencing exceptions in the Commitment (Exception Documents) other than the standard printed exceptions. Seller authorizes the Title Company to deliver the Commitment and Exception Documents to Buyer at Buyer's address shown in Paragraph 21. If the Commitment and Exception Documents are not delivered to Buyer within the specified time, the time for delivery will be automatically extended up to 15 days or 3 days before the Closing Date, whichever is earlier. If, due to factors beyond Seller's control, the Commitment and Exception Documents are not delivered within the time required, Buyer may terminate this contract and the earnest money will be refunded to Buyer.
   C. SURVEY: The survey must be made after the Substantial Completion Date by a registered professional land surveyor acceptable to the Title Company and Buyer's lender(s). (Check one box only)
   ❑ (1)At least _____days prior to the Closing Date, Seller, at Seller's expense, shall provide a new survey to Buyer.
   ❑ (2)At least _____ days prior to the Closing Date, Buyer, at Buyer's expense, shall obtain a new survey. Buyer is deemed to receive the survey on the date of actual receipt or the date specified in this paragraph, whichever is earlier.

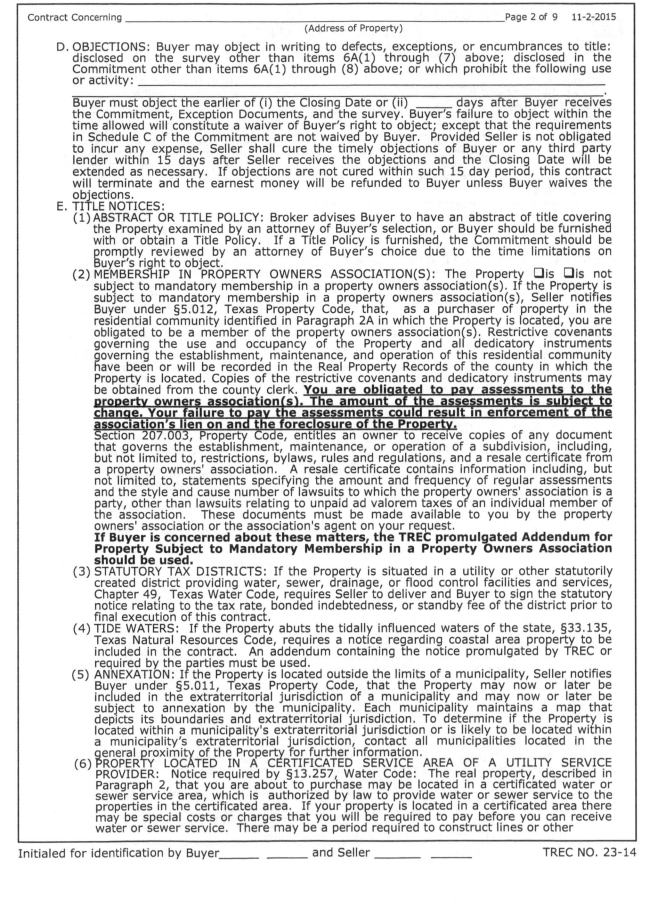

D. OBJECTIONS: Buyer may object in writing to defects, exceptions, or encumbrances to title: disclosed on the survey other than items 6A(1) through (7) above; disclosed in the Commitment other than items 6A(1) through (8) above; or which prohibit the following use or activity: _____ .
_____ Buyer must object the earlier of (i) the Closing Date or (ii) _____ days after Buyer receives the Commitment, Exception Documents, and the survey. Buyer's failure to object within the time allowed will constitute a waiver of Buyer's right to object; except that the requirements in Schedule C of the Commitment are not waived by Buyer. Provided Seller is not obligated to incur any expense, Seller shall cure the timely objections of Buyer or any third party lender within 15 days after Seller receives the objections and the Closing Date will be extended as necessary. If objections are not cured within such 15 day period, this contract will terminate and the earnest money will be refunded to Buyer unless Buyer waives the objections.

E. TITLE NOTICES:
   (1) ABSTRACT OR TITLE POLICY: Broker advises Buyer to have an abstract of title covering the Property examined by an attorney of Buyer's selection, or Buyer should be furnished with or obtain a Title Policy. If a Title Policy is furnished, the Commitment should be promptly reviewed by an attorney of Buyer's choice due to the time limitations on Buyer's right to object.
   (2) MEMBERSHIP IN PROPERTY OWNERS ASSOCIATION(S): The Property ❑is ❑is not subject to mandatory membership in a property owners association(s). If the Property is subject to mandatory membership in a property owners association(s), Seller notifies Buyer under §5.012, Texas Property Code, that, as a purchaser of property in the residential community identified in Paragraph 2A in which the Property is located, you are obligated to be a member of the property owners association(s). Restrictive covenants governing the use and occupancy of the Property and all dedicatory instruments governing the establishment, maintenance, and operation of this residential community have been or will be recorded in the Real Property Records of the county in which the Property is located. Copies of the restrictive covenants and dedicatory instruments may be obtained from the county clerk. **You are obligated to pay assessments to the property owners association(s). The amount of the assessments is subject to change. Your failure to pay the assessments could result in enforcement of the association's lien on and the foreclosure of the Property.**
   Section 207.003, Property Code, entitles an owner to receive copies of any document that governs the establishment, maintenance, or operation of a subdivision, including, but not limited to, restrictions, bylaws, rules and regulations, and a resale certificate from a property owners' association. A resale certificate contains information including, but not limited to, statements specifying the amount and frequency of regular assessments and the style and cause number of lawsuits to which the property owners' association is a party, other than lawsuits relating to unpaid ad valorem taxes of an individual member of the association. These documents must be made available to you by the property owners' association or the association's agent on your request.
   If Buyer is concerned about these matters, the TREC promulgated Addendum for Property Subject to Mandatory Membership in a Property Owners Association should be used.
   (3) STATUTORY TAX DISTRICTS: If the Property is situated in a utility or other statutorily created district providing water, sewer, drainage, or flood control facilities and services, Chapter 49, Texas Water Code, requires Seller to deliver and Buyer to sign the statutory notice relating to the tax rate, bonded indebtedness, or standby fee of the district prior to final execution of this contract.
   (4) TIDE WATERS: If the Property abuts the tidally influenced waters of the state, §33.135, Texas Natural Resources Code, requires a notice regarding coastal area property to be included in the contract. An addendum containing the notice promulgated by TREC or required by the parties must be used.
   (5) ANNEXATION: If the Property is located outside the limits of a municipality, Seller notifies Buyer under §5.011, Texas Property Code, that the Property may now or later be included in the extraterritorial jurisdiction of a municipality and may now or later be subject to annexation by the municipality. Each municipality maintains a map that depicts its boundaries and extraterritorial jurisdiction. To determine if the Property is located within a municipality's extraterritorial jurisdiction or is likely to be located within a municipality's extraterritorial jurisdiction, contact all municipalities located in the general proximity of the Property for further information.
   (6) PROPERTY LOCATED IN A CERTIFICATED SERVICE AREA OF A UTILITY SERVICE PROVIDER: Notice required by §13.257, Water Code: The real property, described in Paragraph 2, that you are about to purchase may be located in a certificated water or sewer service area, which is authorized by law to provide water or sewer service to the properties in the certificated area. If your property is located in a certificated area there may be special costs or charges that you will be required to pay before you can receive water or sewer service. There may be a period required to construct lines or other

Initialed for identification by Buyer_____ _____ and Seller _____ _____   TREC NO. 23-14

facilities necessary to provide water or sewer service to your property. You are advised to determine if the property is in a certificated area and contact the utility service provider to determine the cost that you will be required to pay and the period, if any, that is required to provide water or sewer service to your property. The undersigned Buyer hereby acknowledges receipt of the foregoing notice at or before the execution of a binding contract for the purchase of the real property described in Paragraph 2 or at closing of purchase of the real property.

(7) PUBLIC IMPROVEMENT DISTRICTS: If the Property is in a public improvement district, §5.014, Property Code, requires Seller to notify Buyer as follows: As a purchaser of this parcel of real property you are obligated to pay an assessment to a municipality or county for an improvement project undertaken by a public improvement district under Chapter 372, Local Government Code. The assessment may be due annually or in periodic installments. More information concerning the amount of the assessment and the due dates of that assessment may be obtained from the municipality or county levying the assessment. The amount of the assessments is subject to change. Your failure to pay the assessments could result in a lien on and the foreclosure of your property.

(8) TRANSFER FEES: If the Property is subject to a private transfer fee obligation, §5.205, Property Code, requires Seller to notify Buyer as follows: The private transfer fee obligation may be governed by Chapter 5, Subchapter G of the Texas Property Code.

(9) PROPANE GAS SYSTEM SERVICE AREA: If the Property is located in a propane gas system service area owned by a distribution system retailer, Seller must give Buyer written notice as required by §141.010, Texas Utilities Code. An addendum containing the notice approved by TREC or required by the parties should be used.

(10) NOTICE OF WATER LEVEL FLUCTUATIONS: If the Property adjoins an impoundment of water, including a reservoir or lake, constructed and maintained under Chapter 11, Water Code, that has a storage capacity of at least 5,000 acre-feet at the impoundment's normal operating level, Seller hereby notifies Buyer: "The water level of the impoundment of water adjoining the Property fluctuates for various reasons, including as a result of: (1) an entity lawfully exercising its right to use the water stored in the impoundment; or (2) drought or flood conditions."

7. PROPERTY CONDITION:

A. ACCESS AND INSPECTIONS: Seller shall permit Buyer and Buyer's agents access to the Property at reasonable times. Buyer may have the Property inspected by inspectors selected by Buyer and licensed by TREC or otherwise permitted by law to make inspections.

B. CONSTRUCTION DOCUMENTS: Seller shall complete all improvements to the Property with due diligence in accordance with the Construction Documents. "Construction Documents" means the plans and specifications, the finish out schedules, any change orders, and any allowances related to the plans and specifications, finish out schedules, and change orders. The Construction Documents have been signed by the parties and are incorporated into this contract by reference.

C. COST ADJUSTMENTS: All change orders must be in writing. Increase in costs resulting from change orders or items selected by Buyer which exceed the allowances specified in the Construction Documents will be paid by Buyer as follows:_____
_____.
A decrease in costs resulting from change orders and unused allowances will reduce the Sales Price, with proportionate adjustments to the amounts in Paragraphs 3A and 3B as required by lender.

D. BUYER'S SELECTIONS: If the Construction Documents permit selections by Buyer, Buyer's selections will conform to Seller's normal standards as set out in the Construction Documents or will not, in Seller's judgment, adversely affect the marketability of the Property. Buyer will make required selections within _____ days after notice from Seller.

E. COMPLETION: Seller must commence construction no later than _____ days after the effective date of this contract. The improvements will be substantially completed in accordance with the Construction Documents and ready for occupancy not later than _____, 20____ . The improvements will be deemed to be substantially completed in accordance with the Construction Documents upon the final inspection and approval by all applicable governmental authorities and any lender (Substantial Completion Date). Construction delays caused by acts of God, fire or other casualty, strikes, boycotts or nonavailability of materials for which no substitute of comparable quality and price is available will be added to the time allowed for substantial completion of the construction. However, in no event may the time for substantial completion extend beyond the Closing Date. Seller may substitute materials, equipment and appliances of comparable quality for those specified in the Construction Documents.

F. WARRANTIES: Except as expressly set forth in this contract, a separate writing, or provided by law, Seller makes no other express warranties. Seller shall assign to Buyer at closing all assignable manufacturer warranties.

G. INSULATION: As required by Federal Trade Commission Regulations, the information relating to the insulation installed or to be installed in the Improvements at the Property is: (check only one box below)
☐ (1) as shown in the attached specifications.
☐ (2) as follows:
  (a) Exterior walls of improved living areas: insulated with _____ insulation to a thickness of _____ inches which yields an R-Value of _____.
  (b) Walls in other areas of the home: insulated with_____ insulation to a thickness of _____ inches which yields an R-Value of _____.
  (c) Ceilings in improved living areas: insulated with_____ insulation to a thickness of _____ inches which yields an R-Value of _____.
  (d) Floors of improved living areas not applied to a slab foundation: insulated with_____ _____ insulation to a thickness of __ inches which yields an R-Value of _.
  (e) Other insulated areas: insulated with _____insulation to a thickness of _____ inches which yields an R-Value of _____.
  All stated R-Values are based on information provided by the manufacturer of the insulation.
H. ENVIRONMENTAL MATTERS: Buyer is advised that the presence of wetlands, toxic substances, including asbestos and wastes or other environmental hazards, or the presence of a threatened or endangered species or its habitat may affect Buyer's intended use of the Property. If Buyer is concerned about these matters, an addendum promulgated by TREC or required by the parties should be used.
I. SELLER'S DISCLOSURE: Except as otherwise disclosed in this contract, Seller has no knowledge of the following:
  (1) any flooding of the Property which has had a material adverse effect on the use of the Property;
  (2) any pending or threatened litigation, condemnation, or special assessment affecting the Property;
  (3) any environmental hazards that materially and adversely affect the Property;
  (4) any dumpsite, landfill, or underground tanks or containers now or previously located on the Property;
  (5) any wetlands, as defined by federal or state law or regulation, affecting the Property; or any threatened or endangered species or their habitat affecting the Property.

8. BROKERS' FEES: All obligations of the parties for payment of brokers' fees are contained in separate written agreements.

9. CLOSING:
  A. The closing of the sale will be on or before _____, 20 _____, or within 7 days after objections made under Paragraph 6D have been cured or waived, whichever date is later (Closing Date). If either party fails to close the sale by the Closing Date, the non-defaulting party may exercise the remedies contained in Paragraph 15.
  B. At closing:
    (1) Seller shall execute and deliver a general warranty deed conveying title to the Property to Buyer and showing no additional exceptions to those permitted in Paragraph 6 and furnish tax statements or certificates showing no delinquent taxes on the Property.
    (2) Buyer shall pay the Sales Price in good funds acceptable to the escrow agent.
    (3) Seller and Buyer shall execute and deliver any notices, statements, certificates, affidavits, releases, loan documents and other documents reasonably required for the closing of the sale and the issuance of the Title Policy.
    (4) There will be no liens, assessments, or security interests against the Property which will not be satisfied out of the sales proceeds unless securing payment of any loans assumed by Buyer and assumed loans will not be in default.

10. POSSESSION:
  A. Buyer's Possession: Seller shall deliver to Buyer possession of the Property: ☐ upon closing and funding ☐ according to a temporary residential lease form promulgated by TREC or other written lease required by the parties. Any possession by Buyer prior to closing or by Seller after closing which is not authorized by a written lease will establish a tenancy at sufferance relationship between the parties. **Consult your insurance agent prior to change of ownership and possession because insurance coverage may be limited or terminated. The absence of a written lease or appropriate insurance coverage may expose the parties to economic loss.**
  B. Leases: After the Effective Date, Seller may not execute any lease (including but not limited to mineral leases) or convey any interest in the Property without Buyer's written consent.

11. SPECIAL PROVISIONS: (Insert only factual statements and business details applicable to the sale. TREC rules prohibit license holders from adding factual statements or business details for which a contract addendum, lease or other form has been promulgated by TREC for mandatory use.)

Contract Concerning _____ Page 5 of 9   11-2-2015
(Address of Property)

12. SETTLEMENT AND OTHER EXPENSES:
  A. The following expenses must be paid at or prior to closing:
    (1) Expenses payable by Seller (Seller's Expenses):
      (a) Releases of existing liens, including prepayment penalties and recording fees; release of Seller's loan liability; tax statements or certificates; preparation of deed; one-half of escrow fee; and other expenses payable by Seller under this contract.
      (b) Seller shall also pay an amount not to exceed $ _____ to be applied in the following order: Buyer's Expenses which Buyer is prohibited from paying by FHA, VA, Texas Veterans Land Board or other governmental loan programs, and then to other Buyer's Expenses as allowed by the lender.
    (2) Expenses payable by Buyer (Buyer's Expenses): Appraisal fees; loan application fees; origination charges; credit reports; preparation of loan documents; interest on the notes from date of disbursement to one month prior to dates of first monthly payments; recording fees; copies of easements and restrictions; loan title policy with endorsements required by lender; loan-related inspection fees; photos; amortization schedules; one-half of escrow fee; all prepaid items, including required premiums for flood and hazard insurance, reserve deposits for insurance, ad valorem taxes and special governmental assessments; final compliance inspection; courier fee; repair inspection; underwriting fee; wire transfer fee; expenses incident to any loan; Private Mortgage Insurance Premium (PMI), VA Loan Funding Fee, or FHA Mortgage Insurance Premium (MIP) as required by the lender; and other expenses payable by Buyer under this contract.
  B. If any expense exceeds an amount expressly stated in this contract for such expense to be paid by a party, that party may terminate this contract unless the other party agrees to pay such excess. Buyer may not pay charges and fees expressly prohibited by FHA, VA, Texas Veterans Land Board or other governmental loan program regulations.

13. PRORATIONS AND ROLLBACK TAXES:
  A. PRORATIONS: Taxes for the current year, maintenance fees, assessments, dues and rents will be prorated through the Closing Date. The tax proration may be calculated taking into consideration any change in exemptions that will affect the current year's taxes. If taxes for the current year vary from the amount prorated at closing, the parties shall adjust the prorations when tax statements for the current year are available. If taxes are not paid at or prior to closing, Buyer will be obligated to pay taxes for the current year.
  B. ROLLBACK TAXES: If additional taxes, penalties, or interest (Assessments) are imposed because of Seller's use or change in use of the Property prior to closing, the Assessments will be the obligation of Seller. Obligations imposed by this paragraph will survive closing.

14. CASUALTY LOSS: If any part of the Property is damaged or destroyed by fire or other casualty after the effective date of this contract, Seller shall restore the Property to its previous condition as soon as reasonably possible, but in any event by the Closing Date. If Seller fails to do so due to factors beyond Seller's control, Buyer may (a) terminate this contract and the earnest money will be refunded to Buyer (b) extend the time for performance up to 45 days and the Closing Date will be extended as necessary or (c) accept the Property in its damaged condition with an assignment of insurance proceeds, if permitted by Seller's insurance carrier, and receive credit from Seller at closing in the amount of the deductible under the insurance policy. Seller's obligations under this paragraph are independent of any other obligations of Seller under this contract.

15. DEFAULT: If Buyer fails to comply with this contract, Buyer will be in default, and Seller may (a) enforce specific performance, seek such other relief as may be provided by law, or both, or (b) terminate this contract and receive the earnest money as liquidated damages, thereby releasing both parties from this contract. If Seller fails to comply with this contract Seller will be in default and Buyer may (a) enforce specific performance, seek such other relief as may be provided by law, or both, or (b) terminate this contract and receive the earnest money, thereby releasing both parties from this contract.

16. MEDIATION: It is the policy of the State of Texas to encourage resolution of disputes through alternative dispute resolution procedures such as mediation. Subject to applicable law, any dispute between Seller and Buyer related to this contract which is not resolved through informal discussion will be submitted to a mutually acceptable mediation service or provider. The parties to the mediation shall bear the mediation costs equally. This paragraph does not preclude a party from seeking equitable relief from a court of competent jurisdiction.

17. ATTORNEY'S FEES: A Buyer, Seller, Listing Broker, Other Broker, or escrow agent who prevails in any legal proceeding related to this contract is entitled to recover reasonable attorney's fees and all costs of such proceeding.

18. ESCROW:
  A. ESCROW: The escrow agent is not (i) a party to this contract and does not have liability for the performance or nonperformance of any party to this contract, (ii) liable for interest on the earnest money and (iii) liable for the loss of any earnest money caused by the failure of any financial institution in which the earnest money has been deposited unless the financial institution is acting as escrow agent.

Initialed for identification by Buyer_____ _____ and Seller _____ _____   TREC NO. 23-14

Contract Concerning _____Page 6 of 9   11-2-2015
(Address of Property)

B. **EXPENSES:** At closing, the earnest money must be applied first to any cash down payment, then to Buyer's Expenses and any excess refunded to Buyer. If no closing occurs, escrow agent may: (i) require a written release of liability of the escrow agent from all parties, (ii) require payment of unpaid expenses incurred on behalf of a party, and (iii) only deduct from the earnest money the amount of unpaid expenses incurred on behalf of the party receiving the earnest money.

C. **DEMAND:** Upon termination of this contract, either party or the escrow agent may send a release of earnest money to each party and the parties shall execute counterparts of the release and deliver same to the escrow agent. If either party fails to execute the release, either party may make a written demand to the escrow agent for the earnest money. If only one party makes written demand for the earnest money, escrow agent shall promptly provide a copy of the demand to the other party. If escrow agent does not receive written objection to the demand from the other party within 15 days, escrow agent may disburse the earnest money to the party making demand reduced by the amount of unpaid expenses incurred on behalf of the party receiving the earnest money and escrow agent may pay the same to the creditors. If escrow agent complies with the provisions of this paragraph, each party hereby releases escrow agent from all adverse claims related to the disbursal of the earnest money.

D. **DAMAGES:** Any party who wrongfully fails or refuses to sign a release acceptable to the escrow agent within 7 days of receipt of the request will be liable to the other party for (i) damages (ii) the earnest money; (iii) reasonable attorney's fees; and (iv) all costs of suit.

E. **NOTICES:** Escrow agent's notices will be effective when sent in compliance with Paragraph 21. Notice of objection to the demand will be deemed effective upon receipt by escrow agent.

19. **REPRESENTATIONS:** All covenants, representations and warranties in this contract survive closing. If any representation of Seller in this contract is untrue on the Closing Date, Seller will be in default. Unless expressly prohibited by written agreement, Seller may continue to show the Property and receive, negotiate and accept back up offers.

20. **FEDERAL TAX REQUIREMENTS:** If Seller is a "foreign person," as defined by applicable law, or if Seller fails to deliver an affidavit to Buyer that Seller is not a "foreign person," then Buyer shall withhold from the sales proceeds an amount sufficient to comply with applicable tax law and deliver the same to the Internal Revenue Service together with appropriate tax forms. Internal Revenue Service regulations require filing written reports if currency in excess of specified amounts is received in the transaction.

21. **NOTICES:** All notices from one party to the other must be in writing and are effective when mailed to, hand-delivered at, or transmitted by fax or electronic transmission as follows:

To Buyer at: _____   **To Seller at:** _____

_____   _____

Phone: (   ) _____   Phone: (   ) _____

Fax: (   ) _____   Fax: (   ) _____

E-mail: _____   E-mail: _____

Initialed for identification by Buyer_____ _____ and Seller _____ _____   TREC NO. 23-14

Contract Concerning _____ Page 7 of 9   11-2-2015
(Address of Property)

22. AGREEMENT OF PARTIES: This contract contains the entire agreement of the parties and cannot be changed except by their written agreement. Addenda which are a part of this contract are (check all applicable boxes):

❑ Third Party Financing Addendum

❑ Seller Financing Addendum

❑ Addendum for Property Subject to Mandatory Membership in a Property Owners Association

❑ Buyer's Temporary Residential Lease

❑ Loan Assumption Addendum

❑ Addendum for Sale of Other Property by Buyer

❑ Addendum for Reservation of Oil, Gas and Other Minerals

❑ Addendum for "Back-Up" Contract

❑ Addendum for Coastal Area Property

❑ Environmental Assessment, Threatened or Endangered Species and Wetlands Addendum

❑ Seller's Temporary Residential Lease

❑ Short Sale Addendum

❑ Addendum for Property Located Seaward of the Gulf Intracoastal Waterway

❑ Addendum for Property in a Propane Gas System Service Area

❑ Other (list): _____

_____

23. TERMINATION OPTION: For nominal consideration, the receipt of which is hereby acknowledged by Seller, and Buyer's agreement to pay Seller $_____ (Option Fee) within 3 days after the effective date of this contract, Seller grants Buyer the unrestricted right to terminate this contract by giving notice of termination to Seller within _____ days after the effective date of this contract (Option Period). Notices under this paragraph must be given by 5:00 p.m. (local time where the Property is located) by the date specified. If no dollar amount is stated as the Option Fee or if Buyer fails to pay the Option Fee to Seller within the time prescribed, this paragraph will not be a part of this contract and Buyer shall not have the unrestricted right to terminate this contract. If Buyer gives notice of termination within the time prescribed, the Option Fee will not be refunded; however, any earnest money will be refunded to Buyer. The Option Fee ❑will ❑will not be credited to the Sales Price at closing. **Time is of the essence for this paragraph and strict compliance with the time for performance is required.**

24. CONSULT AN ATTORNEY BEFORE SIGNING: TREC rules prohibit real estate license holders from giving legal advice. READ THIS CONTRACT CAREFULLY.

Buyer's
Attorney is: _____

_____

Phone: (   ) _____

Fax: (   ) _____

E-mail: _____

Seller's
Attorney is: _____

_____

Phone: (   ) _____

Fax: (   ) _____

E-mail: _____

Initialed for identification by Buyer_____ _____ and Seller _____ _____   TREC NO. 23-14

Contract Concerning _____ Page 8 of 9   11-2-2015

(Address of Property)

EXECUTED the _____day of _____, 20_____ (EFFECTIVE DATE).
(BROKER: FILL IN THE DATE OF FINAL ACCEPTANCE.)

This contract is subject to Chapter 27 of the Texas Property Code. The provisions of that chapter may affect your right to recover damages arising from a construction defect. If you have a complaint concerning a construction defect and that defect has not been corrected as may be required by law or by contract, you must provide the notice required by Chapter 27 of the Texas Property Code to the contractor by certified mail, return receipt requested, not later than the 60th day before the date you file suit to recover damages in a court of law or initiate arbitration. The notice must refer to Chapter 27 of the Texas Property Code and must describe the construction defect. If requested by the contractor, you must provide the contractor an opportunity to inspect and cure the defect as provided by Section 27.004 of the Texas Property Code.

_____
Buyer

_____
Buyer

_____
Seller

_____
Seller

Contract Concerning _____ Page 9 of 9   11-2-2015
(Address of Property)

BROKER   INFORMATION
(Print name(s) only. Do not sign)

| Other Broker Firm | License No. | Listing Broker Firm | License No. |

represents ☐ Buyer only as Buyer's agent   represents ☐ Seller and Buyer as an intermediary
☐ Seller as Listing Broker's subagent   ☐ Seller only as Seller's agent

Associate's Name   License No.   Listing Associate's Name   License No.

Licensed Supervisor of Associate   License No.   Licensed Supervisor of Listing Associate   License No.

Other Broker's Address   Fax   Listing Broker's Office Address   Fax

City   State   Zip   City   State   Zip

Associate's Email Address   Phone   Listing Associate's Email Address   Phone

Selling Associate's Name   License No.

Licensed Supervisor of Selling Associate   License No.

Selling Associate's Office Address   Fax

City   State   Zip

Selling Associate's Email Address   Phone

Listing Broker has agreed to pay Other Broker_____ of the total sales price when the Listing Broker's fee is received. Escrow agent is authorized and directed to pay other Broker from Listing Broker's fee at closing.

OPTION FEE RECEIPT

Receipt of $_____ (Option Fee) in the form of _____ is acknowledged.

_____   _____
Seller or Listing Broker   Date

CONTRACT AND EARNEST MONEY RECEIPT

Receipt of ☐Contract and ☐$_____ Earnest Money in the form of _____
is acknowledged.

Escrow Agent: _____   Date: _____

By: _____   _____
                                        Email Address
_____   Phone: (_____) _____
Address
_____   Fax: (_____) _____
City   State   Zip

TREC NO. 23-14

FARM AND RANCH CONTRACT

11-2-2015

1. PARTIES: The parties to this contract are _____
(Seller) and _____ (Buyer). Seller agrees to sell and convey to Buyer and Buyer agrees to buy from Seller the Property defined below.

2. PROPERTY: The land, improvements, accessories and crops except for the exclusions and reservations, are collectively referred to as the "Property".

  A. LAND: The land situated in the County of _____, Texas, described as follows:_____
  _____
  or as described on attached exhibit, also known as _____
  (address/zip code), together with all rights, privileges, and appurtenances pertaining thereto, including but not limited to: water rights, claims, permits, strips and gores, easements, and cooperative or association memberships.

  B. IMPROVEMENTS:
   (1) FARM and RANCH IMPROVEMENTS: The following **permanently installed and built-in items**, if any: windmills, tanks, barns, pens, fences, gates, sheds, outbuildings, and corrals.
   (2) RESIDENTIAL IMPROVEMENTS: The house, garage, and all other fixtures and improvements attached to the above-described real property, including without limitation, the following **permanently installed and built-in items,** if any: all equipment and appliances, valances, screens, shutters, awnings, wall-to-wall carpeting, mirrors, ceiling fans, attic fans, mail boxes, television antennas, mounts and brackets for televisions and speakers, heating and air-conditioning units, security and fire detection equipment, wiring, plumbing and lighting fixtures, chandeliers, water softener system, kitchen equipment, garage door openers, cleaning equipment, shrubbery, landscaping, outdoor cooking equipment, and all other property owned by Seller and attached to the above described real property.

  C. ACCESSORIES:
   (1) FARM AND RANCH ACCESSORIES: The following described related accessories: (check boxes of conveyed accessories) ❏ portable buildings ❏ hunting blinds ❏ game feeders ❏ livestock feeders and troughs ❏ irrigation equipment ❏ fuel tanks ❏ submersible pumps ❏ pressure tanks ❏ corrals ❏ gates ❏ chutes ❏ other:_____
   _____
   (2) RESIDENTIAL ACCESSORIES: The following described related accessories, if any: window air conditioning units, stove, fireplace screens, curtains and rods, blinds, window shades, draperies and rods, door keys, mailbox keys, above ground pool, swimming pool equipment and maintenance accessories, artificial fireplace logs, and controls for: (i) garages, (ii) entry gates, and (iii) other improvements and accessories.

  D. CROPS: Unless otherwise agreed in writing, Seller has the right to harvest all growing crops until delivery of possession of the Property.

  E. EXCLUSIONS: The following improvements, accessories, and crops will be retained by Seller and must be removed prior to delivery of possession: _____
  _____.

  F. RESERVATIONS: Any reservation for oil, gas, or other minerals, water, timber, or other interests is made in accordance with an attached addendum or Special Provisions.

3. SALES PRICE:
  A. Cash portion of Sales Price payable by Buyer at closing .... $_____
  B. Sum of all financing described in the attached: ❏ Third Party Financing Addendum, ❏ Loan Assumption Addendum, ❏ Seller Financing Addendum ... $_____
  C. Sales Price (Sum of A and B) .... $_____
  D. The Sales Price ❏ will ❏ will not be adjusted based on the survey required by Paragraph 6C. If the Sales Price is adjusted, the Sales Price will be calculated on the basis of $ _____ per acre. If the Sales Price is adjusted by more than 10%, either party may terminate this contract by providing written notice to the other party within _____ days after the terminating party receives the survey. If neither party terminates this contract or if the variance is 10% or less, the adjustment will be made to the amount in ❏ 3A ❏ 3B ❏ proportionately to 3A and 3B.

4. LICENSE HOLDER DISCLOSURE: Texas Law requires a real estate license holder who is a party to a transaction or acting on behalf of a spouse, parent, child, business entity in which the license holder owns more than 10%, or a trust for which the license holder acts as trustee or of which the license holder or the license holder's spouse, parent or child is a beneficiary, to notify the other party in writing before entering into a contract of sale. Disclose if applicable:_____
_____.

5. EARNEST MONEY: Upon execution of this contract by all parties, Buyer shall deposit $_____ as earnest money with _____,
as escrow agent, at _____
(address). Buyer shall deposit additional earnest money of $_____ with escrow agent within _____ days after the effective date of this contract. If Buyer fails to deposit the earnest money as required by this contract, Buyer will be in default.

Contract Concerning _____ Page 2 of 10   11-2-2015
(Address of Property)

6. TITLE POLICY AND SURVEY:

A. TITLE POLICY: Seller shall furnish to Buyer at ☐Seller's ☐Buyer's expense an owner policy of title insurance (Title Policy) issued by: _____ (Title Company) in the amount of the Sales Price, dated at or after closing, insuring Buyer against loss under the provisions of the Title Policy, subject to the promulgated exclusions (including existing building and zoning ordinances) and the following exceptions:
   (1) The standard printed exception for standby fees, taxes and assessments.
   (2) Liens created as part of the financing described in Paragraph 3.
   (3) Reservations or exceptions otherwise permitted by this contract or as may be approved by Buyer in writing.
   (4) The standard printed exception as to marital rights.
   (5) The standard printed exception as to waters, tidelands, beaches, streams, and related matters.
   (6) The standard printed exception as to discrepancies, conflicts, shortages in area or boundary lines, encroachments or protrusions, or overlapping improvements: ☐ (i) will not be amended or deleted from the title policy; or ☐(ii) will be amended to read, "shortages in area" at the expense of ☐Buyer ☐Seller.

B. COMMITMENT: Within 20 days after the Title Company receives a copy of this contract, Seller shall furnish to Buyer a commitment for title insurance (Commitment) and, at Buyer's expense, legible copies of restrictive covenants and documents evidencing exceptions in the Commitment (Exception Documents) other than the standard printed exceptions. Seller authorizes the Title Company to deliver the Commitment and Exception Documents to Buyer at Buyer's address shown in Paragraph 21. If the Commitment and Exception Documents are not delivered to Buyer within the specified time, the time for delivery will be automatically extended up to 15 days or 3 days before the Closing Date, whichever is earlier. If, due to factors beyond Seller's control, the Commitment and Exception Documents are not delivered within the time required, Buyer may terminate this contract and the earnest money will be refunded to Buyer.

C. SURVEY: The survey must be made by a registered professional land surveyor acceptable to the Title Company and Buyer's lender(s). (Check one box only):
☐ (1) Within _____ days after the effective date of this contract, Seller shall furnish to Buyer and Title Company Seller's existing survey of the Property and a Residential Real Property Affidavit promulgated by the Texas Department of Insurance (T-47 Affidavit). **If Seller fails to furnish the existing survey or affidavit within the time prescribed, Buyer shall obtain a new survey at Seller's expense no later than 3 days prior to Closing Date.** The existing survey ☐ will ☐ will not be recertified to a date subsequent to the effective date of this contract at the expense of ☐ Buyer ☐ Seller. If the existing survey is not approved by the Title Company or Buyer's lender(s), a new survey will be obtained at the expense of ☐ Buyer ☐ Seller no later than 3 days prior to Closing Date.
☐ (2) Within _____ days after the effective date of this contract, Buyer shall obtain a new survey at Buyer's expense. Buyer is deemed to receive the survey on the date of actual receipt or the date specified in this paragraph, whichever is earlier.
☐ (3) Within _____ days after the effective date of this contract, Seller, at Seller's expense shall furnish a new survey to Buyer.
☐ (4) No survey is required.

D. OBJECTIONS: Buyer may object in writing to (i) defects, exceptions, or encumbrances to title disclosed on the survey other than items 6A(1) through (5) above; or disclosed in the Commitment other than items 6A(1) through (6) above; (ii) any portion of the Property lying in a special flood hazard area (Zone V or A) as shown on the current Federal Emergency Management Agency map; or (iii) any exceptions which prohibit the following use or activity:_____
_____.
Buyer must object the earlier of (i) the Closing Date or (ii) _____ days after Buyer receives the Commitment, Exception Documents, and the survey. Buyer's failure to object within the time allowed will constitute a waiver of Buyer's right to object; except that the requirements in Schedule C of the Commitment are not waived by Buyer. Provided Seller is not obligated to incur any expense, Seller shall cure the timely objections of Buyer or any third party lender within 15 days after Seller receives the objections and the Closing Date will be extended as necessary. If objections are not cured within such 15 day period, this contract will terminate and the earnest money will be refunded to Buyer unless Buyer waives the objections.

E. EXCEPTION DOCUMENTS: Prior to the execution of the contract, Seller has provided Buyer with copies of the Exception Documents listed below or on the attached exhibit. Matters reflected in the Exception Documents listed below or on the attached exhibit will be permitted exceptions in the Title Policy and will not be a basis for objection to title:

Document	Date	Recording Reference
_____	_____	_____
_____	_____	_____
_____	_____	_____

Initialed for identification by Buyer_____ _____ and Seller _____ _____   TREC NO. 25-11

Contract Concerning _____ Page 3 of 10   11-2-2015
(Address of Property)

F. SURFACE LEASES: Prior to the execution of the contract, Seller has provided Buyer with copies of written leases and given notice of oral leases (Leases) listed below or on the attached exhibit. The following Leases will be permitted exceptions in the Title Policy and will not be a basis for objection to title:_____
_____

G. TITLE NOTICES:
  (1) ABSTRACT OR TITLE POLICY: Broker advises Buyer to have an abstract of title covering the Property examined by an attorney of Buyer's selection, or Buyer should be furnished with or obtain a Title Policy. If a Title Policy is furnished, the Commitment should be promptly reviewed by an attorney of Buyer's choice due to the time limitations on Buyer's right to object.
  (2) STATUTORY TAX DISTRICTS: If the Property is situated in a utility or other statutorily created district providing water, sewer, drainage, or flood control facilities and services, Chapter 49, Texas Water Code, requires Seller to deliver and Buyer to sign the statutory notice relating to the tax rate, bonded indebtedness, or standby fee of the district prior to final execution of this contract.
  (3) TIDE WATERS: If the Property abuts the tidally influenced waters of the state, §33.135, Texas Natural Resources Code, requires a notice regarding coastal area property to be included in the contract. An addendum containing the notice promulgated by TREC or required by the parties must be used.
  (4) ANNEXATION: If the Property is located outside the limits of a municipality, Seller notifies Buyer under §5.011, Texas Property Code, that the Property may now or later be included in the extraterritorial jurisdiction of a municipality and may now or later be subject to annexation by the municipality. Each municipality maintains a map that depicts its boundaries and extraterritorial jurisdiction. To determine if the Property is located within a municipality's extraterritorial jurisdiction or is likely to be located within a municipality's extraterritorial jurisdiction, contact all municipalities located in the general proximity of the Property for further information.
  (5) PROPERTY LOCATED IN A CERTIFICATED SERVICE AREA OF A UTILITY SERVICE PROVIDER: Notice required by §13.257, Water Code: The real property, described in Paragraph 2, that you are about to purchase may be located in a certificated water or sewer service area, which is authorized by law to provide water or sewer service to the properties in the certificated area. If your property is located in a certificated area there may be special costs or charges that you will be required to pay before you can receive water or sewer service. There may be a period required to construct lines or other facilities necessary to provide water or sewer service to your property. You are advised to determine if the property is in a certificated area and contact the utility service provider to determine the cost that you will be required to pay and the period, if any, that is required to provide water or sewer service to your property. The undersigned Buyer hereby acknowledges receipt of the foregoing notice at or before the execution of a binding contract for the purchase of the real property described in Paragraph 2 or at closing of purchase of the real property.
  (6) PUBLIC IMPROVEMENT DISTRICTS: If the Property is in a public improvement district, §5.014, Property Code, requires Seller to notify Buyer as follows: As a purchaser of this parcel of real property you are obligated to pay an assessment to a municipality or county for an improvement project undertaken by a public improvement district under Chapter 372, Local Government Code. The assessment may be due annually or in periodic installments. More information concerning the amount of the assessment and the due dates of that assessment may be obtained from the municipality or county levying the assessment. The amount of the assessments is subject to change. Your failure to pay the assessments could result in a lien on and the foreclosure of your property.
  (7) TEXAS AGRICULTURAL DEVELOPMENT DISTRICT: The Property ☐ is ☐ is not located in a Texas Agricultural Development District. For additional information contact the Texas Department of Agriculture
  (8) TRANSFER FEES: If the Property is subject to a private transfer fee obligation, §5.205, Property Code, requires Seller to notify Buyer as follows: The private transfer fee obligation may be governed by Chapter 5, Subchapter G of the Texas Property Code.
  (9) PROPANE GAS SYSTEM SERVICE AREA: If the Property is located in a propane gas system service area owned by a distribution system retailer, Seller must give Buyer written notice as required by §141.010, Texas Utilities Code. An addendum containing the notice approved by TREC or required by the parties should be used.
  (10) NOTICE OF WATER LEVEL FLUCTUATIONS: If the Property adjoins an impoundment of water, including a reservoir or lake, constructed and maintained under Chapter 11, Water Code, that has a storage capacity of at least 5,000 acre-feet at the impoundment's normal operating level, Seller hereby notifies Buyer: "The water level of the impoundment of water adjoining the Property fluctuates for various reasons, including as a result of: (1) an entity lawfully exercising its right to use the water stored in the impoundment; or (2) drought or flood conditions."

Contract Concerning _____ Page 4 of 10   11-2-2015
(Address of Property)

7. PROPERTY CONDITION:

A. ACCESS, INSPECTIONS AND UTILITIES: Seller shall permit Buyer and Buyer's agents access to the Property at reasonable times. Buyer may have the Property inspected by inspectors selected by Buyer and licensed by TREC or otherwise permitted by law to make inspections. Any hydrostatic testing must be separately authorized by Seller in writing. Seller at Seller's expense shall immediately cause existing utilities to be turned on and shall keep the utilities on during the time this contract is in effect .
NOTICE: Buyer should determine the availability of utilities to the Property suitable to satisfy Buyer's needs.

B. SELLER'S DISCLOSURE NOTICE PURSUANT TO §5.008, TEXAS PROPERTY CODE (Notice):
(Check one box only)
❏ (1) Buyer has received the Notice
❏ (2) Buyer has not received the Notice. Within _____ days after the effective date of this contract, Seller shall deliver the Notice to Buyer. If Buyer does not receive the Notice, Buyer may terminate this contract at any time prior to the closing and the earnest money will be refunded to Buyer. If Seller delivers the Notice, Buyer may terminate this contract for any reason within 7 days after Buyer receives the Notice or prior to the closing, whichever first occurs, and the earnest money will be refunded to Buyer.
❏ (3) The Texas Property Code does not require this Seller to furnish the Notice.

C. SELLER'S DISCLOSURE OF LEAD-BASED PAINT AND LEAD-BASED PAINT HAZARDS is required by Federal law for a residential dwelling constructed prior to 1978.

D. ACCEPTANCE OF PROPERTY CONDITION: "As Is" means the present condition of the Property with any and all defects and without warranty except for the warranties of title and the warranties in this contract. Buyer's agreement to accept the Property As Is under Paragraph 7D (1) or (2) does not preclude Buyer from inspecting the Property under Paragraph 7A, from negotiating repairs or treatments in a subsequent amendment, or from terminating this contract during the Option Period, if any.
(Check one box only)
❏ (1) Buyer accepts the Property As Is.
❏ (2) Buyer accepts the Property As Is provided Seller, at Seller's expense, shall complete the following specific repairs and treatments: _____
_____.
(Do not insert general phrases, such as "subject to inspections," that do not identify specific repairs and treatments.)

E. COMPLETION OF REPAIRS: Unless otherwise agreed in writing: (i) Seller shall complete all agreed repairs and treatments prior to the Closing Date; and (ii) all required permits must be obtained, and repairs and treatments must be performed by persons who are licensed to provide such repairs or treatments or, if no license is required by law, are commercially engaged in the trade of providing such repairs or treatments. At Buyer's election, any transferable warranties received by Seller with respect to the repairs will be transferred to Buyer at Buyer's expense. If Seller fails to complete any agreed repairs prior to the Closing Date, Buyer may exercise remedies under Paragraph 15 or extend the Closing Date up to 5 days if necessary for Seller to complete repairs.

F. LENDER REQUIRED REPAIRS AND TREATMENTS: Unless otherwise agreed in writing, neither party is obligated to pay for lender required repairs, which includes treatment for wood destroying insects. If the parties do not agree to pay for the lender required repairs or treatments, this contract will terminate and the earnest money will be refunded to Buyer. If the cost of lender required repairs and treatments exceeds 5% of the Sales Price, Buyer may terminate this contract and the earnest money will be refunded to Buyer.

G. ENVIRONMENTAL MATTERS: Buyer is advised that the presence of wetlands, toxic substances, including asbestos and wastes or other environmental hazards, or the presence of a threatened or endangered species or its habitat may affect Buyer's intended use of the Property. If Buyer is concerned about these matters, an addendum promulgated by TREC or required by the parties should be used.

H. SELLER'S DISCLOSURES: Except as otherwise disclosed in this contract, Seller has no knowledge of the following:
(1) any flooding of the Property which has had a material adverse effect on the use of the Property;
(2) any pending or threatened litigation, condemnation, or special assessment affecting the Property;
(3) any environmental hazards that materially and adversely affect the Property;
(4) any dumpsite, landfill, or underground tanks or containers now or previously located on the Property;
(5) any wetlands, as defined by federal or state law or regulation, affecting the Property; or
(6) any threatened or endangered species or their habitat affecting the Property.

I. RESIDENTIAL SERVICE CONTRACTS: Buyer may purchase a residential service contract from a residential service company licensed by TREC. If Buyer purchases a residential service contract, Seller shall reimburse Buyer at closing for the cost of the residential service contract in an amount not exceeding $_____. Buyer should review any residential service contract

Initialed for identification by Buyer_____ _____ and Seller _____ _____   TREC NO. 25-11

for the scope of coverage, exclusions and limitations. **The purchase of a residential service contract is optional. Similar coverage may be purchased from various companies authorized to do business in Texas.**

J. GOVERNMENT PROGRAMS: The Property is subject to the government programs listed below or on the attached exhibit:_____.

Seller shall provide Buyer with copies of all governmental program agreements. Any allocation or proration of payment under governmental programs is made by separate agreement between the parties which will survive closing.

8. BROKERS' FEES: All obligations of the parties for payment of brokers' fees are contained in separate written agreements.

9. CLOSING:
A. The closing of the sale will be on or before _____, 20_____, or within 7 days after objections made under Paragraph 6D have been cured or waived, whichever date is later (Closing Date). If either party fails to close the sale by the Closing Date, the non-defaulting party may exercise the remedies contained in Paragraph 15.
B. At closing:
(1) Seller shall execute and deliver a general warranty deed conveying title to the Property to Buyer and showing no additional exceptions to those permitted in Paragraph 6, an assignment of Leases, and furnish tax statements or certificates showing no delinquent taxes on the Property.
(2) Buyer shall pay the Sales Price in good funds acceptable to the escrow agent.
(3) Seller and Buyer shall execute and deliver any notices, statements, certificates, affidavits, releases, loan documents and other documents reasonably required for the closing of the sale and the issuance of the Title Policy.
(4) There will be no liens, assessments, or security interests against the Property which will not be satisfied out of the sales proceeds unless securing the payment of any loans assumed by Buyer and assumed loans will not be in default.
(5) If the Property is subject to a residential lease, Seller shall transfer security deposits (as defined under §92.102, Property Code), if any, to Buyer. In such an event, Buyer shall deliver to the tenant a signed statement acknowledging that the Buyer has acquired the Property and is responsible for the return of the security deposit, and specifying the exact dollar amount of the security deposit.

10. POSSESSION:
A. Buyer's Possession: Seller shall deliver to Buyer possession of the Property in its present or required condition, ordinary wear and tear excepted: ❑ upon closing and funding ❑ according to a temporary residential lease form promulgated by TREC or other written lease required by the parties. Any possession by Buyer prior to closing or by Seller after closing which is not authorized by a written lease will establish a tenancy at sufferance relationship between the parties. **Consult your insurance agent prior to change of ownership and possession because insurance coverage may be limited or terminated. The absence of a written lease or appropriate insurance coverage may expose the parties to economic loss.**
B. Leases:
(1) After the Effective Date, Seller may not execute any lease (including but not limited to mineral leases) or convey any interest in the Property without Buyer's written consent.
(2) If the Property is subject to any lease to which Seller is a party, Seller shall deliver to Buyer copies of the lease(s) and any move-in condition form signed by the tenant within 7 days after the Effective Date of the contract.

11. SPECIAL PROVISIONS: (Insert only factual statements and business details applicable to the sale. TREC rules prohibit license holders from adding factual statements or business details for which a contract addendum or other form has been promulgated by TREC for mandatory use.

Contract Concerning _____ Page 6 of 10   11-2-2015
                                        (Address of Property)

12. SETTLEMENT AND OTHER EXPENSES:
   A. The following expenses must be paid at or prior to closing:
      (1) Expenses payable by Seller (Seller's Expenses):
         (a) Releases of existing liens, including prepayment penalties and recording fees; release of Seller's loan liability; tax statements or certificates; preparation of deed; one-half of escrow fee; and other expenses payable by Seller under this contract.
         (b) Seller shall also pay an amount not to exceed $ _____ to be applied in the following order: Buyer's Expenses which Buyer is prohibited from paying by FHA, VA, Texas Veterans Land Board or other governmental loan programs, and then to other Buyer's Expenses as allowed by the lender.
      (2) Expenses payable by Buyer (Buyer's Expenses) Appraisal fees; loan application fees; origination charges; credit reports; preparation of loan documents; interest on the notes from date of disbursement to one month prior to dates of first monthly payments; recording fees; copies of easements and restrictions; loan title policy with endorsements required by lender; loan-related inspection fees; photos; amortization schedules; one-half of escrow fee; all prepaid items, including required premiums for flood and hazard insurance, reserve deposits for insurance, ad valorem taxes and special governmental assessments; final compliance inspection; courier fee; repair inspection; underwriting fee; wire transfer fee; expenses incident to any loan; Private Mortgage Insurance Premium (PMI), VA Loan Funding Fee, or FHA Mortgage Insurance Premium (MIP) as required by the lender; and other expenses payable by Buyer under this contract.
   B. If any expense exceeds an amount expressly stated in this contract for such expense to be paid by a party, that party may terminate this contract unless the other party agrees to pay such excess. Buyer may not pay charges and fees expressly prohibited by FHA, VA, Texas Veterans Land Board or other governmental loan program regulations.

13. PRORATIONS AND ROLLBACK TAXES:
   A. PRORATIONS: Taxes for the current year, interest, maintenance fees, assessments, dues and rents will be prorated through the Closing Date. The tax proration may be calculated taking into consideration any change in exemptions that will affect the current year's taxes. If taxes for the current year vary from the amount prorated at closing, the parties shall adjust the prorations when tax statements for the current year are available. If taxes are not paid at or prior to closing, Buyer shall pay taxes for the current year. Rentals which are unknown at time of closing will be prorated between Buyer and Seller when they become known.
   B. ROLLBACK TAXES: If this sale or Buyer's use of the Property after closing results in the assessment of additional taxes, penalties or interest (Assessments) for periods prior to closing, the Assessments will be the obligation of Buyer. If Assessments are imposed because of Seller's use or change in use of the Property prior to closing, the Assessments will be the obligation of Seller. Obligations imposed by this paragraph will survive closing.

14. CASUALTY LOSS: If any part of the Property is damaged or destroyed by fire or other casualty after the effective date of this contract, Seller shall restore the Property to its previous condition as soon as reasonably possible, but in any event by the Closing Date. If Seller fails to do so due to factors beyond Seller's control, Buyer may (a) terminate this contract and the earnest money will be refunded to Buyer, (b) extend the time for performance up to 15 days and the Closing Date will be extended as necessary or (c) accept the Property in its damaged condition with an assignment of insurance proceeds, if permitted by Seller's insurance carrier, and receive credit from Seller at closing in the amount of the deductible under the insurance policy. Seller's obligations under this paragraph are independent of any other obligations of Seller under this contract.

15. DEFAULT: If Buyer fails to comply with this contract, Buyer will be in default, and Seller may (a) enforce specific performance, seek such other relief as may be provided by law, or both, or (b) terminate this contract and receive the earnest money as liquidated damages, thereby releasing both parties from this contract. If Seller fails to comply with this contract for any other reason, Seller will be in default and Buyer may (a) enforce specific performance, seek such other relief as may be provided by law, or both, or (b) terminate this contract and receive the earnest money, thereby releasing both parties from this contract.

16. MEDIATION: It is the policy of the State of Texas to encourage resolution of disputes through alternative dispute resolution procedures such as mediation. Any dispute between Seller and Buyer related to this contract which is not resolved through informal discussion will be submitted to a mutually acceptable mediation service or provider. The parties to the mediation shall bear the mediation costs equally. This paragraph does not preclude a party from seeking equitable relief from a court of competent jurisdiction.

17. ATTORNEY'S FEES: A Buyer, Seller, Listing Broker, Other Broker, or escrow agent who prevails in any legal proceeding related to this contract is entitled to recover reasonable attorney's fees and all costs of such proceeding.

Initialed for identification by Buyer_____ _____ and Seller _____ _____   TREC NO. 25-11

Contract Concerning _____Page 7 of 10   11-2-2015
(Address of Property)

18. ESCROW:

A. ESCROW: The escrow agent is not (i) a party to this contract and does not have liability for the performance or nonperformance of any party to this contract, (ii) liable for interest on the earnest money and (iii) liable for the loss of any earnest money caused by the failure of any financial institution in which the earnest money has been deposited unless the financial institution is acting as escrow agent.

B. EXPENSES: At closing, the earnest money must be applied first to any cash down payment, then to Buyer's Expenses and any excess refunded to Buyer. If no closing occurs, escrow agent may: (i) require a written release of liability of the escrow agent from all parties, (ii) require payment of unpaid expenses incurred on behalf of a party, and (iii) only deduct from the earnest money the amount of unpaid expenses incurred on behalf of the party receiving the earnest money.

C. DEMAND: Upon termination of this contract, either party or the escrow agent may send a release of earnest money to each party and the parties shall execute counterparts of the release and deliver same to the escrow agent. If either party fails to execute the release, either party may make a written demand to the escrow agent for the earnest money. If only one party makes written demand for the earnest money, escrow agent shall promptly provide a copy of the demand to the other party. If escrow agent does not receive written objection to the demand from the other party within 15 days, escrow agent may disburse the earnest money to the party making demand reduced by the amount of unpaid expenses incurred on behalf of the party receiving the earnest money and escrow agent may pay the same to the creditors. If escrow agent complies with the provisions of this paragraph, each party hereby releases escrow agent from all adverse claims related to the disbursal of the earnest money.

D. DAMAGES: Any party who wrongfully fails or refuses to sign a release acceptable to the escrow agent within 7 days of receipt of the request will be liable to the other party for (i) damages; (iii) reasonable attorney's fees; and (iv) all costs of suit.

E. NOTICES: Escrow agent's notices will be effective when sent in compliance with Paragraph 21. Notice of objection to the demand will be deemed effective upon receipt by escrow agent.

19. **REPRESENTATIONS:** All covenants, representations and warranties in this contract survive closing. If any representation of Seller in this contract is untrue on the Closing Date, Seller will be in default. Unless expressly prohibited by written agreement, Seller may continue to show the Property and receive, negotiate and accept back up offers.

20. **FEDERAL TAX REQUIREMENTS:** If Seller is a "foreign person," as defined by applicable law, or if Seller fails to deliver an affidavit to Buyer that Seller is not a "foreign person," then Buyer shall withhold from the sales proceeds an amount sufficient to comply with applicable tax law and deliver the same to the Internal Revenue Service together with appropriate tax forms. Internal Revenue Service regulations require filing written reports if currency in excess of specified amounts is received in the transaction.

21. **NOTICES:** All notices from one party to the other must be in writing and are effective when mailed to, hand-delivered at, or transmitted by fax or electronic transmission as follows:

To Buyer	**To Seller**
at: _____	at: _____
_____	_____
Phone: ( ) _____	Phone: ( ) _____
Fax: ( ) _____	Fax: ( ) _____
E-mail: _____	E-mail: _____

Initialed for identification by Buyer_____ _____ and Seller _____ _____   TREC NO. 25-11

Contract Concerning _____ Page 8 of 10   11-2-2015
(Address of Property)

22. AGREEMENT OF PARTIES: This contract contains the entire agreement of the parties and cannot be changed except by their written agreement. Addenda which are a part of this contract are (check all applicable boxes):

- ❏ Third Party Financing Addendum

- ❏ Seller Financing Addendum

- ❏ Addendum for Property Subject to Mandatory Membership in a Property Owners Association

- ❏ Buyer's Temporary Residential Lease

- ❏ Loan Assumption Addendum

- ❏ Addendum for Sale of Other Property by Buyer

- ❏ Addendum for "Back-Up" Contract

- ❏ Addendum for Coastal Area Property

- ❏ Environmental Assessment, Threatened or Endangered Species and Wetlands Addendum

- ❏ Seller's Temporary Residential Lease

- ❏ Short Sale Addendum

- ❏ Addendum for Property Located Seaward of the Gulf Intracoastal Waterway

- ❏ Addendum for Seller's Disclosure of Information on Lead-based Paint and Lead-based Paint Hazards as Required by Federal Law

- ❏ Addendum for Property in a Propane Gas System Service Area

- ❏ Other (list): _____
  _____

23. TERMINATION OPTION: For nominal consideration, the receipt of which is hereby acknowledged by Seller, and Buyer's agreement to pay Seller $_____ (Option Fee) within 3 days after the effective date of this contract, Seller grants Buyer the unrestricted right to terminate this contract by giving notice of termination to Seller within _____ days after the effective date of this contract (Option Period). Notices under this paragraph must be given by 5:00 p.m. (local time where the Property is located) by the date specified. If no dollar amount is stated as the Option Fee or if Buyer fails to pay the Option Fee to Seller within the time prescribed, this paragraph will not be a part of this contract and Buyer shall not have the unrestricted right to terminate this contract. If Buyer gives notice of termination within the time prescribed, the Option Fee will not be refunded; however, any earnest money will be refunded to Buyer. The Option Fee ❏will ❏will not be credited to the Sales Price at closing. **Time is of the essence for this paragraph and strict compliance with the time for performance is required.**

24. CONSULT AN ATTORNEY BEFORE SIGNING: TREC rules prohibit real estate license holders from giving legal advice. READ THIS CONTRACT CAREFULLY.

Buyer's
Attorney is: _____

Phone: (___) _____

Fax: (___) _____

E-mail: _____

Seller's
Attorney is: _____

Phone: (___) _____

Fax: (___) _____

E-mail: _____

EXECUTED the _____ day of _____, 20_____ (EFFECTIVE DATE).
(BROKER: FILL IN THE DATE OF FINAL ACCEPTANCE.)

_____
Buyer

_____
Buyer

_____
Seller

_____
Seller

The form of this contract has been approved by the Texas Real Estate Commission. TREC forms are intended for use only by trained real estate. No representation is made as to the legal validity or adequacy of any provision in any specific transactions. It is not intended for complex transactions. Texas Real Estate Commission, P.O. Box 12188, Austin, TX 78711-2188, (512) 936-3000 (http://www.trec.texas.gov) TREC NO. 25-11. This form replaces TREC NO. 25-10.

TREC NO. 25-11

Contract Concerning _____Page 9 of 10   11-2-2015
(Address of Property)

RATIFICATION OF FEE

Listing Broker has agreed to pay Other Broker_____ of the total Sales Price when Listing Broker's fee is received. Escrow Agent is authorized and directed to pay Other Broker from Listing Broker's fee at closing.

Other Broker: Listing Broker:

By: _____   By: _____

BROKER INFORMATION AND AGREEMENT FOR PAYMENT OF BROKERS' FEES

Other Broker	License No.	Listing or Principal Broker	License No.
Associate's Name	License No.	Listing Associate's Name	License No.
Licensed Supervisor of Associate	License No.	Licensed Supervisor of Listing Associate	License No.
Other Broker's Office Address		Listing Broker's Office Address	
City State Zip		City State Zip	
Phone Fax		Phone Fax	
Associate's Email Address		Listing Associate's Email Address	

represents ☐ Buyer only as Buyer's agent
☐ Seller as Listing Broker's subagent

Selling Associate   License No.

Licensed Supervisor of Selling Associate   License No.

Selling Associate's Office Address   Fax

City   State   Zip

Selling Associate's Email Address

represents ☐ Seller only
☐ Buyer only
☐ Seller and Buyer as an intermediary

Upon closing of the sale by Seller to Buyer of the Property described in the contract to which this fee agreement is attached: (a) ☐ Seller ☐ Buyer will pay Listing/Principal Broker ☐ a cash fee of $_____ or ☐ _____% of the total Sales Price; and (b) ☐ Seller ☐ Buyer will pay Other Broker ☐ a cash fee of $_____ or ☐ _____% of the total Sales Price. Seller/Buyer authorizes and directs Escrow Agent to pay the brokers from the proceeds at closing.

Brokers' fees are negotiable. Brokers' fees or the sharing of fees between brokers are not fixed, controlled, recommended, suggested or maintained by the Texas Real Estate Commission.

_____   _____
Seller   Buyer

_____   _____
Seller   Buyer
Do not sign if there is a separate written agreement for payment of Brokers' fees.

TREC NO. 25-11

Contract Concerning _____Page 10 of 10   11-2-2015
(Address of Property)

OPTION FEE RECEIPT

Receipt of $_____ (Option Fee) in the form of _____ is acknowledged.

_____   _____
Seller or Listing Broker   Date

CONTRACT AND EARNEST MONEY RECEIPT

Receipt of ☐Contract and ☐$_____ Earnest Money in the form of _____
is acknowledged.

Escrow Agent: _____   Date: _____

By: _____   _____
                                                               Email Address
_____   Phone: (_____) _____
Address
_____   Fax: (_____) _____
City   State   Zip

Initialed for identification by Buyer_____ _____ and Seller _____ _____   TREC NO. 25-11

PROMULGATED BY THE TEXAS REAL ESTATE COMMISSION (TREC)   11-2-2015
NOTICE: Not For Use Where Seller Owns Fee Simple Title To Land Beneath Unit

RESIDENTIAL CONDOMINIUM CONTRACT (RESALE)

1. PARTIES: The parties to this contract are _____(Seller) and
_____(Buyer). Seller agrees to
sell and convey to Buyer and Buyer agrees to buy from Seller the Property defined below.

2. PROPERTY AND CONDOMINIUM DOCUMENTS:

A. The Condominium Unit, improvements and accessories described below are collectively referred to as the "Property".

(1) CONDOMINIUM UNIT: Unit _____, in Building _____,
of _____, a condominium project, located at
_____
_____
(address/zip code), City of _____,County of _____
Texas, described in the Condominium Declaration and Plat and any amendments thereto of record in said County; together with such Unit's undivided interest in the Common Elements designated by the Declaration, including those areas reserved as Limited Common Elements appurtenant to the Unit and such other rights to use the Common Elements which have been specifically assigned to the Unit in any other manner. Parking areas assigned to the Unit are:_____.

(2) IMPROVEMENTS: All fixtures and improvements attached to the above described real property including without limitation, the following **permanently installed and built-in items**, if any: all equipment and appliances, valances, screens, shutters, awnings, wall-to-wall carpeting, mirrors, ceiling fans, attic fans, mail boxes, television antennas, mounts and brackets for televisions and speakers, heating and air conditioning units, security and fire detection equipment, wiring, plumbing and lighting fixtures, chandeliers, shrubbery, landscaping, outdoor cooking equipment, and all other property owned by Seller and attached to the above described Condominium Unit.

(3) ACCESSORIES: The following described related accessories, if any: window air conditioning units, stove, fireplace screens, curtains and rods, blinds, window shades, draperies and rods, door keys, mailbox keys, above ground pool, swimming pool equipment and maintenance accessories, artificial fireplace logs, and controls for: (i) garage doors, (ii) entry gates, and (iii) other improvements and accessories.

(4) EXCLUSIONS: The following improvements and accessories will be retained by Seller and must be removed prior to delivery of possession:_____.

B. The Declaration, Bylaws and any Rules of the Association are called "Documents". (Check one box only):

❑ (1) Buyer has received a copy of the Documents. Buyer is advised to read the Documents before signing the contract.

❑ (2)Buyer has not received a copy of the Documents. Seller shall deliver the Documents to Buyer within _____ days after the effective date of the contract. Buyer may cancel the contract before the sixth day after Buyer receives the Documents by hand-delivering or mailing written notice of cancellation to Seller by certified United States mail, return receipt requested. If Buyer cancels the contract pursuant to this paragraph, the contract will terminate and the earnest money will be refunded to Buyer.

C. The Resale Certificate from the condominium owners association (the Association) is called the "Certificate". The Certificate must be in a form promulgated by TREC or required by the parties. The Certificate must have been prepared no more than 3 months before the date it is delivered to Buyer and must contain at a minimum the information required by Section 82.157, Texas Property Code.
(Check one box only):

❑ (1) Buyer has received the Certificate.

❑ (2) Buyer has not received the Certificate. Seller shall deliver the Certificate to Buyer within _____days after the effective date of the contract. Buyer may cancel the contract before the sixth day after the date Buyer receives the Certificate by hand-delivering or mailing written notice of cancellation to Seller by certified United States mail, return receipt requested. If Buyer cancels the contract pursuant to this paragraph, the contract will terminate and the earnest money will be refunded to Buyer.

❑ (3) Buyer has received Seller's affidavit that Seller requested information from the Association concerning its financial condition as required by the Texas Property Code, and that the Association did not provide a Certificate or information required in the Certificate. Buyer and Seller agree to waive the requirement to furnish the Certificate.

D. If the Documents reveal that the Property is subject to a right of refusal under which the Association or a member of the Association may purchase the Property, the effective date shall be amended to the date that Buyer receives a copy of the Association's certification that: (i) Seller has complied with the requirements under the right of refusal; and (ii) all persons who may exercise the right of refusal have not exercised or have waived the right to buy the Property. If Buyer does not receive the Association's certification within _____days after the effective date or if the right of refusal is exercised, this contract shall terminate and the earnest money shall be refunded to Buyer.

Initialed for identification by Buyer_____ _____ and Seller _____ _____   TREC NO. 30-12

Contract Concerning_____Page 2 of 8 11-2-2015
(Address of Property)

3. SALES PRICE:
   A. Cash portion of Sales Price payable by Buyer at closing................... $_____
   B. Sum of all financing described in the attached: ❑   Third Party Financing Addendum,
      ❑   Loan Assumption Addendum, ❑   Seller Financing Addendum ... $_____
   C. Sales Price (Sum of A and B).. $_____

4. LICENSE HOLDER DISCLOSURE: Texas law requires a real estate license holder who is a party to a transaction or acting on behalf of a spouse, parent, child, business entity in which the license holder owns more than 10%, or a trust for which the license holder acts as trustee or of which the license holder or the license holder's spouse, parent or child is a beneficiary, to notify the other party in writing before entering into a contract of sale. Disclose if applicable:_____
_____.

5. EARNEST MONEY: Upon execution of this contract by all parties, Buyer shall deposit $_____ as earnest money with _____, as escrow agent, at _____(address). Buyer shall deposit additional earnest money of $_____with escrow agent within _____ days after the effective date of this contract. If Buyer fails to deposit the earnest money as required by this contract, Buyer will be in default.

6. TITLE POLICY:
   A. TITLE POLICY: Seller shall furnish to Buyer at ❑Seller's ❑Buyer's expense an owner policy of title insurance (Title Policy) issued by _____(Title Company) in the amount of the Sales Price, dated at or after closing, insuring Buyer against loss under the provisions of the Title Policy, subject to the promulgated exclusions (including existing building and zoning ordinances) and the following exceptions:
      (1) Restrictive covenants common to the platted subdivision in which the Property is located.
      (2) The standard printed exception for standby fees, taxes and assessments.
      (3) Liens created as part of the financing described in Paragraph 3.
      (4) Terms and provisions of the Documents including the assessments and platted easements.
      (5) Reservations or exceptions otherwise permitted by this contract or as may be approved by Buyer in writing.
      (6) The standard printed exception as to marital rights.
      (7) The standard printed exception as to waters, tidelands, beaches, streams, and related matters.
      (8) The standard printed exception as to discrepancies, conflicts, shortages in area or boundary lines, encroachments or protrusions, or overlapping improvements.
   B. COMMITMENT: Within 20 days after the Title Company receives a copy of this contract, Seller shall furnish to Buyer a commitment for title insurance (Commitment) and, at Buyer's expense, legible copies of restrictive covenants and documents evidencing exceptions in the Commitment (Exception Documents) other than the standard printed exceptions. Seller authorizes the Title Company to deliver the Commitment and Exception Documents to Buyer at Buyer's address shown in Paragraph 21. If the Commitment and Exception Documents are not delivered to Buyer within the specified time, the time for delivery will be automatically extended up to 15 days or 3 days before the Closing Date, whichever is earlier. If, due to factors beyond Seller's control, the Commitment and Exception Documents are not delivered within the time required, Buyer may terminate this contract and the earnest money will be refunded to Buyer.
   C. OBJECTIONS: Buyer may object in writing to defects, exceptions, or encumbrances to title: disclosed in the Commitment other than items 6A(1) through (8) above; or which prohibit the following use or activity: _____
   _____.
   Buyer must object the earlier of (i) the Closing Date or (ii) _____ days after Buyer receives the Commitment and Exception Documents. Buyer's failure to object within the time allowed will constitute a waiver of Buyer's right to object; except that the requirements in Schedule C of the Commitment are not waived by Buyer. Provided Seller is not obligated to incur any expense, Seller shall cure the timely objections of Buyer or any third party lender within 15 days after Seller receives the objections and the Closing Date will be extended as necessary. If objections are not cured within such 15 day period, this contract will terminate and the earnest money will be refunded to Buyer unless Buyer waives the objections.
   D. TITLE NOTICES:
      (1) ABSTRACT OR TITLE POLICY: Broker advises Buyer to have an abstract of title covering the Property examined by an attorney of Buyer's selection, or Buyer should be furnished with or obtain a Title Policy. If a Title Policy is furnished, the Commitment should be promptly reviewed by an attorney of Buyer's choice due to the time limitations on Buyer's right to object.
      (2) STATUTORY TAX DISTRICTS: If the Property is situated in a utility or other statutorily created district providing water, sewer, drainage, or flood control facilities and services, Chapter 49, Texas Water Code, requires Seller to deliver and Buyer to sign the statutory notice relating to the tax rate, bonded indebtedness, or standby fee of the district prior to final execution of this contract.

Initialed for identification by Buyer_____ _____ and Seller _____ _____   TREC NO. 30-12

Contract Concerning_____Page 3 of 8   11-2-2015
(Address of Property)

(3) TIDE WATERS: If the Property abuts the tidally influenced waters of the state, §33.135, Texas Natural Resources Code, requires a notice regarding coastal area property to be included in the contract. An addendum containing the notice promulgated by TREC or required by the parties must be used.

(4) ANNEXATION: If the Property is located outside the limits of a municipality, Seller notifies Buyer under §5.011, Texas Property Code, that the Property may now or later be included in the extraterritorial jurisdiction of a municipality and may now or later be subject to annexation by the municipality. Each municipality maintains a map that depicts its boundaries and extraterritorial jurisdiction. To determine if the Property is located within a municipality's extraterritorial jurisdiction or is likely to be located within a municipality's extraterritorial jurisdiction, contact all municipalities located in the general proximity of the Property for further information.

(5) PROPERTY LOCATED IN A CERTIFICATED SERVICE AREA OF A UTILITY SERVICE PROVIDER: Notice required by §13.257, Water Code: The real property, described in Paragraph 2, that you are about to purchase may be located in a certificated water or sewer service area, which is authorized by law to provide water or sewer service to the properties in the certificated area. If your property is located in a certificated area there may be special costs or charges that you will be required to pay before you can receive water or sewer service. There may be a period required to construct lines or other facilities necessary to provide water or sewer service to your property. You are advised to determine if the property is in a certificated area and contact the utility service provider to determine the cost that you will be required to pay and the period, if any, that is required to provide water or sewer service to your property. The undersigned Buyer hereby acknowledges receipt of the foregoing notice at or before the execution of a binding contract for the purchase of the real property described in Paragraph 2 or at closing of purchase of the real property.

(6) TRANSFER FEES: If the Property is subject to a private transfer fee obligation, §5.205, Property Code, requires Seller to notify Buyer as follows: The private transfer fee obligation may be governed by Chapter 5, Subchapter G of the Texas Property Code.

(7) PROPANE GAS SYSTEM SERVICE AREA: If the Property is located in a propane gas system service area owned by a distribution system retailer, Seller must give Buyer written notice as required by §141.010, Texas Utilities Code. An addendum containing the notice approved by TREC or required by the parties should be used.

(8) NOTICE OF WATER LEVEL FLUCTUATIONS: If the Property adjoins an impoundment of water, including a reservoir or lake, constructed and maintained under Chapter 11, Water Code, that has a storage capacity of at least 5,000 acre-feet at the impoundment's normal operating level, Seller hereby notifies Buyer: "The water level of the impoundment of water adjoining the Property fluctuates for various reasons, including as a result of: (1) an entity lawfully exercising its right to use the water stored in the impoundment; or (2) drought or flood conditions."

7. PROPERTY CONDITION:
A. ACCESS, INSPECTIONS AND UTILITIES: Seller shall permit Buyer and Buyer's agents access to the Property at reasonable times. Buyer may have the Property inspected by inspectors selected by Buyer and licensed by TREC or otherwise permitted by law to make inspections. Any hydrostatic testing must be separately authorized by Seller in writing. Seller at Seller's expense shall immediately cause existing utilities to be turned on and shall keep the utilities on during the time this contract is in effect .
B. SELLER'S DISCLOSURE NOTICE PURSUANT TO §5.008, TEXAS PROPERTY CODE (Notice): (Check one box only)
❏ (1) Buyer has received the Notice.
❏ (2) Buyer has not received the Notice. Within _____ days after the effective date of this contract, Seller shall deliver the Notice to Buyer. If Buyer does not receive the Notice, Buyer may terminate this contract at any time prior to the closing and the earnest money will be refunded to Buyer. If Seller delivers the Notice, Buyer may terminate this contract for any reason within 7 days after Buyer receives the Notice or prior to the closing, whichever first occurs, and the earnest money will be refunded to Buyer.
❏ (3) The Texas Property Code does not require this Seller to furnish the Notice.
C. SELLER'S DISCLOSURE OF LEAD-BASED PAINT AND LEAD-BASED PAINT HAZARDS is required by Federal law for a residential dwelling constructed prior to 1978.
D. ACCEPTANCE OF PROPERTY CONDITION: "As Is" means the present condition of the Property with any and all defects and without warranty except for the warranties of title and the warranties in this contract. Buyer's agreement to accept the Property As Is under Paragraph 7D(1) or (2) does not preclude Buyer from inspecting the Property under Paragraph 7A, from negotiating repairs or treatments in a subsequent amendment, or from terminating this contract during the Option Period, if any. (Check one box only)
❏ (1) Buyer accepts the Property As Is.
❏ (2) Buyer accepts the Property As Is provided Seller, at Seller's expense, shall complete the following specific repairs and treatments:_____.

(Do not insert general phrases, such as "subject to inspections," that do not identify specific repairs and treatments.)
E. LENDER REQUIRED REPAIRS AND TREATMENTS: Unless otherwise agreed in writing, neither party is obligated to pay for lender required repairs, which includes treatment for wood

Initialed for identification by Buyer_____ _____ and Seller _____ _____   TREC NO. 30-12

Contract Concerning_____Page 4 of 8   11-2-2015
(Address of Property)

destroying insects. If the parties do not agree to pay for the lender required repairs or treatments, this contract will terminate and the earnest money will be refunded to Buyer. If the cost of lender required repairs and treatments exceeds 5% of the Sales Price, Buyer may terminate this contract and the earnest money will be refunded to Buyer.

F. COMPLETION OF REPAIRS AND TREATMENTS: Unless otherwise agreed in writing: (i) Seller shall complete all agreed repairs and treatments prior to the Closing Date; and (ii) all required permits must be obtained, and repairs and treatments must be performed by persons who are licensed to provide such repairs or treatments or, if no license is required by law, are commercially engaged in the trade of providing such repairs or treatments. At Buyer's election, any transferable warranties received by Seller with respect to the repairs and treatments will be transferred to Buyer at Buyer's expense. If Seller fails to complete any agreed repairs and treatments prior to the Closing Date, Buyer may exercise remedies under Paragraph 15 or extend the Closing Date up to 5 days if necessary for Seller to complete repairs and treatments.

G. ENVIRONMENTAL MATTERS: Buyer is advised that the presence of wetlands, toxic substances, including asbestos and wastes or other environmental hazards or the presence of a threatened or endangered species or its habitat may affect Buyer's intended use of the Property. If Buyer is concerned about these matters, an addendum promulgated by TREC or required by the parties should be used.

H. RESIDENTIAL SERVICE CONTRACTS: Buyer may purchase a residential service contract from a residential service company licensed by TREC. If Buyer purchases a residential service contract, Seller shall reimburse Buyer at closing for the cost of the residential service contract in an amount not exceeding $_____. Buyer should review any residential service contract for the scope of coverage, exclusions and limitations. **The purchase of a residential service contract is optional. Similar coverage may be purchased from various companies authorized to do business in Texas.**

8. BROKERS' FEES: All obligations of the parties for payment of brokers' fees are contained in separate written agreements.

9. CLOSING:

A. The closing of the sale will be on or before _____, 20____, or within 7 days after objections to matters disclosed in the Commitment have been cured, whichever date is later (Closing Date). If either party fails to close the sale by the Closing Date, the non-defaulting party may exercise the remedies contained in Paragraph 15.

B.   At closing:

(1) Seller shall execute and deliver a general warranty deed conveying title to the Property to Buyer and showing no additional exceptions to those permitted in Paragraph 6 and furnish tax statements or certificates showing no delinquent taxes on the Property.

(2) Buyer shall pay the Sales Price in good funds acceptable to the escrow agent.

(3) Seller and Buyer shall execute and deliver any notices, statements, certificates, affidavits, releases, loan documents and other documents reasonably required for the closing of the sale and the issuance of the Title Policy.

(4) There will be no liens, assessments, or security interests against the Property which will not be satisfied out of the sales proceeds unless securing the payment of any loans assumed by Buyer and assumed loans will not be in default.

(5) If the Property is subject to a residential lease, Seller shall transfer security deposits (as defined under §92.102, Property Code), if any, to Buyer. In such an event, Buyer shall deliver to the tenant a signed statement acknowledging that the Buyer has acquired the Property and is responsible for the return of the security deposit, and specifying the exact dollar amount of the security deposit.

10. POSSESSION:

A. Buyers Possession: Seller shall deliver to Buyer possession of the Property in its present or required condition, ordinary wear and tear excepted: ❑ upon closing and funding ❑ according to a temporary residential lease form promulgated by TREC or other written lease required by the parties. Any possession by Buyer prior to closing or by Seller after closing which is not authorized by a written lease will establish a tenancy at sufferance relationship between the parties. **Consult your insurance agent prior to change of ownership and possession because insurance coverage may be limited or terminated. The absence of a written lease or appropriate insurance coverage may expose the parties to economic loss.**

B. Leases:

(1) After the Effective Date, Seller may not execute any lease (including but not limited to mineral leases) or convey any interest in the Property without Buyer's written consent.

(2) If the Property is subject to any lease to which Seller is a party, Seller shall deliver to Buyer copies of the lease(s) and any move-in condition form signed by the tenant within 7 days after the Effective Date of the contract.

11. SPECIAL PROVISIONS: (Insert only factual statements and business details applicable to the sale. TREC rules prohibit license holders from adding factual statements or business details for which a contract addendum, lease or other form has been promulgated by TREC for mandatory use.)

Initialed for identification by Buyer_____ _____ and Seller _____ _____   TREC NO. 30-12

Contract Concerning_____Page 5 of 8   11-2-2015
(Address of Property)

12. SETTLEMENT AND OTHER EXPENSES:
    A. The following expenses must be paid at or prior to closing:
        (1) Expenses payable by Seller (Seller's Expenses):
            (a) Releases of existing liens, including prepayment penalties and recording fees; lender, FHA, or VA completion requirements; tax statements or certificates; preparation of deed; one-half of escrow fee; and other expenses payable by Seller under this contract.
            (b) Seller shall also pay an amount not to exceed $_____ to be applied in the following order: Buyer's Expenses which Buyer is prohibited from paying by FHA, VA, Texas Veterans Land Board or other governmental loan programs, and then to other Buyer's Expenses as allowed by the lender.
        (2) Expenses payable by Buyer (Buyer's Expenses): Appraisal fees; loan application fees; origination charges; credit reports; preparation of loan documents; interest on the notes from date of disbursement to one month prior to dates of first monthly payments; recording fees; copies of easements and restrictions; loan title policy with endorsements required by lender; loan-related inspection fees; photos; amortization schedules; one-half of escrow fee; all prepaid items, including required premiums for flood and hazard insurance, reserve deposits for insurance, ad valorem taxes and special governmental assessments; final compliance inspection; courier fee; repair inspection; underwriting fee; wire transfer fee; expenses incident to any loan; Private Mortgage Insurance Premium (PMI), VA Loan Funding Fee, or FHA Mortgage Insurance Premium (MIP) as required by the lender; and other expenses payable by Buyer under this contract.
        (3) Except as provided by 12(A)(4) below, Buyer shall pay any and all Association fees or other charges resulting from the transfer of the Property not to exceed $_____ and Seller shall pay any excess.
        (4) Buyer shall pay any deposits for reserves required at closing by the Association.
    B. If any expense exceeds an amount expressly stated in this contract for such expense to be paid by a party, that party may terminate this contract unless the other party agrees to pay such excess. Buyer may not pay charges and fees expressly prohibited by FHA, VA, Texas Veterans Land Board or other governmental loan program regulations.

13. PRORATIONS: Taxes for the current year, interest, maintenance fees, regular condominium assessments, dues and rents will be prorated through the Closing Date. The tax proration may be calculated taking into consideration any change in exemptions that will affect the current year's taxes. If taxes for the current year vary from the amount prorated at closing, the parties shall adjust the prorations when tax statements for the current year are available. If taxes are not paid at or prior to closing, Buyer shall pay taxes for the current year. Cash reserves from regular condominium assessments for deferred maintenance or capital improvements established by the Association will not be credited to Seller. Any special condominium assessment due and unpaid at closing will be the obligation of Seller.

14. CASUALTY LOSS: If any part of the Unit which Seller is solely obligated to maintain and repair under the terms of the Declaration is damaged or destroyed by fire or other casualty, Seller shall restore the same to its previous condition as soon as reasonably possible, but in any event by the Closing Date. If Seller fails to do so due to factors beyond Seller's control, Buyer may (a) terminate this contract and the earnest money will be refunded to Buyer, (b) extend the time for performance up to 15 days and the Closing Date will be extended as necessary or (c) accept the Property in its damaged condition with an assignment of insurance proceeds, if permitted by Seller's insurance carrier, and receive credit from Seller at closing in the amount of the deductible under the insurance policy. If any part of the Common Elements or Limited Common Elements appurtenant to the Unit is damaged or destroyed by fire or other casualty loss, Buyer will have 7 days from receipt of notice of such casualty loss within which to notify Seller in writing that the contract will be terminated unless Buyer receives written confirmation from the Association that the damaged condition will be restored to its previous condition within a reasonable time at no cost to Buyer. Unless Buyer gives such notice within such time, Buyer will be deemed to have accepted the Property without confirmation of such restoration. Seller will have 7 days from the date of receipt of Buyer's notice within which to cause to be delivered to Buyer such confirmation. If written confirmation is not delivered to Buyer as required above, Buyer may terminate this contract and the earnest money will be refunded to Buyer. Seller's obligations under this paragraph are independent of any other obligations of Seller under this contract.

15. DEFAULT: If Buyer fails to comply with this contract, Buyer will be in default, and Seller may (a) enforce specific performance, seek such other relief as may be provided by law, or both, or (b) terminate this contract and receive the earnest money as liquidated damages, thereby releasing both parties from this contract. If Seller fails to comply with this contract for any other reason, Seller will be in default and Buyer may (a) enforce specific performance, seek such other relief as may be provided by law, or both, or (b) terminate this contract and receive the earnest money, thereby releasing both parties from this contract.

16. MEDIATION: It is the policy of the State of Texas to encourage resolution of disputes through alternative dispute resolution procedures such as mediation. Any dispute between Seller and Buyer related to this contract which is not resolved through informal discussion will be submitted to a mutually acceptable mediation service or provider. The parties to the mediation shall bear the mediation costs equally. This paragraph does not preclude a party from seeking equitable relief from a court of competent jurisdiction.

17. ATTORNEY'S FEES: A Buyer, Seller, Listing Broker, Other Broker, or escrow agent who prevails in any legal proceeding related to this contract is entitled to recover reasonable attorney's fees and all costs of such proceeding.

Initialed for identification by Buyer_____ _____ and Seller _____ _____   TREC NO. 30-12

Contract Concerning_____Page 6 of 8   11-2-2015
(Address of Property)

18. ESCROW:
    A. ESCROW: The escrow agent is not (i) a party to this contract and does not have liability for the performance or nonperformance of any party to this contract, (ii) liable for interest on the earnest money and (iii) liable for the loss of any earnest money caused by the failure of any financial institution in which the earnest money has been deposited unless the financial institution is acting as escrow agent.
    B. EXPENSES: At closing, the earnest money must be applied first to any cash down payment, then to Buyer's Expenses and any excess refunded to Buyer. If no closing occurs, escrow agent may: (i) require a written release of liability of the escrow agent from all parties, (ii) require payment of unpaid expenses incurred on behalf of a party, and (iii) only deduct from the earnest money the amount of unpaid expenses incurred on behalf of the party receiving the earnest money.
    C. DEMAND: Upon termination of this contract, either party or the escrow agent may send a release of earnest money to each party and the parties shall execute counterparts of the release and deliver same to the escrow agent. If either party fails to execute the release, either party may make a written demand to the escrow agent for the earnest money. If only one party makes written demand for the earnest money, escrow agent shall promptly provide a copy of the demand to the other party. If escrow agent does not receive written objection to the demand from the other party within 15 days, escrow agent may disburse the earnest money to the party making demand reduced by the amount of unpaid expenses incurred on behalf of the party receiving the earnest money and escrow agent may pay the same to the creditors. If escrow agent complies with the provisions of this paragraph, each party hereby releases escrow agent from all adverse claims related to the disbursal of the earnest money.
    D. DAMAGES: Any party who wrongfully fails or refuses to sign a release acceptable to the escrow agent within 7 days of receipt of the request will be liable to the other party for (i) damages; (ii) the earnest money; (iii) reasonable attorney's fees; and (iv) all costs of suit.
    E. NOTICES: Escrow agent's notices will be effective when sent in compliance with Paragraph 21. Notice of objection to the demand will be deemed effective upon receipt by escrow agent.

19. REPRESENTATIONS: All covenants, representations and warranties in this contract survive closing. If any representation of Seller in this contract is untrue on the Closing Date, Seller will be in default. Unless expressly prohibited by written agreement, Seller may continue to show the Property and receive, negotiate and accept back up offers.

20. FEDERAL TAX REQUIREMENTS: If Seller is a "foreign person," as defined by applicable law, or if Seller fails to deliver an affidavit to Buyer that Seller is not a "foreign person," then Buyer shall withhold from the sales proceeds an amount sufficient to comply with applicable tax law and deliver the same to the Internal Revenue Service together with appropriate tax forms. Internal Revenue Service regulations require filing written reports if currency in excess of specified amounts is received in the transaction.

21. NOTICES: All notices from one party to the other must be in writing and are effective when mailed to, hand-delivered at, or transmitted by fax or electronic transmission as follows:

To Buyer at: _____	**To Seller** at: _____
_____	_____
Phone: ( ) _____	Phone: ( ) _____
Fax: ( ) _____	Fax: ( ) _____
E-mail: _____	E-mail: _____

22. AGREEMENT OF PARTIES: This contract contains the entire agreement of the parties and cannot be changed except by their written agreement. Addenda which are a part of this contract are (check all applicable boxes):

❑ Third Party Financing Addendum
❑ Loan Assumption Addendum
❑ Buyer's Temporary Residential Lease
❑ Seller's Temporary Residential Lease
❑ Addendum for Sale of Other Property by Buyer
❑ Addendum for "Back-Up" Contract
❑ Seller Financing Addendum
❑ Addendum for Coastal Area Property
❑ Short Sale Addendum
❑ Addendum for Seller's Disclosure of Information on Lead-based Paint and Lead-based Paint Hazards as Required by Federal Law

❑ Environmental Assessment, Threatened or Endangered Species and Wetlands Addendum
❑ Addendum for Property Located Seaward of the Gulf Intracoastal Waterway
❑ Addendum for Release of Liability on Assumption of FHA, VA, or Conventional Loan Restoration of Seller's Entitlement for VA Guaranteed Loan
❑ Addendum for Property in a Propane Gas System Service Area
❑ Other (list): _____
_____

Initialed for identification by Buyer_____ _____ and Seller _____ _____   TREC NO. 30-12

Contract Concerning_____Page 7 of 8 11-2-2015
(Address of Property)

23. TERMINATION OPTION: For nominal consideration, the receipt of which is hereby acknowledged by Seller, and Buyer's agreement to pay Seller $_____ (Option Fee) within 3 days after the effective date of this contract, Seller grants Buyer the unrestricted right to terminate this contract by giving notice of termination to Seller within _____ days after the effective date of this contract (Option Period). Notices under this paragraph must be given by 5:00 p.m. (local time where the Property is located) by the date specified. If no dollar amount is stated as the Option Fee or if Buyer fails to pay the Option Fee to Seller within the time prescribed, this paragraph will not be a part of this contract and Buyer shall not have the unrestricted right to terminate this contract. If Buyer gives notice of termination within the time prescribed, the Option Fee will not be refunded; however, any earnest money will be refunded to Buyer. The Option Fee ❑will ❑will not be credited to the Sales Price at closing. **Time is of the essence for this paragraph and strict compliance with the time for performance is required.**

24. CONSULT AN ATTORNEY BEFORE SIGNING: TREC rules prohibit real estate license holders from giving legal advice. READ THIS CONTRACT CAREFULLY.

Buyer's
Attorney is: _____

Seller's
Attorney is: _____

_____

_____

Phone: (____)_____

Phone: (____)_____

Fax: (____)_____

Fax: (____)_____

E-mail: _____

E-mail: _____

EXECUTED the _____day of _____, 20_____ (EFFECTIVE DATE).
(BROKER: FILL IN THE DATE OF FINAL ACCEPTANCE.)

_____
Buyer

_____
Seller

_____
Buyer

_____
Seller

The form of this contract has been approved by the Texas Real Estate Commission.   TREC forms are intended for use only by trained real estate license holders. No representation is made as to the legal validity or adequacy of any provision in any specific transactions. It is not intended for complex transactions. Texas Real Estate Commission, P.O. Box 12188, Austin, TX 78711-2188, (512) 936-3000 (http://www.trec.texas.gov) TREC NO. 30-12. This form replaces TREC NO. 30-11.

Initialed for identification by Buyer_____ _____ and Seller _____ _____   TREC NO. 30-12

Contract Concerning_____Page 8 of 8 11-2-2015
(Address of Property)

BROKER INFORMATION
(Print name(s) only. Do not sign)

Other Broker Firm _____ License No.

represents ☐ Buyer only as Buyer's agent
☐ Seller as Listing Broker's subagent

Associate's Name _____ License No.

Licensed Supervisor of Associate _____ License No.

Other Broker's Address _____ Fax

City   State   Zip

Associate's Email Address _____ Phone

Listing Broker Firm _____ License No.

represents ☐ Seller and Buyer as an intermediary
☐ Seller only as Seller's agent

Listing Associate's Name _____ License No.

Licensed Supervisor of Listing Associate _____ License No.

Listing Broker's Office Address _____ Fax

City   State   Zip

Listing Associate's Email Address _____ Phone

Selling Associate's Name _____ License No.

Licensed Supervisor of Selling Associate _____ License No.

Selling Associate's Office Address _____ Fax

City   State   Zip

Selling Associate's Email Address _____ Phone

Listing Broker has agreed to pay Other Broker_____of the total sales price when the Listing Broker's fee is received. Escrow agent is authorized and directed to pay other Broker from Listing Broker's fee at closing.

OPTION FEE RECEIPT

Receipt of $_____ (Option Fee) in the form of _____ is acknowledged.

_____   _____
Seller or Listing Broker   Date

CONTRACT AND EARNEST MONEY RECEIPT

Receipt of ☐ Contract and ☐ $_____ Earnest Money in the form of _____
is acknowledged.
Escrow Agent: _____   Date: _____

By: _____

_____   Email Address
Address

_____   Phone: (_____) _____
City   State   Zip

Fax: (_____) _____

Initialed for identification by Buyer_____ _____ and Seller _____ _____   TREC NO. 30-12

PROMULGATED BY THE TEXAS REAL ESTATE COMMISSION (TREC)

12-05-11

ADDENDUM FOR
SALE OF OTHER PROPERTY BY BUYER

TO CONTRACT CONCERNING THE PROPERTY AT

_____
(Address of Property)

A. The contract is contingent upon Buyer's **receipt of the proceeds** from the sale of Buyer's property at_____
(Address) on or before _____, 20_____ (the Contingency). If the Contingency is not satisfied or waived by Buyer by the above date, the contract will terminate automatically and the earnest money will be refunded to Buyer.

NOTICE: The date inserted in this Paragraph should be no later than the Closing Date specified in Paragraph 9 of the contract.

B. If Seller accepts a written offer to sell the Property, Seller shall notify Buyer (1) of such acceptance **AND** (2) that Seller requires Buyer to waive the Contingency. Buyer must waive the Contingency on or before the _____ day after Seller's notice to Buyer; otherwise the contract will terminate automatically and the earnest money will be refunded to Buyer.

C. Buyer may waive the Contingency only by notifying Seller of the waiver and depositing $_____ with escrow agent as additional earnest money. All notices and waivers must be in writing and are effective when delivered in accordance with the contract.

D. If Buyer waives the Contingency and fails to close and fund solely due to Buyer's non-receipt of proceeds from Buyer's property described in Paragraph A above, Buyer will be in default. If such default occurs, Seller may exercise the remedies specified in Paragraph 15 of the contract.

E. For purposes of this Addendum time is of the essence; strict compliance with the times for performance stated herein is required.

_____   _____
Buyer   Seller

_____   _____
Buyer   Seller

TREC No. 10-6

PROMULGATED BY THE TEXAS REAL ESTATE COMMISSION (TREC)   12-05-11

ADDENDUM FOR
"BACK-UP" CONTRACT

TO CONTRACT CONCERNING THE PROPERTY AT

_____

(Address of Property)

A. The contract to which this Addendum is attached (the Back-Up Contract) is binding upon execution by the parties, and the earnest money and any Option Fee must be paid as provided in the Back-Up Contract. The Back-Up Contract is contingent upon the termination of a previous contract (the First Contract) dated _____, 20_____, for the sale of Property. Except as provided by this Addendum, neither party is required to perform under the Back-Up Contract while it is contingent upon the termination of the First Contract.

B. If the First Contract does not terminate on or before _____, 20_____, the Back-Up Contract terminates and the earnest money will be refunded to Buyer. Seller must notify Buyer immediately of the termination of the First Contract. For purposes of performance, the effective date of the Back-Up Contract changes to the date Buyer receives notice of termination of the First Contract (Amended Effective Date).

C. An amendment or modification of the First Contract will not terminate the First Contract.

D. If Buyer has the unrestricted right to terminate the Back-Up Contract, the time for giving notice of termination begins on the effective date of the Back-Up Contract, continues after the Amended Effective Date and ends upon the expiration of Buyer's unrestricted right to terminate the Back-Up Contract.

E. For purposes of this Addendum, time is of the essence. Strict compliance with the times for performance stated herein is required.

_____   _____
Buyer   Seller

_____   _____
Buyer   Seller

This form has been approved by the Texas Real Estate Commission for use with similarly approved or promulgated contract forms. Such approval relates to this form only. TREC forms are intended for use only by trained real estate licensees. No representation is made as to the legal validity or adequacy of any provision in any specific transactions. It is not suitable for complex transactions. Texas Real Estate Commission, P.O. Box 12188, Austin, TX 78711-2188, 512-936-3000 (http://www.trec.texas.gov) TREC No. 11-7. This form replaces TREC No. 11-6.

TREC No. 11-7

PROMULGATED BY THE TEXAS REAL ESTATE COMMISSION (TREC)   12-05-11
(NOTICE: For use only when SELLER occupies the property for no more than 90 days AFTER the closing)

SELLER'S TEMPORARY RESIDENTIAL LEASE

1. **PARTIES:** The parties to this Lease are_____
(Landlord) and _____(Tenant).

2. **LEASE:** Landlord leases to Tenant the Property described in the Contract between Landlord as Buyer and Tenant as Seller known as _____
_____(address).

3. **TERM:** The term of this Lease commences on the date the sale covered by the Contract is closed and funded and terminates _____, unless terminated earlier by reason of other provisions.

4. **RENTAL:** Tenant shall pay to Landlord as rental $_____ per day (excluding the day of closing and funding) with the full amount of rental for the term of the Lease to be paid at the time of funding of the sale. Tenant will not be entitled to a refund of rental if this Lease terminates early due to Tenant's default or voluntary surrender of the Property.

5. **DEPOSIT:** Tenant shall pay to Landlord at the time of funding of the sale $_____as a deposit to secure performance of this Lease by Tenant. Landlord may use the deposit to satisfy Tenant's obligations under this Lease. Landlord shall refund any unused portion of the deposit to Tenant with an itemized list of all deductions from the deposit within 30 days after Tenant (a) surrenders possession of the Property and (b) provides Landlord written notice of Tenant's forwarding address.

6. **UTILITIES:** Tenant shall pay all utility charges except _____
which Landlord shall pay.

7. **USE OF PROPERTY:** Tenant may use the Property only for residential purposes. Tenant may not assign this Lease or sublet any part of the Property.

8. **PETS:** Tenant may not keep pets on the Property except _____.

9. **CONDITION OF PROPERTY:** Tenant accepts the Property in its present condition and state of repair at the commencement of the Lease. Upon termination, Tenant shall surrender the Property to Landlord in the condition required under the Contract, except normal wear and tear and any casualty loss.

10. **ALTERATIONS:** Tenant may not alter the Property or install improvements or fixtures without the prior written consent of the Landlord. Any improvements or fixtures placed on the Property during the Lease become the Property of Landlord.

11. **SPECIAL PROVISIONS:**

12. **INSPECTIONS:** Landlord may enter at reasonable times to inspect the Property. Tenant shall provide Landlord door keys and access codes to allow access to the Property during the term of Lease.

13. **LAWS:** Tenant shall comply with all applicable laws, restrictions, ordinances, rules and regulations with respect to the Property.

14. **REPAIRS AND MAINTENANCE:** Except as otherwise provided in this Lease, Tenant shall bear all expense of repairing and maintaining the Property, including but not limited to the yard, trees and shrubs, unless otherwise required by the Texas Property Code. Tenant shall promptly repair at Tenant's expense any damage to the Property caused directly or indirectly by any act or omission of the Tenant or any person other than the Landlord, Landlord's agents or invitees.

Initialed for identification by Landlord _____ and Tenant_____   TREC NO. 15-5

Seller's Temporary Residential Lease _____Page 2 of 2   12-05-11
(Address of Property)

15. **INDEMNITY:** Tenant indemnifies Landlord from the claims of all third parties for injury or damage to the person or property of such third party arising from the use or occupancy of the Property by Tenant. This indemnification includes attorney's fees, costs and expenses incurred by Landlord.

16. **INSURANCE:** Landlord and Tenant shall each maintain such insurance on the contents and Property as each party may deem appropriate during the term of this Lease. <u>NOTE</u>: CONSULT YOUR INSURANCE AGENT; POSSESSION OF THE PROPERTY BY SELLER AS TENANT MAY CHANGE INSURANCE POLICY COVERAGE.

17. **DEFAULT:** If Tenant fails to perform or observe any provision of this Lease and fails, within 24 hours after notice by Landlord, to commence and diligently pursue to remedy such failure, Tenant will be in default.

18. **TERMINATION:** This Lease terminates upon expiration of the term specified in Paragraph 3 or upon Tenant's default under this Lease.

19. **HOLDING OVER:** Tenant shall surrender possession of the Property upon termination of this Lease. Any possession by Tenant after termination creates a tenancy at sufferance and will not operate to renew or extend this Lease. Tenant shall pay $_____ per day during the period of any possession after termination as damages, in addition to any other remedies to which Landlord is entitled.

20. **ATTORNEY'S FEES:** The prevailing party in any legal proceeding brought under or with respect to this Lease is entitled to recover from the non-prevailing party all costs of such proceeding and reasonable attorney's fees.

21. **SMOKE ALARMS:** The Texas Property Code requires Landlord to install smoke alarms in certain locations within the Property at Landlord's expense. <u>Tenant expressly waives Landlord's duty to inspect and repair smoke alarms</u>.

22. **SECURITY DEVICES:** The requirements of the Texas Property Code relating to security devices do not apply to a residential lease for a term of 90 days or less.

23. **CONSULT YOUR ATTORNEY:** Real estate licensees cannot give legal advice. This Lease is intended to be legally binding. READ IT CAREFULLY. If you do not understand the effect of this Lease, consult your attorney BEFORE signing.

24. **NOTICES:** All notices from one party to the other must be in writing and are effective when mailed to, hand-delivered at, or transmitted by facsimile or electronic transmission as follows:

To Landlord: _____   **To Tenant:** _____

_____   _____

_____   _____

_____   _____

Telephone: (   ) _____   Telephone: (   ) _____

Facsimile: (   ) _____   Facsimile: (   ) _____

E-mail: _____   E-mail: _____

_____   _____
Landlord   Tenant

_____   _____
Landlord   Tenant

The form of this contract has been approved by the Texas Real Estate Commission.   TREC forms are intended for use only by trained real estate licensees. No representation is made as to the legal validity or adequacy of any provision in any specific transactions. It is not intended for complex transactions. Texas Real Estate Commission, P.O. Box 12188, Austin, TX 78711-2188, 512-936-3000 (http://www.trec.texas.gov) TREC NO. 15-5. This form replaces TREC NO. 15-4.

TREC NO. 15-5

Source: Reprinted with permission from Texas Real Estate Commission (TREC)

PROMULGATED BY THE TEXAS REAL ESTATE COMMISSION (TREC)   12-05-11
(NOTICE: For use only when BUYER occupies the property for no more than 90 days PRIOR the closing)

BUYER'S TEMPORARY RESIDENTIAL LEASE

1. PARTIES: The parties to this Lease are_____
(Landlord) and _____(Tenant).

2. LEASE: Landlord leases to Tenant the Property described in the Contract between Landlord as Seller and Tenant as Buyer known as _____
_____(address).

3. TERM: The term of this Lease commences _____ and terminates as specified in Paragraph 18.

4. RENTAL: Rental will be $_____ per day. Upon commencement of this Lease, Tenant shall pay to Landlord the full amount of rental of $ _____ for the anticipated term of the Lease (commencement date to the Closing Date specified in Paragraph 9 of the Contract). If the actual term of this Lease differs from the anticipated term, any additional rent or reimbursement will be paid at closing. No portion of the rental will be applied to payment of any items covered by the Contract.

5. DEPOSIT: Tenant has paid to Landlord $_____ as a deposit to secure performance of this Lease by Tenant. If this Lease is terminated before the Closing Date, Landlord may use the deposit to satisfy Tenant's obligations under this Lease. Landlord shall refund to Tenant any unused portion of the deposit together with an itemized list of all deductions from the deposit within 30 days after Tenant (a) surrenders possession of the Property and (b) provides Landlord written notice of Tenant's forwarding address. If this Lease is terminated by the closing and funding of the sale of the Property, the deposit will be refunded to Tenant at closing and funding.
NOTICE: The deposit must be in addition to the earnest money under the Contract.

6. UTILITIES: Tenant shall pay all utility connections, deposits and charges except _____
_____, which Landlord shall pay.

7. USE OF PROPERTY: Tenant may use the Property only for residential purposes. Tenant may not assign this Lease or sublet any part of the Property.

8. PETS: Tenant may not keep pets on the Property except _____.

9. CONDITION OF PROPERTY: Tenant accepts the Property in its present condition and state of repair, but Landlord shall make all repairs and improvements required by the Contract. If this Lease is terminated prior to closing, Tenant shall surrender possession of the Property to Landlord in its present condition, as improved by Landlord, except normal wear and tear and any casualty loss.

10. ALTERATIONS: Tenant may not: (a) make any holes or drive nails into the woodwork, floors, walls or ceilings (b) alter, paint or decorate the Property or (c) install improvements or fixtures without the prior written consent of Landlord. Any improvements or fixtures placed on the Property during the Lease become a part of the Property.

11. SPECIAL PROVISIONS:

12. INSPECTIONS: Landlord may enter at reasonable times to inspect, replace, repair or complete the improvements. Tenant shall provide Landlord door keys and access codes to allow access to the Property during the term of the Lease.

13. LAWS: Tenant shall comply with all applicable laws, restrictions, ordinances, rules and regulations with respect to the Property.

14. REPAIRS AND MAINTENANCE: Except as otherwise provided in this Lease, Tenant shall bear all expense of repairing, replacing and maintaining the Property, including but not limited to the yard, trees, shrubs, and all equipment and appliances, unless otherwise required by the Texas Property Code. Tenant shall promptly repair at Tenant's expense any damage to the Property caused directly or indirectly by any act or omission of the Tenant or any person other than the Landlord, Landlord's agents or invitees.

15. INDEMNITY: Tenant indemnifies Landlord from the claims of all third parties for injury or damage to the person or property of such third party arising from the use or occupancy of the Property by Tenant. This indemnification includes attorney's fees, costs and expenses incurred by Landlord.

16. INSURANCE: Landlord and Tenant shall each maintain such insurance on the contents and Property as each party may deem appropriate during the term of this Lease. NOTE: CONSULT YOUR INSURANCE AGENT; POSSESSION OF THE PROPERTY BY BUYER AS TENANT MAY CHANGE INSURANCE POLICY COVERAGE.

17. DEFAULT: If Tenant fails to perform or observe any provision of this Lease and fails, within 24 hours after notice by Landlord, to commence and diligently pursue to remedy such failure, Tenant will be in default.

18. TERMINATION: This Lease terminates upon (a) closing and funding of the sale under the Contract, (b) termination of the Contract prior to closing, (c) Tenant's default under this Lease, or (d) Tenant's default under the Contract, whichever occurs first. Upon termination other than by closing and funding of the sale, Tenant shall surrender possession of the property.

19. HOLDING OVER: Any possession by Tenant after termination creates a tenancy at sufferance and will not operate to renew or extend this Lease. Tenant shall pay $_____ per day during the period of any possession after termination as damages, in addition to any other remedies to which Landlord is entitled.

20. ATTORNEY'S FEES: The prevailing party in any legal proceeding brought under or with respect to this Lease is entitled to recover from the non-prevailing party all costs of such proceeding and reasonable attorney's fees.

21. SMOKE ALARMS: The Texas Property Code requires Landlord to install smoke alarms in certain locations within the Property at Landlord's expense. Tenant expressly waives Landlord's duty to inspect and repair smoke alarms.

22. SECURITY DEVICES: The requirements of the Texas Property Code relating to security devices do not apply to a residential lease for a term of 90 days or less.

23. CONSULT YOUR ATTORNEY: Real estate licensees cannot give legal advice. This Lease is intended to be legally binding. READ IT CAREFULLY. If you do not understand the effect of this Lease, consult your attorney BEFORE signing.

24. NOTICES: All notices from one party to the other must be in writing and are effective when mailed to, hand-delivered at, or transmitted by facsimile or electronic transmission as follows:

To Landlord: _____

_____

_____

_____

Telephone: ( ) _____

Facsimile: ( ) _____

E-mail: _____

To Tenant: _____

_____

_____

_____

Telephone: ( ) _____

Facsimile: ( ) _____

E-mail: _____

_____
Landlord

_____
Landlord

_____
Tenant

_____
Tenant

TREC NO. 16-5

PROMULGATED BY THE TEXAS REAL ESTATE COMMISSION (TREC)

12-05-11

ENVIRONMENTAL ASSESSMENT, THREATENED OR ENDANGERED SPECIES, AND WETLANDS ADDENDUM

TO CONTRACT CONCERNING THE PROPERTY AT

_____

(Address of Property)

❑ A. ENVIRONMENTAL ASSESSMENT: Buyer, at Buyer's expense, may obtain an environmental assessment report prepared by an environmental specialist.

❑ B. THREATENED OR ENDANGERED SPECIES: Buyer, at Buyer's expense, may obtain a report from a natural resources professional to determine if there are any threatened or endangered species or their habitats as defined by the Texas Parks and Wildlife Department or the U.S. Fish and Wildlife Service.

❑ C. WETLANDS: Buyer, at Buyer's expense, may obtain a report from an environmental specialist to determine if there are wetlands, as defined by federal or state law or regulation.

Within _____ days after the effective date of the contract, Buyer may terminate the contract by furnishing Seller a copy of any report noted above that adversely affects the use of the Property and a notice of termination of the contract. Upon termination, the earnest money will be refunded to Buyer.

_____   _____
Buyer   Seller

_____   _____
Buyer   Seller

TREC No. 28-2

PROMULGATED BY THE TEXAS REAL ESTATE COMMISSION (TREC)

12-05-11

ADDENDUM FOR
COASTAL AREA PROPERTY
(SECTION 33.135, TEXAS NATURAL RESOURCES CODE)

TO CONTRACT CONCERNING THE PROPERTY AT

_____

(Address of Property)

NOTICE REGARDING COASTAL AREA PROPERTY

1. The real property described in and subject to this contract adjoins and shares a common boundary with the tidally influenced submerged lands of the state. The boundary is subject to change and can be determined accurately only by a survey on the ground made by a licensed state land surveyor in accordance with the original grant from the sovereign. The owner of the property described in this contract may gain or lose portions of the tract because of changes in the boundary.

2. The seller, transferor, or grantor has no knowledge of any prior fill as it relates to the property described in and subject to this contract except:_____
_____
_____.

3. State law prohibits the use, encumbrance, construction, or placing of any structure in, on, or over state-owned submerged lands below the applicable tide line, without proper permission.

4. The purchaser or grantee is hereby advised to seek the advice of an attorney or other qualified person as to the legal nature and effect of the facts set forth in this notice on the property described in and subject to this contract. Information regarding the location of the applicable tide line as to the property described in and subject to this contract may be obtained from the surveying division of the General Land Office in Austin.

_____   _____
Buyer   Seller

_____   _____
Buyer   Seller

TREC No. 33-2

PROMULGATED BY THE TEXAS REAL ESTATE COMMISSION (TREC)
12-05-11

ADDENDUM FOR
PROPERTY LOCATED SEAWARD OF THE
GULF INTRACOASTAL WATERWAY
(SECTION 61.025, TEXAS NATURAL RESOURCES CODE)

TO CONTRACT CONCERNING THE PROPERTY AT

_____

(Address of Property)

DISCLOSURE NOTICE CONCERNING LEGAL AND ECONOMIC RISKS OF PURCHASING COASTAL REAL PROPERTY NEAR A BEACH

WARNING: THE FOLLOWING NOTICE OF POTENTIAL RISKS OF ECONOMIC LOSS TO YOU AS THE PURCHASER OF COASTAL REAL PROPERTY IS REQUIRED BY STATE LAW.

- READ THIS NOTICE CAREFULLY. DO NOT SIGN THIS CONTRACT UNTIL YOU FULLY UNDERSTAND THE RISKS YOU ARE ASSUMING.

- BY PURCHASING THIS PROPERTY, YOU MAY BE ASSUMING ECONOMIC RISKS OVER AND ABOVE THE RISKS INVOLVED IN PURCHASING INLAND REAL PROPERTY.

- IF YOU OWN A STRUCTURE LOCATED ON COASTAL REAL PROPERTY NEAR A GULF COAST BEACH, IT MAY COME TO BE LOCATED ON THE PUBLIC BEACH BECAUSE OF COASTAL EROSION AND STORM EVENTS.

- AS THE OWNER OF A STRUCTURE LOCATED ON THE PUBLIC BEACH, YOU COULD BE SUED BY THE STATE OF TEXAS AND ORDERED TO REMOVE THE STRUCTURE.

- THE COSTS OF REMOVING A STRUCTURE FROM THE PUBLIC BEACH AND ANY OTHER ECONOMIC LOSS INCURRED BECAUSE OF A REMOVAL ORDER WOULD BE SOLELY YOUR RESPONSIBILITY.

The real property described in this contract is located seaward of the Gulf Intracoastal Waterway to its southernmost point and then seaward of the longitudinal line also known as 97 degrees, 12', 19" which runs southerly to the international boundary from the intersection of the centerline of the Gulf Intracoastal Waterway and the Brownsville Ship Channel. If the property is in close proximity to a beach fronting the Gulf of Mexico, the purchaser is hereby advised that the public has acquired a right of use or easement to or over the area of any public beach by prescription, dedication, or presumption, or has retained a right by virtue of continuous right in the public since time immemorial, as recognized in law and custom.

The extreme seaward boundary of natural vegetation that spreads continuously inland customarily marks the landward boundary of the public easement. If there is no clearly marked natural vegetation line, the landward boundary of the easement is as provided by Sections 61.016 and 61.017, Natural Resources Code.

Much of the Gulf of Mexico coastline is eroding at rates of more than five feet per year. Erosion rates for all Texas Gulf property subject to the open beaches act are available from the Texas General Land Office.

State law prohibits any obstruction, barrier, restraint, or interference with the use of the public easement, including the placement of structures seaward of the landward boundary of the easement. OWNERS OF STRUCTURES ERECTED SEAWARD OF THE VEGETATION LINE (OR OTHER APPLICABLE EASEMENT BOUNDARY) OR THAT BECOME SEAWARD OF THE VEGETATION LINE AS A RESULT OF PROCESSES SUCH AS SHORELINE EROSION ARE SUBJECT TO A LAWSUIT BY THE STATE OF TEXAS TO REMOVE THE STRUCTURES.

The purchaser is hereby notified that the purchaser should: (1) determine the rate of shoreline erosion in the vicinity of the real property; and (2) seek the advice of an attorney or other qualified person before executing this contract or instrument of conveyance as to the relevance of these statutes and facts to the value of the property the purchaser is hereby purchasing or contracting to purchase.

_____   _____
Buyer   Seller

_____   _____
Buyer   Seller

TREC No. 34-4

PROMULGATED BY THE TEXAS REAL ESTATE COMMISSION (TREC)　　08-18-2014

ADDENDUM FOR PROPERTY SUBJECT TO MANDATORY MEMBERSHIP IN A PROPERTY OWNERS ASSOCIATION
(NOT FOR USE WITH CONDOMINIUMS)
ADDENDUM TO CONTRACT CONCERNING THE PROPERTY AT

_____

(Street Address and City)

_____

(Name of Property Owners Association, (Association) and Phone Number)

A. SUBDIVISION INFORMATION: "Subdivision Information" means: (i) a current copy of the restrictions applying to the subdivision and bylaws and rules of the Association, and (ii) a resale certificate, all of which are described by Section 207.003 of the Texas Property Code.

(Check only one box):

❑ 1. Within _____ days after the effective date of the contract, Seller shall obtain, pay for, and deliver the Subdivision Information to the Buyer. If Seller delivers the Subdivision Information, Buyer may terminate the contract within 3 days after Buyer receives the Subdivision Information or prior to closing, whichever occurs first, and the earnest money will be refunded to Buyer. If Buyer does not receive the Subdivision Information, Buyer, as Buyer's sole remedy, may terminate the contract at any time prior to closing and the earnest money will be refunded to Buyer.

❑ 2. Within _____ days after the effective date of the contract, Buyer shall obtain, pay for, and deliver a copy of the Subdivision Information to the Seller. If Buyer obtains the Subdivision Information within the time required, Buyer may terminate the contract within 3 days after Buyer receives the Subdivision Information or prior to closing, whichever occurs first, and the earnest money will be refunded to Buyer. If Buyer, due to factors beyond Buyer's control, is not able to obtain the Subdivision Information within the time required, Buyer may, as Buyer's sole remedy, terminate the contract within 3 days after the time required or prior to closing, whichever occurs first, and the earnest money will be refunded to Buyer.

❑ 3. Buyer has received and approved the Subdivision Information before signing the contract. Buyer ❑ does ❑ does not require an updated resale certificate. If Buyer requires an updated resale certificate, Seller, at Buyer's expense, shall deliver it to Buyer within 10 days after receiving payment for the updated resale certificate from Buyer. Buyer may terminate this contract and the earnest money will be refunded to Buyer if Seller fails to deliver the updated resale certificate within the time required.

❑ 4. Buyer does not require delivery of the Subdivision Information.

The title company or its agent is authorized to act on behalf of the parties to obtain the Subdivision Information ONLY upon receipt of the required fee for the Subdivision Information from the party obligated to pay.

B. MATERIAL CHANGES. If Seller becomes aware of any material changes in the Subdivision Information, Seller shall promptly give notice to Buyer. Buyer may terminate the contract prior to closing by giving written notice to Seller if: (i) any of the Subdivision Information provided was not true; or (ii) any material adverse change in the Subdivision Information occurs prior to closing, and the earnest money will be refunded to Buyer.

C FEES: Except as provided by Paragraphs A, D and E, Buyer shall pay any and all Association fees or other charges associated with the transfer of the Property not to exceed $_____ and Seller shall pay any excess.

D. DEPOSITS FOR RESERVES: Buyer shall pay any deposits for reserves required at closing by the Association.

E. AUTHORIZATION: Seller authorizes the Association to release and provide the Subdivision Information and any updated resale certificate if requested by the Buyer, the Title Company, or any broker to this sale. If Buyer does not require the Subdivision Information or an updated resale certificate, and the Title Company requires information from the Association (such as the status of dues, special assessments, violations of covenants and restrictions, and a waiver of any right of first refusal), ❑ Buyer ❑ Seller shall pay the Title Company the cost of obtaining the information prior to the Title Company ordering the information.

NOTICE TO BUYER REGARDING REPAIRS BY THE ASSOCIATION: The Association may have the sole responsibility to make certain repairs to the Property. If you are concerned about the condition of any part of the Property which the Association is required to repair, you should not sign the contract unless you are satisfied that the Association will make the desired repairs.

_____   _____
Buyer   Seller

_____   _____
Buyer   Seller

TREC NO. 36-8

Source: Reprinted with permission from Texas Real Estate Commission (TREC)

PROMULGATED BY THE TEXAS REAL ESTATE COMMISSION (TREC)

12-05-11

ADDENDUM FOR RESERVATION OF OIL, GAS, AND OTHER MINERALS

ADDENDUM TO CONTRACT CONCERNING THE PROPERTY AT

_____

(Street Address and City)

_____

NOTICE: For use only if Seller reserves all or a portion of the Mineral Estate.

A. "Mineral Estate" means all oil, gas, and other minerals in or under the Property, any royalty under any existing or future lease covering any part of the Property, surface rights (including rights of ingress and egress), production and drilling rights, lease payments, and all related benefits.

B. The Mineral Estate owned by Seller, if any, will be conveyed unless reserved as follows (check one box only):

☐ (1) Seller reserves all of the Mineral Estate owned by Seller.

☐ (2) Seller reserves an undivided _____% interest in the Mineral Estate owned by Seller. *NOTE: If Seller does not own all of the Mineral Estate, Seller reserves only this percentage of Seller's interest.*

C. Seller ☐ waives ☐ does not waive Seller's surface rights (including rights of ingress and egress). *NOTE: Any waiver of surface rights by Seller does not affect any surface rights that may be held by others.*

D. If B(2) applies, Seller shall, on or before the Closing Date, provide Buyer contact information known to Seller for any existing lessee.

If either party is concerned about the legal rights or impact of the above provisions, that party is advised to consult an attorney BEFORE signing.

TREC rules prohibit real estate licensees from giving legal advice.

_____   _____
Buyer   Seller

_____   _____
Buyer   Seller

TREC NO. 44-1

PROMULGATED BY THE TEXAS REAL ESTATE COMMISSION (TREC)   12-05-11

SHORT SALE ADDENDUM

ADDENDUM TO CONTRACT CONCERNING THE PROPERTY AT

_____

(Street Address and City)

A. This contract involves a "short sale" of the Property. As used in this Addendum, "short sale" means that:

   (1) Seller's net proceeds at closing will be insufficient to pay the balance of Seller's mortgage loan; and

   (2) Seller requires:
     (a) the consent of the lienholder to sell the Property pursuant to this contract; and
     (b) the lienholder's agreement to:
       (i) accept Seller's net proceeds in full satisfaction of Seller's liability under the mortgage loan; and
       (ii) provide Seller an executed release of lien against the Property in a recordable format.

B. As used in this Addendum, "Seller's net proceeds" means the Sales Price less Seller's Expenses under Paragraph 12 of the contract and Seller's obligation to pay any brokerage fees.

C. The contract to which this Addendum is attached is binding upon execution by the parties and the earnest money and the Option Fee must be paid as provided in the contract. The contract is contingent on the satisfaction of Seller's requirements under Paragraph A(2) of this Addendum (Lienholder's Consent and Agreement). Seller shall apply promptly for and make every reasonable effort to obtain Lienholder's Consent and Agreement, and shall furnish all information and documents required by the lienholder. Except as provided by this Addendum, neither party is required to perform under the contract while it is contingent upon obtaining Lienholder's Consent and Agreement.

D. If Seller does not notify Buyer that Seller has obtained Lienholder's Consent and Agreement on or before _____, this contract terminates and the earnest money will be refunded to Buyer. Seller must notify Buyer immediately if Lienholder's Consent and Agreement is obtained. For purposes of performance, the effective date of the contract changes to the date Seller provides Buyer notice of the Lienholder's Consent and Agreement (Amended Effective Date).

E. This contract will terminate and the earnest money will be refunded to Buyer if the Lienholder refuses or withdraws its Consent and Agreement prior to closing and funding. Seller shall promptly notify Buyer of any lienholder's refusal to provide or withdrawal of a Lienholder's Consent and Agreement.

F. If Buyer has the unrestricted right to terminate this contract, the time for giving notice of termination begins on the effective date of the contract, continues after the Amended Effective Date and ends upon the expiration of Buyer's unrestricted right to terminate the contract under Paragraph 23.

G. For the purposes of this Addendum, time is of the essence. Strict compliance with the times for performance stated in this Addendum is required.

H. Seller authorizes any lienholder to furnish to Buyer or Buyer's representatives information relating to the status of the request for a Lienholder's Consent and Agreement.

I. If there is more than one lienholder or loan secured by the Property, this Addendum applies to each lienholder.

_____   _____
Buyer   Seller

_____   _____
Buyer   Seller

TREC NO. 45-1

Source: Reprinted with permission from Texas Real Estate Commission (TREC)

PROMULGATED BY THE TEXAS REAL ESTATE COMMISSION (TREC)

2-10-2014

ADDENDUM FOR PROPERTY IN A
PROPANE GAS SYSTEM SERVICE AREA
(Section 141.010, Utilities Code)

CONCERNING THE PROPERTY AT _____

(Street Address and City)

NOTICE

The above referenced real property that you are about to purchase may be located in a propane gas system service area, which is authorized by law to provide propane gas service to the properties in the area pursuant to Chapter 141, Utilities Code. If your property is located in a propane gas system service area, there may be special costs or charges that you will be required to pay before you can receive propane gas service. There may be a period required to construct lines or other facilities necessary to provide propane gas service to your property. You are advised to determine if the property is in a propane gas system service area and contact the distribution system retailer to determine the cost that you will be required to pay and the period, if any, that is required to provide propane gas service to your property.

Buyer hereby acknowledges receipt of this notice at or before execution of a binding contract for the purchase of the above referenced real property or at the closing of the real property.

Section 141.010(a), Utilities Code, requires this notice to include a copy of the notice the distribution system retailer is required to record in the real property records. A copy of the recorded notice is attached.

NOTE: Seller can obtain a copy of the required recorded notice from the county clerk's office where the property is located or from the distribution system retailer.

_____ _____   _____ _____
Buyer   Date   Seller   Date

_____ _____   _____ _____
Buyer   Date   Seller   Date

TREC NO. 47-0

Source: Reprinted with permission from Texas Real Estate Commission (TREC)

PROMULGATED BY THE TEXAS REAL ESTATE COMMISSION (TREC)   11-2-2015

AMENDMENT
TO CONTRACT CONCERNING THE PROPERTY AT

_____
(Street Address and City)

Seller and Buyer amend the contract as follows: (check each applicable box)

❑(1) The Sales Price in Paragraph 3 of the contract is:
  A. Cash portion of Sales Price payable by Buyer at closing .... $_____
  B. Sum of financing described in the contract... $_____
  C. Sales Price (Sum of A and B) .... $_____

❑(2) In addition to any repairs and treatments otherwise required by the contract, Seller, at Seller's expense, shall complete the following repairs and treatments:

❑(3) The date in Paragraph 9 of the contract is changed to _____, 20_____.

❑(4) The amount in Paragraph 12A(1)(b) of the contract is changed to $ _____.

❑(5) The cost of lender required repairs and treatment, as itemized on the attached list, will be paid as follows: $ _____ by Seller; $ _____ by Buyer.

❑(6) Buyer has paid Seller an additional Option Fee of $ _____ for an extension of the unrestricted right to terminate the contract on or before 5:00 p.m. on _____, 20_____. This additional Option Fee ❑ will ❑ will not be credited to the Sales Price.

❑(7) Buyer waives the unrestricted right to terminate the contract for which the Option Fee was paid.

❑(8) The date for Buyer to give written notice to Seller that Buyer cannot obtain Buyer Approval as set forth in the Third Party Financing Addendum is changed to _____, 20_____.

❑(9) **Other Modifications**: (Insert only factual statements and business details applicable to this sale.)

EXECUTED the _____day of _____, 20_____ . (BROKER: FILL IN THE DATE OF FINAL ACCEPTANCE.)

_____   _____
Buyer   Seller

_____   _____
Buyer   Seller

TREC NO. 39-8

PROMULGATED BY THE TEXAS REAL ESTATE COMMISSION (TREC)   8-17-2015

CONDOMINIUM RESALE CERTIFICATE
(Section 82.157, Texas Property Code)

Condominium Certificate concerning Condominium Unit _____, in Building _____, of _____
_____,a condominium project, located at _____
_____(Address), City of _____,
County of _____, Texas, on behalf of the condominium owners' association (the Association) by the Association's governing body (the Board).

A. The Declaration ☐does ☐does not contain a right of first refusal or other restraint that restricts the right to transfer the Unit. If a right of first refusal or other restraint exists, see Section _____of the Declaration.

B. The periodic common expense assessment for the Unit is $_____ per _____.

C. There ☐ is ☐is not a common expense or special assessment due and unpaid by the Seller to the Association. The total unpaid amount is $_____ and is for _____.

D. Other amounts ☐are ☐are not payable by Seller to the Association. The total unpaid amount is $_____and is for _____.

E. Capital expenditures approved by the Association for the next 12 months are $_____.

F. Reserves for capital expenditures are $_____;of this amount $_____ has been designated for_____.

G. The current operating budget and balance sheet of the Association is attached.

H. The amount of unsatisfied judgments against the Association is $ _____.

I. There ☐are ☐are not any suits pending against the Association. The nature of the suits is _____.

J. The Association ☐does ☐does not provide insurance coverage for the benefit of unit owners as per the attached summary from the Association's insurance agent.

K. The Board ☐has ☐has no knowledge of alterations or improvements to the Unit or to the limited common elements assigned to the Unit or any portion of the project that violate any provision of the Declaration, by-laws or rules of the Association. Known violations are:_____
_____.

L. The Board ☐has ☐has not received notice from a governmental authority concerning violations of health or building codes with respect to the Unit, the limited common elements assigned to the Unit, or any other portion of the condominium project. Notices received are: _____
_____.

M. The remaining term of any leasehold estate that affects the condominium is _____ and the provisions governing an extension or a renewal of the lease are: _____
_____
_____.

N. The Association's managing agent is _____
(Name of Agent)

_____
(Mailing Address)

_____   _____
(Phone)   (Fax)

_____
(E-mail Address)

TREC NO. 32-4

Condominium Resale Certificate Concerning | Page 2 of 2

_____
(Address of Property)

O. Association fees resulting from the transfer of the unit described above:

Description | Paid To | Amount

_____   _____   _____

_____   _____   _____

_____   _____   _____

P. Required contribution, if any, to the capital reserves account $_____.

REQUIRED ATTACHMENTS:
1. Operating Budget
2. Insurance Summary
3. Balance Sheet

NOTICE: The Certificate must be prepared no more than three months before the date it is delivered to Buyer.

_____
Name of Association

By: _____

Name: _____

Title: _____

Date:_____

Mailing Address: _____

E-mail: _____

TREC NO. 32-4

Source: Reprinted with permission from Texas Real Estate Commission (TREC)

PROMULGATED BY THE TEXAS REAL ESTATE COMMISSION (TREC)

2-10-2014

SUBDIVISION INFORMATION, INCLUDING
RESALE CERTIFICATE FOR PROPERTY SUBJECT TO
MANDATORY MEMBERSHIP IN A PROPERTY OWNERS' ASSOCIATION
(Chapter 207, Texas Property Code)

Resale Certificate concerning the Property (including any common areas assigned to the Property) located at _____(Street Address), City of _____, County of _____, Texas, prepared by the property owners' association (Association).

A. The Property ☐is ☐ is not subject to a right of first refusal (other than a right of first refusal prohibited by statute) or other restraint contained in the restrictions or restrictive covenants that restricts the owner's right to transfer the owner's property.

B. The current regular assessment for the Property is $_____ per _____.

C. A special assessment for the Property due after this resale certificate is delivered is $_____
   payable as follows_____
   for the following purpose:_____.

D. The total of all amounts due and unpaid to the Association that are attributable to the Property is
   $ _____ .

E. The capital expenditures approved by the Association for its current fiscal year are
   $ _____.

F. The amount of reserves for capital expenditures is $_____.

G. Unsatisfied judgments against the Association total $_____.

H. Other than lawsuits relating to unpaid ad valorem taxes of an individual member of the association, there ☐ are ☐ are not any suits pending in which the Association is a party. The style and cause number of each pending suit is: _____.

I. The Association's board ☐has actual knowledge ☐has no actual knowledge of conditions on the Property in violation of the restrictions applying to the subdivision or the bylaws or rules of the Association. Known violations are: _____.

J. The Association ☐has ☐has not received notice from any governmental authority regarding health or building code violations with respect to the Property or any common areas or common facilities owned or leased by the Association. A summary or copy of each notice is attached.

K. The amount of any administrative transfer fee charged by the Association for a change of ownership of property in the subdivision is $_____. Describe all fees associated with the transfer of ownership (include a description of each fee, to whom each fee is payable and the amount of each fee)._____

_____

_____

TREC NO. 37=5

Subdivision Information Concerning _____ Page 2 of 2   2-10-2014
(Address of Property)

L. The Association's managing agent is_____
(Name of Agent)

_____
(Mailing Address)

_____   _____
(Telephone Number)   (Fax Number)

_____
(E-mail Address)

M. The restrictions ❑ do ❑ do not allow foreclosure of the Association's lien on the Property for failure to pay assessments.
    REQUIRED ATTACHMENTS:

    1. Restrictions   5. Current Operating Budget

    2. Rules   6. Certificate of Insurance concerning Property and Liability Insurance for Common Areas and Facilities

    3. Bylaws

    4. Current Balance Sheet   7. Any Governmental Notices of Health or Housing Code Violations

NOTICE: This Subdivision Information may change at any time.

_____
Name of Association

By: _____

Print Name: _____

Title: _____

Date:_____

Mailing Address: _____

E-mail: _____

TREC NO. 37=5

Source: Reprinted with permission from Texas Real Estate Commission (TREC)

11-2-15

PROMULGATED BY THE TEXAS REAL ESTATE COMMISSION (TREC)

NOTICE OF BUYER'S TERMINATION OF CONTRACT

CONCERNING THE CONTRACT FOR THE SALE OF THE PROPERTY AT

_____
(Street Address and City)

BETWEEN THE UNDERSIGNED BUYER AND_____

_____ (SELLER)

Buyer notifies Seller that the contract is terminated pursuant to the following:

☐(1) the unrestricted right of Buyer to terminate the contract under Paragraph 23 of the contract.

☐(2) Buyer cannot obtain Buyer Approval in accordance with the Third Party Financing Addendum to the contract.

☐(3) the Property does not satisfy Property Approval in accordance with the Third Party Financing Addendum to the contract.

☐(4) Buyer elects to terminate under Paragraph A of the Addendum for Property Subject to Mandatory Membership in a Property Owners' Association.

☐(5) Buyer elects to terminate under Paragraph 7B(2) of the contract relating to the Seller's Disclosure Notice.

☐(6) Other _(identify the paragraph number of contract or the addendum)_: _____

_____

_____

_____

_____

NOTE: Release of the earnest money is governed by the terms of the contract.

_____   _____
Buyer   Date   Buyer   Date

This form has been approved by the Texas Real Estate Commission for use with similarly approved or promulgated contract forms. Such approval relates to this form only. TREC forms are intended for use only by trained real estate license holders. No representation is made as to the legal validity or adequacy of any provision in any specific transactions. It is not suitable for complex transactions. Texas Real Estate Commission, P.O. Box 12188, Austin, TX 78711-2188, (512) 936-3000 (http://www.trec.texas.gov) TREC No. 38-5. This form replaces TREC No. 38-4.

TREC No.38-5

Source: Reprinted with permission from Texas Real Estate Commission (TREC)

THIS FIRM IS

LICENSED AND REGULATED

BY THE

TEXAS REAL ESTATE

COMMISSION (TREC)

TREC ADMINISTERS TWO RECOVERY FUNDS

WHICH MAY BE USED TO SATISFY JUDGMENTS

AGAINST INSPECTORS AND REAL ESTATE

LICENSEES INVOLVING A VIOLATION OF THE LAW.

COMPLAINTS OR INQUIRIES SHOULD

BE DIRECTED TO

TEXAS REAL ESTATE COMMISSION
P.O. BOX 12188
AUSTIN, TEXAS 78711-2188

(512) 936-3005

PROMULGATED BY THE TEXAS REAL ESTATE COMMISSION (TREC)   11-02-2015
DISCLOSURE OF RELATIONSHIP
WITH RESIDENTIAL SERVICE COMPANY

RESIDENTIAL SERVICE CONTRACTS. A residential service contract is a product under which a residential service company, for a fee, agrees to repair or replace certain equipment or items in a property. Co-payments typically apply to most service calls. Residential service companies are licensed and regulated by the Texas Real Estate Commission. The extent of coverage and the cost of coverage will vary. Before buying a residential service contract, the buyer should read the contract and consider comparing it with the extent of coverage and costs from several other residential service companies. You may obtain a list of the residential service companies licensed in Texas at http://www.trec.texas.gov. **YOU MAY CHOOSE ANY COMPANY.**

THE PURCHASE OF A RESIDENTIAL SERVICE CONTRACT IS OPTIONAL. The TREC promulgated residential contract forms contain a paragraph in which the parties may negotiate whether the seller will reimburse the buyer the cost of a residential service contract. The choice of the residential service company and extent of coverage lies with the buyer. **NEITHER A BROKER/SALES AGENT NOR A SELLER MAY CONDITION THE SALE OF A PROPERTY ON THE BUYER'S PURCHASE OF A RESIDENTIAL SERVICE CONTRACT.**

☐ Other Broker/Sales Agent will receive no compensation from a residential service company.

☐ Listing Broker/Sales Agent will receive no compensation from a residential service company.

☐ Other Broker/Sales Agent receives compensation from the following residential service company:

☐ Listing Broker/Sales Agent receives compensation from the following residential service company:

_____

_____

_____

_____

for providing the following services:

for providing the following services:

_____

_____

_____

_____

The compensation is not contingent upon a party to the real estate transaction purchasing a contract or services from the residential service company.

The compensation is the fee for the services that Listing Broker or Other Broker, either directly or through an agent, provides to the company. As required by the Real Estate Settlement Procedures Act and HUD Regulation X, any fees paid to a settlement services provider are limited to the reasonable value of services actually rendered.

Other Broker's Name	License No.	Listing Broker's Name	License No.

By: _____   By: _____

The undersigned acknowledges receipt of this notice:

_____   _____
Buyer   Seller

_____   _____
Buyer   Seller

APPROVED BY THE TEXAS REAL ESTATE COMMISSION   10-10-11

NOTICE TO PROSPECTIVE BUYER

As required by law, I advise you to have the abstract covering the property known as

_____

_____ (Address) examined by an attorney of your own selection OR you should be furnished with or obtain a policy of title insurance.

If the property is situated in a Utility District, Chapter 49 of the Texas Water Code requires you to sign and acknowledge the statutory notice from the seller of the property relating to the tax rate, bonded indebtedness or standby fee of the District.

DATED: _____ , _____ .

_____
Brokerage Company Name

_____
Broker or Sales Associate

I have received a copy of this **NOTICE TO PROSPECTIVE BUYER.**

_____
Prospective Buyer

_____
Prospective Buyer

This form has been approved by the Texas Real Estate Commission (TREC) for use when a contract of sale has not been promulgated by TREC. The form should be presented before an offer to purchase is signed by the prospective buyer. Texas real Estate Commission, P.O. Box 12188, Austin, Texas 78711-2188, 512-936-3000 (http://www.trec.texas.gov). TREC Notice to Prospective Buyer. OP-C replaces MA-C.

TREC NO. OP-C

8-17-2015

APPROVED BY THE TEXAS REAL ESTATE COMMISSION (TREC)

SELLER'S DISCLOSURE OF PROPERTY CONDITION

CONCERNING THE PROPERTY AT_____

(Street Address and City)

THIS NOTICE IS A DISCLOSURE OF SELLER'S KNOWLEDGE OF THE CONDITION OF THE PROPERTY AS OF THE DATE SIGNED BY SELLER AND IS NOT A SUBSTITUTE FOR ANY INSPECTIONS OR WARRANTIES THE PURCHASER MAY WISH TO OBTAIN. IT IS NOT A WARRANTY OF ANY KIND BY SELLER OR SELLER'S AGENTS.

Seller ☐ is ☐ is not occupying the Property. If unoccupied, how long since Seller has occupied the Property? _____

1. The Property has the items checked below [Write Yes (Y), No (N), or Unknown (U)]:

_____ Range	_____ Oven	_____ Microwave
_____ Dishwasher	_____ Trash Compactor	_____ Disposal
_____ Washer/Dryer Hookups	_____ Window Screens	_____ Rain Gutters
_____ Security System	_____ Fire Detection Equipment	_____ Intercom System
	_____ Smoke Detector	
	_____ Smoke Detector-Hearing Impaired	
	_____ Carbon Monoxide Alarm	
	_____ Emergency Escape Ladder(s)	
_____ TV Antenna	_____ Cable TV Wiring	_____ Satellite Dish
_____ Ceiling Fan(s)	_____ Attic Fan(s)	_____ Exhaust Fan(s)
_____ Central A/C	_____ Central Heating	_____ Wall/Window Air Conditioning
_____ Plumbing System	_____ Septic System	_____ Public Sewer System
_____ Patio/Decking	_____ Outdoor Grill	_____ Fences
_____ Pool	_____ Sauna	_____ Spa _____ Hot Tub
_____ Pool Equipment	_____ Pool Heater	_____ Automatic Lawn Sprinkler System
_____ Fireplace(s) & Chimney (Wood burning)		_____ Fireplace(s) & Chimney (Mock)
_____ Natural Gas Lines		_____ Gas Fixtures
_____ Liquid Propane Gas	_____ LP Community (Captive)	_____ LP on Property

Garage: _____ Attached   _____ Not Attached   _____ Carport

Garage Door Opener(s):   _____ Electronic   _____ Control(s)

Water Heater: _____ Gas   _____ Electric

Water Supply: _____ City   _____ Well   _____ MUD   _____ Co-op

Roof Type:_____ Age:_____ (approx.)

Are you (Seller) aware of any of the above items that are not in working condition, that have known defects, or that are in need of repair? ☐ Yes ☐ No ☐ Unknown. If yes, then describe. (Attach additional sheets if necessary):_____

_____

_____

_____

Seller's Disclosure Notice Concerning the Property at _____ Page 2 8-17-2015

(Street Address and City)

2. Does the property have working smoke detectors installed in accordance with the smoke detector requirements of Chapter 766, Health and Safety Code? ☐ Yes ☐ No ☐ Unknown. If the answer to this question is no or unknown, explain (Attach additional sheets if necessary): _____

_____

_____

_____

* Chapter 766 of the Health and Safety Code requires one-family or two-family dwellings to have working smoke detectors installed in accordance with the requirements of the building code in effect in the area in which the dwelling is located, including performance, location, and power source requirements. If you do not know the building code requirements in effect in your area, you may check unknown above or contact your local building official for more information. A buyer may require a seller to install smoke detectors for the hearing impaired if: (1) the buyer or a member of the buyer's family who will reside in the dwelling is hearing impaired; (2) the buyer gives the seller written evidence of the hearing impairment from a licensed physician; and (3) within 10 days after the effective date, the buyer makes a written request for the seller to install smoke detectors for the hearing impaired and specifies the locations for the installation. The parties may agree who will bear the cost of installing the smoke detectors and which brand of smoke detectors to install.

3. Are you (Seller) aware of any known defects/malfunctions in any of the following? Write Yes (Y) if you are aware, write No (N) if you are not aware.

_____ Interior Walls	_____ Ceilings	_____ Floors
_____ Exterior Walls	_____ Doors	_____ Windows
_____ Roof	_____ Foundation/Slab(s)	_____ Sidewalks
_____ Walls/Fences	_____ Driveways	_____ Intercom System
_____ Plumbing/Sewers/Septics	_____ Electrical Systems	_____ Lighting Fixtures

_____ Other Structural Components (Describe): _____

_____

_____

If the answer to any of the above is yes, explain. (Attach additional sheets if necessary):_____

_____

_____

4. Are you (Seller) aware of any of the following conditions? Write Yes (Y) if you are aware, write No (N) if you are not aware.

_____ Active Termites (includes wood destroying insects)	_____ Previous Structural or Roof Repair
_____ Termite or Wood Rot Damage Needing Repair	_____ Hazardous or Toxic Waste
_____ Previous Termite Damage	_____ Asbestos Components
_____ Previous Termite Treatment	_____ Urea-formaldehyde Insulation
_____ Previous Flooding	_____ Radon Gas
_____ Improper Drainage	_____ Lead Based Paint
_____ Water Penetration	_____ Aluminum Wiring
_____ Located in 100-Year Floodplain	_____ Previous Fires
_____ Present Flood Insurance Coverage	_____ Unplatted Easements
_____ Landfill, Settling, Soil Movement, Fault Lines	_____ Subsurface Structure or Pits
_____ Single Blockable Main Drain in Pool/Hot Tub/Spa*	_____ Previous Use of Premises for Manufacture of Methamphetamine

If the answer to any of the above is yes, explain. (Attach additional sheets if necessary):_____

_____

_____

* A single blockable main drain may cause a section entrapment hazard for an individual.

TREC No. OP-H

Seller's Disclosure Notice Concerning the Property at _____ Page 3 8-17-2015
(Street Address and City)

5.   Are you (Seller) aware of any item, equipment, or system in or on the Property that is in need of repair?☐ Yes (if you are aware)
☐ No (if you are not aware) If yes, explain. (Attach additional sheets if necessary): _____

_____

_____

6.   Are you (Seller) aware of any of the following? Write Yes (Y) if you are aware, write No (N) if you are not aware.

_____ Room additions, structural modifications, or other alterations or repairs made without necessary permits or not in compliance with building codes in effect at that time.

_____ Homeowners' Association or maintenance fees or assessments.

_____ Any "common area" (facilities such as pools, tennis courts, walkways, or other areas) co-owned in undivided interest with others.

_____ Any notices of violations of deed restrictions or governmental ordinances affecting the condition or use of the Property.

_____ Any lawsuits directly or indirectly affecting the Property.

_____ Any condition on the Property which materially affects the physical health or safety of an individual.

_____ Any rainwater harvesting system located on the property that is larger than 500 gallons and that uses a public water supply as an auxiliary water source.

_____ Any portion of the property that is located in a groundwater conservation district or a subsidence district.

If the answer to any of the above is yes, explain. (Attach additional sheets if necessary):_____

_____

_____

7.   If the property is located in a costal area that is seaward of the Gulf Intracoastal Waterway or within 1,000 feet of the mean high tide bordering the Gulf of Mexico, the property may be subject to the Open Beaches Act or the Dune Protection Act (Chapter 61 or 63, Natural Resources Code, respectively) and a beachfront construction certificate or dune protection permit maybe required for repairs or improvements. Contact the local government with ordinance authority over construction adjacent to public beaches for more information.

_____   _____   _____   _____
Signature of Seller   Date   Signature of Seller   Date

The undersigned purchaser hereby acknowledges receipt of the foregoing notice.

_____   _____   _____   _____
Signature of Purchaser   Date   Signature of Purchaser   Date

TREC No. OP-H

11-2-2015

Information About Brokerage Services

Texas law requires all real estate license holders to give the following information about brokerage services to prospective buyers, tenants, sellers and landlords.

TYPES OF REAL ESTATE LICENSE HOLDERS:
- **A BROKER** is responsible for all brokerage activities, including acts performed by sales agents sponsored by the broker.
- **A SALES AGENT** must be sponsored by a broker and works with clients on behalf of the broker.

A BROKER'S MINIMUM DUTIES REQUIRED BY LAW (A client is the person or party that the broker represents):
- Put the interests of the client above all others, including the broker's own interests;
- Inform the client of any material information about the property or transaction received by the broker;
- Answer the client's questions and present any offer to or counter-offer from the client; and
- Treat all parties to a real estate transaction honestly and fairly.

A LICENSE HOLDER CAN REPRESENT A PARTY IN A REAL ESTATE TRANSACTION:

AS AGENT FOR OWNER (SELLER/LANDLORD): The broker becomes the property owner's agent through an agreement with the owner, usually in a written listing to sell or property management agreement. An owner's agent must perform the broker's minimum duties above and must inform the owner of any material information about the property or transaction known by the agent, including information disclosed to the agent or subagent by the buyer or buyer's agent.

AS AGENT FOR BUYER/TENANT: The broker becomes the buyer/tenant's agent by agreeing to represent the buyer, usually through a written representation agreement. A buyer's agent must perform the broker's minimum duties above and must inform the buyer of any material information about the property or transaction known by the agent, including information disclosed to the agent by the seller or seller's agent.

AS AGENT FOR BOTH - INTERMEDIARY: To act as an intermediary between the parties the broker must first obtain the written agreement of *each party* to the transaction. The written agreement must state who will pay the broker and, in conspicuous bold or underlined print, set forth the broker's obligations as an intermediary. A broker who acts as an intermediary:
- Must treat all parties to the transaction impartially and fairly;
- May, with the parties' written consent, appoint a different license holder associated with the broker to each party (owner and buyer) to communicate with, provide opinions and advice to, and carry out the instructions of each party to the transaction.
- Must not, unless specifically authorized in writing to do so by the party, disclose:
  - that the owner will accept a price less than the written asking price;
  - that the buyer/tenant will pay a price greater than the price submitted in a written offer; and
  - any confidential information or any other information that a party specifically instructs the broker in writing not to disclose, unless required to do so by law.

AS SUBAGENT: A license holder acts as a subagent when aiding a buyer in a transaction without an agreement to represent the buyer. A subagent can assist the buyer but does not represent the buyer and must place the interests of the owner first.

TO AVOID DISPUTES, ALL AGREEMENTS BETWEEN YOU AND A BROKER SHOULD BE IN WRITING AND CLEARLY ESTABLISH:
- The broker's duties and responsibilities to you, and your obligations under the representation agreement.
- Who will pay the broker for services provided to you, when payment will be made and how the payment will be calculated.

LICENSE HOLDER CONTACT INFORMATION: This notice is being provided for information purposes. It does not create an obligation for you to use the broker's services. Please acknowledge receipt of this notice below and retain a copy for your records.

Licensed Broker /Broker Firm Name or Primary Assumed Business Name	License No.	Email	Phone
Designated Broker of Firm	License No.	Email	Phone
Licensed Supervisor of Sales Agent/ Associate	License No.	Email	Phone
Sales Agent/Associate's Name	License No.	Email	Phone

Buyer/Tenant/Seller/Landlord Initials   Date

Regulated by the Texas Real Estate Commission   **Information available at www.trec.texas.gov**

IABS 1-0

Source: Reprinted with permission from Texas Real Estate Commission (TREC)

APPROVED BY THE TEXAS REAL ESTATE COMMISSION   10-10-11

ADDENDUM FOR SELLER'S DISCLOSURE OF INFORMATION ON LEAD-BASED PAINT AND LEAD-BASED PAINT HAZARDS AS REQUIRED BY FEDERAL LAW

CONCERNING THE PROPERTY AT _____
(Street Address and City)

A. LEAD WARNING STATEMENT: "Every purchaser of any interest in residential real property on which a residential dwelling was built prior to 1978 is notified that such property may present exposure to lead from lead-based paint that may place young children at risk of developing lead poisoning. Lead poisoning in young children may produce permanent neurological damage, including learning disabilities, reduced intelligence quotient, behavioral problems, and impaired memory. Lead poisoning also poses a particular risk to pregnant women. The seller of any interest in residential real property is required to provide the buyer with any information on lead-based paint hazards from risk assessments or inspections in the seller's possession and notify the buyer of any known lead-based paint hazards. A risk assessment or inspection for possible lead-paint hazards is recommended prior to purchase."
 NOTICE: Inspector must be properly certified as required by federal law.
B. SELLER'S DISCLOSURE:
 1. PRESENCE OF LEAD-BASED PAINT AND/OR LEAD-BASED PAINT HAZARDS (check one box only):
  ❑(a) Known lead-based paint and/or lead-based paint hazards are present in the Property (explain): _____
  _____ .
  ❑(b) Seller has no actual knowledge of lead-based paint and/or lead-based paint hazards in the Property.
 2. RECORDS AND REPORTS AVAILABLE TO SELLER (check one box only):
  ❑(a) Seller has provided the purchaser with all available records and reports pertaining to lead-based paint and/or lead-based paint hazards in the Property (list documents):_____
  _____ .
  ❑(b) Seller has no reports or records pertaining to lead-based paint and/or lead-based paint hazards in the Property.
C. BUYER'S RIGHTS (check one box only):
 ❑1. Buyer waives the opportunity to conduct a risk assessment or inspection of the Property for the presence of lead-based paint or lead-based paint hazards.
 ❑2. Within ten days after the effective date of this contract, Buyer may have the Property inspected by inspectors selected by Buyer. If lead-based paint or lead-based paint hazards are present, Buyer may terminate this contract by giving Seller written notice within 14 days after the effective date of this contract, and the earnest money will be refunded to Buyer.
D. BUYER'S ACKNOWLEDGMENT (check applicable boxes):
 ❑1. Buyer has received copies of all information listed above.
 ❑2. Buyer has received the pamphlet *Protect Your Family from Lead in Your Home.*
E. BROKERS' ACKNOWLEDGMENT: Brokers have informed Seller of Seller's obligations under 42 U.S.C. 4852d to: (a) provide Buyer with the federally approved pamphlet on lead poisoning prevention; (b) complete this addendum; (c) disclose any known lead-based paint and/or lead-based paint hazards in the Property; (d) deliver all records and reports to Buyer pertaining to lead-based paint and/or lead-based paint hazards in the Property; (e) provide Buyer a period of up to 10 days to have the Property inspected; and (f) retain a completed copy of this addendum for at least 3 years following the sale. Brokers are aware of their responsibility to ensure compliance.
F. CERTIFICATION OF ACCURACY: The following persons have reviewed the information above and certify, to the best of their knowledge, that the information they have provided is true and accurate.

_____ _____   _____ _____
Buyer   Date   Seller   Date

_____ _____   _____ _____
Buyer   Date   Seller   Date

_____ _____   _____ _____
Other Broker   Date   Listing Broker   Date

> The form of this addendum has been approved by the Texas Real Estate Commission for use only with similarly approved or promulgated forms of contracts. Such approval relates to this contract form only. TREC forms are intended for use only by trained real estate licensees. No representation is made as to the legal validity or adequacy of any provision in any specific transactions. It is not suitable for complex transactions. Texas Real Estate Commission, P.O. Box 12188, Austin, TX 78711-2188, 512-936-3000 (http://www.trec.texas.gov)

TREC NO. OP-L

EQUAL HOUSING
OPPORTUNITY

APPROVED BY THE TEXAS REAL ESTATE COMMISSION (TREC)
FOR VOLUNTARY USE

10-10-11

NON-REALTY ITEMS ADDENDUM

TO CONTRACT CONCERNING THE PROPERTY AT

_____
(Address of Property)

A. For an additional sum of $_____and other and good valuable consideration, Seller shall convey to Buyer at closing the following personal property (specify each item carefully, include description, model numbers, serial numbers, location, and other information):

_____
_____
_____
_____
_____
_____
_____
_____
_____
_____
_____
_____

B. Seller represents and warrants that Seller owns the personal property described in Paragraph A free and clear of all encumbrances.

C. Seller does not warrant or guarantee the condition or future performance of the personal property conveyed by this document.

_____   _____
Buyer   Seller

_____   _____
Buyer   Seller

This form has been approved by the Texas Real Estate Commission for voluntary use by its licensees. Copies of TREC rules governing real estate brokers, salesperson and real estate inspectors are available at nominal cost from TREC. Texas Real Estate Commission, P.O. Box 12188, Austin, TX 78711-2188, 512-936-3000 (http://www.trec.texas.gov)

TREC NO. OP-M

Chapter 3

Parties, Property, and Financing

LEARNING OBJECTIVES

When you have completed this chapter, you should be able to:

1. Recall the salient parts of the promulgated One to Four Family Residential Contract (Resale).

2. Accurately incorporate most of the relevant material needed to create a correctly written earnest money contract.

3. Identify the potential problems areas within an improperly written earnest money contract when submitted to you by another licensee.

KEY TERMS

administrator (trix)

community property

effective date

executor (trix)

improvements, accessories, and exclusions (per earnest money contract)

joint tenants

legal description/lot and block

separate property

tenants in common

ONE TO FOUR FAMILY RESIDENTIAL CONTRACT (RESALE)

There is little doubt that the most frequently used form in Texas real estate is the One to Four Family Residential Contract (Resale). Given its frequency of use, it seems prudent to begin our tutorial with that one. We will attempt in this chapter to support the reader by taking a step-by-step approach to some of the various contract parts and pieces, systematically going through this important document in a paragraph-by-paragraph manner. This format will be used in upcoming chapters as well. We have included some of the other finance-related forms that likely will be attached to the "standard" contract at the back of the chapter, and offered some insights into their use.

As we look at the first few lines of this contract, note that it is promulgated by TREC. (In Chapter 2, we discussed the authority of TREC, the Broker-Lawyer Committee, and other important foundational rules and regulations.) Please remember that this contract is *not* to be used for condominium transactions. Condominium buildings may go by many different names, including town homes, townhouses, garden homes, etc.

When deciding whether the One to Four Family Residential Contract (Resale) is to be used, ask yourself a couple of simple questions:

1. Does the unit in discussion share a common wall with another separate unit?
2. Does ownership of this unit carry with it a fractional ownership of certain common elements, like a pool, stairways, party house, etc.

If the answer to the two questions above is *yes*, <u>do not use the contract we are discussing here</u>.

CHECKLIST FOR CONTRACT COMPLETION

Before we dive into our section-by-section discussion of the One to Four Family Residential Contract (Resale) form, we would like to offer you a concentrated checklist on the items you will need to successfully complete the document. Below is a list of the types of information you will need to obtain.

1. Complete names of the parties to the contract.
2. A correct legal description. Confirm this from reliable sources.
3. Items not included in the sales agreement. Be as specific as possible.
4. Financing information, including down payment amount, loan amounts, and type of financing, as well as total sales price.
5. Earnest money, including initial amount and any additional amounts to be deposited later on, if any, as well as name and address of escrow officer.
6. Title company and escrow officer information. This may be negotiated later on, but having some idea of this is important.

7. Disclosure notices and timelines to include repair limits and responsibilities.

8. Closing and possession dates. If not the same, is a lease required?

9. Any other business details not outlined elsewhere.

10. Accurate contact information for all the parties, including attorneys.

11. Option fees and anything else being attached to the nine-page contract.

PARTIES: PARAGRAPH 1

It is important to establish all of the parties to the contract early on. Hence, in the very first paragraph, we identify the seller(s) and buyer(s). It is beyond the scope of this book to present extensive material on the various ways that property ownership can be established. That topic should be covered well in a principles of real estate class. Here, we will simply provide a sampling of some of the more common ways that the parties might be identified.

COMMUNITY PROPERTY

Given that Texas is a **community property** state, this form of ownership is frequent, so an entry like "Brad Boyd and wife Nan Boyd" is commonly used. But keep in mind, in today's society, spouses may not use the same last name. Johnnie Rosenauer and Danell Mackey may also be husband and wife.

MARRIED BUT SEPARATE PROPERTY

A married person can own property separate and apart from his/her spouse under certain conditions, such as if the property was purchased before marriage, acquired through gift or inheritance (where the separate property ownership is specifically spelled out), or purchased with separate, non comingled funds. Any of these situations could be illustrated by filling in the appropriate blank in this manner: "Jessica Alene Rosenauer, as her sole and separate property."

AN UNMARRIED PERSON TAKING TITLE AS A SOLE OWNER

"Rhonda Kay, a single person," is adequate if the individual has never married, is divorced, or is widowed.

TENANTS IN COMMON OR JOINT TENANTS

This entry would be used in cases where two or more people are taking title in their own names, but hopefully have some written agreement as to how their relationships are established. As in all the situations illustrated here, and in others we may not include, it would be best to specifically state the status of the parties as it relates to the contract. Joint tenancy is way that husband and wife take title in some states. However, since we are a community property state, this method does not apply, and you may discover some potential purchasers new to Texas who will be confused by this difference. An example such as "Carmen Garcia and Juan Crespin as Tenants in Common" could clearly define the type of ownership, but not necessarily the percentage owned by each party.

ESTATES

Sometimes, a licensee will create a contract with an **executor/executrix** that is named in the deceased person's will, or an **administrator/administratrix** that is appointed by the court when there is no valid will. Making an entry of "Janet Lozano, Executrix for the Estate of Rose M. Gonzalez, Deceased" clearly shows the role Ms. Lozano has. Further documentation to include a copy of the will and probate order may be required later for title work, but relating to the earnest money contract, the above should be an adequate reflection of the capacity of that party.

PARTNERSHIPS

Whether a General Partnership or a Limited Partnership, the contract should indicate the business name and the parties who represent the group. This would include the name of a general partner for the Limited Partnership, and may include the names of all or just one of the partners in the General Partnership. Once again, later on in the transaction, evidence may be required to show the authority of the signing party.

CORPORATIONS

The company name and the officer who holds the legal authority to sign on behalf of the entity is generally part of the contract. An entry of "John W. Price, CEO of ABC, Inc." is a good example. Past experience has taught that a copy of a resolution allowing the sale and identifying the person(s) (including his/her title) who can sign on behalf of the corporation is required.

There may be other examples, but hopefully, the point is clear regarding identification of the parties. Make sure you get this correct, or all the other many details associated with the documents involved are of no value.

1. PARTIES: The parties to this contract are _____
(Seller) and _____(Buyer).
Seller agrees to sell and convey to Buyer and Buyer agrees to buy from Seller the Property defined
below.

PROPERTY: PARAGRAPH 2

The importance of having a correct **legal description** cannot be overstated. In the agriculture real estate side, I cannot count how many contracts have come to me with the legal description being stated as something like "720 acres in Rooster County commonly referred to as (or known as) the Yellow Gates Ranch." Or there will be an attached topographical map or picture from the site with the boundaries drawn in. While helpful in marketing efforts, this kind of documentation is *not* adequate for a sale contract.

In the urban sector, usually there will be a **lot and block** reference, along with a subdivision name—for example, "Lot 13 Block 7 in the Wildflower Heights Subdivision." The TREC forms go on to include the street address as a matter of convenience and further identification, but as you may recall from your principles of real estate class, a street address alone is *not* considered an adequate legal description.

With regards to the last section of paragraph 2, while a large number of **"Improvements and Accessories"** are often included in the promulgated earnest money contract, bear in mind that if something is to be excluded, those items should be deleted from the improvements and accessories list by placing them in the **"Exclusions"** section.

2. PROPERTY: The land, improvements and accessories are collectively referred to as the "Property".
    A. LAND: Lot _____ Block_____, _____
        Addition, City of _____ , County of _____,
        Texas, known as _____
        (address/zip code), or as described on attached exhibit.
    B. IMPROVEMENTS: The house, garage and all other fixtures and improvements attached to the above-described real property, including without limitation, the following **permanently installed and built-in items,** if any: all equipment and appliances, valances, screens, shutters, awnings, wall-to-wall carpeting, mirrors, ceiling fans, attic fans, mail boxes, television antennas, mounts and brackets for televisions and speakers, heating and air-conditioning units, security and fire detection equipment, wiring, plumbing and lighting fixtures, chandeliers, water softener system, kitchen equipment, garage door openers, cleaning equipment, shrubbery, landscaping, outdoor cooking equipment, and all other property owned by Seller and attached to the above described real property.
    C. ACCESSORIES: The following described related accessories, if any: window air conditioning units, stove, fireplace screens, curtains and rods, blinds, window shades, draperies and rods, door keys, mailbox keys, above ground pool, swimming pool equipment and maintenance accessories, artificial fireplace logs, and controls for: (i) garage doors, (ii) entry gates, and (iii) other improvements and accessories.
    D. EXCLUSIONS: The following improvements and accessories will be retained by Seller and must be removed prior to delivery of possession:_____

Sales Price: Paragraph 3

In prior versions of the promulgated contracts forms, Paragraphs 3 and 4 were both used to address financing issues. The most current versions focus on the finance details only in Paragraph 3. Various addenda that have the specifics about finance options are still found in paragraph 22.

3. SALES PRICE:
  A. Cash portion of Sales Price payable by Buyer at closing .... $_____
  B. Sum of all financing described in the attached: ❑   Third Party Financing Addendum,
     ❑   Loan Assumption Addendum, ❑   Seller Financing Addendum .... $_____
  C. Sales Price (Sum of A and B) .... $_____

License Holder Disclosure: Paragraph 4

Paragraph 4 is about required disclosure for a real estate license holder who is involved in this transaction. Please note the requirement is not limited to the listing or selling agent. If a license holder is involved personally or represents a child, parent, spouse, or as an owner of a business entity where the license holder has a 10% or greater interests, disclosure is required. This required disclosure expands to include personal or familial interests as a trustee or beneficiary.

4. LICENSE HOLDER DISCLOSURE: Texas law requires a real estate license holder who is a party to a transaction or acting on behalf of a spouse, parent, child, business entity in which the license holder owns more than 10%, or a trust for which the license holder acts as a trustee or of which the license holder or the license holder's spouse, parent or child is a beneficiary, to notify the other party in writing before entering into a contract of sale. Disclose if applicable:_____.

Earnest Money: Paragraph 5

How much earnest money to deposit is a matter of negotiation between the principals involved in the sale. Make certain that you have the correct name and address of the escrow agent, and be very clear on whether or not additional earnest money will be deposited. If so, how much and by what date needs to be clearly established.

5. EARNEST MONEY: Upon execution of this contract by all parties, Buyer shall deposit $_____ as earnest money with _____, as escrow agent, at _____ (address). Buyer shall deposit additional earnest money of $_____ with escrow agent within _____ days after the effective date of this contract. If Buyer fails to deposit the earnest money as required by this contract, Buyer will be in default.

TITLE POLICY AND SURVEY: PARAGRAPH 6

This is one of those areas where the "devil is in the details." Lots of information regarding the physical survey and title objections is found in this piece. There are lots of blanks in this section of the form that simply cannot be ignored. This part of the contract also addresses several additional issues that range from property owners' associations to utility and tax districts. In our opinion, paragraph 6 is one that requires the greatest amount of attention. Like paragraph 4, this one can have more than one of the approved addenda associated with it.

6. TITLE POLICY AND SURVEY:

A. TITLE POLICY: Seller shall furnish to Buyer at ❑ Seller's ❑ Buyer's expense an owner policy of title insurance (Title Policy) issued by _____ (Title Company) in the amount of the Sales Price, dated at or after closing, insuring Buyer against loss under the provisions of the Title Policy, subject to the promulgated exclusions (including existing building and zoning ordinances) and the following exceptions:

(1) Restrictive covenants common to the platted subdivision in which the Property is located.

(2) The standard printed exception for standby fees, taxes and assessments.

(3) Liens created as part of the financing described in Paragraph 3.

(4) Utility easements created by the dedication deed or plat of the subdivision in which the Property is located.

(5) Reservations or exceptions otherwise permitted by this contract or as may be approved by Buyer in writing.

(6) The standard printed exception as to marital rights.

(7) The standard printed exception as to waters, tidelands, beaches, streams, and related matters.

(8) The standard printed exception as to discrepancies, conflicts, shortages in area or boundary lines, encroachments or protrusions, or overlapping improvements: ❑(i) will not be amended or deleted from the title policy; or ❑(ii) will be amended to read, "shortages in area" at the expense of ❑Buyer ❑Seller.

B. COMMITMENT: Within 20 days after the Title Company receives a copy of this contract, Seller shall furnish to Buyer a commitment for title insurance (Commitment) and, at Buyer's expense, legible copies of restrictive covenants and documents evidencing exceptions in the Commitment (Exception Documents) other than the standard printed exceptions. Seller authorizes the Title Company to deliver the Commitment and Exception Documents to Buyer at Buyer's address shown in Paragraph 21. If the Commitment and Exception Documents are not delivered to Buyer within the specified time, the time for delivery will be automatically extended up to 15 days or 3 days before the Closing Date, whichever is earlier. If, due to factors beyond Seller's control, the Commitment and Exception Documents are not delivered within the time required, Buyer may terminate this contract and the earnest money will be refunded to Buyer.

C. SURVEY: The survey must be made by a registered professional land surveyor acceptable to the Title Company and Buyer's lender(s). (Check one box only)

❑(1) Within _____ days after the effective date of this contract, Seller shall furnish to Buyer and Title Company Seller's existing survey of the Property and a Residential Real Property Affidavit promulgated by the Texas Department of Insurance (T-47 Affidavit). **If Seller fails to furnish the existing survey or affidavit within the time prescribed, Buyer shall obtain a new survey at Seller's expense no later than 3 days prior to Closing Date.** If the existing survey or affidavit is not acceptable to Title Company or Buyer's lender(s), Buyer shall obtain a new survey at ❑Seller's ❑Buyer's expense no later than 3 days prior to Closing Date.

❑(2) Within _____ days after the effective date of this contract, Buyer shall obtain a new survey at Buyer's expense. Buyer is deemed to receive the survey on the date of actual receipt or the date specified in this paragraph, whichever is earlier.

❑(3) Within _____ days after the effective date of this contract, Seller, at Seller's expense shall furnish a new survey to Buyer.

D. OBJECTIONS: Buyer may object in writing to defects, exceptions, or encumbrances to title: disclosed on the survey other than items 6A(1) through (7) above; disclosed in the Commitment other than items 6A(1) through (8) above; or which prohibit the following use or activity: _____.
Buyer must object the earlier of (i) the Closing Date or (ii) _____ days after Buyer receives the Commitment, Exception Documents, and the survey. Buyer's failure to object within the time allowed will constitute a waiver of Buyer's right to object; except that the requirements in Schedule C of the Commitment are not waived by Buyer. Provided Seller is not obligated to incur any expense, Seller shall cure the timely objections of Buyer or any third party lender within 15 days after Seller receives the objections and the Closing Date will be extended as necessary. If objections are not cured within such 15 day period, this contract will terminate and the earnest money will be refunded to Buyer unless Buyer waives the objections.

E. TITLE NOTICES:
  (1) ABSTRACT OR TITLE POLICY: Broker advises Buyer to have an abstract of title covering the Property examined by an attorney of Buyer's selection, or Buyer should be furnished with or obtain a Title Policy. If a Title Policy is furnished, the Commitment should be promptly reviewed by an attorney of Buyer's choice due to the time limitations on Buyer's right to object.
  (2) MEMBERSHIP IN PROPERTY OWNERS ASSOCIATION(S): The Property ❑is ❑is not subject to mandatory membership in a property owners association(s). If the Property is subject to mandatory membership in a property owners association(s), Seller notifies Buyer under §5.012, Texas Property Code, that, as a purchaser of property in the residential community identified in Paragraph 2A in which the Property is located, you are obligated to be a member of the property owners association(s). Restrictive covenants governing the use and occupancy of the Property and all dedicatory instruments governing the establishment, maintenance, or operation of this residential community have been or will be recorded in the Real Property Records of the county in which the Property is located. Copies of the restrictive covenants and dedicatory instruments may be obtained from the county clerk. **You are obligated to pay assessments to the property owners association(s). The amount of the assessments is subject to change. Your failure to pay the assessments could result in enforcement of the association's lien on and the foreclosure of the Property.**
  Section 207.003, Property Code, entitles an owner to receive copies of any document that governs the establishment, maintenance, or operation of a subdivision, including, but not limited to, restrictions, bylaws, rules and regulations, and a resale certificate from a property owners' association. A resale certificate contains information including, but not limited to, statements specifying the amount and frequency of regular assessments and the style and cause number of lawsuits to which the property owners' association is a party, other than lawsuits relating to unpaid ad valorem taxes of an individual member of the association. These documents must be made available to you by the property owners' association or the association's agent on your request.
  If Buyer is concerned about these matters, the TREC promulgated Addendum for Property Subject to Mandatory Membership in a Property Owners Association(s) should be used.
  (3) STATUTORY TAX DISTRICTS: If the Property is situated in a utility or other statutorily created district providing water, sewer, drainage, or flood control facilities and services, Chapter 49, Texas Water Code, requires Seller to deliver and Buyer to sign the statutory notice relating to the tax rate, bonded indebtedness, or standby fee of the district prior to final execution of this contract.
  (4) TIDE WATERS: If the Property abuts the tidally influenced waters of the state, §33.135, Texas Natural Resources Code, requires a notice regarding coastal area property to be included in the contract. An addendum containing the notice promulgated by TREC or required by the parties must be used.
  (5) ANNEXATION: If the Property is located outside the limits of a municipality, Seller notifies Buyer under §5.011, Texas Property Code, that the Property may now or later be included in the extraterritorial jurisdiction of a municipality and may now or later be subject to annexation by the municipality. Each municipality maintains a map that depicts its boundaries and extraterritorial jurisdiction. To determine if the Property is located within a municipality's extraterritorial jurisdiction or is likely to be located within a municipality's extraterritorial jurisdiction, contact all municipalities located in the general proximity of the Property for further information.

(6) PROPERTY LOCATED IN A CERTIFICATED SERVICE AREA OF A UTILITY SERVICE PROVIDER: Notice required by §13.257, Water Code: The real property, described in Paragraph 2, that you are about to purchase may be located in a certificated water or sewer service area, which is authorized by law to provide water or sewer service to the properties in the certificated area. If your property is located in a certificated area there may be special costs or charges that you will be required to pay before you can receive water or sewer service. There may be a period required to construct lines or other facilities necessary to provide water or sewer service to your property. You are advised to determine if the property is in a certificated area and contact the utility service provider to determine the cost that you will be required to pay and the period, if any, that is required to provide water or sewer service to your property. The undersigned Buyer hereby acknowledges receipt of the foregoing notice at or before the execution of a binding contract for the purchase of the real property described in Paragraph 2 or at closing of purchase of the real property.

(7) PUBLIC IMPROVEMENT DISTRICTS: If the Property is in a public improvement district, §5.014, Property Code, requires Seller to notify Buyer as follows: As a purchaser of this parcel of real property you are obligated to pay an assessment to a municipality or county for an improvement project undertaken by a public improvement district under Chapter 372, Local Government Code. The assessment may be due annually or in periodic installments. More information concerning the amount of the assessment and the due dates of that assessment may be obtained from the municipality or county levying the assessment. The amount of the assessments is subject to change. Your failure to pay the assessments could result in a lien on and the foreclosure of your property.

(8) TRANSFER FEES: If the Property is subject to a private transfer fee obligation, §5.205, Property Code, requires Seller to notify Buyer as follows: The private transfer fee obligation may be governed by Chapter 5, Subchapter G of the Texas Property Code.

(9) PROPANE GAS SYSTEM SERVICE AREA: If the Property is located in a propane gas system service area owned by a distribution system retailer, Seller must give Buyer written notice as required by §141.010, Texas Utilities Code. An addendum containing the notice approved by TREC or required by the parties should be used.

(10) NOTICE OF WATER LEVEL FLUCTUATIONS: If the Property adjoins an impoundment of water, including a reservoir or lake, constructed and maintained under Chapter 11, Water Code, that has a storage capacity of at least 5,000 acre-feet at the impoundment's normal operating level, Seller hereby notifies Buyer: "The water level of the impoundment of water adjoining the Property fluctuates for various reasons, including as a result of: (1) an entity lawfully exercising its right to use the water stored in the impoundment; or (2) drought or flood conditions."

PROPERTY CONDITION: PARAGRAPH 7

This paragraph goes back to one of the most important principles in real estate as it relates to consumer protection. The old term *caveat emptor* has changed somewhat through the years in terms of implications, but the concept of inspection of the property from a physical as well as title (paragraph 6) perspective remains alive and well. From the Seller's Disclosure of Property Condition to lender requirements to who pays for the repairs ... there is the need for lots of investigation and careful, deliberate communications.

It seems almost repetitious, but this paragraph, much like the financing paragraph above, can also have numerous addenda associated with it. Paragraphs 3, 5, and 7 are in many ways the heart of the contract, outside of sales price. Become very familiar with the implications of these important areas in terms of your training.

7.PROPERTY CONDITION:
  A. ACCESS, INSPECTIONS AND UTILITIES: Seller shall permit Buyer and Buyer's agents access to the Property at reasonable times. Buyer may have the Property inspected by inspectors selected by Buyer and licensed by TREC or otherwise permitted by law to make inspections. Any hydrostatic testing must be separately authorized by Seller in writing. Seller at Seller's expense shall immediately cause existing utilities to be turned on and shall keep the utilities on during the time this contract is in effect.
  B. SELLER'S DISCLOSURE NOTICE PURSUANT TO §5.008, TEXAS PROPERTY CODE (Notice): (Check one box only)
  ❑ (1) Buyer has received the Notice.
  ❑ (2) Buyer has not received the Notice. Within _____ days after the effective date of this contract, Seller shall deliver the Notice to Buyer. If Buyer does not receive the Notice, Buyer may terminate this contract at any time prior to the closing and the earnest money will be refunded to Buyer. If Seller delivers the Notice, Buyer may terminate this contract for any reason within 7 days after Buyer receives the Notice or prior to the closing, whichever first occurs, and the earnest money will be refunded to Buyer.
  ❑ (3)The Seller is not required to furnish the notice under the Texas Property Code.
  C. SELLER'S DISCLOSURE OF LEAD-BASED PAINT AND LEAD-BASED PAINT HAZARDS is required by Federal law for a residential dwelling constructed prior to 1978.
  D. ACCEPTANCE OF PROPERTY CONDITION: "As Is" means the present condition of the Property with any and all defects and without warranty except for the warranties of title and the warranties in this contract. Buyer's agreement to accept the Property As Is under Paragraph 7D(1) or (2) does not preclude Buyer from inspecting the Property under Paragraph 7A, from negotiating repairs or treatments in a subsequent amendment, or from terminating this contract during the Option Period, if any.
  (Check one box only)
  ❑ (1) Buyer accepts the Property As Is.
  ❑ (2) Buyer accepts the Property As Is provided Seller, at Seller's expense, shall complete the following specific repairs and treatments: _____
  _____.
  (Do not insert general phrases, such as "subject to inspections" that do not identify specific repairs and treatments.)
  E. LENDER REQUIRED REPAIRS AND TREATMENTS: Unless otherwise agreed in writing, neither party is obligated to pay for lender required repairs, which includes treatment for wood destroying insects. If the parties do not agree to pay for the lender required repairs or treatments, this contract will terminate and the earnest money will be refunded to Buyer. If the cost of lender required repairs and treatments exceeds 5% of the Sales Price, Buyer may terminate this contract and the earnest money will be refunded to Buyer.
  F. COMPLETION OF REPAIRS AND TREATMENTS: Unless otherwise agreed in writing: (i) Seller shall complete all agreed repairs and treatments prior to the Closing Date; and (ii) all required permits must be obtained, and repairs and treatments must be performed by persons who are licensed to provide such repairs or treatments or, if no license is required by law, are commercially engaged in the trade of providing such repairs or treatments. At Buyer's election, any transferable warranties received by Seller with respect to the repairs and treatments will be transferred to Buyer at Buyer's expense. If Seller fails to complete any agreed repairs and treatments prior to the Closing Date, Buyer may exercise remedies under Paragraph 15 or extend the Closing Date up to 5 days if necessary for Seller to complete the repairs and treatments.
  G. ENVIRONMENTAL MATTERS: Buyer is advised that the presence of wetlands, toxic substances, including asbestos and wastes or other environmental hazards, or the presence of a threatened or endangered species or its habitat may affect Buyer's intended use of the Property. If Buyer is concerned about these matters, an addendum promulgated by TREC or required by the parties should be used.
  H. RESIDENTIAL SERVICE CONTRACTS: Buyer may purchase a residential service contract from a residential service company licensed by TREC. If Buyer purchases a residential service contract, Seller shall reimburse Buyer at closing for the cost of the residential service contract in an amount not exceeding $_____. Buyer should review any residential service contract for the scope of coverage, exclusions and limitations. **The purchase of a residential service contract is optional. Similar coverage may be purchased from various companies authorized to do business in Texas.**

BROKER'S FEES: PARAGRAPH 8

It certainly seems time to have a nice and short one-sentence piece to this already complex contract. However, think of the implications. The sales contract is between the buyer and seller. The listing agreement is between the listing broker and seller, and a buyer's representation agreement is between the buyer's rep and the buyer. The document we are addressing here has *little or nothing* to do with a formal agreement between the principals and agents involved. The point is, make sure you have your own documentation well established in order to protect your professional interests in the transaction being formalized with this contract. The one exception to the above statement is the Farm and Ranch Sales Contract, where there is a ratification of fee and agreement for broker fees section. It is found right at the end of the contract, and even it points out that if there exists a separate written agreement regarding broker fees payment, it should not be filled out. The point is, take care of yourself and get your agreements for your professional services fee well established early in the transaction. Then you can fully concentrate on the important task at hand, which is taking care of your principal.

8.BROKERS' FEES: All obligations of the parties for payment of brokers' fees are contained in separate written agreements.

CLOSING: PARAGRAPH 9

There are fewer things nicer about a real estate transaction than drawing near to its completion and funding *if* everything is well planned out and moving smoothly towards a close. Paragraph 9 is much more than just an on or before closing date. Please pay careful attention to the buyer and seller obligations found in 9B. As is virtually always the case in a real estate deal, there are a number of documents that are required to be created and/or obtained. Make sure some of these important pieces of paper are properly created and delivered to the escrow officer in a timely manner. (P.S. "Timely" does not mean 15 minutes before closing, at least not if you want to keep that escrow officer happily doing business with you!)

A very important aspect of putting in the closing date is to insure that *all* of the other dates that have been incorporated in a way so that one is not conflicting with another. Some of the key sections that may have dates to insert include paragraphs 5, 6, 7, 9, and 24 (effective date), as well as financing attachments. Obviously, Date D cannot come before Date A any more than April can come before February. Make sure you have thought this part through very carefully, or you run the risk of having a contract that cannot be enforced.

9.CLOSING:

A. The closing of the sale will be on or before _____, 20____, or within 7 days after objections made under Paragraph 6D have been cured or waived, whichever date is later (Closing Date). If either party fails to close the sale by the Closing Date, the non-defaulting party may exercise the remedies contained in Paragraph 15.

B. At closing:
(1) Seller shall execute and deliver a general warranty deed conveying title to the Property to Buyer and showing no additional exceptions to those permitted in Paragraph 6 and furnish tax statements or certificates showing no delinquent taxes on the Property.
(2) Buyer shall pay the Sales Price in good funds acceptable to the escrow agent.
(3) Seller and Buyer shall execute and deliver any notices, statements, certificates, affidavits, releases, loan documents and other documents reasonably required for the closing of the sale and the issuance of the Title Policy.
(4) There will be no liens, assessments, or security interests against the Property which will not be satisfied out of the sales proceeds unless securing the payment of any loans assumed by Buyer and assumed loans will not be in default.
(5)If the Property is subject to a residential lease, Seller shall transfer security deposits (as defined under §92.102, Property Code), if any, to Buyer. In such an event, Buyer shall deliver to the tenant a signed statement acknowledging that the Buyer has acquired the Property and is responsible for the return of the security deposit, and specifying the exact dollar amount of the security deposit.

POSSESSION: PARAGRAPH 10

Is this transaction going to be one where the seller gets paid and never looks back as the buyer pays and takes over the place? Or is there going to be some form of continuance of the seller's occupancy, or even a prior-to-closing possession by the buyer? Any of these situations create the need for additional documentation and use of additional TREC promulgated forms. Potential insurance coverage issues rear their ugly head when a soon-to-be buyer becomes a "now tenant," or the reverse if the seller stays on the property after closing.

10.POSSESSION:

A Buyer's Possession: Seller shall deliver to Buyer possession of the Property in its present or required condition, ordinary wear and tear excepted: ❑upon closing and funding ❑according to a temporary residential lease form promulgated by TREC or other written lease required by the parties. Any possession by Buyer prior to closing or by Seller after closing which is not authorized by a written lease will establish a tenancy at sufferance relationship between the parties. **Consult your insurance agent prior to change of ownership and possession because insurance coverage may be limited or terminated. The absence of a written lease or appropriate insurance coverage may expose the parties to economic loss.**

B. Leases:
(1)After the Effective Date, Seller may not execute any lease (including but not limited to mineral leases) or convey any interest in the Property without Buyer's written consent.
(2) If the Property is subject to any lease to which Seller is a party, Seller shall deliver to Buyer copies of the lease(s) and any move-in condition form signed by the tenant within 7 days after the Effective Date of the contract.

SPECIAL PROVISIONS: PARAGRAPH 11

There are certain details to a transaction that cannot be fitted into the various promulgated documents that licensees work with. These details are frequently best suited to include here. Pay *special attention* to the guidance TREC gives you about what to insert and what *not* to insert in this important paragraph.

11.SPECIAL PROVISIONS: (Insert only factual statements and business details applicable to the sale. TREC rules prohibit license holders from adding factual statements or business details for which a contract addendum, lease or other form has been promulgated by TREC for mandatory use.)

SETTLEMENT AND OTHER EXPENSES: PARAGRAPH 12

This paragraph can cause serious problems in situations where a consumer is not *fully* aware of the various costs that they are agreeing to pay. This is why it is so important to prepare an estimation of closing costs *in advance* for your buyer or seller. While you cannot guarantee a 100% accurate estimate, it is wise to discuss the respective costs ahead of time so that there are no problems at closing. To be safe, we prefer to have a slightly higher number for the buyer's costs, and a slightly lower number for the seller's net, when compared to the Closing Disclosure that the escrow officer will provide before closing.

12. SETTLEMENT AND OTHER EXPENSES:
   A. The following expenses must be paid at or prior to closing:
      (1) Expenses payable by Seller (Seller's Expenses):
         (a) Releases of existing liens, including prepayment penalties and recording fees; release of Seller's loan liability; tax statements or certificates; preparation of deed; one-half of escrow fee; and other expenses payable by Seller under this contract.
         (b) Seller shall also pay an amount not to exceed $_____ to be applied in the following order: Buyer's Expenses which Buyer is prohibited from paying by FHA, VA, Texas Veterans Land Board or other governmental loan programs, and then to other Buyer's Expenses as allowed by the lender.
      (2) Expenses payable by Buyer (Buyer's Expenses): Appraisal fees; loan application fees; origination charges; credit reports; preparation of loan documents; interest on the notes from date of disbursement to one month prior to dates of first monthly payments; recording fees; copies of easements and restrictions; loan title policy with endorsements required by lender; loan-related inspection fees; photos; amortization schedules; one-half of escrow fee; all prepaid items, including required premiums for flood and hazard insurance, reserve deposits for insurance, ad valorem taxes and special governmental assessments; final compliance inspection; courier fee; repair inspection; underwriting fee; wire transfer fee; expenses incident to any loan; Private Mortgage Insurance Premium (PMI), VA Loan Funding Fee, or FHA Mortgage Insurance Premium (MIP) as required by the lender; and other expenses payable by Buyer under this contract.
   B. If any expense exceeds an amount expressly stated in this contract for such expense to be paid by a party, that party may terminate this contract unless the other party agrees to pay such excess. Buyer may not pay charges and fees expressly prohibited by FHA, VA, Texas Veterans Land Board or other governmental loan program regulations.

PRORATIONS: PARAGRAPH 13

An important follow-up to paragraph 12 is the brief discussion found in paragraph 13 which speaks to tax prorations. Prorations are a "dividing up" of income or expense. In the final analysis, what this means is that unless otherwise stated, the seller has a liability from January 1 through the day of closing to pay the current-year taxes and other expenses. Likewise, they have the expectation of receiving the income, if any, for the portion of the year that they held title. Keep in mind that in a rapidly escalating marketplace, there may be an adjustment upward in terms of the amount each party is responsible for with regards to costs, and this can create a problem when sellers move away and/or have expended all of their proceeds from the sale.

13. PRORATIONS: Taxes for the current year, interest, maintenance fees, assessments, dues and rents will be prorated through the Closing Date. The tax proration may be calculated taking into consideration any change in exemptions that will affect the current year's taxes. If taxes for the current year vary from the amount prorated at closing, the parties shall adjust the prorations when tax statements for the current year are available. If taxes are not paid at or prior to closing, Buyer shall pay taxes for the current year.

CASUALTY LOSS: PARAGRAPH 14

Sometimes, a tragedy will occur after a contract has been signed (executory) but before closing (fully executed), and the subject property has a partial or total loss. Review carefully what is stated in this important information. Like most things in life, this issue is not a problem until it is a *big* problem.

14. CASUALTY LOSS: If any part of the Property is damaged or destroyed by fire or other casualty after the effective date of this contract, Seller shall restore the Property to its previous condition as soon as reasonably possible, but in any event by the Closing Date. If Seller fails to do so due to factors beyond Seller's control, Buyer may (a) terminate this contract and the earnest money will be refunded to Buyer (b) extend the time for performance up to 15 days and the Closing Date will be extended as necessary or (c) accept the Property in its damaged condition with an assignment of insurance proceeds, if permitted by Seller's insurance carrier, and receive credit from Seller at closing in the amount of the deductible under the insurance policy. Seller's obligations under this paragraph are independent of any other obligations of Seller under this contract.

DEFAULT: PARAGRAPH 15

As addressed in another part of this book, a default occurs when one of the parties under contract does not do what they committed to do. This small paragraph addresses options available to the respective parties in the event of default. Our caution to you is that this paragraph gets into legal issues beyond the scope of a real estate licensee's ability to give advice.

15. DEFAULT: If Buyer fails to comply with this contract, Buyer will be in default, and Seller may (a) enforce specific performance, seek such other relief as may be provided by law, or both, or (b) terminate this contract and receive the earnest money as liquidated damages, thereby releasing both parties from this contract. If Seller fails to comply with this contract, Seller will be in default and Buyer may (a) enforce specific performance, seek such other relief as may be provided by law, or both, or (b) terminate this contract and receive the earnest money, thereby releasing both parties from this contract.

Mediation: Paragraph 16

While mediation does not take away the right to legal action, sometimes a skilled party, knowledgeable in real estate and trained in negotiations, can provide a solution that all parties can agree to. A word to the wise: Legal proceedings can be lengthy and draining, both financially and emotionally. In many cases, mediation resolution may have some real merit.

16. MEDIATION: It is the policy of the State of Texas to encourage resolution of disputes through alternative dispute resolution procedures such as mediation. Any dispute between Seller and Buyer related to this contract which is not resolved through informal discussion will be submitted to a mutually acceptable mediation service or provider. The parties to the mediation shall bear the mediation costs equally. This paragraph does not preclude a party from seeking equitable relief from a court of competent jurisdiction.

Attorney's Fees: 17

This 2-1/2 line paragraph is pretty well clear. If you are one of the parties involved in a legal proceeding, the prevailing (winning) party can expect to receive costs associated with the legal efforts.

17. ATTORNEY'S FEES: A Buyer, Seller, Listing Broker, Other Broker, or escrow agent who prevails in any legal proceeding related to this contract is entitled to recover reasonable attorney's fees and all costs of such proceeding.

Escrow: Paragraph 18

This portion of the contract has lots of details that deal with how the funds held by the escrow agent will flow from this transaction. Escrow people do not take sides; they must follow what the contract says, and this paragraph attempts to address their role and responsibility. From a licensee point of view, we encourage you to get to know the policies and practices of the escrow agents you will frequently come into contact with in order to make this very important relationship as smooth as possible during the potentially stressful times leading up to a closing.

18. ESCROW:

A. ESCROW: The escrow agent is not (i) a party to this contract and does not have liability for the performance or nonperformance of any party to this contract, (ii) liable for interest on the earnest money and (iii) liable for the loss of any earnest money caused by the failure of any financial institution in which the earnest money has been deposited unless the financial institution is acting as escrow agent.

B. EXPENSES: At closing, the earnest money must be applied first to any cash down payment, then to Buyer's Expenses and any excess refunded to Buyer. If no closing occurs, escrow agent may: (i) require a written release of liability of the escrow agent from all parties, (ii) require payment of unpaid expenses incurred on behalf of a party, and (iii) only deduct from the earnest money the amount of unpaid expenses incurred on behalf of the party receiving the earnest money.

C. DEMAND: Upon termination of this contract, either party or the escrow agent may send a release of earnest money to each party and the parties shall execute counterparts of the release and deliver same to the escrow agent. If either party fails to execute the release, either party may make a written demand to the escrow agent for the earnest money. If only one party makes written demand for the earnest money, escrow agent shall promptly provide a copy of the demand to the other party. If escrow agent does not receive written objection to the demand from the other party within 15 days, escrow agent may disburse the earnest money to the party making demand reduced by the amount of unpaid expenses incurred on behalf of the party receiving the earnest money and escrow agent may pay the same to the creditors. If escrow agent complies with the provisions of this paragraph, each party hereby releases escrow agent from all adverse claims related to the disbursal of the earnest money.

D. DAMAGES: Any party who wrongfully fails or refuses to sign a release acceptable to the escrow agent within 7 days of receipt of the request will be liable to the other party for (i) damages; (ii) the earnest money; (iii) reasonable attorney's fees; and (iv) all costs of suit.

E. NOTICES: Escrow agent's notices will be effective when sent in compliance with Paragraph 21. Notice of objection to the demand will be deemed effective upon receipt by escrow agent.

REPRESENTATIONS: PARAGRAPH 19

This small paragraph really addresses two issues: The accuracy of the parties' representations *and* the Seller's right (or non-right, if agreed by the parties) to continue to show the property and take back-up offers. Obviously, the first part is always an important concern. Whatever is being represented continues (survives) past closing and can come back to haunt all parties should an intentional untruth be presented.

19. REPRESENTATIONS: All covenants, representations and warranties in this contract survive closing. If any representation of Seller in this contract is untrue on the Closing Date, Seller will be in default. Unless expressly prohibited by written agreement, Seller may continue to show the Property and receive, negotiate and accept back up offers.

FEDERAL TAX REQUIREMENTS: PARAGRAPH 20

This short piece speaks to the disclosure of "foreign persons" and the reporting of funds from a transaction, if beyond a certain amount. With so much international investing in Texas currently taking place, this small paragraph may have implications to some of your transactions. Better to ask and be told that it's not applicable than to fail to ask and wish you had pursued the issue further in advance of closing! Our best resources tell us that at the time of this writing, the magic number that an escrow officer uses to trigger tax withholdingsfrom the transaction is *$300,000* for a sales price. Like many things in life, this may be subject to change in the future.

20. FEDERAL TAX REQUIREMENTS: If Seller is a "foreign person," as defined by applicable law, or if Seller fails to deliver an affidavit to Buyer that Seller is not a "foreign person," then Buyer shall withhold from the sales proceeds an amount sufficient to comply with applicable tax law and deliver the same to the Internal Revenue Service together with appropriate tax forms. Internal Revenue Service regulations require filing written reports if currency in excess of specified amounts is received in the transaction.

NOTICES: PARAGRAPH 21

It is critical to know how to track down the principals in your transactions. Make sure you get *accurate and numerous* contact points. As an aside, the end of page 7 on the One to Four Family Residential Contract (Resale) is the last page for the sellers and buyers to initial. Don't forget this important detail, and make sure all of the previous pages have those initials. Better to go back and correct such oversights *before* submitting a contract to the other parties.

21. NOTICES: All notices from one party to the other must be in writing and are effective when mailed to, hand-delivered at, or transmitted by fax or electronic transmission as follows:

To Buyer at:	_____	To Seller at:	_____
	_____		_____
Phone:	( ) _____	Phone:	( ) _____
Fax:	( ) _____	Fax:	( ) _____
E-mail:	_____	E-mail:	_____

AGREEMENT OF PARTIES: PARAGRAPH 22

This important part is basically a review of what all is included in this contract. We consider it to be sort of the Table of Contents of the entire document. Please make sure you have all of the appropriate addenda needed to accurately reflect this transaction noted. Further, use this checklist to go back and make sure that all of your addenda are correctly completed to the best of your ability. It is always wise, if at all possible, to have another person in your office go over your contract before you obtain your customer's or client's signature on it.

22. AGREEMENT OF PARTIES: This contract contains the entire agreement of the parties and cannot be changed except by their written agreement. Addenda which are a part of this contract are (Check all applicable boxes):

❏ Third Party Financing Addendum

❏ Seller Financing Addendum

❏ Addendum for Property Subject to Mandatory Membership in a Property Owners Association

❏ Buyer's Temporary Residential Lease

❏ Loan Assumption Addendum

❏ Addendum for Sale of Other Property by Buyer

❏ Addendum for Reservation of Oil, Gas and Other Minerals

❏ Addendum for "Back-Up" Contract

❏ Addendum for Coastal Area Property

❏ Environmental Assessment, Threatened or Endangered Species and Wetlands Addendum

❏ Seller's Temporary Residential Lease

❏ Short Sale Addendum

❏ Addendum for Property Located Seaward of the Gulf Intracoastal Waterway

❏ Addendum for Seller's Disclosure of Information on Lead-based Paint and Lead-based Paint Hazards as Required by Federal Law

❏ Addendum for Property in a Propane Gas System Service Area

❏ Other (list): _____
_____

TERMINATION OPTION: PARAGRAPH 23

We have written in another part of this book about the unilateral nature of an option period. There are three questions to be addressed on this section of the contract:

1. How much money will be paid? (Remember, this goes to the seller and not the escrow agent.)

2. How long does the buyer have to decide to buy?

3. Will the option fee count toward the sales price at closing?

23. TERMINATION OPTION: For nominal consideration, the receipt of which is hereby acknowledged by Seller, and Buyer's agreement to pay Seller $_____ (Option Fee) within 3 days after the effective date of this contract, Seller grants Buyer the unrestricted right to terminate this contract by giving notice of termination to Seller within _____ days after the effective date of this contract (Option Period). Notices under this paragraph must be given by 5:00 p.m. (local time where the Property is located) by the date specified. If no dollar amount is stated as the Option Fee or if Buyer fails to pay the Option Fee to Seller within the time prescribed, this paragraph will not be a part of this contract and Buyer shall not have the unrestricted right to terminate this contract. If Buyer gives notice of termination within the time prescribed, the Option Fee will not be refunded; however, any earnest money will be refunded to Buyer. The Option Fee ❏will ❏will not be credited to the Sales Price at closing. **Time is of the essence for this paragraph and strict compliance with the time for performance is required.**

CONSULT AN ATTORNEY: PARAGRAPH 24

As licensees, our job is to fill in the blanks of these contracts and forms in a competent manner. If there is a need to discuss the *legal* implications of these respective documents, we need to encourage our consumer to seek legal advice from someone licensed in the state of Texas. Keep in mind, just because you know how to turn on a light switch, that does not make you an electrical engineer! Just like in paragraph 21 (Notices), make sure you have accurate and ample ways to contact the respective attorneys involved. If one or more of the parties does not choose to have legal representation, our opinion is that there should be a "None" or "NA" placed in the correct position in this paragraph. Please note that right under the attorney contacts is the **EFFECTIVE DATE** portion. This little piece is *critical* to fill in once final agreement has been reached, as many the dates in the entire contract use this point in time as the starting point.

24. CONSULT AN ATTORNEY BEFORE SIGNING: TREC rules prohibit real estate license holders from giving legal advice. READ THIS CONTRACT CAREFULLY.

Buyer's
Attorney is: _____

Seller's
Attorney is: _____

_____

_____

Phone: ( ) _____

Phone: ( ) _____

Fax: ( ) _____

Fax: ( ) _____

E-mail: _____

E-mail: _____

EXECUTED the _____day of _____, 20_____ (EFFECTIVE DATE).
(BROKER: FILL IN THE DATE OF FINAL ACCEPTANCE.)

_____
Buyer

_____
Seller

_____
Buyer

_____
Seller

BROKER INFORMATION
(Print name(s) only. Do not sign)

| Other Broker Firm | License No. | Listing Broker Firm | License No. |

represents ☐ Buyer only as Buyer's agent
☐ Seller as Listing Broker's subagent

represents ☐ Seller and Buyer as an intermediary
☐ Seller only as Seller's agent

Associate's Name   License No.

Listing Associate's Name   License No.

Licensed Supervisor of Associate   License No.

Licensed Supervisor of Listing Associate   License No.

Other Broker's Address   Fax

Listing Broker's Office Address   Fax

City   State   Zip

City   State   Zip

Associate's Email Address   Phone

Listing Associate's Email Address   Phone

Selling Associate's Name   License No.

Licensed Supervisor of Selling Associate   License No.

Selling Associate's Office Address   Fax

City   State   Zip

Selling Associate's Email Address   Phone

Listing Broker has agreed to pay Other Broker_____of the total sales price when the Listing Broker's fee is received. Escrow agent is authorized and directed to pay other Broker from Listing Broker's fee at closing.

OPTION FEE RECEIPT

Receipt of $_____ (Option Fee) in the form of _____ is acknowledged.

_____   _____
Seller or Listing Broker   Date

CONTRACT AND EARNEST MONEY RECEIPT

Receipt of ☐Contract and ☐$_____Earnest Money in the form of _____ is acknowledged.

Escrow Agent: _____   Date: _____

By: _____

_____   _____
                              Email Address

Address   Phone: (____)_____

_____   Fax: (____)_____
City   State   Zip

TREC NO. 20-13

Page 9 of this particular contract (One to Four Family Residential - Resale) has the appropriate broker information, option fee (signed on behalf of the seller by the listing agent/broker), and earnest money receipt (signed by an escrow agent representative). Page 9 is also the last one where the property is identified at the top of the page. Use your review of this last page to make sure a correct address is placed on top of this one as well as the previous eight pages.

PUTTING IT INTO PRACTICE

The ability to formalize a contract that correctly reflects the wishes of the parties you represent is essential for success in the real estate industry. Of equal significance is that you be able to create a document that will stand the test of being valid.

To that extent, we have created for you a time to practice this important skill. At the end of this chapter, you will find the details of two transactions, along with information about the appropriate forms. Keep in mind, we would rather you make your mistakes here and now rather than out in the field, where the consequences are far greater.

COMMON AND IMPORTANT FORMS ASSOCIATED WITH THE EARNEST MONEY CONTRACT

While we sometimes have cash offers to create, most of the time, there will be some third party financing involved. Form 40-7 Third Party Financing Addendum is the most common financing-related addendum that is used with paragraph 4.

Please ensure *you check only the appropriate boxes* relevant to this particular transaction, and also make certain of your inserted dollar amounts so that purchase price, down payment, and loan amounts all "balance out" correctly. You should note that credit approval is a *time sensitive* aspect of this addendum, and consequently, of the entire agreement. This is an especially important piece of the finance puzzle, and details of proper interest rates, loan origination fees, and other information inserted into the form blanks *must* be accurate. Money is a commodity, like stocks, bonds and other investment products; the interest rates can vary widely and, at times, change quickly. Make sure you are as current as possible to be able to address *all* aspects of the information regarding financing. Your sponsoring broker may have some thoughts on who to seek out for financing options, assuming the prospective buyer does not already have contacts in place with one or more particular lenders. Our suggestion is that you establish good working relationships with several loan officers who offer financing in the marketplaces where you are working. Not all lenders offer financing in all marketplaces. For example, a strong residential lender may not be at all interested in a farm and ranch loan or a commercial development loan.

If a situation arises where you know the buyer you are working with will need to secure third party financing, it is prudent to begin that process very early in the working relationship. Included below is a checklist of the information that most loan officers will be seeking from a potential borrower.

PROMULGATED BY THE TEXAS REAL ESTATE COMMISSION (TREC)

THIRD PARTY FINANCING ADDENDUM

TO CONTRACT CONCERNING THE PROPERTY AT

_____

(Street Address and City)

A. TYPE OF FINANCING AND DUTY TO APPLY AND OBTAIN APPROVAL: Buyer shall apply promptly for all financing described below and make every reasonable effort to obtain approval for the financing, including but not limited to furnishing all information and documents required by Buyer's lender. (Check applicable boxes):

❑ 1. Conventional Financing:
    ❑ (a) A first mortgage loan in the principal amount of $ _____ (excluding any financed PMI premium), due in full in _____ year(s), with interest not to exceed _____% per annum for the first _____ year(s) of the loan with Origination Charges as shown on Buyer's Loan Estimate for the loan not to exceed _____% of the loan.
    ❑ (b) A second mortgage loan in the principal amount of $_____(excluding any financed PMI premium), due in full in _____year(s), with interest not to exceed _____% per annum for the first _____year(s) of the loan with Origination Charges as shown on Buyer's Loan Estimate for the loan not to exceed _____% of the loan.

❑ 2. Texas Veterans Loan: A loan(s) from the Texas Veterans Land Board of $ _____ for a period in the total amount of _____years at the interest rate established by the Texas Veterans Land Board.

❑ 3. FHA Insured Financing: A Section _____ FHA insured loan of not less than $_____(excluding any financed MIP), amortizable monthly for not less than _____years, with interest not to exceed _____% per annum for the first _____ year(s) of the loan with Origination Charges as shown on Buyer's Loan Estimate for the loan not to exceed _____ % of the loan.

❑ 4. VA Guaranteed Financing: A VA guaranteed loan of not less than $_____(excluding any financed Funding Fee), amortizable monthly for not less than_____years, with interest not to exceed_____% per annum for the first _____year(s) of the loan with Origination Charges as shown on Buyer's Loan Estimate for the loan not to exceed _____% of the loan.

❑ 5. USDA Guaranteed Financing: A USDA-guaranteed loan of not less than $ _____ (excluding any financed Funding Fee), amortizable monthly for not less than_____years, with interest not to exceed _____% per annum for the first _____year(s) of the loan with Origination Charges as shown on Buyer's Loan Estimate for the loan not to exceed _____% of the loan.

❑ 6. Reverse Mortgage Financing: A reverse mortgage loan (also known as a Home Equity Conversion Mortgage loan) in the original principal amount of $ _____ (excluding any financed PMI premium or other costs), with interest not to exceed _____% per annum for the first _____ year(s) of the loan with Origination Charges as shown on Buyer's Loan Estimate for the loan not to exceed _____% of the loan. The reverse mortgage loan ❑will ❑ will not be an FHA insured loan.

Third Party Financing Addendum Concerning   Page 2 of 2

_____
(Address of Property)

B. APPROVAL OF FINANCING: Approval for the financing described above will be deemed to have been obtained when Buyer Approval and Property Approval are obtained.
1. Buyer Approval:
   ❑ This contract is subject to Buyer obtaining Buyer Approval. If Buyer cannot obtain Buyer Approval, Buyer may give written notice to Seller within_____days after the effective date of this contract and this contract will terminate and the earnest money will be refunded to Buyer. If Buyer does not terminate the contract under this provision, the contract shall no longer be subject to the Buyer obtaining Buyer Approval. Buyer Approval will be deemed to have been obtained when (i) the terms of the loan(s) described above are available and (ii) lender determines that Buyer has satisfied all of lender's requirements related to Buyer's assets, income and credit history.
   ❑ This contract is not subject to Buyer obtaining Buyer Approval.
2. Property Approval: Property Approval will be deemed to have been obtained when the Property has satisfied lender's underwriting requirements for the loan, including but not limited to appraisal, insurability, and lender required repairs. If Property Approval is not obtained, Buyer may terminate this contract by giving notice to Seller before closing and the earnest money will be refunded to Buyer.
3. **Time is of the essence for this paragraph and strict compliance with the time for performance is required.**

C. SECURITY: Each note for the financing described above must be secured by vendor's and deed of trust liens.

D. FHA/VA REQUIRED PROVISION: If the financing described above involves FHA insured or VA financing, it is expressly agreed that, notwithstanding any other provision of this contract, the purchaser (Buyer) shall not be obligated to complete the purchase of the Property described herein or to incur any penalty by forfeiture of earnest money deposits or otherwise: (i) unless the Buyer has been given in accordance with HUD/FHA or VA requirements a written statement issued by the Federal Housing Commissioner, Department of Veterans Affairs, or a Direct Endorsement Lender setting forth the appraised value of the Property of not less than $_____; or (ii) if the contract purchase price or cost exceeds the reasonable value of the Property established by the Department of Veterans Affairs.
(1) The Buyer shall have the privilege and option of proceeding with consummation of the contract without regard to the amount of the appraised valuation or the reasonable value established by the Department of Veterans Affairs.
(2) If FHA financing is involved, the appraised valuation is arrived at to determine the maximum mortgage the Department of Housing and Urban Development will insure. HUD does not warrant the value or the condition of the Property. The Buyer should satisfy himself/herself that the price and the condition of the Property are acceptable.
(3) If VA financing is involved and if Buyer elects to complete the purchase at an amount in excess of the reasonable value established by the VA, Buyer shall pay such excess amount in cash from a source which Buyer agrees to disclose to the VA and which Buyer represents will not be from borrowed funds except as approved by VA. If VA reasonable value of the Property is less than the Sales Prices, Seller may reduce the Sales Price to an amount equal to the VA reasonable value and the sale will be closed at the lower Sales Price with proportionate adjustments to the down payment and the loan amount.

E. AUTHORIZATION TO RELEASE INFORMATION:
(1) Buyer authorizes Buyer's lender to furnish to Seller or Buyer or their representatives information relating to the status of the approval for the financing.
(2) Seller and Buyer authorize Buyer's lender, title company, and escrow agent to disclose and furnish a copy of the closing disclosures provided in relation to the closing of this sale to the parties' respective brokers and sales agents identified on the last page of the contract.

_____   _____
Buyer   Seller

_____   _____
Buyer   Seller

Source: Reprinted with permission of Texas Real Estate Commission

TREC NO. 40-7
11-2-2015

Items Needed For Loan Application
**** Please do not take a phone picture of items needed

- Clear Enlarged Copies of current Driver's License and resident alien (if applicable) We must be able to see a clear picture and read all information on front. If card has expired, will need copy of renewal receipt.

- Current consecutive paystubs covering a minimum 30 day period. If you are paid weekly, this will be four paystubs, bi weekly, two stubs, monthly, one paystub.

- Copies of 2014 and 2015 W-2s and 1099s

- Complete copies of 2014 & 2015 (2015 if filed with the IRS) tax returns – all schedules. We are looking at any Schedule A (unreimbursed expenses), Schedule C (any business losses) & Schedule E (Rental Loss)

- Copies of the recent benefit letters for any social security or retirement income. Letter must be dated within the last 12 months.

- Current 2 months bank statements on any checking, savings, and retirement or investment accounts. All pages to all statements will be required. Bank name, your name and account number must be shown on the bank statements. Transaction history doesn't print all information. We will need a copy of your cancelled earnest money check once it has cleared your bank.

- Copies of Divorce Decrees or child support orders if applicable – All Pages & the one signed by Judge

- If you receive income for child support and are using it to qualify a current 12 month printout showing timely payments received will be required and proof it will continue for 3 years.

- Copy of Bankruptcy Papers and Discharge from Bankruptcy if applicable. All pages including the discharge page.

- We will require a complete 2 year employment history. This is to include names, addresses, phone numbers, positions held and dates of employment for the most recent 24 month period. Any phone numbers to the HR department. Write on blank piece of paper or email.

- A complete 24 month residential history will be required to included addresses and dates of history, along with amount paid. Write on blank piece of paper or email.

- Current contact information to include home, work, cell phone numbers and current e-mail address if applicable.

- If you currently own any real estate provide a mortgage payment statement to show if taxes and insurance are included with payment. If they are not, provide insurance information and property tax statement.

From a practical point of view, loan approval can take some time. From the seller's point of view, signing a contract subject to the buyer obtaining financing is a cloud hovering over the deal. If you can present a contract with documentation from a lender showing that the buyer has been qualified (pre-approved) for a large enough loan to purchase the seller's property, that is a major negotiating advantage over a buyer with unknown capacity to borrow. Our recommendation is that you have your buyers start working on this aspect of the transaction ASAP.

At the time of this book's publication, financing real estate is at an interesting place when considering this next document, the Loan Assumption Addendum. For a number of years, the cost of borrowing money for real estate has been at historically low rates when compared to the average rates over the last 30+ years. As a consequence, the vast majority of conventional loans have a provision that says if the property sells, the loan must be paid off. This is called a "due on sale" clause and is found in the Promissory Note. *Before* you begin to structure any kind of an offer based upon the assumption of a Promissory Note—on the rare occasions where that opportunity exists—be sure you have reviewed the original terms and conditions to confirm whether an assumption is even allowed. It is very important to have current loan balances on any and all existing Notes in order to structure this agreement because, as noted in paragraph E, the Note holder may be able to say no to such an agreement.

Another really significant piece of the assumption form is the costs to assume. Lenders may have an assumption fee and/or an increase in the interest rate charge. No purpose is served by beginning this assumption journey until you have determined the possibility of it being feasible. Sometimes, situations arise where the seller is asked to finance the sale. In those cases, Form 26-6, Seller Financing Addendum, becomes the form of choice. Because there will be no loan officer or underwriter involved from a lending company, the licensee involved in seller financing transactions needs to be extremely careful to seek help in evaluating the terms, conditions, and buyer qualifications. Involve the seller's relevant professional service providers in the review process. In nearly all cases, the seller's accountant, banker, and attorney should be consulted in making such important decisions. In fact, conversations with these valuable resources should be done *in advance* of offering seller financing as an option.

Every single paragraph of this document has significant ramifications to the seller, and advice from parties more experienced that nearly all licensees is appropriate.

Seller financing can be a valuable alternative for both parties in certain cases. For a seller, becoming "the banker" and not the owner might provide

PROMULGATED BY THE TEXAS REAL ESTATE COMMISSION (TREC)   12-05-11

EQUAL HOUSING
OPPORTUNITY

LOAN ASSUMPTION ADDENDUM
TO CONTRACT CONCERNING THE PROPERTY AT

_____
(Address of Property)

A. CREDIT DOCUMENTATION. To establish Buyer's creditworthiness, Buyer shall deliver to Seller within_____days after the effective date of this contract ☞ credit report ❑ verification of employment, including salary ❑ verification of funds on deposit in financial institutions ❑ current financial statement and ❑_____ .
Buyer hereby authorizes any credit reporting agency to furnish copies of Buyer's credit reports to Seller at Buyer's sole expense.

B. CREDIT APPROVAL. If the credit documentation described in Paragraph A is not delivered within the specified time, Seller may terminate this contract by notice to Buyer within 7 days after expiration of the time for delivery, and the earnest money will be paid to Seller. If the credit documentation is timely delivered, and Seller determines in Seller's sole discretion that Buyer's credit is unacceptable, Seller may terminate this contract by notice to Buyer within 7 days after expiration of the time for delivery and the earnest money will be refunded to Buyer. If Seller does not terminate this contract within the time specified, Seller will be deemed to have approved Buyer's creditworthiness.

C. ASSUMPTION. Buyer's assumption of an existing note includes all obligations imposed by the deed of trust securing the note.
❑ (1) The unpaid principal balance of a first lien promissory note payable to_____
_____which unpaid balance at closing will be $ _____.
The total current monthly payment including principal, interest and any reserve deposits is $ _____. Buyer's initial payment will be the first payment due after closing.

❑ (2) The unpaid principal balance of a second lien promissory note payable to _____
_____which unpaid balance at closing will be $ _____.
The total current monthly payment including principal, interest and any reserve deposits is $ _____. Buyer's initial payment will be the first payment due after closing.

If the unpaid principal balance of any assumed loan as of the Closing Date varies from the loan balance stated above, the ❑ cash payable at closing ❑ Sales Price will be adjusted by the amount of any variance. If the total principal balance of all assumed loans varies in an amount greater than $500 at closing, either party may terminate this contract and the earnest money will be refunded to Buyer unless the other party elects to pay the excess of the variance.

D. LOAN ASSUMPTION TERMS. Buyer may terminate this contract and the earnest money will be refunded to Buyer if the noteholder requires:
(1) payment of an assumption fee in excess of $ _____in C(1) or $ _____in C(2) and Seller declines to pay such excess, or
(2) an increase in the interest rate to more than _____% in C(1) or_____% in C(2), or
(3) any other modification of the loan documents.

E. CONSENT BY NOTEHOLDER. If the noteholder fails to consent to the assumption of the loan, either Seller or Buyer may terminate this contract by notice to the other party and the earnest money will be refunded to the Buyer.

F. SELLER'S LIENS. Unless Seller is released from liability on any assumed note, a vendor's lien and deed of trust to secure assumption will be required. The vendor's lien will automatically be released on delivery of an executed release by noteholder.

Initialed for identification by Buyer_____ and Seller_____   TREC NO. 41-2

_____
(Address of Property)

G. TAX AND INSURANCE ESCROW. If noteholder maintains an escrow account for ad valorem taxes, casualty insurance premiums or mortgage insurance premiums, Seller shall transfer the escrow account to Buyer without any deficiency. Buyer shall reimburse Seller for the amount in the transferred accounts.

NOTICE TO BUYER: If you are concerned about the possibility of future adjustments, monthly payments, interest rates or other terms, do not sign the contract without examining the notes and deeds of trust.

NOTICE TO SELLER: Your liability to pay the notes assumed by Buyer will continue unless you obtain a release of liability from the noteholders. If you are concerned about future liability, you should use the TREC Release of Liability Addendum.

_____   _____
Buyer   Seller

_____   _____
Buyer   Seller

Source: Reprinted with permission of Texas Real Estate Commission

PROMULGATED BY THE TEXAS REAL ESTATE COMMISSION (TREC)   11-2-2015

SELLER FINANCING ADDENDUM
TO CONTRACT CONCERNING THE PROPERTY AT

_____

(Address of Property)

A. CREDIT DOCUMENTATION. To establish Buyer's creditworthiness, Buyer shall deliver to Seller within_____days after the effective date of this contract, ❑ credit report ❑ verification of employment, including salary ❑ verification of funds on deposit in financial institutions ❑ current financial statement and ❑ _____
_____. Buyer hereby authorizes any credit reporting agency to furnish copies of Buyer's credit reports to Seller at Buyer's sole expense.

B. BUYER'S CREDIT APPROVAL. If the credit documentation described in Paragraph A is not delivered within the specified time, Seller may terminate this contract by notice to Buyer within 7 days after expiration of the time for delivery, and the earnest money will be paid to Seller. If the credit documentation is timely delivered, and Seller determines in Seller's sole discretion that Buyer's credit is unacceptable, Seller may terminate this contract by notice to Buyer within 7 days after expiration of the time for delivery and the earnest money will be refunded to Buyer. If Seller does not terminate this contract, Seller will be deemed to have approved Buyer's creditworthiness.

C. PROMISSORY NOTE. The promissory note in the amount of $_____(Note), included in Paragraph 3B of the contract payable by Buyer to the order of Seller will bear interest at the rate of _____% per annum and be payable at the place designated by Seller. Buyer may prepay the Note in whole or in part at any time without penalty. Any prepayments are to be applied to the payment of the installments of principal last maturing and interest will immediately cease on the prepaid principal. The Note will contain a provision for payment of a late fee of 5% of any installment not paid within 10 days of the due date. Matured unpaid amounts will bear interest at the rate of 1½% per month or at the highest lawful rate, whichever is less. The Note will be payable as follows:

❑ (1) In one payment due _____ after the date of the Note with interest payable ❑ at maturity ❑ monthly ❑ quarterly. (check one box only)

❑ (2) In monthly installments of $ _____ ❑ including interest ❑plus interest (check one box only) beginning _____ after the date of the Note and continuing monthly thereafter for_____ months when the balance of the Note will be due and payable.

❑ (3) Interest only in monthly installments for the first _____ month(s) and thereafter in installments of $_____ ❑ including interest ❑ plus interest (check one box only) beginning _____ after the date of the Note and continuing monthly thereafter for_____ months when the balance of the Note will be due and payable.

D. DEED OF TRUST. The deed of trust securing the Note will provide for the following:

(1) PROPERTY TRANSFERS: (check one box only)

❑ (a) Consent Not Required: The Property may be sold, conveyed or leased without the consent of Seller, provided any subsequent buyer assumes the Note.

❑ (b) Consent Required: If all or any part of the Property is sold, conveyed, leased for a period longer than 3 years, leased with an option to purchase, or otherwise sold (including any contract for deed), without Seller's prior written consent, which consent may be withheld in Seller's sole discretion, Seller may declare the balance of the Note

Initialed for identification by Buyer_____ and Seller_____   TREC NO. 26-7

(Address of Property)

to be immediately due and payable. The creation of a subordinate lien, any conveyance under threat or order of condemnation, any deed solely between buyers, or the passage of title by reason of the death of a buyer or by operation of law will not entitle Seller to exercise the remedies provided in this paragraph.

NOTE: _Under (a) or (b), Buyer's liability to pay the Note will continue unless Buyer obtains a release of liability from Seller._

(2) TAX AND INSURANCE ESCROW: (check one box only)

☐ (a) Escrow Not Required: Buyer shall furnish Seller, before each year's ad valorem taxes become delinquent, evidence that all ad valorem taxes on the Property have been paid. Buyer shall annually furnish Seller evidence of paid-up casualty insurance naming Seller as a mortgagee loss payee.

☐ (b) Escrow Required: With each installment Buyer shall deposit in escrow with Seller a pro rata part of the estimated annual ad valorem taxes and casualty insurance premiums for the Property. Buyer shall pay any deficiency within 30 days after notice from Seller. Buyer's failure to pay the deficiency will be a default under the deed of trust. Buyer is not required to deposit any escrow payments for taxes and insurance that are deposited with a superior lienholder. The casualty insurance must name Seller as a mortgagee loss payee.

(3) PRIOR LIENS: Any default under any lien superior to the lien securing the Note will be a default under the deed of trust securing the Note.

_____   _____
Buyer   Seller

_____   _____
Buyer   Seller

a stable cash flow with a return rate higher than possible with other alternatives. When you seriously consider paragraph A, would you want to carry a Note without some assurances of the borrower's creditworthiness? If you represent the seller, we would suggest asking for every single one of the items outlined in this section. In paragraph B, if the buyer does not/will not provide the required information, the seller can terminate. If the seven-day preprinted timeframe is not appropriate, it needs to be negotiated and adjustments made to the document to reflect the principals' agreement.

Note that in paragraph C, some of the conditions are already established, and may or may not reflect the wishes of the parties. For example, the ability to prepay some or all of the Note has been preprinted in the document, as has the late fee percentage to be charged. The decisions regarding C(1), C(2), or C(3) could have some serious tax implications, furthering the need for professional advice and counsel from a tax attorney or accountant. Paragraph D looks to the future and, again, a seller has to ask how much continuing control is desired. Both points D(1) and D(2) have some significant implications, and the decisions should not be made without expert professional advice.

As stated earlier, we have very few conventional loan assumptions taking place. On the other situations where a seller seeking to be released from liability and/or seeking to have VA entitlement benefits restored are more common in many of our marketplaces. A word to the wise regarding this form: *Before* even starting a proposed sale that includes the condition of a Restoration of Entitlement, make certain you can answer "yes" to all three points (a, b, and c) covered under paragraph B. Regarding paragraph A, especially the conventional loan aspects, make sure the loan in question is even assumable. Please note in the form that the seller is responsible for paying the costs of the necessary documents. The thoughtful seller's agent will determine what those costs might be in advance so there is no disappointment about the potentially expensive fees to the seller.

No purpose is served without all these factors being confirmed as possible at the front of negotiations and discussions. Keep in mind that under either scenario in paragraphs A or B, there are two options to consider: The parties involved can agree to continue the sale if release or restoration cannot be done, or they can terminate the sale and earnest money will be refunded. Rarely are consumers satisfied with a licensee's services if such an endeavor as this was not feasible at the outset.

PROMULGATED BY THE TEXAS REAL ESTATE COMMISSION (TREC)

12-05-11

ADDENDUM FOR
RELEASE OF LIABILITY ON ASSUMED LOAN
AND/OR RESTORATION OF SELLER'S VA ENTITLEMENT

TO CONTRACT CONCERNING THE PROPERTY AT

_____

(Address of Property)

❏ **A. RELEASE OF SELLER'S LIABILITY ON LOAN TO BE ASSUMED:**

Within _____ days after the effective date of this contract Seller and Buyer shall apply for release of Seller's liability from (a) any conventional lender, (b) VA and any lender whose loan has been guaranteed by VA, or (c) FHA and any lender whose loan has been insured by FHA. Seller and Buyer shall furnish all required information and documents. If any release of liability has not been approved by the Closing Date: (check one box only)

❏ (1) This contract will terminate and the earnest money will be refunded to Buyer.

❏ (2) Failure to obtain release approval will not delay closing.

❏ **B. RESTORATION OF SELLER'S ENTITLEMENT FOR VA LOAN:**

Within _____ days after the effective date of this contract Seller and Buyer shall apply for restoration of Seller's VA entitlement and shall furnish all information and documents required by VA. If restoration has not been approved by the Closing Date: (check one box only)

❏ (1) This contract will terminate and the earnest money will be refunded to Buyer.

❏ (2) Failure to obtain restoration approval will not delay closing.

NOTICE: VA will not restore Seller's VA entitlement unless Buyer: (a) is a veteran, (b) has sufficient unused VA entitlement and (c) is otherwise qualified. If Seller desires restoration of VA entitlement, paragraphs A and B should be used.

Seller shall pay the cost of securing the release and restoration.

Seller's deed will contain any loan assumption clause required by FHA, VA or any lender.

_____   _____
Buyer   Seller

_____   _____
Buyer   Seller

TREC No. 12-3

Source: Reprinted with permission of Texas Real Estate Commission

In summary, in order to be a successful real estate practitioner, it is crucial to know the *appropriate forms to use in a particular setting* and to know *how to correctly complete those forms*.

Each of the individual paragraphs has details you need to review and understand for your own comfort and for the comfort of those consumers you serve. While you are *not* to provide legal advice, it is imperative for your long-term success to have a full understanding of the documents used in your everyday professional life. Seek help to become competent and confident in using these important tools.

PRACTICE TIME #1

Sergei Karabailonov is a Russian national legally living in the USA. He has for sale a large single-family dwelling in Big Town, Texas 78231. The street address is 51398 Tatar Avenue and the property has a legal description of Lot 9 Block 7 NCB 6391 in the Golden Heights Subdivision. Sergei is represented by G.E. Mack, Attorney at Law, whose law office is located at 32894 N. Ash in Big Town. The attorney's phone number is 555-114-1994 and his email is sumnow@hotspot.org.

The listing company is Vela Realty and the list price is $1,657,000. Robert Vela is the listing agent. Vela Realty is located at 1951 Frio Town Trail in Big Town. His phone number is 555-818-2014 and his license number is 20140818. There is a 5% broker performance fee associated with the listing, and Robert has agreed to split the fees evenly with a seller firm. His email is newboss@hotstuff.org.

Susan Blizzard and Mai Lei Eng own a real estate investment firm called BlizEng Real Estate Investments, LLC. They have a mailing address of P.O. Box 1300, Miguel, Texas 78010, and a phone number of 555-777-1984. Their email is blizenginvestments@xyz.com.

They are represented by Connie McKeag of Talbot Realty. Talbot Realty has an address of 1103 Mission Trails in Big Town. The phone number is 555-602-1954 and the email is talbotsells@topdrawer.org. The broker license number is 0196301.

The buyers have decided to offer $1,525,000, with $325,000 down, and obtain a third party loan for the balance. They will put up $25,000 in escrow with Araujo Title and Abstract Company in Big Town. Delia Araujo is the escrow agent, and the company is located at 197 Venado Grande. Her email is delia@araujotitle.com and her phone is 555-696-1522. The buyers have offered a $1,000 option fee for a 10-day option, and the option funds will be counted as part of the sales price.

There needs to be a new survey done within 30 days of the effective date, and closing will be within 75 days of the effective date. The effective date is the day you are doing this assignment. Buyers have not received a notice of property condition, and they have requested that the custom pool table in the den, along with all pool-related equipment, be included in the sale.

Please prepare this offer.

PRACTICE TIME #2

Lt. Colonel (retired) Berle T. Barnett and wife Barbara S. Barnett occupy a property they own in Walkertown, Texas 78007. The address is 1948 Avenida del Toro, and the legal description is Lot 14 Block 11 in Avenida del Sol Subdivision. They have a phone number of 555-393-0654 and an email of LTCBB@southsan.com. The Barnetts are selling their home without the aid of a licensee, although they do have an attorney. She is Debra Crowther from Walkertown. Her phone number is 555-393-1257 and her email is crowtherlaw@legal.org.

Elmer W. Lindsey and wife Helen Elizabeth looked at the property with their buyer rep agent, and they desire to attempt to purchase this property. They are paying a 2% finder's fee to their agent to handle the details of the contract, negotiations, etc. Mr. Lindsey is a veteran with adequate VA entitlement to assume the existing loan of $69,000. The Lindseys live at 4242 Lighthouse Way in Walkertown and have a phone number of 555-393-0270. They have no email.

The Lindseys want to offer $100,000 down for a purchase price of $169,000. They wish to give a $500 option fee for 15 days to be used as part of the sales price, and have agreed to place $10,000 in escrow as earnest money with Pam Jason at Jodaro Title Company, located at 15022 Red Robin Drive in Walkertown. Pam's phone number is 555-422-3131 and her email is pam@jodarotitle.org. The offer is contingent upon the buyers being able to assume the existing mortgage, and closing is scheduled to be on or before September 9th. The Lindseys' attorney is Christene Stanley, whose mailing address is P.O. Box 2309 in Walkertown. Her phone number is 555-223-2250 and her email is chris@stanleylaw.org. The Lindseys want any and all documents they are to sign to be sent to Ms. Stanley for review prior to them signing.

Buyer rep for the Lindseys is Betty Anderson at CB Anderson Realty. Her license number is 8181937. CB Anderson Realty is located at 303 Langford Blvd., Suite 144, in Smallerville, Texas 78281. Phone number is 555-822-1765 and email is betty@cbarealty.com.

Please prepare this offer.

REVIEW AND DISCUSSION QUESTIONS

1. When would you NOT use the promulgated One to Four Family Residential Contract (Resale)?

2. When a buyer asks you how much money should be put down for earnest money, how should you respond?

3. Assume a party to the contract does not have an email address. What should you put in paragraph 21 (Notices)?

4. What does the term *proration* mean as it relates to ad valorem taxes on a property involved in an ownership transfer?

5. Who "chooses" the escrow agent?

6. How is an executrix different from an administratrix?

LESSONS TO LEARN

You have recently finished your pre-licensing coursework, prepared for and passed your Real Estate Salesperson's Exam, chosen a sponsoring broker, and yesterday completed your two-week New Agent Training Program. Congratulations!

This morning, an old family friend, Della Fischer (a widower) called you and asked that you show her a new listing your company has just taken that was owned by a recently deceased neighbor of hers, Lena Walker (also a widower). Ms. Walker died with a valid will. The listing was taken by Tammy Perez of your office. Ms. Walker's estate is being handled by her daughter, Verna Dell Walker Rosen.

How should you proceed with the request from Della?

Chapter 4

Covenants, Commitments, and Notices

LEARNING OBJECTIVES

When you have completed this chapter, you will be able to:

- Complete paragraphs 5 through 8 of the contract.
- Describe the requirement of the buyer and the buyer's agent for depositing the earnest money with the escrow agent.
- Identify who must furnish a Seller's Disclosure and who is exempt, according to the Texas Property Code.
- Describe when you must furnish the Lead-Based Paint Addendum.
- Describe when to use the Environmental Assessment, Threatened or Endangered Species, and Wetlands Addendum.

KEY TERMS

earnest money	seller's disclosure
option fee	survey
commitment	title policy
escrow	restrictive covenants

EARNEST MONEY

TREC promulgated contracts include a provision for earnest money in paragraph 5. **Earnest money** is the "good faith money" presented by the prospective buyer as an indication of the buyer's intention to carry out the terms of the contract. Not only does earnest money show good faith and serious intent on the part of the buyer, it may also serve as liquidated damages in the event of default as addressed in the identified remedies listed in paragraph 15. Earnest money is not necessary to bind the contract. The promise of the purchaser to buy, and the promise of the seller to deliver title, are adequate consideration to create a legally binding executory contract. There is no set rule of thumb on the amount of earnest money required. Typically, 1% to 3% of the purchase price is ideal; however, the parties may determine that a smaller or larger amount is appropriate for their particular transaction.

Additional earnest money can be required when the buyer is unable to make the full, desired deposit at the time of signing the agreement, or if the contract needs to be extended or amended. Paragraph 5 includes a blank space specifically for additional earnest money. If the buyer fails to deposit the earnest money as required by the contract, the buyer will be in default. This gives the seller the right to exercise the default remedies established by agreement of the parties in paragraph 15. Upon execution of the contract, the buyer is required to deposit the earnest money with the title company that was negotiated between the parties.

TREC rule 535.146(a)(b) requires that earnest money be deposited with the escrow agent selected by the parties no later than the close of the second business day after the date the broker receives it. When the buyer has presented the offer in writing, the seller has accepted the offer by signing the contract, and the buyer has been notified of the seller's acceptance, an executory contract exists, and the agent or buyer should deliver the earnest money to the escrow agent named in paragraph 5 of the contract. The only exception occurs when the principals agree that a deposit may be delayed and a different time is expressly defined in paragraph 11 of the contract [TREC Rule 535.146 (a)(b)(3)].

The agent should deposit the contract and earnest money, if any, with the escrow agent immediately and obtain a receipted copy of the contract for each party. The receipt is issued by the escrow agent, not the listing or selling licensee.

5. EARNEST MONEY: Upon execution of this contract by all parties, Buyer shall deposit $_____ as earnest money with _____, as escrow agent, at _____ (address). Buyer shall deposit additional earnest money of $_____ with escrow agent within _____days after the effective date of this contract. If Buyer fails to deposit the earnest money as required by this contract, Buyer will be in default.

OPTION FEE

The **option fee** is separate from the earnest money and allows the buyer the unrestricted right to terminate the contract by giving notice of termination to the seller within a predetermined number of days after the effective date of the contract ("Option Period"). Most option periods are used by the buyer to conduct due diligence on the property. Property inspections typically uncover repairs that the buyer most likely will want to negotiate with the seller. Having an option period in place will allow the buyer to negotiate any property repairs or defects with the seller without the risk of losing the earnest money. The option fee is a nominal amount—typically $10.00 per day for the length of the option period. For example, if the option period is seven days, then typically the option fee will be $70.00. If a termination option is agreed to by the seller as specified in paragraph 23, the buyer must deliver the option fee to the seller within three *calendar* days after the effective date of the contract. If no dollar amount is stated as the option fee, or the buyer fails to pay the option fee to the seller within the time required, the paragraph will *not* be a part of the contract and the buyer will *not* have the unrestricted right to terminate the contract. If the buyer gives notice of termination within the time prescribed, the option fee will not be refunded; however, any earnest money will be refunded to the buyer. All notices under this paragraph must be given by 5:00 p.m. local time where the property is located by the date specified. As stated in bold print in paragraph 23 of the contract, time is of the essence for this paragraph, and strict compliance with the time for performance is required.

Paragraph 23 of the contract says that the buyer's option fee will be delivered to the seller within three days of effective date of the contract. If it is delivered to an agent at the listing broker's office, legally it has been delivered to the seller. The agent will sign the receipt form. One of the ways to prove delivery within the proper time frame is the Option Fee Receipt on page 9 of the contract. If proof is provided in a different manner (for example, via postal service delivery confirmation), then it is not necessary to use the receipt on page 9 of the sales contract.

23. **TERMINATION OPTION:** For nominal consideration, the receipt of which is hereby acknowledged by Seller, and Buyer's agreement to pay Seller $_____ (Option Fee) within 3 days after the effective date of this contract, Seller grants Buyer the unrestricted right to terminate this contract by giving notice of termination to Seller within _____ days after the effective date of this contract (Option Period). Notices under this paragraph must be given by 5:00 p.m. (local time where the Property is located) by the date specified. If no dollar amount is stated as the Option Fee or if Buyer fails to pay the Option Fee to Seller within the time prescribed, this paragraph will not be a part of this contract and Buyer shall not have the unrestricted right to terminate this contract. If Buyer gives notice of termination within the time prescribed, the Option Fee will not be refunded; however, any earnest money will be refunded to Buyer. The Option Fee ☐will ☐will not be credited to the Sales Price at closing. **Time is of the essence for this paragraph and strict compliance with the time for performance is required.**

TITLE COMMITMENT, TITLE POLICY, AND ENDORSEMENTS

Most transactions closed in Texas involve the issuance of a title policy to the buyer of the property. **Title policy** is title insurance that indemnifies the buyer from financial loss in the event of title failure. Providing title insurance is the best way for the seller to show evidence of clear title. Usually, the company selected in paragraph 6 to issue the owner's title policy is the same chosen in paragraph five to serve as escrow agent;

however, it is not mandatory. The owner's title policy is a contract between the buyer and the title company, and neither party is allowed to dictate which title company must be used. To do so would be a violation of the Real Estate Settlement Procedures Act (RESPA). Federal regulation prohibits the seller from requiring the buyer to use the services of a particular title provider.

Typically, the owner's policy of title insurance to be furnished to the buyer will be at the seller's expense. A buyer who is asking the seller to pay for the policy might be willing to allow the seller to choose which title company will be used for the transaction. However, because it is the buyer who must live with the coverage and deal with the insurance company if a title problem arises, the buyer may want to be able to select the title insurance company. Ultimately, the choice of the title company and who pays for it is a point to be negotiated by the parties. When the parties have come to an agreement on this matter, check the appropriate box in paragraph 6A.

In addition to identifying who issues and who pays for the title policy, paragraph 6A establishes that the policy is subject to the exclusions published by the state insurance board in Austin, Texas. The standard printed exception relates to discrepancies, conflicts, and shortages in area or boundary lines. It may be amended to include only shortages in area by the payment of an additional 15% to the title insurance premium and by providing a survey acceptable to the title company. Check with the title company about the amount and identify who will pay it as an additional business detail in paragraph 11 of the contract. The additional cost is 5% of the title insurance premium for homestead properties, and 15% for others.

6. TITLE POLICY AND SURVEY:
   A. TITLE POLICY: Seller shall furnish to Buyer at ❑ Seller's ❑ Buyer's expense an owner policy of title insurance (Title Policy) issued by _____ (Title Company) in the amount of the Sales Price, dated at or after closing, insuring Buyer against loss under the provisions of the Title Policy, subject to the promulgated exclusions (including existing building and zoning ordinances) and the following exceptions:
   (1) Restrictive covenants common to the platted subdivision in which the Property is located.
   (2) The standard printed exception for standby fees, taxes and assessments.
   (3) Liens created as part of the financing described in Paragraph 3.
   (4) Utility easements created by the dedication deed or plat of the subdivision in which the Property is located.
   (5) Reservations or exceptions otherwise permitted by this contract or as may be approved by Buyer in writing.
   (6) The standard printed exception as to marital rights.
   (7) The standard printed exception as to waters, tidelands, beaches, streams, and related matters.
   (8) The standard printed exception as to discrepancies, conflicts, shortages in area or boundary lines, encroachments or protrusions, or overlapping improvements: ❑(i) will not be amended or deleted from the title policy; or ❑(ii) will be amended to read, "shortages in area" at the expense of ❑Buyer ❑Seller.

The agreement calls for the seller to furnish the buyer a **commitment** for title insurance, and at the buyer's expense, legible copies of deed restrictions (restrictive covenants) and documentation of any exceptions in the commitment within 20 days after the title company receives a copy of the contract. The seller requests that the title company mail or hand deliver the commitment to the buyer's address shown in paragraph 21 of the contract form. The parties agreed that if the title company is unable to deliver within 20 days, the time for delivery automatically extends up to 15 days or the closing date, whichever is sooner.

It is extremely important to understand the **restrictive covenants** and other deed restrictions that are in place for a specific piece of real estate because they dictate how the buyer can and cannot use the property. Restrictive covenants are deed restrictions that apply to a group of homes or lots, and property that is part of a specific development or subdivision. Customarily, they are put in place by the original developer and are different for every area of homes.

Restrictive covenants generally stipulate the minimum size dwelling allowed, how many homes may be built on one lot, and what type of construction may or may not be allowed in building the homes. If in a suburban or rural area, the covenants may also stipulate what type of livestock is or is not allowed and how many head of livestock per acre of land is permissible. Other types of restrictive covenants include the following:

- Easements (access for roadways or power lines or other utilities)
- Setbacks (how far homes must be from streets and interior lot lines)
- Fees for road maintenance or amenities
- Regulations dealing with in-home businesses and home rentals
- Rules about pets and other animals
- Rules regarding changing or avoiding the covenants
- Clauses that dictate what type of fencing can be used, if any
- Clauses to reduce clutter on lots, such as prohibiting owners from storing a vehicle that doesn't run within view of others, or parking a vehicle on the property

After the buyer receives the commitment, the buyer will have the negotiated number of days to object in writing to any matters disclosed in the commitment. That number of days negotiated will be determined by agreement of the parties upon execution of the contract.

B. COMMITMENT: Within 20 days after the Title Company receives a copy of this contract, Seller shall furnish to Buyer a commitment for title insurance (Commitment) and, at Buyer's expense, legible copies of restrictive covenants and documents evidencing exceptions in the Commitment (Exception Documents) other than the standard printed exceptions.   Seller authorizes the Title Company to deliver the Commitment and Exception Documents to Buyer at Buyer's address shown in Paragraph 21. If the Commitment and Exception Documents are not delivered to Buyer within the specified time, the time for delivery will be automatically extended up to 15 days or 3 days before the Closing Date, whichever is earlier. If, due to factors beyond Seller's control, the Commitment and Exception Documents are not delivered within the time required, Buyer may terminate this contract and the earnest money will be refunded to Buyer.

SURVEY

There are three **survey** options in the contract. The seller may provide the buyer with the existing survey. If this option is chosen, the seller must also furnish the buyer with a Residential Real Property Affidavit (T-47), published by the Texas Department of Insurance. This affidavit is discussed in the next section.

If the existing survey or affidavit is not acceptable to the title company or to the buyer's lender, the parties will negotiate in paragraph 6C(1) and agree who will pay for a new survey. When using paragraph 6C(1), make sure to check either the seller's or buyer's checkbox to indicate who will pay for the new survey.

Paragraphs 6C(2) and 6C(3) are both for getting a new survey. 6C(2) is at the buyer's expense, and 6C(3) is at the seller's expense.

C. SURVEY: The survey must be made by a registered professional land surveyor acceptable to the Title Company and Buyer's lender(s). (Check one box only)
❑(1) Within _____ days after the effective date of this contract, Seller shall furnish to Buyer and Title Company Seller's existing survey of the Property and a Residential Real Property Affidavit promulgated by the Texas Department of Insurance (T-47 Affidavit). **If Seller fails to furnish the existing survey or affidavit within the time prescribed, Buyer shall obtain a new survey at Seller's expense no later than 3 days prior to Closing Date.** If the existing survey or affidavit is not acceptable to Title Company or Buyer's lender(s), Buyer shall obtain a new survey at ❑Seller's ❑Buyer's expense no later than 3 days prior to Closing Date.
❑(2) Within _____ days after the effective date of this contract, Buyer shall obtain a new survey at Buyer's expense. Buyer is deemed to receive the survey on the date of actual receipt or the date specified in this paragraph, whichever is earlier.
❑(3) Within _____ days after the effective date of this contract, Seller, at Seller's expense shall furnish a new survey to Buyer.

AFFIDAVIT AND NOTICE TO PROSPECTIVE BUYER

If the seller wants to furnish the existing property survey, the listing agent must be sure that the survey is available for the buyer. The contract also calls for the seller to furnish the buyer with a Residential Real Property Affidavit

(T-47), promulgated by the Texas Department of Insurance. If the seller fails to furnish the existing survey or affidavit within the time prescribed by the contract, the buyer will obtain a new survey at the seller's expense no later than three days prior to the closing date of the executed contract.

T-47 RESIDENTIAL REAL PROPERTY AFFIDAVIT
(MAY BE MODIFIED AS APPROPRIATE FOR COMMERCIAL TRANSACTIONS)

Date:_____ GF No._____

Name of Affiant(s):_____

Address of Affiant:_____

Description of Property:_____

County_____, Texas

"Title Company" as used herein is the Title Insurance Company whose policy of title insurance is issued in reliance upon the statements contained herein.

Before me, the undersigned notary for the State of _____, personally appeared Affiant(s) who after by me being sworn, stated:

1. We are the owners of the Property. (Or state other basis for knowledge by Affiant(s) of the Property, such as lease, management, neighbor, etc. For example, "Affiant is the manager of the Property for the record title owners.")

2. We are familiar with the property and the improvements located on the Property.

3. We are closing a transaction requiring title insurance and the proposed insured owner or lender has requested area and boundary coverage in the title insurance policy(ies) to be issued in this transaction. We understand that the Title Company may make exceptions to the coverage of the title insurance as Title Company may deem appropriate. We understand that the owner of the property, if the current transaction is a sale, may request a similar amendment to the area and boundary coverage in the Owner's Policy of Title Insurance upon payment of the promulgated premium.

4. To the best of our actual knowledge and belief, since _____ there have been no:

    a. construction projects such as new structures, additional buildings, rooms, garages, swimming pools or other permanent improvements or fixtures;

    b. changes in the location of boundary fences or boundary walls;

    c. construction projects on immediately adjoining property(ies) which encroach on the Property;

    d. conveyances, replattings, easement grants and/or easement dedications (such as a utility line) by any party affecting the Property.

    EXCEPT for the following (If None, Insert "None" Below:)

5. We understand that Title Company is relying on the truthfulness of the statements made in this affidavit to provide the area and boundary coverage and upon the evidence of the existing real property survey of the Property. This Affidavit is not made for the benefit of any other parties and this Affidavit does not constitute a warranty or guarantee of the location of improvements.

6. We understand that we have no liability to Title Company that will issue the policy(ies) should the information in this Affidavit be incorrect other than information that we personally know to be incorrect and which we do not disclose to the Title Company.

_____

_____

SWORN AND SUBSCRIBED this _____ day of _____, 20_____.

_____
Notary Public

TITLE OBJECTIONS

Paragraph 6D relates to any buyer objections regarding defects, exceptions, or encumbrances to title: disclosed on the survey other than items 6A (1) through (7); disclosed in the commitment other than items 6A(1) through (8) above; or which prohibit specific uses for activities that the buyer requires.

For example: If the buyer is specifically purchasing the property with plans of having an in-home daycare, he or she must disclose this in section 6D. Once the title company furnishes the title commitment and legible copies of restrictive covenants to the buyer, and the restrictive covenants show that in-home businesses are prohibited, the buyer must object to the seller *-in writing-* regarding this matter. If the objection(s) to defects, exceptions, encumbrances to title, or restrictive covenants are not cured within a 15-day period, the contract will terminate and the earnest money will be refunded to the buyer unless buyer waives the objections.

D. OBJECTIONS: Buyer may object in writing to defects, exceptions, or encumbrances to title: disclosed on the survey other than items 6A(1) through (7) above; disclosed in the Commitment other than items 6A(1) through (8) above; or which prohibit the following use or activity: _____.
Buyer must object the earlier of (i) the Closing Date or (ii) _____ days after Buyer receives the Commitment, Exception Documents, and the survey. Buyer's failure to object within the time allowed will constitute a waiver of Buyer's right to object; except that the requirements in Schedule C of the Commitment are not waived by Buyer. Provided Seller is not obligated to incur any expense, Seller shall cure the timely objections of Buyer or any third party lender within 15 days after Seller receives the objections and the Closing Date will be extended as necessary. If objections are not cured within such 15 day period, this contract will terminate and the earnest money will be refunded to Buyer unless Buyer waives the objections.

TITLE NOTICES

The Notice in 6E(1) is a requirement of the Texas Real Estate License Act. Every licensee is required to give this written notice to every buyer, even if the buyer is getting a title policy. Agents actually have three ways to give the notice:

1. Using any TREC promulgated contract form
2. Using TAR's buyer representation agreement
3. Using the separate, approved TREC form, Notice to Prospective Buyer

The notice in 6E(2) notifies the buyer if the property is or is not subject to mandatory membership in a property owners association. If the property is subject to mandatory membership in a property owners association, the seller notifies the buyer under §5.012, Texas Property code, that, as a purchaser of the property of the residential community identified in paragraph 2(A) of the sales contract, he or she will be obligated to become a member of the property owners association. Restrictive covenants showing the use and occupancy requirements of the property and all formal documents governing the establishment, maintenance, or operation of the residential community may be obtained from the county clerk. This paragraph also notifies the buyer that there is an obligation to pay assessments to the property owners association and what the penalties may be if the buyer fails to pay.

The notice in 6E(3) pertains to statutory tax districts. If the property is situated in a utility or other statutorily created district providing water, sewer, drainage, or flood control facilities and services, Chapter 49 of the Texas Water Code, requires the seller to deliver and the buyer to sign the statutory notice relating to the tax rate, bonded indebtedness, or standby fee of the district prior to final execution of the sales contract.

The notice in 6E(4) pertains to tide waters. If the property abuts the tidally influenced waters of the state, § 33.135, Texas Natural Resources Code, requires a notice regarding coastal area property to be included in the contract. There is a promulgated addendum for this particular notice.

Notice 6E(5) pertains to annexation. If the property is located outside the limits of a municipality, the seller must notify the buyer under § 5.011, Texas Property Code, that the property may now or later be included in the extraterritorial jurisdiction of a municipality and may now or later be subject to annexation by the municipality. Each municipality maintains a map that shows the boundaries and its extraterritorial jurisdiction. To determine if the property is located within a municipality's extraterritorial jurisdiction or is likely to be located within a municipality's extraterritorial jurisdiction, the buyer should contact all municipalities located in the general proximity of the property for further information.

Notice 6E(6) pertains to the property located in a certificated service area of a utility service provider. § 13.257 of the Texas Water Code requires that the seller notify the buyer if the real property described in paragraph 2 of the sales contract is located in a certificated water or sewer service area. If the property is located in a certificated area, there may be special costs or charges that will be required to be paid before the buyer can receive water or sewer service. The notice also explains that there may be a time period required to construct lines or other facilities necessary to provide water or sewer service to the property. The buyer is advised to determine if the property is in a certificated area and contact the utility service provider to determine the costs that may be required, and the period, if any, that is required to provide water or sewer service to the property.

Notice 6E(7) pertains to public improvement districts. If the property is in a public improvement district, § 5.014, Texas Property Code, requires that the seller notify the buyer with regards to his or her obligation to pay an assessment to the municipality or county for an improvement project undertaken by a public improvement district under Chapter 372, of the Local Government Code. The assessment may be due annually or in periodic installments. The paragraph also states what penalties could result from failure to pay the assessments.

Notice 6E(8) pertains to transfer fees. If the property is subject to a private transfer fee obligation, § 5.205, of the Texas Property Code, requires the seller to notify the buyer of the private transfer fee obligation that may be governed by Chapter 5, subchapter G, of the Texas Property Code.

Notice 6E(9) pertains to propane Gas System Service Areas. If the property is located in a propane Gas System Service Area owned by a distribution system retailer, the seller must give buyer written notice as required by § 141.010, of the Texas Utilities code. A promulgated addendum form is required to be used for this notice.

Notice 6E (10) pertains to Water Level Fluctuations. Section 5.019 of Chapter 11 of the Water Code was added on September 1, 2015 which notifies the buyer about water fluctuations. If a residential or commercial property adjoins a lake, reservoir, or other impoundment of water that has a storage capacity of at least 5,000 acre-feet at the impoundment's normal operating level, the seller notifies the buyer: "The water level of the impoundment of water adjoining the Property fluctuates for various reasons, including as a result of: (1) an entity lawfully exercising its right to use the water stored in the impoundment; or (2) drought or flood conditions."

(1) ABSTRACT OR TITLE POLICY: Broker advises Buyer to have an abstract of title covering the Property examined by an attorney of Buyer's selection, or Buyer should be furnished with or obtain a Title Policy. If a Title Policy is furnished, the Commitment should be promptly reviewed by an attorney of Buyer's choice due to the time limitations on Buyer's right to object.

(2) MEMBERSHIP IN PROPERTY OWNERS ASSOCIATION(S): The Property ❑is ❑is not subject to mandatory membership in a property owners association(s). If the Property is subject to mandatory membership in a property owners association(s), Seller notifies Buyer under §5.012, Texas Property Code, that, as a purchaser of property in the residential community identified in Paragraph 2A in which the Property is located, you are obligated to be a member of the property owners association(s). Restrictive covenants governing the use and occupancy of the Property and all dedicatory instruments governing the establishment, maintenance, or operation of this residential community have been or will be recorded in the Real Property Records of the county in which the Property is located. Copies of the restrictive covenants and dedicatory instruments may be obtained from the county clerk. **You are obligated to pay assessments to the property owners association(s). The amount of the assessments is subject to change. Your failure to pay the assessments could result in enforcement of the association's lien on and the foreclosure of the Property.** Section 207.003, Property Code, entitles an owner to receive copies of any document that governs the establishment, maintenance, or operation of a subdivision, including, but not limited to, restrictions, bylaws, rules and regulations, and a resale certificate from a property owners' association. A resale certificate contains information including, but not limited to, statements specifying the amount and frequency of regular assessments and the style and cause number of lawsuits to which the property owners' association is a party, other than lawsuits relating to unpaid ad valorem taxes of an individual member of the association. These documents must be made available to you by the property owners' association or the association's agent on your request.

If Buyer is concerned about these matters, the TREC promulgated Addendum for Property Subject to Mandatory Membership in a Property Owners Association(s) should be used.

(3) STATUTORY TAX DISTRICTS: If the Property is situated in a utility or other statutorily created district providing water, sewer, drainage, or flood control facilities and services, Chapter 49, Texas Water Code, requires Seller to deliver and Buyer to sign the statutory notice relating to the tax rate, bonded indebtedness, or standby fee of the district prior to final execution of this contract.

(4) TIDE WATERS: If the Property abuts the tidally influenced waters of the state, §33.135, Texas Natural Resources Code, requires a notice regarding coastal area property to be included in the contract. An addendum containing the notice promulgated by TREC or required by the parties must be used.

(5) ANNEXATION: If the Property is located outside the limits of a municipality, Seller notifies Buyer under §5.011, Texas Property Code, that the Property may now or later be included in the extraterritorial jurisdiction of a municipality and may now or later be subject to annexation by the municipality. Each municipality maintains a map that depicts its boundaries and extraterritorial jurisdiction. To determine if the Property is located within a municipality's extraterritorial jurisdiction or is likely to be located within a municipality's extraterritorial jurisdiction, contact all municipalities located in the general proximity of the Property for further information.

(6) PROPERTY LOCATED IN A CERTIFICATED SERVICE AREA OF A UTILITY SERVICE PROVIDER: Notice required by §13.257, Water Code: The real property, described in Paragraph 2, that you are about to purchase may be located in a certificated water or sewer service area, which is authorized by law to provide water or sewer service to the properties in the certificated area. If your property is located in a certificated area there may be special costs or charges that you will be required to pay before you can receive water or sewer service. There may be a period required to construct lines or other facilities necessary to provide water or sewer service to your property. You are advised to determine if the property is in a certificated area and contact the utility service provider to determine the cost that you will be required to pay and the period, if any, that is required to provide water or sewer service to your property. The undersigned Buyer hereby acknowledges receipt of the foregoing notice at or before the execution of a binding contract for the purchase of the real property described in Paragraph 2 or at closing of purchase of the real property.

(7) PUBLIC IMPROVEMENT DISTRICTS: If the Property is in a public improvement district, §5.014, Property Code, requires Seller to notify Buyer as follows: As a purchaser of this parcel of real property you are obligated to pay an assessment to a municipality or county for an improvement project undertaken by a public improvement district under Chapter 372, Local Government Code. The assessment may be due annually or in periodic installments. More information concerning the amount of the assessment and the due dates of that assessment may be obtained from the municipality or county levying the assessment. The amount of the assessments is subject to change. Your failure to pay the assessments could result in a lien on and the foreclosure of your property.

(8) TRANSFER FEES: If the Property is subject to a private transfer fee obligation, §5.205, Property Code, requires Seller to notify Buyer as follows: The private transfer fee obligation may be governed by Chapter 5, Subchapter G of the Texas Property Code.

(9) PROPANE GAS SYSTEM SERVICE AREA: If the Property is located in a propane gas system service area owned by a distribution system retailer, Seller must give Buyer written notice as required by §141.010, Texas Utilities Code. An addendum containing the notice approved by TREC or required by the parties should be used.

PROPERTY CONDITION: INSPECTION, ACCEPTANCE, REPAIRS

Paragraph 7A gives every buyer the right to perform inspections. This paragraph also makes the seller responsible for immediately turning on utilities and keeping them on during the time the contract is in effect.

Property condition is further discussed in paragraphs 7D, E, and F of the promulgated contract forms. 7D states that the buyer accepts the property in its present condition. If there are specific items the buyer wants repaired, there is space to negotiate for those items in paragraph 7D(2).

Paragraph 7E confirms that neither the buyer nor the seller is obligated to do lender-required repairs. If there are lender-required repairs, and neither party agrees to do them, then the property will not qualify for the loan and the buyer will be refunded their earnest money. This paragraph also gives the buyer the right to terminate, even if the seller agrees to do the lender-required repairs, if the cost of those repairs is going to exceed 5% of the sales price.

If the seller agrees to do any repairs, either in the original offer or later in an amendment, paragraph F explains that any repairs agreed upon will be done by professionals and completed before closing.

SELLER'S DISCLOSURE

Paragraph 7B discusses the **seller's disclosure notice** that is required by the Texas Property Code and gives the parties three choices for negotiations. It is in the seller's best interest to limit any future liability by disclosing everything they know about the property. Previously repaired or replaced items need to be disclosed on the notice.

Making the seller's disclosure available at the time of showing the property will satisfy paragraph 7B(1) in the event the buyer decides to make an offer. Buyers should review the seller's disclosure notice before making an offer. That way, he or she will know that they're making an offer based on the property's present condition and can negotiate appropriately.

Paragraph 7B(2) is for the buyer's agent who is preparing an offer, but has not been able to get a completed seller's disclosure from the listing agent. The buyer can make an offer and ask the seller to provide the notice within a certain number of days. The risk for the seller is that even if the seller delivers the disclosure within the proper time frame, the buyer can terminate the contract, for any reason, within seven days and receive the earnest money back. If the seller never delivers the disclosure, the buyer has the right to terminate and receive their earnest money back, up to the day of closing.

There are certain exceptions to providing the seller's disclosure. Paragraph 7B(3) is for the seller who, by law, is not required to furnish the notice. Investors and relocation companies are not excused from providing the seller's disclosure. The following are the legal exemptions from requiring a seller's disclosure:

1. Person went to a court order or foreclosure sale
2. By a trustee and bankruptcy
3. To a mortgage by a mortgagor or successor in interest, or to a beneficiary of a deed of trust by a trustor or successor in interest;
4. By a mortgagee or beneficiary under a deed of trust who has acquired the real property at a sale conducted pursuant to a power of sale under a deed of trust, or a sale pursuant to a court-ordered foreclosure, or has acquitted the real property by a deed in lieu of foreclosure
5. By a fiduciary in the course of the administration of the decedent's estate, guardianship, conservatorship, or trust

6. From one co-owner to one or more other co-owners

7. Made to a spouse or to a person or persons in the lineal line of consanguinity of one or more of the transferors

8. Between spouses resulting from a decree of dissolution of marriage, or a decree of legal separation, or from a property settlement agreement incidental to such a decree

9. To or from any governmental entity

10. Transfers of new residences of not more than one dwelling unit which have not previously been occupied for residential purposes

Note that the TREC seller's disclosure is an optional form, not a promulgated form. All of the information on this form is required by the Texas Property Code and is also on the TAR Seller's Disclosure form. The TAR forms also include additional disclosure items. Many REALTOR® Associations also have these forms.

LEAD-BASED PAINT ADDENDUM

Paragraph 7C addresses the possibility of the presence of lead-based paint or lead-based paint hazards. If the building permits for the construction of the home were issued prior to January 1, 1978, the addendum must be used to comply with the federal regulation to furnish a lead paint disclosure. Use TREC Form OP-L, Addendum for Seller's Disclosure of Information on Lead-Based Paint and Lead-Based Paint Hazards As Required by Federal Law, or the Closing Disclosure.

A. ACCESS, INSPECTIONS AND UTILITIES: Seller shall permit Buyer and Buyer's agents access to the Property at reasonable times. Buyer may have the Property inspected by inspectors selected by Buyer and licensed by TREC or otherwise permitted by law to make inspections. Any hydrostatic testing must be separately authorized by Seller in writing. Seller at Seller's expense shall immediately cause existing utilities to be turned on and shall keep the utilities on during the time this contract is in effect.

B. SELLER'S DISCLOSURE NOTICE PURSUANT TO §5.008, TEXAS PROPERTY CODE (Notice): (Check one box only)

❑ (1) Buyer has received the Notice.

❑ (2) Buyer has not received the Notice. Within _____ days after the effective date of this contract, Seller shall deliver the Notice to Buyer. If Buyer does not receive the Notice, Buyer may terminate this contract at any time prior to the closing and the earnest money will be refunded to Buyer. If Seller delivers the Notice, Buyer may terminate this contract for any reason within 7 days after Buyer receives the Notice or prior to the closing, whichever first occurs, and the earnest money will be refunded to Buyer.

❑ (3)The Seller is not required to furnish the notice under the Texas Property Code.

C. SELLER'S DISCLOSURE OF LEAD-BASED PAINT AND LEAD-BASED PAINT HAZARDS is required by Federal law for a residential dwelling constructed prior to 1978.

D. ACCEPTANCE OF PROPERTY CONDITION: "As Is" means the present condition of the Property with any and all defects and without warranty except for the warranties of title and the warranties in this contract. Buyer's agreement to accept the Property As Is under Paragraph 7D(1) or (2) does not preclude Buyer from inspecting the Property under Paragraph 7A, from negotiating repairs or treatments in a subsequent amendment, or from terminating this contract during the Option Period, if any.

(Check one box only)
- ☐ (1) Buyer accepts the Property As Is.
- ☐ (2) Buyer accepts the Property As Is provided Seller, at Seller's expense, shall complete the following specific repairs and treatments: _____.

  (Do not insert general phrases, such as "subject to inspections" that do not identify specific repairs and treatments.)

E. LENDER REQUIRED REPAIRS AND TREATMENTS: Unless otherwise agreed in writing, neither party is obligated to pay for lender required repairs, which includes treatment for wood destroying insects. If the parties do not agree to pay for the lender required repairs or treatments, this contract will terminate and the earnest money will be refunded to Buyer. If the cost of lender required repairs and treatments exceeds 5% of the Sales Price, Buyer may terminate this contract and the earnest money will be refunded to Buyer.

F. COMPLETION OF REPAIRS AND TREATMENTS: Unless otherwise agreed in writing: (i) Seller shall complete all agreed repairs and treatments prior to the Closing Date; and (ii) all required permits must be obtained, and repairs and treatments must be performed by persons who are licensed to provide such repairs or treatments or, if no license is required by law, are commercially engaged in the trade of providing such repairs or treatments. At Buyer's election, any transferable warranties received by Seller with respect to the repairs and treatments will be transferred to Buyer at Buyer's expense. If Seller fails to complete any agreed repairs and treatments prior to the Closing Date, Buyer may exercise remedies under Paragraph 15 or extend the Closing Date up to 5 days if necessary for Seller to complete the repairs and treatments.

It is important that sellers fill out the lead paint disclosure to the best of their knowledge and sign and date it prior to the buyer signing it. The seller must check one of the boxes in each section of paragraph **B** of the lead paint disclosure form.

The buyer must check boxes in paragraphs C and D. Paragraph C2 explains the buyer's rights to perform inspections within 10 days and the right to terminate within 14 days. The buyer's agent should also furnish the buyer with a booklet called *Protect Your Family from Lead in Your Home*. The buyer acknowledges receipt of this booklet in paragraph D.

Paragraph E of the lead paint disclosure form explains the broker's obligation, including the obligation to maintain a copy of the addendum for at least three years.

Paragraph F certifies that everyone who signs this—including buyers, sellers, and both agents—is giving information to the best of their knowledge, and that the information they have provided is true and correct.

Environmental Assessment, Threatened or Endangered Species, and Wetlands Addendum

Paragraph 7G addresses environmental matters. Buyers should always be given the opportunity to have the property inspected for environmental hazards. Whether their concern is about radon, asbestos, mold, or any other concern, the buyer should be satisfied that the property does not pose a health hazard to the buyer or the buyer's family.

APPROVED BY THE TEXAS REAL ESTATE COMMISSION   10-10-11

ADDENDUM FOR SELLER'S DISCLOSURE OF INFORMATION ON LEAD-BASED PAINT AND LEAD-BASED PAINT HAZARDS AS REQUIRED BY FEDERAL LAW

CONCERNING THE PROPERTY AT _____
(Street Address and City)

A. LEAD WARNING STATEMENT: "Every purchaser of any interest in residential real property on which a residential dwelling was built prior to 1978 is notified that such property may present exposure to lead from lead-based paint that may place young children at risk of developing lead poisoning. Lead poisoning in young children may produce permanent neurological damage, including learning disabilities, reduced intelligence quotient, behavioral problems, and impaired memory. Lead poisoning also poses a particular risk to pregnant women. The seller of any interest in residential real property is required to provide the buyer with any information on lead-based paint hazards from risk assessments or inspections in the seller's possession and notify the buyer of any known lead-based paint hazards. A risk assessment or inspection for possible lead-paint hazards is recommended prior to purchase."

   NOTICE: Inspector must be properly certified as required by federal law.

B. SELLER'S DISCLOSURE:
   1. PRESENCE OF LEAD-BASED PAINT AND/OR LEAD-BASED PAINT HAZARDS (check one box only):
      ☐(a) Known lead-based paint and/or lead-based paint hazards are present in the Property (explain): _____
      _____ .
      ☐(b) Seller has no actual knowledge of lead-based paint and/or lead-based paint hazards in the Property.
   2. RECORDS AND REPORTS AVAILABLE TO SELLER (check one box only):
      ☐(a) Seller has provided the purchaser with all available records and reports pertaining to lead-based paint and/or lead-based paint hazards in the Property (list documents):_____
      _____ .
      ☐(b) Seller has no reports or records pertaining to lead-based paint and/or lead-based paint hazards in the Property.

C. BUYER'S RIGHTS (check one box only):
   ☐1. Buyer waives the opportunity to conduct a risk assessment or inspection of the Property for the presence of lead-based paint or lead-based paint hazards.
   ☐2. Within ten days after the effective date of this contract, Buyer may have the Property inspected by inspectors selected by Buyer. If lead-based paint or lead-based paint hazards are present, Buyer may terminate this contract by giving Seller written notice within 14 days after the effective date of this contract, and the earnest money will be refunded to Buyer.

D. BUYER'S ACKNOWLEDGMENT (check applicable boxes):
   ☐1. Buyer has received copies of all information listed above.
   ☐2. Buyer has received the pamphlet *Protect Your Family from Lead in Your Home*.

E. BROKERS' ACKNOWLEDGMENT: Brokers have informed Seller of Seller's obligations under 42 U.S.C. 4852d to: (a) provide Buyer with the federally approved pamphlet on lead poisoning prevention; (b) complete this addendum; (c) disclose any known lead-based paint and/or lead-based paint hazards in the Property; (d) deliver all records and reports to Buyer pertaining to lead-based paint and/or lead-based paint hazards in the Property; (e) provide Buyer a period of up to 10 days to have the Property inspected; and (f) retain a completed copy of this addendum for at least 3 years following the sale. Brokers are aware of their responsibility to ensure compliance.

F. CERTIFICATION OF ACCURACY: The following persons have reviewed the information above and certify, to the best of their knowledge, that the information they have provided is true and accurate.

Buyer	Date	Seller	Date
Buyer	Date	Seller	Date
Other Broker	Date	Listing Broker	Date

TREC NO. OP-L

Use TREC's Environmental Assessment, Threatened or Endangered Species, and Wetlands Addendum (TREC Form No. 28-2) to allow the buyer adequate time to have the property inspected by specialists of his or her choice.

Environmental Assessment, Threatened or Endangered Species, and Wetlands Addendum

G. ENVIRONMENTAL MATTERS: Buyer is advised that the presence of wetlands, toxic substances, including asbestos and wastes or other environmental hazards, or the presence of a threatened or endangered species or its habitat may affect Buyer's intended use of the Property. If Buyer is concerned about these matters, an addendum promulgated by TREC or required by the parties should be used.

RESIDENTIAL SERVICE CONTRACT

Paragraph 7H informs the buyer of their right to choose a Residential Service Contract, also known as a home buyer warranty, and to negotiate for the seller to reimburse the buyer for the cost. Buyer's agents should make sure the buyer reads the portion of paragraph 7H that is presented in bold type. It is important that the buyer understand the following:

- Many different companies offer service contracts
- Coverage and exclusions may differ from one company to another
- It is the buyer's responsibility to review and choose the coverage

The Real Estate Settlement Procedures Act (RESPA) prohibits kickbacks for licensees who refer their clients to a particular lender, settlement agent, inspector, residential service company (home warranty company), and the like, unless the licensee renders a service that warrants a payment or fee. If a licensee is to receive a fee for services rendered, this must be disclosed to the client.

If the licensee refers a client to a residential service provider with whom the licensee has an existing relationship, the licensee should disclose this to the client using TREC's Disclosure of Relationship with Residential Service Company form (See Form RSC 1 on page 99). The format provides for the licensee to disclose any compensation received from the residential service company and the services rendered to earn that compensation.

H. RESIDENTIAL SERVICE CONTRACTS: Buyer may purchase a residential service contract from a residential service company licensed by TREC. If Buyer purchases a residential service contract, Seller shall reimburse Buyer at closing for the cost of the residential service contract in an amount not exceeding $_____. Buyer should review any residential service contract for the scope of coverage, exclusions and limitations. **The purchase of a residential service contract is optional. Similar coverage may be purchased from various companies authorized to do business in Texas.**

SUMMARY

Paragraphs 5 and 6 define the agreement of the parties concerning earnest money, the title policy, and the survey.

The notices in paragraph 6E of the promulgated forms describe the legislation of disclosures that must be conveyed to the buyer about various items. The buyer receives notice when they receive the contract.

Paragraph 7 examines property condition and includes the seller's disclosure notice, lead-based paint disclosure, environmental matters, and residential service contracts.

REVIEW QUESTIONS

1. What is earnest money?

2. When must earnest money be deposited with an escrow agent?

3. Who should deliver the earnest money to the escrow agent?

4. What is an option fee?

5. When must the option fee be delivered to the seller?

6. What is a title policy?

LESSONS TO LEARN

Buyer Becky has made an offer that was accepted by Seller Spencer. She has a 10 day option period with her offer. During the inspection, it is discovered that the plumbing in the master bathroom is substantially defective and will need about $3,500 worth of work. There are three days left to Becky's option period. What can be done?

Chapter 5

Closing, Possession, and More

LEARNING OBJECTIVES

When you have completed this chapter, you will be able to:

1. Complete paragraph 9 through the end of the contract.
2. Describe when it is necessary to use a temporary residential lease as an addition to the contract.
3. Determine what is appropriate to write in paragraph 11, Special Provisions.
4. Identify buyers and sellers closing expenses.
5. Describe when to use an amendment to the contract.
6. Describe where all notices to the contract must be sent.

KEY TERMS

amendment	liquidated damages
casualty loss	possession
closing costs	prorations
default	seller's expenses
funding	specific performance
general warranty deed	temporary residential lease

CLOSING PARAGRAPHS AND BUYER'S POSSESSION PARAGRAPHS IN CONTRACT

Paragraphs 9 and 10 address closing the transaction and delivering possession of the property according to the terms of the contract. The parties negotiate the closing date in paragraph 9A. This is an "on or before" date—meaning if the parties agree, they can close earlier, but not later.

The closing of the sale will occur on or before a specific date with one exception: The closing date may be automatically extended if objections have been made regarding the commitment and/or the survey in paragraph 6D. If the closing date needs to be extended for any other reason, it will require all parties to sign an **amendment** to the contract. The amendment form will be discussed later on.

At closing, the seller will execute and deliver a **general warranty deed** conveying title to the property to the buyer. The buyer agrees to pay the sales price in good funds acceptable to the escrow agent. The seller and buyer execute and deliver any documents required for the closing of the sale and the issuance of a title policy. There will be no liens, assessments, or security interests against the property which will not be satisfied out of the sales proceeds. The only exception to this is if the buyer is assuming any existing loans on the property. If this is the case, the seller guarantees that any assumed loans will not be in default. If the purchased property is an investment property and is secured by a residential lease, the seller will transfer security deposits, if any, to the buyer. In such an event, the buyer will deliver a signed statement to the tenant acknowledging that he or she has received the security deposit and will be responsible for the return of the security deposit once the lease has terminated. After the effective date of the contract, the seller may not execute any lease or convey any interest in the property without the buyer's written consent. If the property is subject to any lease to which the seller is a party, the seller will deliver copies of the lease(s) and any move-in condition form signed by the tenant to the buyer within seven days after the effective date of the contract.

A. The closing of the sale will be on or before _____, 20_____, or within 7 days after objections made under Paragraph 6D have been cured or waived, whichever date is later (Closing Date). If either party fails to close the sale by the Closing Date, the non-defaulting party may exercise the remedies contained in Paragraph 15.

B. At closing:
   (1) Seller shall execute and deliver a general warranty deed conveying title to the Property to Buyer and showing no additional exceptions to those permitted in Paragraph 6 and furnish tax statements or certificates showing no delinquent taxes on the Property.
   (2) Buyer shall pay the Sales Price in good funds acceptable to the escrow agent.
   (3) Seller and Buyer shall execute and deliver any notices, statements, certificates, affidavits, releases, loan documents and other documents reasonably required for the closing of the sale and the issuance of the Title Policy.
   (4) There will be no liens, assessments, or security interests against the Property which will not be satisfied out of the sales proceeds unless securing the payment of any loans assumed by Buyer and assumed loans will not be in default.
   (5) If the Property is subject to a residential lease, Seller shall transfer security deposits (as defined under §92.102, Property Code), if any, to Buyer. In such an event, Buyer shall deliver to the tenant a signed statement acknowledging that the Buyer has acquired the Property and is responsible for the return of the security deposit, and specifying the exact dollar amount of the security deposit.

SELLER'S TEMPORARY LEASE FORM AND BUYER'S TEMPORARY LEASE FORM

After closing and funding, seller will deliver to the buyer **possession** of the property in its present or required condition, ordinary wear and tear excepted. If the buyer wants to take possession of the property prior to closing, or if the seller wants to stay in the property after closing, a temporary lease agreement must be used. Notice the bold print in paragraph 10. It requires both parties of the agreement to consult their insurance agents and determine if their interests are protected in the event of a loss during possession of the property under a temporary lease. For example, if the closing takes place on a Monday, but the seller cannot move until the following weekend, and a fire happens in the kitchen due to a grease fire and the cabinets sustain major damage, whose insurance will cover the damage?

- Because the buyer has not moved in yet, is the property covered by the buyer's new homeowner's policy?

- Because the seller is no longer the owner, do they still have coverage on personal items in the property?

When a seller remains after closing and funding, or when a buyer moves in before closing and funding, a landlord/tenant relationship exists. The relationship must clearly be defined by a seller's or buyer's **temporary residential lease**. Failure to use the appropriate temporary lease will create a tenancy at sufferance. Pay attention to the provisions relating to insurance coverage on the property during the tenancy period. A temporary lease may not be used to address any tenancy that lasts longer than 90 days. If the tenancy exceeds 90 days, the owner will need to regard the property as a residential rental property and bring it into compliance with Chapter 92 of the Texas Property code. This chapter defines what features must be provided in a residential rental unit, such as the need for security devices, smoke detectors, and other features that a landlord must provide a tenant.

A Buyer's Possession: Seller shall deliver to Buyer possession of the Property in its present or required condition, ordinary wear and tear excepted: ❑upon closing and funding ❑according to a temporary residential lease form promulgated by TREC or other written lease required by the parties. Any possession by Buyer prior to closing or by Seller after closing which is not authorized by a written lease will establish a tenancy at sufferance relationship between the parties. **Consult your insurance agent prior to change of ownership and possession because insurance coverage may be limited or terminated. The absence of a written lease or appropriate insurance coverage may expose the parties to economic loss.**

B. Leases:
    (1)After the Effective Date, Seller may not execute any lease (including but not limited to mineral leases) or convey any interest in the Property without Buyer's written consent.
    (2) If the Property is subject to any lease to which Seller is a party, Seller shall deliver to Buyer copies of the lease(s) and any move-in condition form signed by the tenant within 7 days after the Effective Date of the contract.

PROMULGATED BY THE TEXAS REAL ESTATE COMMISSION (TREC)   12-05-11
(NOTICE: For use only when SELLER occupies the property for no more than 90 days AFTER the closing)

SELLER'S TEMPORARY RESIDENTIAL LEASE

1. **PARTIES:** The parties to this Lease are_____
(Landlord) and _____(Tenant).

2. **LEASE:** Landlord leases to Tenant the Property described in the Contract between Landlord as Buyer and Tenant as Seller known as _____
_____(address).

3. **TERM:** The term of this Lease commences on the date the sale covered by the Contract is closed and funded and terminates _____, unless terminated earlier by reason of other provisions.

4. **RENTAL:** Tenant shall pay to Landlord as rental $_____ per day (excluding the day of closing and funding) with the full amount of rental for the term of the Lease to be paid at the time of funding of the sale. Tenant will not be entitled to a refund of rental if this Lease terminates early due to Tenant's default or voluntary surrender of the Property.

5. **DEPOSIT:** Tenant shall pay to Landlord at the time of funding of the sale $_____as a deposit to secure performance of this Lease by Tenant. Landlord may use the deposit to satisfy Tenant's obligations under this Lease. Landlord shall refund any unused portion of the deposit to Tenant with an itemized list of all deductions from the deposit within 30 days after Tenant (a) surrenders possession of the Property and (b) provides Landlord written notice of Tenant's forwarding address.

6. **UTILITIES:** Tenant shall pay all utility charges except _____
which Landlord shall pay.

7. **USE OF PROPERTY:** Tenant may use the Property only for residential purposes. Tenant may not assign this Lease or sublet any part of the Property.

8. **PETS:** Tenant may not keep pets on the Property except _____.

9. **CONDITION OF PROPERTY:** Tenant accepts the Property in its present condition and state of repair at the commencement of the Lease. Upon termination, Tenant shall surrender the Property to Landlord in the condition required under the Contract, except normal wear and tear and any casualty loss.

10. **ALTERATIONS:** Tenant may not alter the Property or install improvements or fixtures without the prior written consent of the Landlord. Any improvements or fixtures placed on the Property during the Lease become the Property of Landlord.

11. **SPECIAL PROVISIONS:**

12. **INSPECTIONS:** Landlord may enter at reasonable times to inspect the Property. Tenant shall provide Landlord door keys and access codes to allow access to the Property during the term of Lease.

13. **LAWS:** Tenant shall comply with all applicable laws, restrictions, ordinances, rules and regulations with respect to the Property.

14. **REPAIRS AND MAINTENANCE:** Except as otherwise provided in this Lease, Tenant shall bear all expense of repairing and maintaining the Property, including but not limited to the yard, trees and shrubs, unless otherwise required by the Texas Property Code. Tenant shall promptly repair at Tenant's expense any damage to the Property caused directly or indirectly by any act or omission of the Tenant or any person other than the Landlord, Landlord's agents or invitees.

Initialed for Identification by Landlord _____ and Tenant_____   TREC NO. 15-5

Seller's Temporary Residential Lease _____Page 2 of 2   12-05-11
(Address of Property)

15. **INDEMNITY:** Tenant indemnifies Landlord from the claims of all third parties for injury or damage to the person or property of such third party arising from the use or occupancy of the Property by Tenant. This indemnification includes attorney's fees, costs and expenses incurred by Landlord.

16. **INSURANCE:** Landlord and Tenant shall each maintain such insurance on the contents and Property as each party may deem appropriate during the term of this Lease. NOTE: CONSULT YOUR INSURANCE AGENT; POSSESSION OF THE PROPERTY BY SELLER AS TENANT MAY CHANGE INSURANCE POLICY COVERAGE.

17. **DEFAULT:** If Tenant fails to perform or observe any provision of this Lease and fails, within 24 hours after notice by Landlord, to commence and diligently pursue to remedy such failure, Tenant will be in default.

18. **TERMINATION:** This Lease terminates upon expiration of the term specified in Paragraph 3 or upon Tenant's default under this Lease.

19. **HOLDING OVER:** Tenant shall surrender possession of the Property upon termination of this Lease. Any possession by Tenant after termination creates a tenancy at sufferance and will not operate to renew or extend this Lease. Tenant shall pay $_____ per day during the period of any possession after termination as damages, in addition to any other remedies to which Landlord is entitled.

20. **ATTORNEY'S FEES:** The prevailing party in any legal proceeding brought under or with respect to this Lease is entitled to recover from the non-prevailing party all costs of such proceeding and reasonable attorney's fees.

21. **SMOKE ALARMS:** The Texas Property Code requires Landlord to install smoke alarms in certain locations within the Property at Landlord's expense. Tenant expressly waives Landlord's duty to inspect and repair smoke alarms.

22. **SECURITY DEVICES:** The requirements of the Texas Property Code relating to security devices do not apply to a residential lease for a term of 90 days or less.

23. **CONSULT YOUR ATTORNEY:** Real estate licensees cannot give legal advice. This Lease is intended to be legally binding. READ IT CAREFULLY. If you do not understand the effect of this Lease, consult your attorney BEFORE signing.

24. **NOTICES:** All notices from one party to the other must be in writing and are effective when mailed to, hand-delivered at, or transmitted by facsimile or electronic transmission as follows:

To Landlord: _____   **To Tenant:** _____

_____   _____

_____   _____

_____   _____

Telephone: (____)_____   Telephone: (____)_____

Facsimile: (____)_____   Facsimile: (____)_____

E-mail: _____   E-mail: _____

_____   _____
Landlord   Tenant

_____   _____
Landlord   Tenant

BUYER'S TEMPORARY RESIDENTIAL LEASE

1. PARTIES: The parties to this Lease are_____
(Landlord) and _____(Tenant).

2. LEASE: Landlord leases to Tenant the Property described in the Contract between Landlord as Seller and Tenant as Buyer known as _____
_____(address).

3. TERM: The term of this Lease commences _____ and terminates as specified in Paragraph 18.

4. RENTAL: Rental will be $_____ per day. Upon commencement of this Lease, Tenant shall pay to Landlord the full amount of rental of $ _____ for the anticipated term of the Lease (commencement date to the Closing Date specified in Paragraph 9 of the Contract). If the actual term of this Lease differs from the anticipated term, any additional rent or reimbursement will be paid at closing. No portion of the rental will be applied to payment of any items covered by the Contract.

5. DEPOSIT: Tenant has paid to Landlord $_____ as a deposit to secure performance of this Lease by Tenant. If this Lease is terminated before the Closing Date, Landlord may use the deposit to satisfy Tenant's obligations under this Lease. Landlord shall refund to Tenant any unused portion of the deposit together with an itemized list of all deductions from the deposit within 30 days after Tenant (a) surrenders possession of the Property and (b) provides Landlord written notice of Tenant's forwarding address. If this Lease is terminated by the closing and funding of the sale of the Property, the deposit will be refunded to Tenant at closing and funding.
NOTICE: The deposit must be in addition to the earnest money under the Contract.

6. UTILITIES: Tenant shall pay all utility connections, deposits and charges except _____
_____, which Landlord shall pay.

7. USE OF PROPERTY: Tenant may use the Property only for residential purposes. Tenant may not assign this Lease or sublet any part of the Property.

8. PETS: Tenant may not keep pets on the Property except _____.

9. CONDITION OF PROPERTY: Tenant accepts the Property in its present condition and state of repair, but Landlord shall make all repairs and improvements required by the Contract. If this Lease is terminated prior to closing, Tenant shall surrender possession of the Property to Landlord in its present condition, as improved by Landlord, except normal wear and tear and any casualty loss.

10. ALTERATIONS: Tenant may not: (a) make any holes or drive nails into the woodwork, floors, walls or ceilings (b) alter, paint or decorate the Property or (c) install improvements or fixtures without the prior written consent of Landlord. Any improvements or fixtures placed on the Property during the Lease become a part of the Property.

11. SPECIAL PROVISIONS:

12. INSPECTIONS: Landlord may enter at reasonable times to inspect, replace, repair or complete the improvements. Tenant shall provide Landlord door keys and access codes to allow access to the Property during the term of the Lease.

13. LAWS: Tenant shall comply with all applicable laws, restrictions, ordinances, rules and regulations with respect to the Property.

14. REPAIRS AND MAINTENANCE: Except as otherwise provided in this Lease, Tenant shall bear all expense of repairing, replacing and maintaining the Property, including but not limited to the yard, trees, shrubs, and all equipment and appliances, unless otherwise required by the Texas Property Code. Tenant shall promptly repair at Tenant's expense any damage to the Property caused directly or indirectly by any act or omission of the Tenant or any person other than the Landlord, Landlord's agents or invitees.

Initialed for identification by Landlord _____ and Tenant_____   TREC NO. 16-5

15.INDEMNITY: Tenant indemnifies Landlord from the claims of all third parties for injury or damage to the person or property of such third party arising from the use or occupancy of the Property by Tenant. This indemnification includes attorney's fees, costs and expenses incurred by Landlord.

16.INSURANCE: Landlord and Tenant shall each maintain such insurance on the contents and Property as each party may deem appropriate during the term of this Lease. NOTE: CONSULT YOUR INSURANCE AGENT; POSSESSION OF THE PROPERTY BY BUYER AS TENANT MAY CHANGE INSURANCE POLICY COVERAGE.

17.DEFAULT: If Tenant fails to perform or observe any provision of this Lease and fails, within 24 hours after notice by Landlord, to commence and diligently pursue to remedy such failure, Tenant will be in default.

18.TERMINATION: This Lease terminates upon (a) closing and funding of the sale under the Contract, (b) termination of the Contract prior to closing, (c) Tenant's default under this Lease, or (d) Tenant's default under the Contract, whichever occurs first. Upon termination other than by closing and funding of the sale, Tenant shall surrender possession of the property.

19.HOLDING OVER: Any possession by Tenant after termination creates a tenancy at sufferance and will not operate to renew or extend this Lease. Tenant shall pay $_____ per day during the period of any possession after termination as damages, in addition to any other remedies to which Landlord is entitled.

20.ATTORNEY'S FEES: The prevailing party in any legal proceeding brought under or with respect to this Lease is entitled to recover from the non-prevailing party all costs of such proceeding and reasonable attorney's fees.

21.SMOKE ALARMS: The Texas Property Code requires Landlord to install smoke alarms in certain locations within the Property at Landlord's expense. Tenant expressly waives Landlord's duty to inspect and repair smoke alarms.

22.SECURITY DEVICES: The requirements of the Texas Property Code relating to security devices do not apply to a residential lease for a term of 90 days or less.

23.CONSULT YOUR ATTORNEY: Real estate licensees cannot give legal advice. This Lease is intended to be legally binding. READ IT CAREFULLY. If you do not understand the effect of this Lease, consult your attorney BEFORE signing.

24.NOTICES: All notices from one party to the other must be in writing and are effective when mailed to, hand-delivered at, or transmitted by facsimile or electronic transmission as follows:

To Landlord: _____

_____

_____

_____

Telephone: (   ) _____

Facsimile: (   ) _____

E-mail: _____

_____
Landlord

_____
Landlord

To Tenant: _____

_____

_____

_____

Telephone: (   ) _____

Facsimile: (   ) _____

E-mail: _____

_____
Tenant

_____
Tenant

SPECIAL PROVISIONS

The contract allows special provisions to be noted when factual statements or business details are part of the sales agreement. Licensees are prohibited from including legal rights or remedies in paragraph 11. If the parties want to define legal rights or remedies, they must seek the advice of their own attorney. For example, a *factual statement* states what someone will or will not do, but, a *legal right or remedy* states what will happen if someone does or does not do a particular act.

Here are some examples of things that can be added in paragraph 11 by the licensee:

- Notice that a licensee acting on his own behalf owns a real estate license
- Who will pay for specific costs that may be incurred that are not addressed elsewhere in the contract
- A prior-to-closing walkthrough inspection
- An inventory list
- Documents available for review prior to closing

A licensee must never write "time is of the essence" in paragraph 11 or any place on the contract unless he or she is a state-licensed attorney. The phrase "time of the essence" is considered a legal term, and TREC rules prohibit a licensee from giving legal advice unless he or she is also licensed as an attorney.

11. SPECIAL PROVISIONS: (Insert only factual statements and business details applicable to the sale. TREC rules prohibit licensees from adding factual statements or business details for which a contract addendum, lease or other form has been promulgated by TREC for mandatory use.)

TREC rules prohibit licensees from adding factual statements or business details for which a contract addendum, lease, or other form has been promulgated by TREC for mandatory use. The following are examples of things that may not be addressed in Special Provisions paragraph 11:

- The transaction is contingent upon the sale of another property (*see* TREC Form 10-6, Addendum for Sale of Other Property by Buyer).
- The contract is in a second or backup position (*see* TREC Form 11-7, Addendum for Back-Up Contract).
- The assumption transaction is contingent upon the seller's release of liability, or in the case of a VA-guaranteed loan, restoration of VA entitlement (*see* TREC Form 12-3, Addendum for Release of Liability on Assumption of FHA, VA, or Conventional Loan/Restoration of Seller's Entitlement).

- The buyer and the seller arrange for the seller to stay after closing, or the buyer to possess before closing (*see* TREC Form 15-5, Seller's Temporary Residential Lease, and TREC Form 16-5, Buyer's Temporary Residential Lease).

- The contract is contingent upon satisfactory inspections to the buyer.

- The parties agree that in the event of a dispute, they will try mediation before bringing a lawsuit.

- The licensee uses wording that defines legal rights and remedies such as *contingent upon*, *terminate*, *refund earnest money on demand*, *cancel*, and so forth.

SETTLEMENT AND OTHER EXPENSES

There are various costs and expenses associated with closing a real estate transaction. Paragraph 12 defines all of the various costs, known as **closing costs**, as well as who is responsible for payment (**Seller's Expenses** and Buyer's Expenses). Paragraph 12A(2) lists all of the buyer's expenses. Because of the many expenses allocated to the buyer, the seller may agree to pay a portion of those expenses. Paragraph 12A(1)(b) provides a space in the contract for negotiating these expenses with the seller.

A. The following expenses must be paid at or prior to closing:
  (1) Expenses payable by Seller (Seller's Expenses):
    (a) Releases of existing liens, including prepayment penalties and recording fees; release of Seller's loan liability; tax statements or certificates; preparation of deed; one-half of escrow fee; and other expenses payable by Seller under this contract.
    (b) Seller shall also pay an amount not to exceed $_____ to be applied in the following order: Buyer's Expenses which Buyer is prohibited from paying by FHA, VA, Texas Veterans Land Board or other governmental loan programs, and then to other Buyer's Expenses as allowed by the lender.
  (2) Expenses payable by Buyer (Buyer's Expenses): Appraisal fees; loan application fees; origination charges; credit reports; preparation of loan documents; interest on the notes from date of disbursement to one month prior to dates of first monthly payments; recording fees; copies of easements and restrictions; loan title policy with endorsements required by lender; loan-related inspection fees; photos; amortization schedules; one-half of escrow fee; all prepaid items, including required premiums for flood and hazard insurance, reserve deposits for insurance, ad valorem taxes and special governmental assessments; final compliance inspection; courier fee; repair inspection; underwriting fee; wire transfer fee; expenses incident to any loan; Private Mortgage Insurance Premium (PMI), VA Loan Funding Fee, or FHA Mortgage Insurance Premium (MIP) as required by the lender; and other expenses payable by Buyer under this contract.
B. If any expense exceeds an amount expressly stated in this contract for such expense to be paid by a party, that party may terminate this contract unless the other party agrees to pay such excess. Buyer may not pay charges and fees expressly prohibited by FHA, VA, Texas Veterans Land Board or other governmental loan program regulations.

PRORATIONS, CASUALTY LOSS, DEFAULT, AND MEDIATION OF CONTRACT

PRORATIONS

In Texas, property taxes are paid in arrears. Many times, the tax prorations are based on last year's tax amount because the current year's tax amount is not available yet. Taxes for the current year, interest, maintenance fees, assessments, dues and rents will be prorated through the closing date. The tax **proration** may be calculated taking into consideration any change in exemptions that will affect the current year's taxes. Paragraph 13 says that if there is a variance from what is prorated once the current amounts become available, the parties will work that out on their own. If taxes are not paid at or prior to closing, the buyer will be responsible for paying taxes for the current year. Items subject to proration will be prorated through the day of closing. The seller will be charged the expense for the day of closing regardless of what time the closing occurs.

CASUALTY LOSS

If any part of the property is damaged or destroyed by fire or other casualty after the effective date of the contract, the seller will restore the property to its previous condition as soon as reasonably possible, but no later than the closing date. In the event of a **casualty loss** prior to closing, the buyer has three options:

1. The buyer may terminate the contract and receive their earnest money,

2. The buyer may also extend the time for performance up to 15 days, and the closing date will be extended as necessary, or

3. Accept the property in its currently damaged condition with an assignment of insurance proceeds (if permitted by Seller's insurance carrier) and receive a credit from the seller at closing in the amount of the deductible under the insurance policy.

The seller is responsible for the property up until the closing date.

DEFAULT

If either party fails to comply with the contract, both parties have the same rights regarding **default**. Paragraph 15 clarifies the parties' rights. The non-defaulting party may enforce **specific performance**, seek other relief as may be provided by law, or both, OR terminate the contract and receive the earnest money as **liquidated damages**, thereby releasing both parties from the contract.

MEDIATION

It is the policy of the state of Texas to encourage dispute resolution through alternative dispute resolution procedures such as mediation. Mediation is fair and efficient, and can help the parties avoid a lengthy investigation and litigation. It is an informal and confidential way to resolve disputes with the help of a neutral mediator who is trained to help people discuss their differences. The mediator does not decide who is right or wrong, or issue a decision. Instead, the mediator helps the parties work out their own solutions to problems. If a dispute arises between the seller and buyer related to the contract and cannot be resolved through informal discussions, the dispute will be submitted to a mutually acceptable mediation service or provider. The parties to the mediation will share the mediation costs equally. Paragraph 16 does not prohibit a party from seeking equitable relief from a court of competent jurisdiction after mediation has been exhausted.

OTHER CONTRACT PROVISIONS

Paragraph 17 allows for the buyer, seller, listing broker, other broker, or escrow agent who prevails in any legal proceeding related to the contract to recover reasonable attorney's fees and all costs of such proceedings from the defaulting party.

13. **PRORATIONS:** Taxes for the current year, interest, maintenance fees, assessments, dues and rents will be prorated through the Closing Date. The tax proration may be calculated taking into consideration any change in exemptions that will affect the current year's taxes. If taxes for the current year vary from the amount prorated at closing, the parties shall adjust the prorations when tax statements for the current year are available. If taxes are not paid at or prior to closing, Buyer shall pay taxes for the current year.

14. **CASUALTY LOSS:** If any part of the Property is damaged or destroyed by fire or other casualty after the effective date of this contract, Seller shall restore the Property to its previous condition as soon as reasonably possible, but in any event by the Closing Date. If Seller fails to do so due to factors beyond Seller's control, Buyer may (a) terminate this contract and the earnest money will be refunded to Buyer (b) extend the time for performance up to 15 days and the Closing Date will be extended as necessary or (c) accept the Property in its damaged condition with an assignment of insurance proceeds, if permitted by Seller's insurance carrier, and receive credit from Seller at closing in the amount of the deductible under the insurance policy. Seller's obligations under this paragraph are independent of any other obligations of Seller under this contract.

15. **DEFAULT:** If Buyer fails to comply with this contract, Buyer will be in default, and Seller may (a) enforce specific performance, seek such other relief as may be provided by law, or both, or (b) terminate this contract and receive the earnest money as liquidated damages, thereby releasing both parties from this contract. If Seller fails to comply with this contract, Seller will be in default and Buyer may (a) enforce specific performance, seek such other relief as may be provided by law, or both, or (b) terminate this contract and receive the earnest money, thereby releasing both parties from this contract.

16. **MEDIATION:** It is the policy of the State of Texas to encourage resolution of disputes through alternative dispute resolution procedures such as mediation. Any dispute between Seller and Buyer related to this contract which is not resolved through informal discussion will be submitted to a mutually acceptable mediation service or provider. The parties to the mediation shall bear the mediation costs equally. This paragraph does not preclude a party from seeking equitable relief from a court of competent jurisdiction.

17. **ATTORNEY'S FEES:** A Buyer, Seller, Listing Broker, Other Broker, or escrow agent who prevails in any legal proceeding related to this contract is entitled to recover reasonable attorney's fees and all costs of such proceeding.

ESCROW PROVISIONS

It is important for licensees to understand what the role of the escrow agent is. The escrow agent is not:

1. A party to the contract and does not have liability for the performance or nonperformance of any party to the contract

2. Liable for interest on the earnest money

3. Liable for the loss of any earnest money caused by the failure of any financial institution in which the earnest money has been deposited unless the financial institution is acting as the escrow agent

Paragraph 18C covers two different situations that may arise:

1. Either party can send a Release of Earnest Money form to the other party. If the parties agree on how and to whom the money should be released, and they both signed the release, the escrow agent may release the earnest money. The escrow agent may also send a Release of Earnest Money form to each party, and the parties will acknowledge (sign) their portion of the release and deliver it back to the escrow agent.

2. If either party fails to execute the release, either party may make a written demand to the escrow agent for the earnest money. The escrow agent must provide a copy of the demand to the other party. If the other party does not respond with a written objection to the demand from the other party within 15 days, the escrow agent may disburse the earnest money to the party making the demand. However, if expenses have been incurred on behalf of the party receiving the money, those expenses may be withheld from the earnest money.

Paragraph 18D relates to the party who wrongfully refuses to sign a release and makes that party liable for liquidated damages in an amount equal to:

1. Damages

2. The earnest money

3. Reasonable attorney's fees

4. All costs of the lawsuit

All notices must be sent in compliance with paragraph 21 of the contract.

Paragraph 19 says that all covenants, representations, and warranties in the contract survive closing. If any representation of the seller is untrue on the closing date, the seller will be in default. Unless expressly prohibited by written agreement, the seller may continue to show the property, and receive, negotiate, and accept back-up offers.

A. ESCROW: The escrow agent is not (i) a party to this contract and does not have liability for the performance or nonperformance of any party to this contract, (ii) liable for interest on the earnest money and (iii) liable for the loss of any earnest money caused by the failure of any financial institution in which the earnest money has been deposited unless the financial institution is acting as escrow agent.
B. EXPENSES: At closing, the earnest money must be applied first to any cash down payment, then to Buyer's Expenses and any excess refunded to Buyer. If no closing occurs, escrow agent may: (i) require a written release of liability of the escrow agent from all parties, (ii) require payment of unpaid expenses incurred on behalf of a party, and (iii) only deduct from the earnest money the amount of unpaid expenses incurred on behalf of the party receiving the earnest money.
C. DEMAND: Upon termination of this contract, either party or the escrow agent may send a release of earnest money to each party and the parties shall execute counterparts of the release and deliver same to the escrow agent. If either party fails to execute the release, either party may make a written demand to the escrow agent for the earnest money. If only one party makes written demand for the earnest money, escrow agent shall promptly provide a copy of the demand to the other party. If escrow agent does not receive written objection to the demand from the other party within 15 days, escrow agent may disburse the earnest money to the party making demand reduced by the amount of unpaid expenses incurred on behalf of the party receiving the earnest money and escrow agent may pay the same to the creditors. If escrow agent complies with the provisions of this paragraph, each party hereby releases escrow agent from all adverse claims related to the disbursal of the earnest money.
D. DAMAGES: Any party who wrongfully fails or refuses to sign a release acceptable to the escrow agent within 7 days of receipt of the request will be liable to the other party for (i) damages; (ii) the earnest money; (iii) reasonable attorney's fees; and (iv) all costs of suit.
E. NOTICES: Escrow agent's notices will be effective when sent in compliance with Paragraph 21. Notice of objection to the demand will be deemed effective upon receipt by escrow agent.

FEDERAL TAX REQUIREMENTS

Internal Revenue Service (IRS) procedures must be followed by the escrow agent. Any questions that arise from paragraph 20 should be answered by qualified and competent sources. TREC prohibits licensees from giving legal advice.

NOTICES

All notices from one party to the other must be in writing and are effective when mailed, hand delivered, or transmitted by facsimile or electronic transmission. Paragraph 21 must be completed by both the buyer and the seller, and should include the most up-to-date information. Due to the nature of real estate transactions, sometimes the buyer or seller will be in transition from one city or state to the next. Therefore, it is extremely important to make sure the most current and up-to-date information is provided in the event that either the buyer or seller must be contacted during the transaction.

21. NOTICES: All notices from one party to the other must be in writing and are effective when mailed to, hand-delivered at, or transmitted by fax or electronic transmission as follows:

To Buyer	**To Seller**
at: _____	at: _____
_____	_____
Phone: (___) _____	Phone: (___) _____
Fax: (___) _____	Fax: (___) _____
E-mail: _____	E-mail: _____

AGREEMENT OF PARTIES

Any additional forms or addenda that are part of the negotiated contract must be identified in paragraph 22. Failure to list or reference an addendum in the agreement can cause confusion at a later date. If it is not referenced in the contract, a court will most likely not accept it as part of the agreement. It is extremely important that the licensee note any and all additional forms or addenda to the agreement in paragraph 22.

Forms not to be listed in paragraph 22 include:

- Seller's disclosure notice
- Information about brokerage services

These documents are part of the transaction file, not the contract. Some title companies may request this information to ensure compliance with disclosure laws, so it is wise to check with the title company before proceeding.

22. AGREEMENT OF PARTIES: This contract contains the entire agreement of the parties and cannot be changed except by their written agreement. Addenda which are a part of this contract are (Check all applicable boxes):

❑ Third Party Financing Addendum

❑ Seller Financing Addendum

❑ Addendum for Property Subject to Mandatory Membership in a Property Owners Association

❑ Buyer's Temporary Residential Lease

❑ Environmental Assessment, Threatened or Endangered Species and Wetlands Addendum

❑ Seller's Temporary Residential Lease

❑ Short Sale Addendum

❑ Addendum for Property Located Seaward of the Gulf Intracoastal Waterway

❏ Loan Assumption Addendum

❏ Addendum for Sale of Other Property by Buyer

❏ Addendum for Reservation of Oil, Gas and Other Minerals

❏ Addendum for "Back-Up" Contract

❏ Addendum for Coastal Area Property

❏ Addendum for Seller's Disclosure of Information on Lead-based Paint and Lead-based Paint Hazards as Required by Federal Law

❏ Addendum for Property in a Propane Gas System Service Area

❏ Other (list): _____
_____

TERMINATION OPTION

The option fee is separate from the earnest money and allows the buyer the unrestricted right to terminate the contract by giving notice of termination to the seller within a predetermined number of days after the effective date of the contract ("Option Period"). If the buyer gives notice of termination within the time prescribed, the option fee will not be refunded; however, any earnest money will be refunded to the buyer. As stated in bold print in paragraph 23 of the contract, time is of the essence for this paragraph, and strict compliance with the time for performance is required. With regard to time, days in the contract are calendar days.

To terminate the contract under this paragraph, the buyer should use a Notice of Buyer's Termination of Contract form (TREC Form 38-4) to terminate the contract. If the Notice of Buyer's Termination of Contract is faxed or emailed, then an electronic return receipt should be used to verify the seller's receipt of the termination.

CONSULT AN ATTORNEY

Paragraph 24 allows for the names of any attorneys representing either the buyer or the seller to be inserted. This is not a requirement, but can be included at the request of the parties.

EXECUTING THE CONTRACT AND FINALIZING THE AGREEMENT

EXECUTING THE CONTRACT

Once the parties have signed the contract, the contract is complete. The effective date of the contract is the date on which the last party accepts the offer. The signatures must match the names of the parties listed in paragraph 1. Once the contract has been fully executed, it can no longer be changed. Any changes must be done with the promulgated Amendment (TREC Form 39-7). The sales contract will have an executed date, and each amendment will have its own executed date—providing a history of the original agreement along with the dates of any further changes.

```
EXECUTED the _____day of _____, 20____ (EFFECTIVE DATE).
(BROKER: FILL IN THE DATE OF FINAL ACCEPTANCE.)
```

FINALIZING THE AGREEMENT

The final page of the contract is for information only. The buyer and the seller signatures complete the agreement between the parties at the end of page 8.

BROKER INFORMATION

Page 9 of the contract asks for the name of the brokerage firms representing the parties (if any), as well as the name of any licensed supervisors overseeing either agent in the transaction. This page should be filled out as completely as possible. This information will be of great service to the escrow agent when preparing the Closing Disclosure. It will also be used in the event that either brokerage or licensee must be contacted. Be sure that the most up-to-date and current information is included on page 9.

After the broker's information is listed, there is space provided for the inclusion of the Other Broker's commission (if any). The Other Broker is the broker responsible for procuring the buyer in the transaction. Furthermore, the other broker is often referred to as the selling broker. Do not confuse "selling broker" with "listing broker." The Listing Broker represents the seller, and the selling broker procures the buyer. Authorization is given to the escrow agent to distribute the commission fee from the listing broker's fee accordingly at closing.

OPTION FEE RECEIPT

The option fee must be delivered to the seller or the seller's agent within three days of the effective date of the contract. Once the seller or seller's agent receives the option fee, the option fee receipt is filled out and acknowledged. The acknowledgment includes the signature of the seller or listing broker, as well as the date it was received.

CONTRACT AND EARNEST MONEY RECEIPT

Upon receiving the fully executed contract, the agent should immediately deposit the contract and earnest money—if any—to the escrow agent.

Contract Concerning _____ Page 9 of 9   11-2-2015
(Address of Property)

BROKER INFORMATION
(Print name(s) only. Do not sign)

| Other Broker Firm | License No. | Listing Broker Firm | License No. |

represents ☐ Buyer only as Buyer's agent
☐ Seller as Listing Broker's subagent

represents ☐ Seller and Buyer as an intermediary
☐ Seller only as Seller's agent

| Associate's Name | License No. |

| Listing Associate's Name | License No. |

| Licensed Supervisor of Associate | License No. |

| Licensed Supervisor of Listing Associate | License No. |

| Other Broker's Address | Fax |

| Listing Broker's Office Address | Fax |

| City | State | Zip |

| City | State | Zip |

| Associate's Email Address | Phone |

| Listing Associate's Email Address | Phone |

| Selling Associate's Name | License No. |

| Licensed Supervisor of Selling Associate | License No. |

| Selling Associate's Office Address | Fax |

| City | State | Zip |

| Selling Associate's Email Address | Phone |

Listing Broker has agreed to pay Other Broker_____of the total sales price when the Listing Broker's fee is received. Escrow agent is authorized and directed to pay other Broker from Listing Broker's fee at closing.

OPTION FEE RECEIPT

Receipt of $_____ (Option Fee) in the form of _____ is acknowledged.

_____   _____
Seller or Listing Broker   Date

CONTRACT AND EARNEST MONEY RECEIPT

Receipt of ☐Contract and ☐$_____Earnest Money in the form of _____ is acknowledged.

Escrow Agent: _____   Date: _____

By: _____   _____
                                                                                    Email Address
_____   Phone: (_____)_____
Address
_____   Fax: (_____) _____
City   State   Zip

TREC NO. 20-13

The escrow agent will acknowledge receipt of the contract as well as the earnest money, if any was provided. It is important to note that once the parties have fully executed the contract, TREC rules [Rule 535.159 (I)] require that the licensee deposit the earnest money with the escrow agent on or before the close of the second business day of the escrow company. The only exception would be if the parties agree that a deposit may be delayed and a different time is expressly defined in paragraph 11 of the contract.

SUMMARY

Paragraphs 9 through 24 discuss parts of the contract agreement covering closing, possession, use of temporary lease agreements if possession is different from closing, closing costs of the buyer and the seller, default and default remedies, mediation, and the buyer's rights to terminate. Special attention should be paid to paragraph 11, as it is only to be used to insert factual business statements.

Any changes to the contract agreement after the executed date must be done using the promulgated Amendment form.

CASE STUDY/WORKSHOP

1. Using the One to Four Family Residential (Resale) Contract, where are the seller's expenses found? The buyer's?

2. According to paragraph 23, the option money is to be delivered to whom?

3. If the option money is not delivered to the proper party within the proper time frame, what is the status of the contract?

4. A property closes on February 2. The buyer and seller agreed to a 10-day Seller's Temporary Residential Lease. On February 15, the seller is still in the home. What, if any, remedies does the buyer have?

5. What happens if the buyer fails to pay the option fee to the seller within the required time period? How many days does the buyer have to give the option money to the seller?

6. A property appraises for $200,000 and, prior to closing, sustains $14,000 worth of fire damage. The seller refuses to pay for the repairs. Does the buyer have to cover the expense of the repairs? Why or why not?

LESSONS TO LEARN

Seller Steven and Buyer Barry have contracted to close on a sale on July 31. On July 26, Seller Steven finds out that the moving company that is suppose to move him to another state will be delayed for 7 days. What can Steven do to prevent delaying his closing with Barry?

Chapter 6

The Remaining Promulgated Forms

LEARNING OBJECTIVES

When you have completed this chapter, you will be able to:

1. Describe the differences between the One to Four Family Contract and the new home contracts.

2. Describe the differences between the One to Four Family Contract and the Farm and Ranch Contract.

3. Describe the differences between the One to Four Family Contract and the Residential Condominium Contract.

4. Describe the differences between the One to Four Family Contract and the Unimproved Property Contract.

5. Describe when rollback taxes might affect the parties and how the contracts treat the issue.

KEY TERMS

completed construction	rollback tax
incomplete construction	surface leases
mineral leases	timber interests
mineral rights	water rights
R-value	

OVERVIEW OF FORMS

TREC promulgates six contract forms, 15 addenda (including two residential temporary leases), one amendment, two resale certificates, one notice, two consumer disclosures, and six approved forms. Because the forms change regularly, licensees should visit TREC's website for information about the most current forms. Here are the titles:

PROMULGATED CONTRACTS

- Unimproved Property Contract
- One to Four Family Residential Contract (Resale)
- New Home Contract (Incomplete Construction)
- New Home Contract (Completed Construction)
- Farm and Ranch Contract
- Residential Condominium Contract (Resale)

PROMULGATED ADDENDA

- Addendum for Sale of Other Property by Buyer
- Addendum for Back-Up Contract
- Addendum for Release of Liability on Assumed Loans and/or Restoration of
- Seller's VA Entitlement
- Seller's Temporary Residential Lease
- Buyer's Temporary Residential Lease
- Seller Financing Addendum
- Environmental Assessment, Threatened or Endangered Species, and Wetlands Addendum
- Addendum for Coastal Area Property
- Addendum for Property Located Seaward of the Gulf Intracoastal Waterway
- Addendum for Property Subject to Mandatory Membership in an Owners' Association
- Third Party Financing Addendum for Credit Approval
- Loan Assumption Addendum
- Addendum for Reservation of Oil, Gas and Other Minerals
- Short Sale Addendum
- Addendum for Property in a Propane Gas System Service Area

PROMULGATED AMENDMENT

- Amendment to Contract

PROMULGATED RESALE CERTIFICATES

- Condominium Resale Certificate
- Subdivision Information, Including Resale Certificate for Property Subject to Mandatory Membership in an Owners' Association

PROMULGATED NOTICE

- Notice of Buyer's Termination of Contract

PROMULGATED CONSUMER DISCLOSURES

- Consumer Information Form 1-1
- Disclosure of Relationship with Residential Service Company

APPROVED OPTIONAL/VOLUNTARY USE FORMS

- Notice to Prospective Buyer
- Seller's Disclosure of Property Condition
- Texas Real Estate Consumer Notice Concerning Hazards or Deficiencies
- Information About Brokerage Services
- Lead-Based Paint Addendum
- Non-Realty Items Addendum

The previous chapters discussed the One to Four Family Residential Contract (Resale). Although all six of the promulgated contracts are similar, there are important distinctions that will be discussed in this chapter.

DIFFERENCES BETWEEN ONE TO FOUR FAMILY RESIDENTIAL (RESALE) AND OTHER CONTRACTS

The following is a list of the important distinctions between the One to Four Family Residential Contract (Resale) and the other five contracts:

1. Paragraph 2 is different in each contract, describing the type of property that is covered.
2. Paragraph 3 is only different in the Farm and Ranch Contract because the sales price can be adjusted by the survey.

3. Paragraph 6 is different in the Condominium Contract and the Farm and Ranch Contract. The Farm and Ranch Contract allows for information regarding exception documents and surface leases. Paragraph 6G7 discusses Texas agricultural development districts.

4. Paragraph 7 is different in both of the New Home Contracts, as well as in the Unimproved Property Contract, and the Farm and Ranch Contract. Different seller's disclosures are required by the type of property and are contained in these paragraphs.

5. Paragraph 12 is only different on the Condominium Contract. It addresses Association fees and deposits.

6. Paragraph 13 is different in both of the New Home Contracts, as well as in the Unimproved Property Contract, the Farm and Ranch Contract, and the Condominium Contract, but for different reasons.

   a. For the New Home Contract, the Unimproved Property Contract, and the Farm and Ranch Contract, Paragraph 13 explains that there is a possibility of the assessment of rollback taxes. Rollback taxes can be assessed when the property's zoning is changing. The amount of rollback taxes can be a significant amount. The contract forms require that the party changing the property's use be responsible for the rollback assessment. It is important that the parties do thorough due diligence and understand rollback taxes and the amount of the assessment before agreeing to be responsible for them.

   b. Paragraph 13 of the condominium contract states the following regarding prorations: "Cash reserves from regular condominium assessments for deferred maintenance or capital improvements established by the Association will not be credited to seller. Any special condominium assessment due and unpaid at closing will be the obligation of the seller."

7. Due to the nature of condominium ownership, and because the seller is only obligated to maintain and repair his or her unit, paragraph 14 is different only in the Condominium Contract. The casualty loss is clearly defined.

RESIDENTIAL CONDOMINIUM CONTRACT

Except for the provisions relating solely to condominium transactions and the statutory requirements of the Texas Uniform Condominium Act (Chapters 81 and 82 of the Texas Property Code), the Residential Condominium Contract is comparable to the One to Four Family Residential Contract (Resale). Ownership of a condominium involves individual ownership of the air space within the unit itself, plus shared ownership of common facilities such as halls, elevators, and the land as undivided interests.

Paragraph 2 reveals the primary difference between the condominium form and the single-family form. The condominium form includes information about the condominium project, as well as parking areas assigned to the unit. Paragraph 2 also discloses the declaration, bylaws and any rules of the Association that the buyer will need. The Resale Certificate from the condominium owners' association is also required and must have been prepared no more than three months before the date it is delivered to the buyer. It must contain, at a minimum, the information required by section 82.157 of the Texas Property Code. TREC has promulgated a Resale Certificate for condominium resale contracts.

A. The Condominium Unit, improvements and accessories described below are collectively referred to as the "Property".
(1) CONDOMINIUM UNIT: Unit _____, in Building _____,
of _____, a condominium project, located at
_____
(address/zip code), City of _____,County of _____
_____,
Texas, described in the Condominium Declaration and Plat and any amendments thereto of record in said County; together with such Unit's undivided interest in the Common Elements designated by the Declaration, including those areas reserved as Limited Common Elements appurtenant to the Unit and such other rights to use the Common Elements which have been specifically assigned to the Unit in any other manner. Parking areas assigned to the Unit are:_____
_____.

The other significant difference is found in paragraph 6, where the survey provisions have been deleted. Because the owners of a condominium project own the land as undivided interests, no survey is required.

Paragraphs 12A(3) and 12A(4) address Association fees and deposits.

(3) Except as provided by 12(A)(4) below, Buyer shall pay any and all Association fees or other charges resulting from the transfer of the Property not to exceed $___ and Seller shall pay any excess.
(4) Buyer shall pay any deposits for reserves required at closing by the Association.

As noted earlier, paragraph 13 addresses cash reserves from regular condominium assessments for deferred maintenance for capital improvements established by the Association. Paragraph 14 clearly defines casualty loss.

FARM AND RANCH CONTRACT

Farm and ranch properties have many unique features that differ from urban or suburban single-family dwellings. The Farm and Ranch Contract calls for a metes and bounds legal description rather than reference to a recorded plat. The other unique features include:

- Equipment
- Crops

- **Mineral rights**
- Oil and gas rights
- **Water rights**
- Other restrictions and exceptions already existing
- Other restrictions and exceptions to be created
- Royalties
- **Surface leases**
- **Mineral leases**
- **Timber interests**
- Rights and obligations of applicable government programs and cooperative or Association memberships

A unique feature of the contract is the provision in paragraph 3 that allows for an adjustment to the sales price based on the results of the survey that may be done after the effective date of the contract. The contract limits the adjustment to 10% of the sales price and allows either party the right to terminate the agreement based on the adjustment, if needed.

D. The Sales Price ❑ will ❑ will not be adjusted based on the survey required by Paragraph 6C. If the Sales Price is adjusted, the Sales Price will be calculated on the basis of $ _____ per acre. If the Sales Price is adjusted by more than 10%, either party may terminate this contract by providing written notice to the other party within ____ days after the terminating party receives the survey. If neither party terminates this contract or if the variance is 10% or less, the adjustment will be made to the amount in ❑ 3A ❑ 3B ❑ proportionately to 3A and 3B.

Paragraph 13 is unique to the Farm and Ranch, the New Home, and the Unimproved Property Contracts. This paragraph discusses the possibility of the assessment of rollback taxes. For a farm or ranch property, a **rollback tax** is an additional tax that is collected when an agricultural-use property is no longer used for agricultural purposes and no longer qualifies for a reduced tax rate. When the property is changed to non-agricultural use, the difference between the reduced agricultural rate and the higher non-agricultural rate must be paid for a statutory number of years prior to the year of the change in use.

If the sale or buyer's use of the property after closing results in the assessment of additional taxes, penalties or interest (assessments) for periods prior to closing, the assessments will be the obligation of the buyer. If the seller changes the use of the property prior to closing, or a denial of a special-use valuation on the property claimed by the seller results in assessments for periods prior to closing, the assessments will be the obligation of the seller.

It is imperative that the buyer and seller agree about who will pay the roll-back taxes. The county appraisal district that the property is located in will be a valuable resource for calculating an estimate of the rollback tax. The obligations imposed by this paragraph will survive closing.

13. PRORATIONS: Taxes for the current year, interest, maintenance fees, assessments, dues and rents will be prorated through the Closing Date. The tax proration may be calculated taking into consideration any change in exemptions that will affect the current year's taxes. If taxes for the current year vary from the amount prorated at closing, the parties shall adjust the prorations when tax statements for the current year are available. If taxes are not paid at or prior to closing, Buyer shall pay taxes for the current year.

UNIMPROVED PROPERTY CONTRACT

Because there are no improvements, fixtures, or accessories found on an unimproved property, paragraph 2 of the Unimproved Property Contract only provides for a legal description. Prior to purchasing unimproved property, the buyer should research availability of utilities, access, restrictive covenants, zoning ordinances, property tax exemptions, and any other matter that may affect the suitability of the property for the buyer's intended use of it.

2. PROPERTY: Lot _____, Block _____, _____Addition, City of _____, County of_____, Texas, known as_____ (address/zip code), or as described on attached exhibit together with all rights, privileges and appurtenances pertaining thereto, including but not limited to: water rights, claims, permits, strips and gores, easements, and cooperative or association memberships (the Property).

NEW HOME CONTRACT

Most builders will require the contract form that they provide, and property owners may instruct licensees to use a form they prefer rather than a TREC promulgated form. If the builder or property owner does not specify a particular contract use, new homes may be sold using one of two promulgated TREC forms:

- **Completed Construction**
- **Incomplete Construction**

The main differences in these two contracts involve the property and the property condition (paragraphs 2 and 7, respectively).

2. PROPERTY: Lot _____,Block_____,
_____Addition, City
of_____,County of_____,
Texas, known as _____
(address/zip code), or as described on attached exhibit, together with: (i) improvements, fixtures and all other property located thereon; and (ii) all rights, privileges and appurtenances thereto, including but not limited to: permits, easements, and cooperative and association memberships. All property sold by this contract is called the "Property".

2. PROPERTY: Lot _____,Block_____, _____
Addition, City of_____,County of _____Texas, known
as _____(address/zip code), or as
described on attached exhibit, together with: (i) improvements, fixtures and all other property described in the Construction Documents; and (ii) all rights, privileges and appurtenances thereto, including but not limited to: permits, easements, and cooperative and association memberships. All property sold by this contract is called the "Property".

Federal law requires that builders disclose to the buyer the **R-value** of the insulation installed in the new home. The R-value is a measure of insulation. The higher the R-value, the better resistance to the transfer of heat. This value may be included in the contract or in an addendum attached to the contract. The TREC promulgated contracts address the R-value factors in the property condition paragraph. Other topics that should be addressed include the following:

■ Access and inspections

■ Construction documents

■ Cost adjustments (change orders)

■ Buyer's selections

■ Dates of completion

■ Warranties

It is important that a buyer not assume that everything in a new home is correctly installed and working properly. Licensees should advise the client to have the property inspected by licensed inspectors throughout the home-building process, as well as seek legal counsel before signing a builder's contract.

7. PROPERTY CONDITION:
A. ACCESS, INSPECTIONS AND UTILITIES: Seller shall permit Buyer and Buyer's agents access to the Property at reasonable times. Buyer may have the Property inspected by inspectors selected by Buyer and licensed by TREC or otherwise permitted by law to make inspections. Seller at Seller's expense shall immediately cause existing utilities to be turned on and shall keep the utilities on during the time this contract is in effect.

B. ACCEPTANCE OF PROPERTY CONDITION: "As Is" means the present condition of the Property with any and all defects and without warranty except for the warranties of title and the warranties in this contract. Buyer's agreement to accept the Property As Is under Paragraph 7B(1) or (2) does not preclude Buyer from inspecting the Property under Paragraph 7A, from negotiating repairs or treatments in a subsequent amendment, or from terminating this contract during the Option Period, if any.
(Check one box only)
❏ (1) Buyer accepts the Property As Is.
❏ (2) Buyer accepts the Property As Is provided Seller, at Seller's expense, shall complete the following specific repairs and treatments:_____
_____(Do not insert general phrases, such as "subject to inspections," that do not identify specific repairs and treatments.)

C. WARRANTIES: Except as expressly set forth in this contract, a separate writing, or provided by law, Seller makes no other express warranties. Seller shall assign to Buyer at closing all assignable manufacturer warranties.

D. INSULATION: As required by Federal Trade Commission Regulations, the information relating to the insulation installed or to be installed in the Improvements at the Property is: (check only one box below)
❏ (1) as shown in the attached specifications.
❏ (2) as follows:
   (a) Exterior walls of improved living areas: insulated with_____
       insulation to a thickness of _____ inches which yields an R-Value of _____.
   (b) Walls in other areas of the home: insulated with_____
       insulation to a thickness of _____ inches which yields an R-Value of _____.
   (c) Ceilings in improved living areas: insulated with___
       insulation to a thickness of _____ inches which yields an R-Value of _____.
   (d) Floors of improved living areas not applied to a slab foundation: insulated with_____
       _____ insulation to a thickness of _____ inches which yields an R-Value of _____.
   (e) Other insulated areas: insulated with _____insulation to a thickness of _____ inches which yields an R-Value of _____.
All stated R-Values are based on information provided by the manufacturer of the insulation.

E. LENDER REQUIRED REPAIRS AND TREATMENTS: Unless otherwise agreed in writing, neither party is obligated to pay for lender required repairs, which includes treatment for wood destroying insects. If the parties do not agree to pay for the lender required repairs or treatments, this contract will terminate and the earnest money will be refunded to Buyer. If the cost of lender required repairs and treatments exceeds 5% of the Sales Price, Buyer may terminate this contract and the earnest money will be refunded to Buyer.

F. COMPLETION OF REPAIRS, TREATMENTS, AND IMPROVEMENTS: Unless otherwise agreed in writing: (i) Seller shall complete all agreed repairs, treatments, and improvements (Work) prior to the Closing Date; and (ii) all required permits must be obtained, and Work must be performed by persons who are licensed to provide such Work or, if no license is required by law, are commercially engaged in the trade of providing such Work. At Buyer's election, any transferable warranties received by Seller with respect to the Work will be transferred to Buyer at Buyer's expense. If Seller fails to complete any agreed Work prior to the Closing Date, Buyer may exercise remedies under Paragraph 15 or extend the Closing Date up to 5 days if necessary for Seller to complete Work.

G. ENVIRONMENTAL MATTERS: Buyer is advised that the presence of wetlands, toxic substances, including asbestos and wastes or other environmental hazards or the presence of a threatened or endangered species or its habitat may affect Buyer's intended use of the Property. If Buyer is concerned about these matters, an addendum promulgated by TREC or required by the parties should be used.

H. SELLER'S DISCLOSURE: Except as otherwise disclosed in this contract, Seller has no knowledge of the following:
   (1) any flooding of the Property which has had a material adverse effect on the use of the Property;
   (2) any pending or threatened litigation, condemnation, or special assessment affecting the Property;
   (3) any environmental hazards that materially and adversely affect the Property;
   (4) any dumpsite, landfill, or underground tanks or containers now or previously located on the Property;
   (5) any wetlands, as defined by federal or state law or regulation, affecting the Property; or
   (6) any threatened or endangered species or their habitat affecting the Property.

    I. RESIDENTIAL SERVICE CONTRACTS: Buyer may purchase a residential service contract from a residential service company licensed by TREC. If Buyer purchases a residential service contract, Seller shall reimburse Buyer at closing for the cost of the residential service contract in an amount not exceeding $_____ . Buyer should review any residential service contract for the scope of coverage, exclusions and limitations. **The purchase of a residential service contract is optional. Similar coverage may be purchased from various companies authorized to do business in Texas.**

7. PROPERTY CONDITION:
    A. ACCESS AND INSPECTIONS: Seller shall permit Buyer and Buyer's agents access to the Property at reasonable times. Buyer may have the Property inspected by inspectors selected by Buyer and licensed by TREC or otherwise permitted by law to make inspections.
    B. CONSTRUCTION DOCUMENTS: Seller shall complete all improvements to the Property with due diligence in accordance with the Construction Documents. "Construction Documents" means the plans and specifications, the finish out schedules, any change orders, and any allowances related to the plans and specifications, finish out schedules, and change orders. The Construction Documents have been signed by the parties and are incorporated into this contract by reference.
    C. COST ADJUSTMENTS: All change orders must be in writing. Increase in costs resulting from change orders or items selected by Buyer which exceed the allowances specified in the Construction Documents will be paid by Buyer as follows:_____
_____.
A decrease in costs resulting from change orders and unused allowances will reduce the Sales Price, with proportionate adjustments to the amounts in Paragraphs 3A and 3B as required by lender.
    D. BUYER'S SELECTIONS: If the Construction Documents permit selections by Buyer, Buyer's selections will conform to Seller's normal standards as set out in the Construction Documents or will not, in Seller's judgment, adversely affect the marketability of the Property. Buyer will make required selections within _____ days after notice from Seller.
    E. COMPLETION: Seller must commence construction no later than _____ days after the effective date of this contract. The improvements will be substantially completed in accordance with the Construction Documents and ready for occupancy not later than _____, 20___ . The improvements will be deemed to be substantially completed in accordance with the Construction Documents upon the final inspection and approval by all applicable governmental authorities and any lender (Substantial Completion Date). Construction delays caused by acts of God, fire or other casualty, strikes, boycotts or nonavailability of materials for which no substitute of comparable quality and price is available will be added to the time allowed for substantial completion of the construction. However, in no event may the time for substantial completion extend beyond the Closing Date. Seller may substitute materials, equipment and appliances of comparable quality for those specified in the Construction Documents.
    F. WARRANTIES: Except as expressly set forth in this contract, a separate writing, or provided by law, Seller makes no other express warranties. Seller shall assign to Buyer at closing all assignable manufacturer warranties.
    G. INSULATION: As required by Federal Trade Commission Regulations, the information relating to the insulation installed or to be installed in the Improvements at the Property is: (check only one box below)
    ☐ (1) as shown in the attached specifications.
    ☐ (2) as follows:
        (a) Exterior walls of improved living areas: insulated with _____ insulation to a thickness of _____ inches which yields an R-Value of _____.
        (b) Walls in other areas of the home: insulated with_____ insulation to a thickness of _____ inches which yields an R-Value of _____.
        (c) Ceilings in improved living areas: insulated with_____ insulation to a thickness of _____ inches which yields an R-Value of _____.
        (d) Floors of improved living areas not applied to a slab foundation: insulated with_____ _____insulation to a thickness of_____ inches which yields an R-Value of _____.
        (e) Other insulated areas: insulated with _____insulation to a thickness of _____ inches which yields an R-Value of _____.
    All stated R-Values are based on information provided by the manufacturer of the insulation.
    H. ENVIRONMENTAL MATTERS: Buyer is advised that the presence of wetlands, toxic substances, including asbestos and wastes or other environmental hazards, or the presence of a threatened or endangered species or its habitat may affect Buyer's intended use of the Property. If Buyer is concerned about these matters, an addendum promulgated by TREC or required by the parties should be used.

I. SELLER'S DISCLOSURE: Except as otherwise disclosed in this contract, Seller has no knowledge of the following:
   (1) any flooding of the Property which has had a material adverse effect on the use of the Property;
   (2) any pending or threatened litigation, condemnation, or special assessment affecting the Property;
   (3) any environmental hazards that materially and adversely affect the Property;
   (4) any dumpsite, landfill, or underground tanks or containers now or previously located on the Property;
   (5) any wetlands, as defined by federal or state law or regulation, affecting the Property; or any threatened or endangered species or their habitat affecting the Property.

SUMMARY

TREC promulgates six contract forms: Complete and Incomplete Construction; Farm and Ranch; Condominium; Unimproved Property; and One to Four Family Residential. The contracts contain much of the same information, but due to differences in property types, their respective contracts will contain different matters.

CASE STUDY/WORKSHOP

1. Which contracts discuss rollback taxes?

2. What happens when paragraph 6G(8) of the Farm and Ranch Contract informs the consumer that the property is subject to a private transfer fee?

3. Which TREC promulgated contract form gives disclosure about the type of insulation in the property?

4. Which TREC promulgated contract form excludes a survey provision?

5. Where does the seller provide disclosure on the Unimproved Property Contract?

6. How many contract forms does TREC promulgate?

LESSONS TO LEARN

REALTOR® Jerry is showing his clients Alex and Julia homes in a newly built subdivision. They fall in a love with a custom builder's spec home. The builder's salesperson is happy to accept Alex and Julia's offer, but writes it on the builder's contract and does not use a TREC promulgated. REALTOR® Jerry is worried about this. What should Jerry do?

Chapter 7

Promulgated Addenda, Notices, and Other Forms

LEARNING OBJECTIVES

When you have completed this chapter, you will be able to:

1. Describe when to use the Addendum for Sale of Other Property by Buyer.

2. Describe when to use the Addendum for Back-Up Contract.

3. Describe when to use the Addendum for Reservation of Oil, Gas and Other Minerals.

4. Describe when to use the Short Sale Addendum.

5. Describe when to use the Addendum for Release of Liability on Assumed Loan and/or Restoration of Seller's VA Entitlement.

6. Describe when to use the Notice of Buyer's Termination of Contract.

7. Describe when to use the Addendum for Coastal Area Property.

8. Describe when to use the Addendum for Property Located Seaward of the Gulf Intracoastal Waterway.

9. Describe when to use the Addendum for Property Subject to Mandatory Membership in a Property Owners' Association.

10. Describe when to use the form Subdivision Information, Including Resale Certificate for Property Subject to Mandatory Membership in a Property Owners' Association.

11. Describe when to use the Condominium Resale Certificate.

12. Describe the purpose of the Consumer Information Form and when to display it.

13. Describe when to use the form Information about Brokerage Services.

14. Describe when to use the Addendum for Property in a Propane Gas System Service Area.

KEY TERMS

Back-Up Contract
short sale
termination

ADDENDUM FOR SALE OF OTHER PROPERTY BY BUYER

If the buyer is unable to purchase a new property unless their existing property closes and funds, it will be necessary to use the Addendum for Sale of Other Property by Buyer. This type of transaction is a contingency agreement, meaning the purchase of the current property is contingent upon the buyer selling their existing property. Typically, this addendum is used when the buyer needs the cash from the first sale to complete the second sale. Use this form when the buyer's present home is already under contract and they're concerned about closing and funding.

Paragraph A is the contingency statement which states that the buyer must receive the proceeds from the sale of the buyer's property on or before a specific date. If the contingency is not satisfied or waived by the buyer by the specified date, the contract will terminate automatically, and the earnest money will be refunded to the buyer.

Paragraph B articulates what will happen if the seller accepts a written offer to sell the property. The seller must notify the buyer of such acceptance and that seller will require the buyer to waive the contingency. The buyer must waive the contingency on or before a specific date after the seller's notice to the buyer; otherwise, the contract will terminate automatically and the earnest money will be refunded to the buyer.

Paragraph C gives the buyer the option to waive the contingency. The buyer must notify the seller of the waiver and deposit an additional amount of earnest money with the escrow agent. All notices and waivers must be in writing and are effective when delivered in accordance with the contract.

Paragraph D warns the buyer that waiving the contingency and failing to close and fund solely due to the buyer's non-receipt of proceeds from the buyer's property described in paragraph A puts the buyer in default to the contract. The seller may exercise the remedies specified in paragraph 15 of the contract.

Paragraph E reminds both parties that time is of the essence and strict compliance with the times for performance is required.

PROMULGATED BY THE TEXAS REAL ESTATE COMMISSION (TREC)

12-05-11

ADDENDUM FOR
SALE OF OTHER PROPERTY BY BUYER

TO CONTRACT CONCERNING THE PROPERTY AT

_____
(Address of Property)

A. The contract is contingent upon Buyer's **receipt of the proceeds** from the sale of Buyer's property
at_____
(Address) on or before _____, 20_____ (the Contingency). If the
Contingency is not satisfied or waived by Buyer by the above date, the contract will terminate
automatically and the earnest money will be refunded to Buyer.

NOTICE: The date inserted in this Paragraph should be no later than the Closing Date specified in
Paragraph 9 of the contract.

B. If Seller accepts a written offer to sell the Property, Seller shall notify Buyer (1) of such acceptance
AND (2) that Seller requires Buyer to waive the Contingency. Buyer must waive the Contingency
on or before the _____ day after Seller's notice to Buyer; otherwise the contract will
terminate automatically and the earnest money will be refunded to Buyer.

C. Buyer may waive the Contingency only by notifying Seller of the waiver and depositing $_____
with escrow agent as additional earnest money. All notices and waivers must be in writing and are
effective when delivered in accordance with the contract.

D. If Buyer waives the Contingency and fails to close and fund solely due to Buyer's non-receipt of
proceeds from Buyer's property described in Paragraph A above, Buyer will be in default. If such
default occurs, Seller may exercise the remedies specified in Paragraph 15 of the contract.

E. For purposes of this Addendum time is of the essence; strict compliance with the times for
performance stated herein is required.

_____   _____
Buyer   Seller

_____   _____
Buyer   Seller

ADDENDUM FOR BACK-UP CONTRACT

A **Back-Up Contract** allows the seller to negotiate with a second buyer and agree upon terms that will be used as a back-up in the event that the first buyer's transaction falls through.

Paragraph A addresses the backup buyer. A Back-Up Contract is binding upon execution by the parties, and the earnest money in any option fee must be paid as provided in the Back-Up Contract. The Back-Up Contract is contingent upon the termination of a previous contract for the sale of the property.

Paragraph B addresses what will happen if the first contract does not terminate on or before a specific date. The seller must notify the buyer immediately upon the termination of the first contract. For purposes of performance, the effective date of the Back-Up Contract changes to the date the buyer receives the notice of termination of the first contract. Simply stated, the effective date will be amended.

Paragraph C says that the seller is free to continue to work with the first buyer, and an amendment or modification of the first contract does not terminate the first contract.

Paragraph D states that if the back-up buyer has an unrestricted right to terminate the Back-Up Contract, the time for giving notice of termination begins on the effective date of the Back-Up Contract. The notice continues after the amended effective date for the number of days agreed to in paragraph 23 of the contract. It ends upon the expiration of the buyer's unrestricted right to terminate the Back-Up Contract.

Paragraph E notifies the parties that time is of the essence and that strict compliance with the times for performance is required.

ADDENDUM FOR RESERVATION OF OIL, GAS AND OTHER MINERALS

The Addendum for Reservation of Oil, Gas and Other Minerals is an addendum for use only if the seller reserves all or a portion of the mineral estate. Mineral estate means all oil, gas, and other minerals in or under the property, any royalty under any existing or future lease covering any part of the property, surface rights (including rights of ingress and egress), production and drilling rights, lease payments, and all related benefits.

Paragraph B states how much of the mineral estate owned by the seller, if any, will be conveyed.

PROMULGATED BY THE TEXAS REAL ESTATE COMMISSION (TREC)   12-05-11

ADDENDUM FOR
"BACK-UP" CONTRACT

TO CONTRACT CONCERNING THE PROPERTY AT

_____

(Address of Property)

A. The contract to which this Addendum is attached (the Back-Up Contract) is binding upon execution by the parties, and the earnest money and any Option Fee must be paid as provided in the Back-Up Contract. The Back-Up Contract is contingent upon the termination of a previous contract (the First Contract) dated _____, 20_____, for the sale of Property. Except as provided by this Addendum, neither party is required to perform under the Back-Up Contract while it is contingent upon the termination of the First Contract.

B. If the First Contract does not terminate on or before _____, 20_____, the Back-Up Contract terminates and the earnest money will be refunded to Buyer. Seller must notify Buyer immediately of the termination of the First Contract. For purposes of performance, the effective date of the Back-Up Contract changes to the date Buyer receives notice of termination of the First Contract (Amended Effective Date).

C. An amendment or modification of the First Contract will not terminate the First Contract.

D. If Buyer has the unrestricted right to terminate the Back-Up Contract, the time for giving notice of termination begins on the effective date of the Back-Up Contract, continues after the Amended Effective Date and ends upon the expiration of Buyer's unrestricted right to terminate the Back-Up Contract.

E. For purposes of this Addendum, time is of the essence. Strict compliance with the times for performance stated herein is required.

_____   _____
Buyer   Seller

_____   _____
Buyer   Seller

Paragraph C instructs whether the seller waives or does not waive their surface rights (including rights of ingress and egress).

Paragraph D states that if Paragraph B(2) applies, then the seller agrees to provide the buyer with the contact information of any existing lessee known to the seller on or before the closing date.

BUYER'S TERMINATION OF CONTRACT

If the buyer exercises his or her right to **terminate** the contract, the Notice of Buyer's Termination of Contract (TREC Form 38-5) must be delivered to the seller prior to the expiration of the option period defined in paragraph 23. Failure to deliver the notice means that the buyer is obligated to close the transaction according to the terms of the contract.

MUTUAL TERMINATION OF CONTRACT

In situations where the termination of an existing contract is mutually agreed upon by both parties, the Mutual Termination of Contract form was created. Although the Broker-Lawyer Committee has been working on the creation of a Mutual Termination of Contract form, the form is still undergoing analysis and has not been approved or adopted at the time of publication of this textbook (December 2015). As always, it is good practice to verify all current and correct contract and addenda forms at the TREC website (http://www.trec.texas.gov/formslawscontracts/forms/forms-contracts.asp).

ADDENDUM FOR PROPERTY LOCATED SEAWARD OF THE GULF INTRACOASTAL WATERWAY

The Addendum for Property Located Seaward of the Gulf Intracoastal Waterway addresses Section 61.025, Texas Natural Resources Code. The form is a disclosure notice concerning legal and economic risks of purchasing coastal real property near a beach.

ADDENDUM FOR COASTAL AREA PROPERTY

The Addendum for Coastal Area Property is a notice for the parties of the transaction regarding coastal area property. The addendum addresses Section 33.135, Texas Natural Resources Code, and addresses properties adjoining or sharing a common boundary with the tidally-influenced, submerged lands of the state. The addendum advises the parties to seek the advice of an attorney or other qualified person as to the legal nature and effect of the addendum.

PROMULGATED BY THE TEXAS REAL ESTATE COMMISSION (TREC)

11-18-14

ADDENDUM FOR RESERVATION OF OIL, GAS, AND OTHER MINERALS

ADDENDUM TO CONTRACT CONCERNING THE PROPERTY AT

_____

(Street Address and City)

NOTICE: For use ONLY if Seller reserves all or a portion of the Mineral Estate.

A. "Mineral Estate" means all oil, gas, and other minerals in and under and that may be produced from the Property, any royalty under any existing or future mineral lease covering any part of the Property, executive rights (including the right to sign a mineral lease covering any part of the Property), implied rights of ingress and egress, exploration and development rights, production and drilling rights, mineral lease payments, and all related rights and benefits. The Mineral Estate does NOT include water, sand, gravel, limestone, building stone, caliche, surface shale, near-surface lignite, and iron, but DOES include the reasonable use of these surface materials for mining, drilling, exploring, operating, developing, or removing the oil, gas, and other minerals from the Property.

B. *Subject to Section C below,* the Mineral Estate owned by Seller, if any, will be conveyed unless reserved as follows (check one box only):

☐ (1) Seller reserves all of the Mineral Estate owned by Seller.

☐ (2) Seller reserves an undivided _____ interest In the Mineral Estate owned by Seller. *NOTE: If Seller does not own all of the Mineral Estate, Seller reserves only this percentage or fraction of Seller's interest.*

C. Seller ☐ does ☐ does *not* reserve and retain implied rights of ingress and egress and of reasonable use of the Property (including surface materials) for mining, drilling, exploring, operating, developing, or removing the oil, gas, and other minerals. *NOTE: Surface rights that may be held by other owners of the Mineral Estate who are not parties to this transaction (including existing mineral lessees) will NOT be affected by Seller's election. Seller's failure to complete Section C will be deemed an election to convey all surface rights described herein.*

D. If Seller does not reserve all of Seller's interest in the Mineral Estate, Seller shall, within 7 days after the Effective Date, provide Buyer with the contact information of any existing mineral lessee known to Seller.

IMPORTANT NOTICE: The Mineral Estate affects important rights, the full extent of which may be unknown to Seller. A full examination of the title to the Property completed by an attorney with expertise in this area is the only proper means for determining title to the Mineral Estate with certainty. In addition, attempts to convey or reserve certain interest out of the Mineral Estate separately from other rights and benefits owned by Seller may have unintended consequences. Precise contract language is essential to preventing disagreements between present and future owners of the Mineral Estate. If Seller or Buyer has any questions about their respective rights and interests in the Mineral Estate and how such rights and interests may be affected by this contract, they are strongly encouraged to consult an attorney with expertise in this area.

CONSULT AN ATTORNEY BEFORE SIGNING: TREC rules prohibit real estate licensees from giving legal advice. READ THIS FORM CAREFULLY.

_____   _____
Buyer   Seller

_____   _____
Buyer   Seller

11-2-15

PROMULGATED BY THE TEXAS REAL ESTATE COMMISSION (TREC)

NOTICE OF BUYER'S TERMINATION OF CONTRACT

CONCERNING THE CONTRACT FOR THE SALE OF THE PROPERTY AT

_____
(Street Address and City)

BETWEEN THE UNDERSIGNED BUYER AND_____

_____ (SELLER)

Buyer notifies Seller that the contract is terminated pursuant to the following:

☐(1) the unrestricted right of Buyer to terminate the contract under Paragraph 23 of the contract.

☐(2) Buyer cannot obtain Buyer Approval in accordance with the Third Party Financing Addendum to the contract.

☐(3) the Property does not satisfy Property Approval in accordance with the Third Party Financing Addendum to the contract.

☐(4) Buyer elects to terminate under Paragraph A of the Addendum for Property Subject to Mandatory Membership in a Property Owners' Association.

☐(5) Buyer elects to terminate under Paragraph 7B(2) of the contract relating to the Seller's Disclosure Notice.

☐(6) Other _(identify the paragraph number of contract or the addendum)_: _____

_____

_____

_____

_____

NOTE: Release of the earnest money is governed by the terms of the contract.

_____   _____
Buyer   Date   Buyer   Date

PROMULGATED BY THE TEXAS REAL ESTATE COMMISSION (TREC)   12-05-11

ADDENDUM FOR
PROPERTY LOCATED SEAWARD OF THE
GULF INTRACOASTAL WATERWAY
(SECTION 61.025, TEXAS NATURAL RESOURCES CODE)

TO CONTRACT CONCERNING THE PROPERTY AT

_____

(Address of Property)

DISCLOSURE NOTICE CONCERNING LEGAL AND ECONOMIC RISKS OF PURCHASING COASTAL REAL PROPERTY NEAR A BEACH

WARNING: THE FOLLOWING NOTICE OF POTENTIAL RISKS OF ECONOMIC LOSS TO YOU AS THE PURCHASER OF COASTAL REAL PROPERTY IS REQUIRED BY STATE LAW.

- READ THIS NOTICE CAREFULLY. DO NOT SIGN THIS CONTRACT UNTIL YOU FULLY UNDERSTAND THE RISKS YOU ARE ASSUMING.

- BY PURCHASING THIS PROPERTY, YOU MAY BE ASSUMING ECONOMIC RISKS OVER AND ABOVE THE RISKS INVOLVED IN PURCHASING INLAND REAL PROPERTY.

- IF YOU OWN A STRUCTURE LOCATED ON COASTAL REAL PROPERTY NEAR A GULF COAST BEACH, IT MAY COME TO BE LOCATED ON THE PUBLIC BEACH BECAUSE OF COASTAL EROSION AND STORM EVENTS.

- AS THE OWNER OF A STRUCTURE LOCATED ON THE PUBLIC BEACH, YOU COULD BE SUED BY THE STATE OF TEXAS AND ORDERED TO REMOVE THE STRUCTURE.

- THE COSTS OF REMOVING A STRUCTURE FROM THE PUBLIC BEACH AND ANY OTHER ECONOMIC LOSS INCURRED BECAUSE OF A REMOVAL ORDER WOULD BE SOLELY YOUR RESPONSIBILITY.

The real property described in this contract is located seaward of the Gulf Intracoastal Waterway to its southernmost point and then seaward of the longitudinal line also known as 97 degrees, 12', 19" which runs southerly to the international boundary from the intersection of the centerline of the Gulf Intracoastal Waterway and the Brownsville Ship Channel. If the property is in close proximity to a beach fronting the Gulf of Mexico, the purchaser is hereby advised that the public has acquired a right of use or easement to or over the area of any public beach by prescription, dedication, or presumption, or has retained a right by virtue of continuous right in the public since time immemorial, as recognized in law and custom.

The extreme seaward boundary of natural vegetation that spreads continuously inland customarily marks the landward boundary of the public easement. If there is no clearly marked natural vegetation line, the landward boundary of the easement is as provided by Sections 61.016 and 61.017, Natural Resources Code.

Much of the Gulf of Mexico coastline is eroding at rates of more than five feet per year. Erosion rates for all Texas Gulf property subject to the open beaches act are available from the Texas General Land Office.

State law prohibits any obstruction, barrier, restraint, or interference with the use of the public easement, including the placement of structures seaward of the landward boundary of the easement. OWNERS OF STRUCTURES ERECTED SEAWARD OF THE VEGETATION LINE (OR OTHER APPLICABLE EASEMENT BOUNDARY) OR THAT BECOME SEAWARD OF THE VEGETATION LINE AS A RESULT OF PROCESSES SUCH AS SHORELINE EROSION ARE SUBJECT TO A LAWSUIT BY THE STATE OF TEXAS TO REMOVE THE STRUCTURES.

The purchaser is hereby notified that the purchaser should: (1) determine the rate of shoreline erosion in the vicinity of the real property; and (2) seek the advice of an attorney or other qualified person before executing this contract or instrument of conveyance as to the relevance of these statutes and facts to the value of the property the purchaser is hereby purchasing or contracting to purchase.

_____   _____
Buyer   Seller

_____   _____
Buyer   Seller

PROMULGATED BY THE TEXAS REAL ESTATE COMMISSION (TREC)

12-05-11

ADDENDUM FOR
COASTAL AREA PROPERTY
(SECTION 33.135, TEXAS NATURAL RESOURCES CODE)

TO CONTRACT CONCERNING THE PROPERTY AT

_____

(Address of Property)

NOTICE REGARDING COASTAL AREA PROPERTY

1. The real property described in and subject to this contract adjoins and shares a common boundary with the tidally influenced submerged lands of the state. The boundary is subject to change and can be determined accurately only by a survey on the ground made by a licensed state land surveyor in accordance with the original grant from the sovereign. The owner of the property described in this contract may gain or lose portions of the tract because of changes in the boundary.

2. The seller, transferor, or grantor has no knowledge of any prior fill as it relates to the property described in and subject to this contract except:_____
_____
_____.

3. State law prohibits the use, encumbrance, construction, or placing of any structure in, on, or over state-owned submerged lands below the applicable tide line, without proper permission.

4. The purchaser or grantee is hereby advised to seek the advice of an attorney or other qualified person as to the legal nature and effect of the facts set forth in this notice on the property described in and subject to this contract. Information regarding the location of the applicable tide line as to the property described in and subject to this contract may be obtained from the surveying division of the General Land Office in Austin.

_____   _____
Buyer   Seller

_____   _____
Buyer   Seller

This form has been approved by the Texas Real Estate Commission for use with similarly approved or promulgated contract forms. Such approval relates to this form only. TREC forms are intended for use only by trained real estate licensees. No representation is made as to the legal validity or adequacy of any provision in any specific transactions. It is not suitable for complex transactions. Texas Real Estate Commission, P.O. Box 12188, Austin, TX 78711-2188, 512-936-3000 (http://www.trec.texas.gov) TREC No. 33-2 This form replaces TREC No. 33-1.

ADDENDUM FOR PROPERTY SUBJECT TO MANDATORY MEMBERSHIP IN AN OWNERS' ASSOCIATION

Paragraph 6E(2) of the contract addresses mandatory membership in an owners' association. The licensee should fill out the addendum for Property Subject to Mandatory Membership in an Owners' Association in order to get details about the owners' association dues, subdivision information, and any deposits for reserves that may be applicable.

SHORT SALE ADDENDUM

The Short Sale Addendum is the form that attaches to the contract involving a "short sale" of the property. **Short sale** means that the seller's net proceeds at closing will be insufficient to pay the balance of the seller's mortgage loan and that the seller must have the consent of the lienholder to sell the property. The lienholder must agree to accept the seller's net proceeds as full satisfaction of the seller's liability under the mortgage loan, and also provide the seller an executed release of lien against the property that will be recorded at closing. If there is more than one lienholder or loan secured by the property, this addendum applies to each lienholder.

It is imperative that the listing agent contact the lender as soon as the property is listed and make sure that all parties follow the lender's instructions precisely. Without the lender's cooperation, a short sale transaction cannot close.

ADDENDUM FOR PROPERTY IN A PROPANE GAS SYSTEM SERVICE AREA

The Addendum for Property in a Propane Gas System Service Area (TREC Form 47-0) is one of the newest TREC promulgated forms. If the property is located in a propane gas system service area, this form notifies the buyer that there may be special costs or charges that he or she will be required to pay before they can receive a propane gas service. The addendum advises the buyer to determine if the property is in a propane gas system service area. Upon finding out that the property IS located in a propane gas service area, the buyer should contact the distribution system retailer to determine the cost that will be required to pay, and the period, if any, that is required to provide propane gas service to the property. The buyer must acknowledge and sign the notice prior to or at the execution of a binding contract for the purchase property.

PROMULGATED BY THE TEXAS REAL ESTATE COMMISSION (TREC)   08-18-2014

ADDENDUM FOR PROPERTY SUBJECT TO MANDATORY MEMBERSHIP IN A PROPERTY OWNERS ASSOCIATION
(NOT FOR USE WITH CONDOMINIUMS)
ADDENDUM TO CONTRACT CONCERNING THE PROPERTY AT

_____

(Street Address and City)

_____

(Name of Property Owners Association, (Association) and Phone Number)

A. SUBDIVISION INFORMATION: "Subdivision Information" means: (i) a current copy of the restrictions applying to the subdivision and bylaws and rules of the Association, and (ii) a resale certificate, all of which are described by Section 207.003 of the Texas Property Code.

(Check only one box):

❑ 1. Within _____ days after the effective date of the contract, Seller shall obtain, pay for, and deliver the Subdivision Information to the Buyer. If Seller delivers the Subdivision Information, Buyer may terminate the contract within 3 days after Buyer receives the Subdivision Information or prior to closing, whichever occurs first, and the earnest money will be refunded to Buyer. If Buyer does not receive the Subdivision Information, Buyer, as Buyer's sole remedy, may terminate the contract at any time prior to closing and the earnest money will be refunded to Buyer.

❑ 2. Within _____ days after the effective date of the contract, Buyer shall obtain, pay for, and deliver a copy of the Subdivision Information to the Seller. If Buyer obtains the Subdivision Information within the time required, Buyer may terminate the contract within 3 days after Buyer receives the Subdivision Information or prior to closing, whichever occurs first, and the earnest money will be refunded to Buyer. If Buyer, due to factors beyond Buyer's control, is not able to obtain the Subdivision Information within the time required, Buyer may, as Buyer's sole remedy, terminate the contract within 3 days after the time required or prior to closing, whichever occurs first, and the earnest money will be refunded to Buyer.

❑ 3.Buyer has received and approved the Subdivision Information before signing the contract. Buyer ❑ does ❑ does not require an updated resale certificate. If Buyer requires an updated resale certificate, Seller, at Buyer's expense, shall deliver it to Buyer within 10 days after receiving payment for the updated resale certificate from Buyer. Buyer may terminate this contract and the earnest money will be refunded to Buyer if Seller fails to deliver the updated resale certificate within the time required.

❑ 4.Buyer does not require delivery of the Subdivision Information.

The title company or its agent is authorized to act on behalf of the parties to obtain the Subdivision Information ONLY upon receipt of the required fee for the Subdivision Information from the party obligated to pay.

B. MATERIAL CHANGES. If Seller becomes aware of any material changes in the Subdivision Information, Seller shall promptly give notice to Buyer. Buyer may terminate the contract prior to closing by giving written notice to Seller if: (i) any of the Subdivision Information provided was not true; or (ii) any material adverse change in the Subdivision Information occurs prior to closing, and the earnest money will be refunded to Buyer.

C FEES: Except as provided by Paragraphs A, D and E, Buyer shall pay any and all Association fees or other charges associated with the transfer of the Property not to exceed $_____ and Seller shall pay any excess.

D. DEPOSITS FOR RESERVES: Buyer shall pay any deposits for reserves required at closing by the Association.

E. AUTHORIZATION: Seller authorizes the Association to release and provide the Subdivision Information and any updated resale certificate if requested by the Buyer, the Title Company, or any broker to this sale. If Buyer does not require the Subdivision Information or an updated resale certificate, and the Title Company requires information from the Association (such as the status of dues, special assessments, violations of covenants and restrictions, and a waiver of any right of first refusal), ❑ Buyer ❑ Seller shall pay the Title Company the cost of obtaining the information prior to the Title Company ordering the information.

NOTICE TO BUYER REGARDING REPAIRS BY THE ASSOCIATION: The Association may have the sole responsibility to make certain repairs to the Property. If you are concerned about the condition of any part of the Property which the Association is required to repair, you should not sign the contract unless you are satisfied that the Association will make the desired repairs.

_____   _____
Buyer   Seller

_____   _____
Buyer   Seller

PROMULGATED BY THE TEXAS REAL ESTATE COMMISSION (TREC)   12-05-11

SHORT SALE ADDENDUM

ADDENDUM TO CONTRACT CONCERNING THE PROPERTY AT

_____

(Street Address and City)

A. This contract involves a "short sale" of the Property. As used in this Addendum, "short sale" means that:

   (1) Seller's net proceeds at closing will be insufficient to pay the balance of Seller's mortgage loan; and

   (2) Seller requires:
      (a) the consent of the lienholder to sell the Property pursuant to this contract; and
      (b) the lienholder's agreement to:
         (i) accept Seller's net proceeds in full satisfaction of Seller's liability under the mortgage loan; and
         (ii) provide Seller an executed release of lien against the Property in a recordable format.

B. As used in this Addendum, "Seller's net proceeds" means the Sales Price less Seller's Expenses under Paragraph 12 of the contract and Seller's obligation to pay any brokerage fees.

C. The contract to which this Addendum is attached is binding upon execution by the parties and the earnest money and the Option Fee must be paid as provided in the contract. The contract is contingent on the satisfaction of Seller's requirements under Paragraph A(2) of this Addendum (Lienholder's Consent and Agreement). Seller shall apply promptly for and make every reasonable effort to obtain Lienholder's Consent and Agreement, and shall furnish all information and documents required by the lienholder. Except as provided by this Addendum, neither party is required to perform under the contract while it is contingent upon obtaining Lienholder's Consent and Agreement.

D. If Seller does not notify Buyer that Seller has obtained Lienholder's Consent and Agreement on or before _____, this contract terminates and the earnest money will be refunded to Buyer. Seller must notify Buyer immediately if Lienholder's Consent and Agreement is obtained. For purposes of performance, the effective date of the contract changes to the date Seller provides Buyer notice of the Lienholder's Consent and Agreement (Amended Effective Date).

E. This contract will terminate and the earnest money will be refunded to Buyer if the Lienholder refuses or withdraws its Consent and Agreement prior to closing and funding. Seller shall promptly notify Buyer of any lienholder's refusal to provide or withdrawal of a Lienholder's Consent and Agreement.

F. If Buyer has the unrestricted right to terminate this contract, the time for giving notice of termination begins on the effective date of the contract, continues after the Amended Effective Date and ends upon the expiration of Buyer's unrestricted right to terminate the contract under Paragraph 23.

G. For the purposes of this Addendum, time is of the essence. Strict compliance with the times for performance stated in this Addendum is required.

H. Seller authorizes any lienholder to furnish to Buyer or Buyer's representatives information relating to the status of the request for a Lienholder's Consent and Agreement.

I. If there is more than one lienholder or loan secured by the Property, this Addendum applies to each lienholder.

_____   _____
Buyer   Seller

_____   _____
Buyer   Seller

PROMULGATED BY THE TEXAS REAL ESTATE COMMISSION (TREC)

2-10-2014

ADDENDUM FOR PROPERTY IN A
PROPANE GAS SYSTEM SERVICE AREA
(Section 141.010, Utilities Code)

CONCERNING THE PROPERTY AT _____

(Street Address and City)

NOTICE

The above referenced real property that you are about to purchase may be located in a propane gas system service area, which is authorized by law to provide propane gas service to the properties in the area pursuant to Chapter 141, Utilities Code. If your property is located in a propane gas system service area, there may be special costs or charges that you will be required to pay before you can receive propane gas service. There may be a period required to construct lines or other facilities necessary to provide propane gas service to your property. You are advised to determine if the property is in a propane gas system service area and contact the distribution system retailer to determine the cost that you will be required to pay and the period, if any, that is required to provide propane gas service to your property.

Buyer hereby acknowledges receipt of this notice at or before execution of a binding contract for the purchase of the above referenced real property or at the closing of the real property.

Section 141.010(a), Utilities Code, requires this notice to include a copy of the notice the distribution system retailer is required to record in the real property records. A copy of the recorded notice is attached.

NOTE: Seller can obtain a copy of the required recorded notice from the county clerk's office where the property is located or from the distribution system retailer.

_____   _____   _____   _____
Buyer   Date   Seller   Date

_____   _____   _____   _____
Buyer   Date   Seller   Date

NON-CONTRACT FORMS

PROMULGATED RESALE CERTIFICATES

The Subdivision Information, Including Resale Certificates for Property Subject to Mandatory Membership in a Property Owners' Association addendum (TREC Form 37-5) is used when a property is subject to mandatory membership in a property owners' association, and the buyer wants more information about the membership and subdivision information. This form is ONLY used for residential purchase transactions and not for condominium transactions.

TREC promulgates a Condominium Resale Certificate (TREC Form 32-4) which addresses section 82.157, Texas Property Code.

The form is filled out by the representative of the homeowners' association—not the licensee. Typically, a fee is assessed for filling out the form.

CONSUMER INFORMATION FORM

The Consumer Information Form (TREC Form CN 1-2) must be prominently displayed in the office of every licensed broker and inspector in Texas.

INFORMATION ABOUT BROKERAGE SERVICES FORM

There are four positions a broker might take when doing business with a seller, buyer, landlord, or tenant. Section 1101.558 of the real estate license act requires that "a licensee shall provide to a party to a real estate transaction at the time of the first substantive dialogue with the party" a "written statement" that sets forth the generalized information relative to seller representation, the agency, buyer representation, and the intermediary position. The TREC promulgated Information about Brokerage Services form (TREC Form IABS 1-0) is approved by the Texas Real Estate Commission for use when disclosing information about brokerage services.

According to the revised Section 1101.558(c) of The Real Estate License Act: (effective on January 01, 2016) (c) A license holder is not required to provide the notice required by Subsection (b-1) if:"

1. the proposed transaction is for a residential lease for less than one year and a sale is not being considered;
2. the license holder meets with a party who the license holder knows is represented by another license holder; or
3. the communication occurs at a property that is held open for any prospective buyer or tenant and the communication concerns that property.

PROMULGATED BY THE TEXAS REAL ESTATE COMMISSION (TREC)

2-10-2014

SUBDIVISION INFORMATION, INCLUDING
RESALE CERTIFICATE FOR PROPERTY SUBJECT TO
MANDATORY MEMBERSHIP IN A PROPERTY OWNERS' ASSOCIATION
(Chapter 207, Texas Property Code)

Resale Certificate concerning the Property (including any common areas assigned to the Property) located at _____(Street Address), City of _____, County of _____, Texas, prepared by the property owners' association (Association).

A. The Property ❑is ❑ is not subject to a right of first refusal (other than a right of first refusal prohibited by statute) or other restraint contained in the restrictions or restrictive covenants that restricts the owner's right to transfer the owner's property.

B. The current regular assessment for the Property is $_____ per _____.

C. A special assessment for the Property due after this resale certificate is delivered is $_____ payable as follows_____ for the following purpose:_____.

D. The total of all amounts due and unpaid to the Association that are attributable to the Property is $ _____ .

E. The capital expenditures approved by the Association for its current fiscal year are $ _____.

F. The amount of reserves for capital expenditures is $_____.

G. Unsatisfied judgments against the Association total $_____.

H. Other than lawsuits relating to unpaid ad valorem taxes of an individual member of the association, there ❑ are ❑ are not any suits pending in which the Association is a party. The style and cause number of each pending suit is: _____.

I. The Association's board ❑has actual knowledge ❑has no actual knowledge of conditions on the Property in violation of the restrictions applying to the subdivision or the bylaws or rules of the Association. Known violations are: _____.

J. The Association ❑has ❑has not received notice from any governmental authority regarding health or building code violations with respect to the Property or any common areas or common facilities owned or leased by the Association. A summary or copy of each notice is attached.

K. The amount of any administrative transfer fee charged by the Association for a change of ownership of property in the subdivision is $_____. Describe all fees associated with the transfer of ownership (include a description of each fee, to whom each fee is payable and the amount of each fee)._____

_____

_____

TREC NO. 37⁼5

Subdivision Information Concerning _____ Page 2 of 2   2-10-2014
(Address of Property)

L. The Association's managing agent is _____
(Name of Agent)

_____
(Mailing Address)

_____   _____
(Telephone Number)   (Fax Number)

_____
(E-mail Address)

M. The restrictions ❑ do ❑ do not allow foreclosure of the Association's lien on the Property for failure to pay assessments.
   REQUIRED ATTACHMENTS:

   1. Restrictions   5. Current Operating Budget

   2. Rules   6. Certificate of Insurance concerning Property and Liability Insurance for Common Areas and Facilities

   3. Bylaws

   4. Current Balance Sheet   7. Any Governmental Notices of Health or Housing Code Violations

NOTICE: This Subdivision Information may change at any time.

_____
Name of Association

By: _____

Print Name: _____

Title: _____

Date: _____

Mailing Address: _____

E-mail: _____

Source: Reprinted with permission of the Texas Real Estate Commission   TREC NO. 37=5

PROMULGATED BY THE TEXAS REAL ESTATE COMMISSION (TREC)   8-17-2015

CONDOMINIUM RESALE CERTIFICATE
(Section 82.157, Texas Property Code)

Condominium Certificate concerning Condominium Unit _____, in Building _____, of _____
_____,a condominium project, located at _____
_____(Address), City of _____,
County of _____, Texas, on behalf of the condominium owners' association
(the Association) by the Association's governing body (the Board).

A. The Declaration ❑does ❑does not contain a right of first refusal or other restraint that restricts
   the right to transfer the Unit. If a right of first refusal or other restraint exists, see Section
   _____of the Declaration.

B. The periodic common expense assessment for the Unit is $_____ per _____.

C. There ❑ is ❑is not a common expense or special assessment due and unpaid by the Seller to the
   Association. The total unpaid amount is $_____ and is for _____.

D. Other amounts ❑are ❑are not payable by Seller to the Association. The total unpaid amount is
   $_____and is for _____.

E. Capital expenditures approved by the Association for the next 12 months are $_____.

F. Reserves for capital expenditures are $_____;of this amount $_____
   has been designated for_____.

G. The current operating budget and balance sheet of the Association is attached.

H. The amount of unsatisfied judgments against the Association is $ _____.

I. There ❑are ❑are not any suits pending against the Association. The nature of the suits is
   _____.

J. The Association ❑does ❑does not provide insurance coverage for the benefit of unit owners as per
   the attached summary from the Association's insurance agent.

K. The Board ❑has ❑has no knowledge of alterations or improvements to the Unit or to the limited
   common elements assigned to the Unit or any portion of the project that violate any provision of the
   Declaration, by-laws or rules of the Association. Known violations are:_____
   _____.

L. The Board ❑has ❑has not received notice from a governmental authority concerning violations
   of health or building codes with respect to the Unit, the limited common elements assigned to the
   Unit, or any other portion of the condominium project. Notices received are: _____
   _____.

M. The remaining term of any leasehold estate that affects the condominium is _____
   and the provisions governing an extension or a renewal of the lease are: _____
   _____
   _____.

N. The Association's managing agent is _____
                                                        (Name of Agent)

   _____
                                        (Mailing Address)

   _____   _____
           (Phone)   (Fax)

   _____
                                      (E-mail Address)

Condominium Resale Certificate Concerning   Page 2 of 2

_____
(Address of Property)

O. Association fees resulting from the transfer of the unit described above:

Description	Paid To	Amount
_____	_____	_____
_____	_____	_____
_____	_____	_____

P. Required contribution, if any, to the capital reserves account $_____.

REQUIRED ATTACHMENTS:
1. Operating Budget
2. Insurance Summary
3. Balance Sheet

NOTICE: The Certificate must be prepared no more than three months before the date it is delivered to Buyer.

_____
Name of Association

By: _____

Name: _____

Title: _____

Date:_____

Mailing Address: _____

E-mail: _____

THE TEXAS REAL ESTATE COMMISSION (TREC) REGULATES
REAL ESTATE BROKERS AND SALES AGENTS, REAL ESTATE INSPECTORS,
HOME WARRANTY COMPANIES, EASEMENT AND RIGHT-OF-WAY AGENTS,
AND TIMESHARE INTEREST PROVIDERS

YOU CAN FIND MORE INFORMATION AND
CHECK THE STATUS OF A LICENSE HOLDER AT

WWW.TREC.TEXAS.GOV

YOU CAN SEND A COMPLAINT AGAINST A LICENSE HOLDER TO TREC

A COMPLAINT FORM IS AVAILABLE ON THE TREC WEBSITE

TREC ADMINISTERS TWO RECOVERY FUNDS WHICH MAY BE USED TO
SATISFY A CIVIL COURT JUDGMENT AGAINST A BROKER, SALES AGENT,
REAL ESTATE INSPECTOR, OR EASEMENT OR RIGHT-OF-WAY AGENT,
IF CERTAIN REQUIREMENTS ARE MET

IF YOU HAVE QUESTIONS OR ISSUES ABOUT THE ACTIVITIES OF
A LICENSE HOLDER, THE COMPLAINT PROCESS OR THE
RECOVERY FUNDS, PLEASE VISIT THE WEBSITE OR CONTACT TREC AT

TEXAS REAL ESTATE COMMISSION
P.O. BOX 12188
AUSTIN, TEXAS 78711-2188

(512) 936-3000

Substantive dialogue means a meeting or written communication that involves a substantive discussion relating to specific real property. A face-to-face meeting with the prospective client in which properties are discussed is considered a substantive dialogue. Any written correspondence, including email or other electronic means, about specific properties constitutes a substantive dialogue.

Substantive dialogue requiring an agent to give a party the information about brokerage services does not include a meeting at an open house or a meeting that occurs after the parties have signed a contract. However, the Real Estate License Act does require that an agent *disclose* to persons visiting an open house (either orally or in writing) that he or she represents the seller [Section 1101.558].

TEXAS REAL ESTATE CONSUMER NOTICE CONCERNING HAZARDS OR DEFICIENCIES

The Texas Real Estate Consumer Notice Concerning Hazards or Deficiencies (TREC Form OP-I) is an optional form that can be used to assist with explaining inspection reports. To ensure that consumers are informed of hazards due to prior-year building codes, the Texas Real Estate Commission has adopted Standards of Practice requiring licensed inspectors to report these conditions as "deficient" when performing an inspection for a buyer or seller, if they can be reasonably determined.

These conditions may not have violated building codes or common practices at the time of the construction of the home, or they may have been "grandfathered" in because they were present prior to the adoption of codes prohibiting such conditions. While the TREC Standards of Practice do not require inspectors to perform a code compliance inspection, TREC considers the potential for injury or property loss from the hazards addressed in the Standards of Practice to be significant enough to warrant this notice.

NON-REALTY ITEMS

The Non-Realty Items Addendum (TREC Form OP-M) is used if the buyer would like to add additional items of personal property that are to stay with the property that are not already listed in paragraph 2B or 2C of the sales contract. Some examples would be the refrigerator, washer, or dryer. The licensee should specify each item carefully and include the description, model numbers, serial numbers, location, and other information that would identify the personal property. The form is then signed by the buyer and seller and attached to the sales contract. Furthermore, the form is also listed in paragraph 22 of the contract.

11-2-2015

Information About Brokerage Services

Texas law requires all real estate license holders to give the following information about brokerage services to prospective buyers, tenants, sellers and landlords.

TYPES OF REAL ESTATE LICENSE HOLDERS:
- **A BROKER** is responsible for all brokerage activities, including acts performed by sales agents sponsored by the broker.
- **A SALES AGENT** must be sponsored by a broker and works with clients on behalf of the broker.

A BROKER'S MINIMUM DUTIES REQUIRED BY LAW (A client is the person or party that the broker represents):
- Put the interests of the client above all others, including the broker's own interests;
- Inform the client of any material information about the property or transaction received by the broker;
- Answer the client's questions and present any offer to or counter-offer from the client; and
- Treat all parties to a real estate transaction honestly and fairly.

A LICENSE HOLDER CAN REPRESENT A PARTY IN A REAL ESTATE TRANSACTION:

AS AGENT FOR OWNER (SELLER/LANDLORD): The broker becomes the property owner's agent through an agreement with the owner, usually in a written listing to sell or property management agreement. An owner's agent must perform the broker's minimum duties above and must inform the owner of any material information about the property or transaction known by the agent, including information disclosed to the agent or subagent by the buyer or buyer's agent.

AS AGENT FOR BUYER/TENANT: The broker becomes the buyer/tenant's agent by agreeing to represent the buyer, usually through a written representation agreement. A buyer's agent must perform the broker's minimum duties above and must inform the buyer of any material information about the property or transaction known by the agent, including information disclosed to the agent by the seller or seller's agent.

AS AGENT FOR BOTH - INTERMEDIARY: To act as an intermediary between the parties the broker must first obtain the written agreement of *each party* to the transaction. The written agreement must state who will pay the broker and, in conspicuous bold or underlined print, set forth the broker's obligations as an intermediary. A broker who acts as an intermediary:
- Must treat all parties to the transaction impartially and fairly;
- May, with the parties' written consent, appoint a different license holder associated with the broker to each party (owner and buyer) to communicate with, provide opinions and advice to, and carry out the instructions of each party to the transaction.
- Must not, unless specifically authorized in writing to do so by the party, disclose:
  - o that the owner will accept a price less than the written asking price;
  - o that the buyer/tenant will pay a price greater than the price submitted in a written offer; and
  - o any confidential information or any other information that a party specifically instructs the broker in writing not to disclose, unless required to do so by law.

AS SUBAGENT: A license holder acts as a subagent when aiding a buyer in a transaction without an agreement to represent the buyer. A subagent can assist the buyer but does not represent the buyer and must place the interests of the owner first.

TO AVOID DISPUTES, ALL AGREEMENTS BETWEEN YOU AND A BROKER SHOULD BE IN WRITING AND CLEARLY ESTABLISH:
- The broker's duties and responsibilities to you, and your obligations under the representation agreement.
- Who will pay the broker for services provided to you, when payment will be made and how the payment will be calculated.

LICENSE HOLDER CONTACT INFORMATION: This notice is being provided for information purposes. It does not create an obligation for you to use the broker's services. Please acknowledge receipt of this notice below and retain a copy for your records.

Licensed Broker /Broker Firm Name or Primary Assumed Business Name	License No.	Email	Phone
Designated Broker of Firm	License No.	Email	Phone
Licensed Supervisor of Sales Agent/ Associate	License No.	Email	Phone
Sales Agent/Associate's Name	License No.	Email	Phone

Buyer/Tenant/Seller/Landlord Initials   Date

Regulated by the Texas Real Estate Commission   **Information available at www.trec.texas.gov**

IABS 1-0

Source: Reprinted with permission of the Texas Real Estate Commission

05-06-13

APPROVED BY THE TEXAS REAL ESTATE COMMISSION (TREC)
P.O. BOX 12188, AUSTIN, TX 78711-2188

EQUAL HOUSING
OPPORTUNITY

TEXAS REAL ESTATE CONSUMER NOTICE
CONCERNING
HAZARDS OR DEFICIENCIES

Each year, Texans sustain property damage and are injured by accidents in the home. While some accidents may not be avoidable, many other accidents, injuries, and deaths may be avoided through the identification and repair of certain hazardous conditions. Examples of such hazards include:

- malfunctioning, improperly installed, or missing ground fault circuit protection (GFCI) devices for electrical receptacles in garages, bathrooms, kitchens, and exterior areas;

- malfunctioning arc fault protection (AFCI) devices;

- ordinary glass in locations where modern construction techniques call for safety glass;

- malfunctioning or lack of fire safety features such as smoke alarms, fire-rated doors in certain locations, and functional emergency escape and rescue openings in bedrooms;

- malfunctioning carbon monoxide alarms;

- excessive spacing between balusters on stairways and porches;

- improperly installed appliances;

- improperly installed or defective safety devices; and

- lack of electrical bonding and grounding.

To ensure that consumers are informed of hazards such as these, the Texas Real Estate Commission (TREC) has adopted Standards of Practice requiring licensed inspectors to report these conditions as "Deficient" when performing an inspection for a buyer or seller, if they can be reasonably determined.

These conditions may not have violated building codes or common practices at the time of the construction of the home, or they may have been "grandfathered" because they were present prior to the adoption of codes prohibiting such conditions. While the TREC Standards of Practice do not require inspectors to perform a code compliance inspection, TREC considers the potential for injury or property loss from the hazards addressed in the Standards of Practice to be significant enough to warrant this notice.

Contract forms developed by TREC for use by its real estate licensees also inform the buyer of the right to have the home inspected and can provide an option clause permitting the buyer to terminate the contract within a specified time. Neither the Standards of Practice nor the TREC contract forms requires a seller to remedy conditions revealed by an inspection. The decision to correct a hazard or any deficiency identified in an inspection report is left to the parties to the contract for the sale or purchase of the home.

NON-REALTY ITEMS ADDENDUM

TO CONTRACT CONCERNING THE PROPERTY AT

_____
(Address of Property)

A. For an additional sum of $_____and other and good valuable consideration, Seller shall convey to Buyer at closing the following personal property (specify each item carefully, include description, model numbers, serial numbers, location, and other information):

_____
_____
_____
_____
_____
_____
_____
_____
_____
_____
_____
_____
_____

B. Seller represents and warrants that Seller owns the personal property described in Paragraph A free and clear of all encumbrances.

C. Seller does not warrant or guarantee the condition or future performance of the personal property conveyed by this document.

_____   _____
Buyer   Seller

_____   _____
Buyer   Seller

SUMMARY

There are situations that merit the use of addenda. TREC promulgates 15 addenda that licensees should become familiar with and understand how to properly fill out. Not all TREC forms and notices are mandatory. Licensees should know which forms are mandatory and which forms are not mandatory but approved for use by licensees.

CASE STUDY/WORKSHOP

1. Who must use the Consumer Information Form?

2. Who must complete the Subdivision Information, Including Resale Certificate for Property Subject to Mandatory Membership in a Property Owners' Association form?

3. If the Back-Up Contract is negotiated with an option period of seven days, with an original effective date of March 3, and an amended effective date of March 14, when does the option period end?

4. What form would a buyer use if he wants to make an offer contingent upon the seller agreeing to allow him to move in two weeks prior to closing?

5. What addendum must be used if the seller is going to carry a second lien for a portion of her equity?

6. What addendum must be used if the property was built prior to 1978?

LESSONS TO LEARN

Seller Patricia receives three offers on her property. She has accepted an offer as well as a back-up offer. The buyer with the Back-up contract would like to have an option period. Is this allowable? Why or why not?

Chapter 8

Other Real Estate Matters

LEARNING OBJECTIVES

When you have finished this chapter, you will be able to:

1. Identify the protected classes under the Fair Housing Act.
2. Address questions about occupancy standards and HIV/AIDS in terms of disclosure requirements.

KEY TERMS

blockbusting	omission
commission	Pick 7/protected classes
fraud	puffing
misrepresentation	steering

OVERVIEW

While the emphasis in this book is on forms and contracts, the Texas Real Estate Commission desires that a few other pieces of information be shared. What follows is a discussion of additional key topics, including real estate fraud, broker's fees, Fair Housing law, occupancy standards, and disclosure issues.

REAL ESTATE FRAUD

Without trying to turn this section into a condensed real estate law book, there is a need to define some of the terms involved within the area of **fraud**. One definition of fraud is: An action conducted with the intent to deceive other parties. One of the key aspects within this definition is the term *action*. Sometimes a person is guilty of doing something wrong. That is called **commission**. Please keep in mind that the word "commission" doesn't just mean an agency (like TREC) or a compensation (brokerage fee). Commission within this context speaks to someone doing something that they knew was false or wrong. On the other side of the coin, fraud can also be accomplished by the *failure* to do something. This is known as **omission**. Keep in mind that both omission and commission have a common aspect of knowingly doing something that is improper. Subchapter N of the Texas Real Estate License Act provides a nice checklist for licensees on how to avoid committing fraud.

It is important that you not confuse a couple of other terms with fraud. One of those terms is **puffing**. Simply put, puffing can be considered "sales talk." The definition we like to use is "telling the truth attractively." The key term here is not *attractively*, but rather, *truth*. One of the authors (JR) mostly sells farm and ranch land. It is a common strategy he uses to show places early or late in the day. A rising or setting sun can "paint" a landscape in a softer and nicer way than the harsh middle of a south Texas day. Sometimes he will ask the potential buyer to just stop and listen really well. The puzzled person usually replies that nothing can be heard, and the response back is, "Precisely." It is about setting the stage and using the positives associated with the property to an advantage. There is nothing wrong with such an action. There is an attempt to influence, but not to deceive.

Another important term is **misrepresentation**, which basically means that a mistake was made in conveying some information about the property. We are all human and we certainly all make mistakes. Some of us more than others! One way of protecting yourself is to share information from reliable sources. We call it "bibliography selling"—meaning that, just as when you were writing term papers or reports in school, you will identify the source of the information.

Such a statement might be: "This tract is believed to be 23.09 acres based upon a survey by Rhonda Kay, Registered Professional Land Surveyor, dated August 22, 2014."

Another example would be: "The property taxes provided to you came from the Harris County Tax Office." Another example: "The square footage quoted is based upon blueprints provided by the builder."

The key here is that you are not a surveyor, ad valorem tax professional, or construction expert. You relied in good faith on material supplied to you from what you believe to be accurate and credible sources.

On the other hand, if you *know* something is wrong with the information given you, then that goes back to the original definition of fraud. If something does not seem right to you, seek help from your manager/broker. And keep in mind that some opportunities are best held in the hands of your worst competitors! Even if a party that you represent instructs you to carry out an action that you believe is less than proper, you are under no obligation to participate in improper business conduct. *No* piece of business is worth losing your credibility and reputation over—much less your license.

Our parting advice on this subject is that you review the topic of real estate fraud in a current Texas real estate law text, and discuss anything you are not understanding with your manager or sponsoring broker.

BROKER'S FEES

In virtually all the earnest money contracts, paragraph 8 outlines that broker's fees are contained in other written agreements. The exception to this as far as promulgated contracts are concerned is the Farm and Ranch Contract. On page 9, there is a Broker Information and Agreement for Payment of Broker's Fees section that is signed by both the buyer and seller in the transaction. With that exception, it is safe to say that broker fee arrangements need to be formalized in different documents than the earnest money contract. There are several reasons for this.

The reasons include:

- Except in a few isolated cases, payment of brokerage fees is not a negotiated item between buyer and seller. The earnest money contract between the two principals deals with the details of the sale of property.

- A listing or buyer representation agreement (signed by the principal or their authorized representative) is between a principal and a broker. Remember: Even if signed by a salesperson or broker associate, these agreements are done in the name of the sponsoring broker.

- Division of fees between brokers does not obligate/involve the principals involved in this transaction. Buyers and sellers (or, for that matter, lessors and lessees) agree to pay $X for professional services. How that money is shared among involved licensees, once performance has occurred, is not relevant to the principals.

- Issues of negotiations between respective licensees to include a review of MLS policies is beyond the scope of this text and better addressed in other classes and publications. Suffice it to say that agreements for payment/division of fees needs to meet all the criteria of a valid contract and should be handled in a professional manner, which translates into a written agreement signed by the involved parties very early (like right away) in the transaction. This eliminates misunderstandings and ill will later on. We suggest you review the documents used in your office and general geographic area, and become proficient with them.

FAIR HOUSING LAW

This topic may be the single most common subject found within the pre-licensing classes for a Texas real estate salesperson's license. It is found in virtually every text and class in some form or fashion. Why? Because it is very important, and from a licensee's perspective, there are no exemptions from following these laws. While certain exemptions do exist in a few circumstances, none of them involve participation by a licensee. Run, don't walk, if a consumer asks you to participate in any form or fashion of violating the Fair Housing Act.

Going back all the way to the Civil Rights Act of 1866 for a foundation, current Fair Housing law simply and clearly states that no one may take discriminatory action in the sale or rental of housing based upon: race, religion, color, national origin, sex, familial status, or disability. These seven categorizations are known as **protected classes**. One of the authors (JR) teaches this concept by calling the above groups the "**Pick 7.**" The learning idea is this: Pick any one of the seven, and if you treat that group differently, you are in serious danger of violating Fair Housing laws.

Certain terms are used in conjunction with the concept of Fair Housing. **Steering**, for example, means guiding people to or away from certain geographic areas due to Pick 7. **Blockbusting**, sometimes also called "panic selling," is inducing or attempting to induce property owners to sell due to the threat or fact of Pick 7 individuals moving into the neighborhood."

The bottom line of this issue is that no person can have terms and conditions or access to facilities/services due to Pick 7. While there are other additions that have been added to this protected class, they are not universal at the federal level. I urge you to clarify what other classes might be included in your trade area.

One of the more challenging areas of Pick 7 is the concept of disability. This can have more than a physical ramification; individuals that have mental and chemical impairments can also be included. It is *very* important to understand that no federal law mandates that a property must be rented or sold to someone who is using or manufacturing an illegal or controlled substance. However, a person involved in a recovery program is protected.

Another area that is easy to become confused about is familial status. This is primarily focused on families with underage children. While there are some exceptions to the law which primarily address housing developments for older persons, certain guidelines must be met to qualify for this designation. Check with your local authorities to determine which, if any, developments apply for these exemptions.

In truth, there are really only two situations where it is considered safe to "steer" or guide a buyer toward or away from a potential area. (1) It is *not* discrimination to deny people access or opportunity due to financial incapacity (not qualifying) for the subject property. Many of us have champagne tastes on a diet soda budget. Wanting something and being able to pay for it (rent or mortgage) are entirely different things. (2) The last thing is that the only really safe discrimination tool a licensee can use is the potential buyers or tenant's own personal preferences. A consumer can decide if they like a neighborhood or area for any number of personal preferences and biases. That is their call to make, and we can honor that self-imposed criteria without being challenged due to Pick 7.

OCCUPANCY STANDARDS

To the best of the authors' knowledge, there are no federal-level occupancy standards in place. This means that you will need to determine what criteria is being used in your state and particular market area. Our best advice here is to discuss this issue with your local apartment association. If you do not have a local chapter, then take a look at the information found at the Texas Apartment Association website (www.taa.org). The Texas Property Code does speak to this issue, as well, establishing a standard for a maximum occupancy of adults per bedroom. However, the Code also allows a city to allow more stringent requirements. Take a look at what your City Occupancy Code has to say. You can ask among the rental specialists what standards are being used within your community. But however you attack this topic, please seek some guidance *before* you find yourself in an uncomfortable situation.

OTHER ISSUES OF DISCLOSURE

At different times through our long careers in real estate, certain "scare topics" have come to the forefront with regards to the issue of disclosure. For a brief period, radon gas was a big topic. So were high-power electrical lines and cell towers. One that comes back pretty often is the issue of haunted or stigmatized properties. The death of someone in a premises and the issue of HIV/AIDS has received lots of press through the years. Using the last example to make a point, HUD, NAR, and TREC have come out with the position that inquiry of, disclosure regarding, or response to questions about HIV/AIDS is not advised.

Specifically, Section 11101.556 of the Texas Real Estate License Act states that:

> *Notwithstanding other law, a license holder is NOT REQUIRED to inquire about, disclose, or release information relating to whether:*
>
> 1. *a previous or current occupant of real property had, may have had, has or may have AIDS, an HIV-related illness, or an HIV infection as defined by the Centers for Disease Control and Prevention of the United States Public Health Service; or*
>
> 2. *A death occurred on a property by natural causes, suicide, or accident unrelated to the condition of the property.*

> *Source:* Added by Acts 2001, 77th Leg., ch. 1421, Sec. 7, eff. June 1, 2003.

In reviewing the relevant documents found on the TREC website, several deserve comment, as discussed below.

OP-H NEW SELLER'S DISCLOSURE OF PROPERTY CONDITION AND OP-I NOTICE CONCERNING HAZARDS OR DEFICIENCIES

It will be noted that there is no reference to disease or deaths.

If there is something wrong with the property due to design, condition, or location, then by all means, disclose, disclose, disclose. It is far better to be safe than sorry about what might be a very important consideration for a consumer.

If relevant, the above two disclosures would be *required*.

OPL LEAD BASE PAINT ADDENDUM

This Addendum is *required* if a dwelling was built prior to 1978. This is particularly significant in resale situations of older neighborhoods.

FORM 47-0 ADDENDUM FOR PROPERTY LOCATED IN A PROPANE GAS SYSTEM SERVICE AREA

This is one of our more recently adopted forms and is applicable where the use of propane gas, not as an individual property, but rather as a system, exists. Please note this is not limited to residential properties.

RSC 2 DISCLOSURE OF RELATIONSHIP
WITH RESIDENTIAL SERVICE COMPANY

This document would be relevant in sales involving residential properties. Please note that the licensees involved, both listing agent and any other, must disclose compensation or no compensation.

SUMMARY

So in summary: You *do not* have to disclose illnesses or deaths in a property as long as they are not related to the condition or design of the property.

You are *required* to disclose information about:

Lead based paint and hazards, depending upon the age of the house (prior to 1978) and hazards and deficiencies, but only in cases where there are residential structures on the property. The same holds true for program gas system service areas and property condition if a system exists. The Seller's Disclosure of Property Condition is a requirement only if there is a useable structure on the land.

Aside from the formal disclosure documents, keep in mind that a licensee is *prohibited* from disclosing information that would place a client in a weakened negotiating position. For example, a seller's motivation to sell—such as impending divorce, health issues (not related to property), financial pressures, or "bottom line" acceptable sales price—would not be the kind of information that should be disclosed. However, such information is *permitted* to be disclosed if the seller allows it. The same would be true when representing a buyer.

It is very important to discuss what your sponsoring broker's policies are on disclosure issues, and we encourage you to have that conversation in the interview stage of your broker selection process.

REVIEW QUESTIONS

1. How is fraud different than puffing and misrepresentation?

2. What are the Pick 7 protected classes?

3. Is it the licensee's responsibility to inquire or inform people about a structural problem with a property that caused an injury or death?

4. Same question as above, but this time regarding the passing of an occupant due to natural causes within the building.

5. What are the two situations wherein a licensee can safely guide people to or away from certain areas?

6. How is the act of commission different from the act of omission?

LESSONS TO LEARN

Edie Huff is a widower that you attend church with. She has come to you with a question regarding a solicitation from another real estate company. The person contacting her had spoken of "changes in the neighborhood" regarding a more diverse group of homeowners acquiring property close to her. Edie has lived in her home nearly 40 years and did not understand the statement. When asked for a clarification, the licensee commented that "it was not too late to sell before any more changes occurred." Edie wants to know what the person is talking about and how she should respond. What is your advice to her?

Chapter 9

Practice Makes Perfect

LEARNING OBJECTIVE

When you have completed this chapter, you should be able to accurately use any number of contracts and addenda in a variety of settings. The following exercises were designed to replicate situations that you can expect to encounter out in the field. While not every document from TREC was used in these scenarios, the majority of the promulgated contracts and forms were incorporated.

As you practice on the scenarios below, keep in mind that while several sets of eyes have reviewed the situations and proposed documents, there may be an error. While regrettable, it is always a possibility. Also, be reminded that different people will choose to prepare offers and attachments in slightly different ways. If you are sponsored under a broker, it is our opinion that the "best approach" when preparing the various documents is to have those documents reviewed and approved by someone in a supervisory position within the firm.

In following TREC curriculum guidelines for the class that this text will accompany, we have not included any listing agreement documents in these scenarios. We also want to remind you that in ALL cases, the Information of Brokerage Services (IBS) form is applicable.

SCENARIO #1

Robert and Mary Zeigler are the sellers of a home located at 1300 San Pedro in Bigfoot, Texas 78000. They have listed their home with John Pursch of Bulverde Springs Realty. The property has a legal description of Lot 12 Block 34 in Hardly Oaks Subdivision. Hardly Oaks has an active and mandatory Home Owners' Association. The home was built in 1977. The sellers have a phone number of 555-222-9999 and an email of PREZ@gogetum.com. Their attorney is Rourke Oeli with a phone number of 555-222-0602 and an email of rourkelaw@umail.com.

John's address is 7551 Olympia in Bulverde Springs, Texas 79123. His phone number is 555-061-1951. His email is sicem@hotshot.net.

The property is listed for $395,000, and the listing agreement is for 5 percent of the sales price. John has offered to split the broker fee with the selling broker.

In the listing agreement, the sellers have agreed to leave the appliances in the kitchen, which includes the stove, refrigerator, dishwasher, and microwave. They have also agreed to leave the drapes in the family room and master bedroom.

Steward and Theresa Rogers have seen the property with their agent, Jackie Hernandez of Top Notch Realty. The Rogers have a phone number of 555-492-6391 and an email address of oilpro@drilling.net. Their mailing address is P.O. Box 12048 in Gusgus, Texas 78400. Jackie has a mailing address of 1409 Gemini Circle in Gusgus, an email of Jackie@topnotch.com, and a phone number of 555-815-6409. The Rogers do not have an attorney.

Jackie has been instructed to offer $365,000 under the following terms and conditions: $10,000 earnest money to Hoyhak Title Company, located at 1665 GarDon Blvd. in Bigfoot. Donna Hoyhak is the escrow officer with a phone number of 555-222-0328. With a down payment at closing of $75,000 and financing of $290,000, the buyers want the seller to pay for the title insurance policy. The buyers will pay for a new survey, if needed, but sellers will provide an existing survey within five days of the effective date of the contract. Closing will be on or 90 days after the effective date of the contract.

This purchase is contingent upon the sale of the Rogers' property located at 3131 Reveille Blvd. in Gusgus. The property is currently under contract and scheduled to close on or before March 7, 2016. Buyers will put down an additional $10,000 in earnest money after Reveille closes. They desire to have 10 days of notice if another acceptable contract is received.

The buyers are offering a $1,000 option fee that will be credited as part of the purchase price for a 10-day option period. In addition to the above-mentioned personal property, they are asking that the free-standing work bench in the garage stay with the property. The sellers have received the Property Condition Report and will accept the property in its present condition, subject to a roof inspection, paid for by the buyers, that shows no needed repairs.

Possession will be a closing and funding. Please prepare this offer.

Scenario #2

Rene Rodriguez is a farm and ranch broker. His address is 218 N. Ash in Whitestone, Texas 78123. His phone is 555-814-0328 and email is rene@ranchsales.com. He has listed 720 acres owned by his sister Debbie, a single person, in Prosperous County. The legal description is 720 acres out of Abstract 31, BS&M Survey No. 6151. There is a survey on the property dated August 15, 2012, that show no easements or encroachment issues outside of an easement allowing Prosperous County Electric Cooperative to bring electricity to and across the ranch.

The property has a working water well, stock tank, and old barn in poor condition. Perimeter fencing is in good shape and interior fencing is in fair condition. Debbie does not plan to fix anything else on the property, but will make sure the water well is working properly at closing. It is listed for sale at $3,000 per acre.

There are no leases on the property of any kind. Debbie owns one-half of the entire mineral estate.

Debbie has a phone number of 555-846-0513. Her email is debbier@grtc.com. Her mailing address is 2070 Bonita Blvd., Whitestone.

Corban Walker and Christopher John, as future co-owners, have been looking for a ranch and responded to an ad by Rene. They looked at Debbie's place and instructed Rene to prepare an offer for $2,750 per acre, cash at closing, with 75 percent of the minerals owned to be conveyed. They will put $80,000 in escrow as earnest money. They will accept the present survey and only require the water well to be in proper working order at closing. Closing will be on or before August 22, 2015, with a title policy at seller's expense coming from Sindon Title Company located at 1939 Miguel Ave., Whitestone. The escrow officer will be Betty James; phone number is 555-334-3691 and email is betty@sindontitle.com.

The buyers do want to conduct an Environmental Assessment of the ranch. They will put down $500 to be credited toward the sale for a 30-day option period. Neither party has an attorney representing them. Please prepare this offer.

Scenario #3

Bobby D. Mackey and daughters Kara B. Jones and Dena R. Smith own an unimproved piece of property located at 1849 Wagon Wheel Drive in Gulf

Coast, Texas 77077. This property has no debt on it and has seashore front-age, seaward of the Gulf Intracoastal Waterway. Bob's phone number is 555-917-0722. His email is wildbob@nail.net. Legal description for the property is Lot 17 Block 4 of the Wildwood Estates Subdivision. Bob's mailing address is P.O. Box 2250 in Roger Mills, Texas 70980. The property is listed by Carolyn Weathersby of MCW Realty at a list price of $97,000. Her email is Carolyn@mcwrealty.org and her phone number is 555-822-1957. Her address is 1413 Vista View in Roger Mills.

Potential buyers Danny and Lovell Harrington (mother and son) have instructed Carolyn to prepare an offer of $90,000, with seller financing of $70,000 for five years at a 5 percent interest rate. Buyers will provide adequate proof of financial ability within seven days, as required by sellers. Buyers will pay taxes themselves and provide evidence each year. The Harringtons' phone number is 555-928-3131 and email is dlh@farming.net. Their mailing address is 32894 Jodaro Street in Frio Town, Texas 78031.

The closing will take place 60 days from the effective date. The earnest money will be $2,500, payable to De Robertis Title Company, located at 1987 Miguel Ave. in Gulf Coast. Charlie De Robertis will be the escrow officer. The phone number at the title company is 555-822-6391. Email is Charlie@derobtitle.com.

There will be a 10-day option period for $250. Seller, at seller's expense, will provide a new survey within 30 days after the option period has expired. The buyers want 15 days to object to the Title Commitment and want to make sure there are no restrictions from building a residence on the property.

The attorney for the sellers is Clint Salyers, who has an email of clint@salyerslaw.com, a phone number of 555-257-7008, and fax is 555-257-3006.

The buyers will be represented by Roberta Young. Ms. Young has an email of ryoung@millstonelaw.org. Her phone number is 555-270-2250 and fax is 555-222-0223. Please prepare this offer.

Scenario #4

P.K. Parker, a single woman, has her condominium under contract to sell. The legal description is Unit 1 in Building 7 of the Fancy Place Condominiums, which has a street address of 831 Upper Crust Blvd. in the city of Silk Stocking, Texas 78711. Her phone is 555-061-1991 and email is pparker@luna.net.

John A. and wife Cynthia C. Price, buyers, have instructed you to put in a Back-Up Contract on Ms. Parker's property. Their address is 11814 Landon James Park in Silk Stocking. Phone is 555-118-1953 and email is JCPrice@itsus.com.

Terms will be for $151,000 cash, with $10,000 earnest money placed to Calvert Title Company located at 82214 Princess Path in Silk Stocking. Buyers have received the Property Disclosure Notice and accept the property in its present condition. The buyers have agreed to pay all Transfer fees from the Condominium Association. There is an $100 option fee for five days.

This contract will be contingent upon the termination of the first contract, which is dated June 3, 2015. If the first contract does not terminate by August 22, 2015, the back-up offer will be terminated.

Closing will be on or before November 1, 2015.

Neither party has an attorney.

Attach a blank copy of the Condominium Resale Certificate.

Put yourself as the Listing Agent and create the Sponsoring Brokerage Information as you desire.

Please prepare the relevant documents that address these details as part of the transaction.

CHAPTER 1

REVIEW AND DISCUSSION

1. How is a valid contract different from a voidable one?

    A valid contract meets all of the requirements to be considered legally binding. A voidable contract is a "maybe yes/maybe no" situation where one party can decide to continue or get out of the contract.

2. What is the difference between and addendum and an amendment?

    An addendum adds details that are important and become part of the contract. An amendment is a change or adjustment to the original contractual agreement.

3. What does the term "bilateral contract" mean?

    Bilateral means there are rights and responsibilities for both parties to the contract. Most real estate contracts are bilateral.

4. Explain the term "time is of the essence" as it relates to the subject matter in this book.

    This means all the timetables outlined in the contract are to be strictly adhered to. Be careful in adding this language where it does not already exist.

5. Please list the essential elements of a valid contract as explained in this chapter.

    Competent Parties
    Offer and Acceptance
    Consideration
    Legal Purpose
    Agreement Signed and in Writing
    Description of the property (legal description)

6. What portion of the Earnest Money Contract speaks to options in the event of default?

    Paragraph 15 speaks to the issue of default

LESSONS TO LEARN

You represent, as the buyer's agent, Gerry and Cynthia Guerra in the purchase of a home located at 923 Winding Way. The Guerras are under contract to purchase. Some time prior to closing, they come to tell you that they have changed their minds about this house and want to back out of the contract. What they want to know is, can they withdraw from the transaction? How do you respond?

I would respond to the Guerras initially by stating that they can back out, but probably only with consequences. We would then review Paragraph 15. We would then discuss their motivation for the decision. Through the years, I have often observed something my Psychology friends label Cognitive Dissonance. In layman's terms, this means a second-guessing of decisions made. Once the excitement of a new property wears off and the reality of the burdens of all that is required to secure financing and arrange to move sets in, that creeping doubt will raise its ugly head.

My advice is to head this type of understandable but potentially destructive human behavior off early. Let the buyers know that they may feel something akin to what is also known as buyer's remorse and that you stand ready to review with them the reasons they wanted the property in the first place.

There may be other motivations that have come to light that deal with something totally different. An impending major surgery or job loss may have a tremendous impact on the buyer's circumstances. In that case, a disclosure to the selling agent and discussion of options may be appropriate.

One thing for certain you should not do: DO NOT offer legal advice on their standing in the contract.

CHAPTER 2

REVIEW AND DISCUSSION

1. What is TRELA?

   TRELA is the **Texas Real Estate License Act (TRELA),** which establishes operating guidelines for real estate practitioners, real estate inspectors, residential service companies, and those offering timeshare interests.

2. Who is TREC?

   The **Texas Real Estate Commission (TREC)** administers the Texas Real Estate License Act. TREC is a nine-member, policymaking commission appointed by the governor and confirmed by the state senate.

Six members must be active in real estate as full-time brokers (including the five years previous to his or her appointment), and three must be members of the public who must have no affiliation with real estate brokerage. Each member must be a qualified voter. The commission has rule-making authority and the rules of the commission have the full force and effect of law.

3. What does TRELA consider "the unauthorized practice of law"?

TRELA specifically prohibits licensees from practicing law by giving opinions or counsel regarding the validity or legal sufficiency of an instrument that addresses real property rights, or as to the status of title to real estate. TRELA clearly establishes that it is illegal for the licensee to draw a deed, note, deed of trust, will, or other written instrument that transfers or may transfer an interest in, or title to, real property. In order to safeguard valid sales contracts, licensees should always advise sellers and buyers to obtain legal counsel if they do not understand the stipulations of the various contract forms that the Act requires licensees to use.

4. Who is the Broker-Lawyer Committee?

The **Broker-Lawyer Committee** is a 13-member committee composed of six licensed real estate brokers (appointed by TREC), six lawyers who are active members of the Texas State Bar (appointed by the president of the State Bar of Texas), and one public member, appointed by the governor. The Broker-Lawyer Committee drafts and revises contract forms for use by real estate licensees. Their purpose is to expedite real estate transactions and reduce controversies, while protecting the interests of the parties involved. The Broker-Lawyer Committee does not **promulgate**, or publish, forms for mandatory use by licensees, but only develops forms and proposes their adoption. TREC is the commission that promulgates the forms for mandatory use.

5. How many promulgated contracts are there? Addenda?

6 promulgated contracts

15 promulgated addenda (including 2 temporary leases)

6. What options does the seller have upon receiving a written offer?

When presented with a written offer, the seller may: accept it, reject it, counter it, or do nothing—that is, ignore it.

LESSONS TO LEARN ANSWER

The Real Estate License Act Sec. 1101.155 allows for a contract form that is prepared by the property owner; or is prepared by an attorney and is required by the property owner. Seller Samantha may use the contract she has. REALTOR Melanie should document her seller's wishes in the file and then proceed with the offer process.

CHAPTER 3

REVIEW AND DISCUSSION

1. When would you NOT use the promulgated One to Four Family Residential Contract (Resale)?

    Do not use when there are common walls with another unit or when there are common elements associated with common elements of ownership.

2. When a buyer asks you how much money should be put down for earnest money, how should you respond?

    Earnest money amounts are a matter of negotiation between the buyer and seller.

3. Assume a party to the contract does not have an email address. What should you put in paragraph 21 (Notices)?

    "N/A"(Not applicable). Keep in mind not all buyers and sellers will have email addresses or facsimile numbers.

4. What does the term *proration* mean as it relates to ad valorem taxes on a property involved in an ownership transfer?

    Proration refers to a dividing up/sharing of certain income or expenses, usually based upon the time of ownership. For example, historically the seller pays the real property taxes from Jan. 1 through the day of closing and the buyer pays for the rest of the year.

5. Who "chooses" the escrow agent?

    Principals decide which escrow agent to use–just like they negotiate the earnest money amount.

6. How is an executrix different from an administratrix?

    While both are female, the executrix has been selected by the testator (maker of a valid will) and the administratrix has been selected by the court when someone days intestate (without a valid will).

APPROVED BY THE TEXAS REAL ESTATE COMMISSION (TREC)
FOR VOLUNTARY USE

10-10-11

NON-REALTY ITEMS ADDENDUM

TO CONTRACT CONCERNING THE PROPERTY AT

51398 Tartar Ave.
(Address of Property)

A. For an additional sum of $_____None_and other and good valuable consideration, Seller shall convey to Buyer at closing the following personal property (specify each item carefully, include description, model numbers, serial numbers, location, and other information):

Pool table and all pool related equipment located in den of subject property at time of showing.

B. Seller represents and warrants that Seller owns the personal property described in Paragraph A free and clear of all encumbrances.

C. Seller does not warrant or guarantee the condition or future performance of the personal property conveyed by this document.

_____   _____
Buyer   Seller

_____   _____
Buyer   Seller

This form has been approved by the Texas Real Estate Commission for voluntary use by its licensees. Copies of TREC rules governing real estate brokers, salesperson and real estate inspectors are available at nominal cost from TREC. Texas Real Estate Commission, P.O. Box 12188, Austin, TX 78711-2188, 512-936-3000 (http://www.trec.texas.gov)

Source: © 2015 OnCourse Learning

TREC NO. OP-M

APPROVED BY THE TEXAS REAL ESTATE COMMISSION (TREC)
FOR VOLUNTARY USE

10-10-11

NON-REALTY ITEMS ADDENDUM

TO CONTRACT CONCERNING THE PROPERTY AT

1300 San Pedro
(Address of Property)

A. For an additional sum of $_____None and other and good valuable consideration, Seller shall convey to Buyer at closing the following personal property (specify each item carefully, include description, model numbers, serial numbers, location, and other information):

Stove, Refrigerator, Dishwasher, Microwave all found in Kitchen will stay. Serial numbers to follow in spaces below.

Drapes in Master Bedroom and in Family Room will stay.

Free Standing Work Bench in Garage to stay.

B. Seller represents and warrants that Seller owns the personal property described in Paragraph A free and clear of all encumbrances.

C. Seller does not warrant or guarantee the condition or future performance of the personal property conveyed by this document.

Buyer _____

Seller _____

Buyer _____

Seller _____

This form has been approved by the Texas Real Estate Commission for voluntary use by its licensees. Copies of TREC rules governing real estate brokers, salesperson and real estate inspectors are available at nominal cost from TREC. Texas Real Estate Commission, P.O. Box 12188, Austin, TX 78711-2188, 512-936-3000 (http://www.trec.texas.gov)

LESSONS TO LEARN

You have recently finished your pre-licensing coursework, prepared for and passed your Real Estate Salesperson's Exam, chosen a sponsoring broker, and yesterday completed your two-week New Agent Training Program. Congratulations!

This morning, an old family friend, Della Fischer (a widower) called you and asked that you show her a new listing your company has just taken that was owned by a recently deceased neighbor of hers, Lena Walker (also a widower). Ms. Walker died with a valid will. The listing was taken by Tammy Perez of your office. Ms. Walker's estate is being handled by her daughter, Verna Dell Walker Rosen.

How should you proceed with the request from Della?

You are very blessed to have such an opportunity so soon! You need to spend some time with your Sales Manager and possibly with Tammy to make certain that the estate is in order and the property can legally go under contract to sell. You will want to get help in preparing as much of the details as you can regarding a potential offer on this property. Does Della plan to pay cash, or will she need financing? Is she qualified to borrow the necessary funds? Does she plan to move into the Walker home, or use it for investment property? Review all these and other relevant questions you can think of with your supervisor at the office. After showing the property, seek help again in order to finish creating a well-crafted offer that meets the expectations of your buyer. It is neither reasonable nor prudent for you or anyone else to think you can draw up this first "real" offer without supervision. Many of us have another set of eyes review the offers or listings we create as a matter of routine, just to insure we have not missed something of importance.

CHAPTER 4

REVIEW AND DISCUSSION

1. What is earnest money?

   Earnest money is the "good faith money" presented by the prospective buyer as an indication of the buyer's intention to carry out the terms of the contract. Not only does earnest money show good faith and serious intent on the part of the buyer, it may also serve

PROMULGATED BY THE TEXAS REAL ESTATE COMMISSION (TREC)

THIRD PARTY FINANCING ADDENDUM

TO CONTRACT CONCERNING THE PROPERTY AT

51398 Tartar Ave Big Town, Texas
_____
(Street Address and City)

A. TYPE OF FINANCING AND DUTY TO APPLY AND OBTAIN APPROVAL: Buyer shall apply promptly for all financing described below and make every reasonable effort to obtain approval for the financing, including but not limited to furnishing all information and documents required by Buyer's lender. (Check applicable boxes):

☑ 1. Conventional Financing:
    ☑ (a) A first mortgage loan in the principal amount of $ _____ 1,200,000 (excluding any financed PMI premium), due in full in ___15___ year(s), with interest not to exceed __5__% per annum for the first ___15___ year(s) of the loan with Origination Charges as shown on Buyer's Loan Estimate for the loan not to exceed ___1___% of the loan.
    ☐ (b) A second mortgage loan in the principal amount of $_____(excluding any financed PMI premium), due in full in _____year(s), with interest not to exceed _____% per annum for the first _____year(s) of the loan with Origination Charges as shown on Buyer's Loan Estimate for the loan not to exceed _____% of the loan.

☐ 2. Texas Veterans Loan: A loan(s) from the Texas Veterans Land Board of $ _____ for a period in the total amount of _____years at the interest rate established by the Texas Veterans Land Board.

☐ 3. FHA Insured Financing: A Section _____ FHA insured loan of not less than $_____(excluding any financed MIP), amortizable monthly for not less than _____years, with interest not to exceed _____% per annum for the first _____year(s) of the loan with Origination Charges as shown on Buyer's Loan Estimate for the loan not to exceed _____ % of the loan.

☐ 4. VA Guaranteed Financing: A VA guaranteed loan of not less than $_____(excluding any financed Funding Fee), amortizable monthly for not less than_____years, with interest not to exceed_____% per annum for the first _____year(s) of the loan with Origination Charges as shown on Buyer's Loan Estimate for the loan not to exceed _____% of the loan.

☐ 5. USDA Guaranteed Financing: A USDA-guaranteed loan of not less than $ _____ (excluding any financed Funding Fee), amortizable monthly for not less than_____years, with interest not to exceed _____% per annum for the first _____year(s) of the loan with Origination Charges as shown on Buyer's Loan Estimate for the loan not to exceed _____% of the loan.

☐ 6. Reverse Mortgage Financing: A reverse mortgage loan (also known as a Home Equity Conversion Mortgage loan) in the original principal amount of $ _____ (excluding any financed PMI premium or other costs), with interest not to exceed _____% per annum for the first _____ year(s) of the loan with Origination Charges as shown on Buyer's Loan Estimate for the loan not to exceed _____% of the loan. The reverse mortgage loan ☐will ☐ will not be an FHA insured loan.

Initialed for identification by Buyer____ _____ and Seller_____ _____

Third Party Financing Addendum Concerning

Page 2 of 2

51398 Tartar Ave.
_____
(Address of Property)

B. APPROVAL OF FINANCING: Approval for the financing described above will be deemed to have been obtained when Buyer Approval and Property Approval are obtained.
1. <u>Buyer Approval</u>:
☑ This contract is subject to Buyer obtaining Buyer Approval. If Buyer cannot obtain Buyer Approval, Buyer may give written notice to Seller within___30___days after the effective date of this contract and this contract will terminate and the earnest money will be refunded to Buyer. If Buyer does not terminate the contract under this provision, the contract shall no longer be subject to the Buyer obtaining Buyer Approval. Buyer Approval will be deemed to have been obtained when (i) the terms of the loan(s) described above are available and (ii) lender determines that Buyer has satisfied all of lender's requirements related to Buyer's assets, income and credit history.
☐ This contract is not subject to Buyer obtaining Buyer Approval.
2. <u>Property Approval</u>: Property Approval will be deemed to have been obtained when the Property has satisfied lender's underwriting requirements for the loan, including but not limited to appraisal, insurability, and lender required repairs. If Property Approval is not obtained, Buyer may terminate this contract by giving notice to Seller before closing and the earnest money will be refunded to Buyer.
3. **Time is of the essence for this paragraph and strict compliance with the time for performance is required.**

C. SECURITY: Each note for the financing described above must be secured by vendor's and deed of trust liens.

D. FHA/VA REQUIRED PROVISION: If the financing described above involves FHA insured or VA financing, it is expressly agreed that, notwithstanding any other provision of this contract, the purchaser (Buyer) shall not be obligated to complete the purchase of the Property described herein or to incur any penalty by forfeiture of earnest money deposits or otherwise: (i) unless the Buyer has been given in accordance with HUD/FHA or VA requirements a written statement issued by the Federal Housing Commissioner, Department of Veterans Affairs, or a Direct Endorsement Lender setting forth the appraised value of the Property of not less than $_____; or (ii) if the contract purchase price or cost exceeds the reasonable value of the Property established by the Department of Veterans Affairs.
(1) The Buyer shall have the privilege and option of proceeding with consummation of the contract without regard to the amount of the appraised valuation or the reasonable value established by the Department of Veterans Affairs.
(2) If FHA financing is involved, the appraised valuation is arrived at to determine the maximum mortgage the Department of Housing and Urban Development will insure. HUD does not warrant the value or the condition of the Property. The Buyer should satisfy himself/herself that the price and the condition of the Property are acceptable.
(3) If VA financing is involved and if Buyer elects to complete the purchase at an amount in excess of the reasonable value established by the VA, Buyer shall pay such excess amount in cash from a source which Buyer agrees to disclose to the VA and which Buyer represents will not be from borrowed funds except as approved by VA. If VA reasonable value of the Property is less than the Sales Prices, Seller may reduce the Sales Price to an amount equal to the VA reasonable value and the sale will be closed at the lower Sales Price with proportionate adjustments to the down payment and the loan amount.

E. AUTHORIZATION TO RELEASE INFORMATION:
(1) Buyer authorizes Buyer's lender to furnish to Seller or Buyer or their representatives information relating to the status of the approval for the financing.
(2) Seller and Buyer authorize Buyer's lender, title company, and escrow agent to disclose and furnish a copy of the closing disclosures provided in relation to the closing of this sale to the parties' respective brokers and sales agents identified on the last page of the contract.

_____   _____
Buyer   Seller

_____   _____
Buyer   Seller

PROMULGATED BY THE TEXAS REAL ESTATE COMMISSION (TREC)
11-2-2015
ONE TO FOUR FAMILY RESIDENTIAL CONTRACT (RESALE)
NOTICE: Not For Use For Condominium Transactions

1. PARTIES: The parties to this contract are <u>Sergei Karabailonov</u>
(Seller) and <u>BlizEng Real Estate Investments, LLC.</u> (Buyer).
Seller agrees to sell and convey to Buyer and Buyer agrees to buy from Seller the Property defined below.

2. PROPERTY: The land, improvements and accessories are collectively referred to as the "Property".

    A. LAND: Lot <u>9</u> Block <u>7</u>, <u>Golden Heights Subdivision</u>
        Addition, City of <u>Big Town</u> , County of <u>Prosperous</u>,
        Texas, known as <u>51398 Tartar Ave.</u>
        (address/zip code), or as described on attached exhibit.

    B. IMPROVEMENTS: The house, garage and all other fixtures and improvements attached to the above-described real property, including without limitation, the following **permanently installed and built-in items,** if any: all equipment and appliances, valances, screens, shutters, awnings, wall-to-wall carpeting, mirrors, ceiling fans, attic fans, mail boxes, television antennas, mounts and brackets for televisions and speakers, heating and air-conditioning units, security and fire detection equipment, wiring, plumbing and lighting fixtures, chandeliers, water softener system, kitchen equipment, garage door openers, cleaning equipment, shrubbery, landscaping, outdoor cooking equipment, and all other property owned by Seller and attached to the above described real property.

    C. ACCESSORIES: The following described related accessories, if any: window air conditioning units, stove, fireplace screens, curtains and rods, blinds, window shades, draperies and rods, door keys, mailbox keys, above ground pool, swimming pool equipment and maintenance accessories, artificial fireplace logs, and controls for: (i) garage doors, (ii) entry gates, and (iii) other improvements and accessories.

    D. EXCLUSIONS: The following improvements and accessories will be retained by Seller and must be removed prior to delivery of possession: <u>None</u>

3. SALES PRICE:
    A. Cash portion of Sales Price payable by Buyer at closing............................. $ <u>325,000</u>
    B. Sum of all financing described in the attached: ☑ Third Party Financing Addendum,
        ☐ Loan Assumption Addendum, ☐ Seller Financing Addendum .... $ <u>1,200,000</u>
    C. Sales Price (Sum of A and B)... $ <u>1,525,000</u>

4. LICENSE HOLDER DISCLOSURE: Texas law requires a real estate license holder who is a party to a transaction or acting on behalf of a spouse, parent, child, business entity in which the license holder owns more than 10%, or a trust for which the license holder acts as a trustee or of which the license holder or the license holder's spouse, parent or child is a beneficiary, to notify the other party in writing before entering into a contract of sale. Disclose if applicable:

5. EARNEST MONEY: Upon execution of this contract by all parties, Buyer shall deposit $ <u>25,000</u> as earnest money with <u>Araujo Title and Abstract Company</u>, as escrow agent, at <u>197 Venado Grande Big Town, Texas 78231</u> (address). Buyer shall deposit additional earnest money of $ <u>None</u> with escrow agent within <u>N/A</u> days after the effective date of this contract. If Buyer fails to deposit the earnest money as required by this contract, Buyer will be in default.

6. TITLE POLICY AND SURVEY:
    A. TITLE POLICY: Seller shall furnish to Buyer at ☑ Seller's ☐ Buyer's expense an owner policy of title insurance (Title Policy) issued by <u>Araujo Title and Abstract Company</u> (Title Company) in the amount of the Sales Price, dated at or after closing, insuring Buyer against loss under the provisions of the Title Policy, subject to the promulgated exclusions (including existing building and zoning ordinances) and the following exceptions:
        (1) Restrictive covenants common to the platted subdivision in which the Property is located.
        (2) The standard printed exception for standby fees, taxes and assessments.
        (3) Liens created as part of the financing described in Paragraph 3.
        (4) Utility easements created by the dedication deed or plat of the subdivision in which the Property is located.

Initialed for identification by Buyer_____ _____ and Seller _____ _____   TREC NO. 20-13

(5) Reservations or exceptions otherwise permitted by this contract or as may be approved by Buyer in writing.

(6) The standard printed exception as to marital rights.

(7) The standard printed exception as to waters, tidelands, beaches, streams, and related matters.

(8) The standard printed exception as to discrepancies, conflicts, shortages in area or boundary lines, encroachments or protrusions, or overlapping improvements: ☐(i) will not be amended or deleted from the title policy; or ☐(ii) will be amended to read, "shortages in area" at the expense of ☐Buyer ☑Seller.

B. COMMITMENT: Within 20 days after the Title Company receives a copy of this contract, Seller shall furnish to Buyer a commitment for title insurance (Commitment) and, at Buyer's expense, legible copies of restrictive covenants and documents evidencing exceptions in the Commitment (Exception Documents) other than the standard printed exceptions. Seller authorizes the Title Company to deliver the Commitment and Exception Documents to Buyer at Buyer's address shown in Paragraph 21. If the Commitment and Exception Documents are not delivered to Buyer within the specified time, the time for delivery will be automatically extended up to 15 days or 3 days before the Closing Date, whichever is earlier. If, due to factors beyond Seller's control, the Commitment and Exception Documents are not delivered within the time required, Buyer may terminate this contract and the earnest money will be refunded to Buyer.

C. SURVEY: The survey must be made by a registered professional land surveyor acceptable to the Title Company and Buyer's lender(s). (Check one box only)

☐(1) Within _____ days after the effective date of this contract, Seller shall furnish to Buyer and Title Company Seller's existing survey of the Property and a Residential Real Property Affidavit promulgated by the Texas Department of Insurance (T-47 Affidavit). **If Seller fails to furnish the existing survey or affidavit within the time prescribed, Buyer shall obtain a new survey at Seller's expense no later than 3 days prior to Closing Date.** If the existing survey or affidavit is not acceptable to Title Company or Buyer's lender(s), Buyer shall obtain a new survey at ☐Seller's ☐Buyer's expense no later than 3 days prior to Closing Date.

☐(2) Within _____ days after the effective date of this contract, Buyer shall obtain a new survey at Buyer's expense. Buyer is deemed to receive the survey on the date of actual receipt or the date specified in this paragraph, whichever is earlier.

☑(3) Within ___30___ days after the effective date of this contract, Seller, at Seller's expense shall furnish a new survey to Buyer.

D. OBJECTIONS: Buyer may object in writing to defects, exceptions, or encumbrances to title: disclosed on the survey other than items 6A(1) through (7) above; disclosed in the Commitment other than items 6A(1) through (8) above; or which prohibit the following use or activity: _None_____.
Buyer must object the earlier of (i) the Closing Date or (ii) __10__ days after Buyer receives the Commitment, Exception Documents, and the survey. Buyer's failure to object within the time allowed will constitute a waiver of Buyer's right to object; except that the requirements in Schedule C of the Commitment are not waived by Buyer. Provided Seller is not obligated to incur any expense, Seller shall cure the timely objections of Buyer or any third party lender within 15 days after Seller receives the objections and the Closing Date will be extended as necessary. If objections are not cured within such 15 day period, this contract will terminate and the earnest money will be refunded to Buyer unless Buyer waives the objections.

E. TITLE NOTICES:

(1) ABSTRACT OR TITLE POLICY: Broker advises Buyer to have an abstract of title covering the Property examined by an attorney of Buyer's selection, or Buyer should be furnished with or obtain a Title Policy. If a Title Policy is furnished, the Commitment should be promptly reviewed by an attorney of Buyer's choice due to the time limitations on Buyer's right to object.

(2) MEMBERSHIP IN PROPERTY OWNERS ASSOCIATION(S): The Property ☐is ☑is not subject to mandatory membership in a property owners association(s). If the Property is subject to mandatory membership in a property owners association(s), Seller notifies Buyer under §5.012, Texas Property Code, that, as a purchaser of property in the residential community identified in Paragraph 2A in which the Property is located, you are obligated to be a member of the property owners association(s). Restrictive covenants governing the use and occupancy of the Property and all dedicatory instruments governing the establishment, maintenance, or operation of this residential community have been or will be recorded in the Real Property Records of the county in which the Property is located. Copies of the restrictive covenants and dedicatory instruments may be obtained from the county clerk. **You are obligated to pay assessments to the property owners association(s). The amount of the assessments is subject to**

Contract Concerning _____ 51398 Tartar Ave. _____ Page 3 of 9   11-2-2015
(Address of Property)

change. Your failure to pay the assessments could result in enforcement of the association's lien on and the foreclosure of the Property.
Section 207.003, Property Code, entitles an owner to receive copies of any document that governs the establishment, maintenance, or operation of a subdivision, including, but not limited to, restrictions, bylaws, rules and regulations, and a resale certificate from a property owners' association. A resale certificate contains information including, but not limited to, statements specifying the amount and frequency of regular assessments and the style and cause number of lawsuits to which the property owners' association is a party, other than lawsuits relating to unpaid ad valorem taxes of an individual member of the association. These documents must be made available to you by the property owners' association or the association's agent on your request.
If Buyer is concerned about these matters, the TREC promulgated Addendum for Property Subject to Mandatory Membership in a Property Owners Association(s) should be used.
(3) STATUTORY TAX DISTRICTS: If the Property is situated in a utility or other statutorily created district providing water, sewer, drainage, or flood control facilities and services, Chapter 49, Texas Water Code, requires Seller to deliver and Buyer to sign the statutory notice relating to the tax rate, bonded indebtedness, or standby fee of the district prior to final execution of this contract.
(4) TIDE WATERS: If the Property abuts the tidally influenced waters of the state, §33.135, Texas Natural Resources Code, requires a notice regarding coastal area property to be included in the contract. An addendum containing the notice promulgated by TREC or required by the parties must be used.
(5) ANNEXATION: If the Property is located outside the limits of a municipality, Seller notifies Buyer under §5.011, Texas Property Code, that the Property may now or later be included in the extraterritorial jurisdiction of a municipality and may now or later be subject to annexation by the municipality. Each municipality maintains a map that depicts its boundaries and extraterritorial jurisdiction. To determine if the Property is located within a municipality's extraterritorial jurisdiction or is likely to be located within a municipality's extraterritorial jurisdiction, contact all municipalities located in the general proximity of the Property for further information.
(6) PROPERTY LOCATED IN A CERTIFICATED SERVICE AREA OF A UTILITY SERVICE PROVIDER: Notice required by §13.257, Water Code: The real property, described in Paragraph 2, that you are about to purchase may be located in a certificated water or sewer service area, which is authorized by law to provide water or sewer service to the properties in the certificated area. If your property is located in a certificated area there may be special costs or charges that you will be required to pay before you can receive water or sewer service. There may be a period required to construct lines or other facilities necessary to provide water or sewer service to your property. You are advised to determine if the property is in a certificated area and contact the utility service provider to determine the cost that you will be required to pay and the period, if any, that is required to provide water or sewer service to your property. The undersigned Buyer hereby acknowledges receipt of the foregoing notice at or before the execution of a binding contract for the purchase of the real property described in Paragraph 2 or at closing of purchase of the real property.
(7) PUBLIC IMPROVEMENT DISTRICTS: If the Property is in a public improvement district, §5.014, Property Code, requires Seller to notify Buyer as follows: As a purchaser of this parcel of real property you are obligated to pay an assessment to a municipality or county for an improvement project undertaken by a public improvement district under Chapter 372, Local Government Code. The assessment may be due annually or in periodic installments. More information concerning the amount of the assessment and the due dates of that assessment may be obtained from the municipality or county levying the assessment. The amount of the assessments is subject to change. Your failure to pay the assessments could result in a lien on and the foreclosure of your property.
(8) TRANSFER FEES: If the Property is subject to a private transfer fee obligation, §5.205, Property Code, requires Seller to notify Buyer as follows: The private transfer fee obligation may be governed by Chapter 5, Subchapter G of the Texas Property Code.
(9) PROPANE GAS SYSTEM SERVICE AREA: If the Property is located in a propane gas system service area owned by a distribution system retailer, Seller must give Buyer written notice as required by §141.010, Texas Utilities Code. An addendum containing the notice approved by TREC or required by the parties should be used.
(10) NOTICE OF WATER LEVEL FLUCTUATIONS: If the Property adjoins an impoundment of water, including a reservoir or lake, constructed and maintained under Chapter 11, Water Code, that has a storage capacity of at least 5,000 acre-feet at the impoundment's normal operating level, Seller hereby notifies Buyer: "The water level of the impoundment of water adjoining the Property fluctuates for various reasons, including as

Initialed for identification by Buyer_____ _____ and Seller _____ _____   TREC NO. 20-13

Contract Concerning _____ 51398 Tartar Ave. _____ Page 4 of 9   11-2-2015
(Address of Property)

a result of: (1) an entity lawfully exercising its right to use the water stored in the impoundment; or (2) drought or flood conditions."

7.PROPERTY CONDITION:

A. ACCESS, INSPECTIONS AND UTILITIES: Seller shall permit Buyer and Buyer's agents access to the Property at reasonable times. Buyer may have the Property inspected by inspectors selected by Buyer and licensed by TREC or otherwise permitted by law to make inspections. Any hydrostatic testing must be separately authorized by Seller in writing. Seller at Seller's expense shall immediately cause existing utilities to be turned on and shall keep the utilities on during the time this contract is in effect.

B. SELLER'S DISCLOSURE NOTICE PURSUANT TO §5.008, TEXAS PROPERTY CODE (Notice): (Check one box only)

☐ (1) Buyer has received the Notice.

☑ (2) Buyer has not received the Notice. Within ___10___ days after the effective date of this contract, Seller shall deliver the Notice to Buyer. If Buyer does not receive the Notice, Buyer may terminate this contract at any time prior to the closing and the earnest money will be refunded to Buyer. If Seller delivers the Notice, Buyer may terminate this contract for any reason within 7 days after Buyer receives the Notice or prior to the closing, whichever first occurs, and the earnest money will be refunded to Buyer.

☐ (3)The Seller is not required to furnish the notice under the Texas Property Code.

C. SELLER'S DISCLOSURE OF LEAD-BASED PAINT AND LEAD-BASED PAINT HAZARDS is required by Federal law for a residential dwelling constructed prior to 1978.

D. ACCEPTANCE OF PROPERTY CONDITION: "As Is" means the present condition of the Property with any and all defects and without warranty except for the warranties of title and the warranties in this contract. Buyer's agreement to accept the Property As Is under Paragraph 7D(1) or (2) does not preclude Buyer from inspecting the Property under Paragraph 7A, from negotiating repairs or treatments in a subsequent amendment, or from terminating this contract during the Option Period, if any.
(Check one box only)

☑ (1) Buyer accepts the Property As Is.

☐ (2) Buyer accepts the Property As Is provided Seller, at Seller's expense, shall complete the following specific repairs and treatments: _____
_____.
(Do not insert general phrases, such as "subject to inspections" that do not identify specific repairs and treatments.)

E. LENDER REQUIRED REPAIRS AND TREATMENTS: Unless otherwise agreed in writing, neither party is obligated to pay for lender required repairs, which includes treatment for wood destroying insects. If the parties do not agree to pay for the lender required repairs or treatments, this contract will terminate and the earnest money will be refunded to Buyer. If the cost of lender required repairs and treatments exceeds 5% of the Sales Price, Buyer may terminate this contract and the earnest money will be refunded to Buyer.

F. COMPLETION OF REPAIRS AND TREATMENTS: Unless otherwise agreed in writing: (i) Seller shall complete all agreed repairs and treatments prior to the Closing Date; and (ii) all required permits must be obtained, and repairs and treatments must be performed by persons who are licensed to provide such repairs or treatments or, if no license is required by law, are commercially engaged in the trade of providing such repairs or treatments.   At Buyer's election, any transferable warranties received by Seller with respect to the repairs and treatments will be transferred to Buyer at Buyer's expense. If Seller fails to complete any agreed repairs and treatments prior to the Closing Date, Buyer may exercise remedies under Paragraph 15 or extend the Closing Date up to 5 days if necessary for Seller to complete the repairs and treatments.

G. ENVIRONMENTAL MATTERS: Buyer is advised that the presence of wetlands, toxic substances, including asbestos and wastes or other environmental hazards, or the presence of a threatened or endangered species or its habitat may affect Buyer's intended use of the Property. If Buyer is concerned about these matters, an addendum promulgated by TREC or required by the parties should be used.

H. RESIDENTIAL SERVICE CONTRACTS: Buyer may purchase a residential service contract from a residential service company licensed by TREC. If Buyer purchases a residential service contract, Seller shall reimburse Buyer at closing for the cost of the residential service contract in an amount not exceeding $_____ None . Buyer should review any residential service contract for the scope of coverage, exclusions and limitations. **The purchase of a residential service contract is optional. Similar coverage may be purchased from various companies authorized to do business in Texas.**

8.BROKERS' FEES: All obligations of the parties for payment of brokers' fees are contained in separate written agreements.

Initialed for identification by Buyer_____ _____ and Seller _____ _____   TREC NO. 20-13

Contract Concerning _____ 51398 Tartar Ave. _____ Page 5 of 9   11-2-2015
(Address of Property)

9. CLOSING:

A. The closing of the sale will be on or before _75 days after effective date of cont_, 20 _15_ , or within 7 days after objections made under Paragraph 6D have been cured or waived, whichever date is later (Closing Date). If either party fails to close the sale by the Closing Date, the non-defaulting party may exercise the remedies contained in Paragraph 15.

B. At closing:
   (1) Seller shall execute and deliver a general warranty deed conveying title to the Property to Buyer and showing no additional exceptions to those permitted in Paragraph 6 and furnish tax statements or certificates showing no delinquent taxes on the Property.
   (2) Buyer shall pay the Sales Price in good funds acceptable to the escrow agent.
   (3) Seller and Buyer shall execute and deliver any notices, statements, certificates, affidavits, releases, loan documents and other documents reasonably required for the closing of the sale and the issuance of the Title Policy.
   (4) There will be no liens, assessments, or security interests against the Property which will not be satisfied out of the sales proceeds unless securing the payment of any loans assumed by Buyer and assumed loans will not be in default.
   (5) If the Property is subject to a residential lease, Seller shall transfer security deposits (as defined under §92.102, Property Code), if any, to Buyer. In such an event, Buyer shall deliver to the tenant a signed statement acknowledging that the Buyer has acquired the Property and is responsible for the return of the security deposit, and specifying the exact dollar amount of the security deposit.

10. POSSESSION:

A. Buyer's Possession: Seller shall deliver to Buyer possession of the Property in its present or required condition, ordinary wear and tear excepted: ☑upon closing and funding ☐according to a temporary residential lease form promulgated by TREC or other written lease required by the parties. Any possession by Buyer prior to closing or by Seller after closing which is not authorized by a written lease will establish a tenancy at sufferance relationship between the parties. **Consult your insurance agent prior to change of ownership and possession because insurance coverage may be limited or terminated. The absence of a written lease or appropriate insurance coverage may expose the parties to economic loss.**

B. Leases:
   (1) After the Effective Date, Seller may not execute any lease (including but not limited to mineral leases) or convey any interest in the Property without Buyer's written consent.
   (2) If the Property is subject to any lease to which Seller is a party, Seller shall deliver to Buyer copies of the lease(s) and any move-in condition form signed by the tenant within 7 days after the Effective Date of the contract.

11. SPECIAL PROVISIONS: (Insert only factual statements and business details applicable to the sale. TREC rules prohibit license holders from adding factual statements or business details for which a contract addendum, lease or other form has been promulgated by TREC for mandatory use.)

Seller to pay for new survey. Buyer will repay Seller at the time of closing the sale.

12. SETTLEMENT AND OTHER EXPENSES:

A. The following expenses must be paid at or prior to closing:
   (1) Expenses payable by Seller (Seller's Expenses):
       (a) Releases of existing liens, including prepayment penalties and recording fees; release of Seller's loan liability; tax statements or certificates; preparation of deed; one-half of escrow fee; and other expenses payable by Seller under this contract.
       (b) Seller shall also pay an amount not to exceed $_____ None to be applied in the following order: Buyer's Expenses which Buyer is prohibited from paying by FHA, VA, Texas Veterans Land Board or other governmental loan programs, and then to other Buyer's Expenses as allowed by the lender.
   (2) Expenses payable by Buyer (Buyer's Expenses): Appraisal fees; loan application fees; origination charges; credit reports; preparation of loan documents; interest on the notes from date of disbursement to one month prior to dates of first monthly payments; recording fees; copies of easements and restrictions; loan title policy with endorsements required by lender; loan-related inspection fees; photos; amortization schedules; one-half of escrow fee; all prepaid items, including required premiums for flood and hazard insurance, reserve deposits for insurance, ad valorem taxes and special governmental assessments; final compliance inspection; courier fee; repair inspection; underwriting fee; wire transfer fee; expenses incident to any loan; Private

Initialed for identification by Buyer_____ _____ and Seller _____ _____   TREC NO. 20-13

Mortgage Insurance Premium (PMI), VA Loan Funding Fee, or FHA Mortgage Insurance Premium (MIP) as required by the lender; and other expenses payable by Buyer under this contract.

B. If any expense exceeds an amount expressly stated in this contract for such expense to be paid by a party, that party may terminate this contract unless the other party agrees to pay such excess. Buyer may not pay charges and fees expressly prohibited by FHA, VA, Texas Veterans Land Board or other governmental loan program regulations.

13. **PRORATIONS:** Taxes for the current year, interest, maintenance fees, assessments, dues and rents will be prorated through the Closing Date. The tax proration may be calculated taking into consideration any change in exemptions that will affect the current year's taxes. If taxes for the current year vary from the amount prorated at closing, the parties shall adjust the prorations when tax statements for the current year are available. If taxes are not paid at or prior to closing, Buyer shall pay taxes for the current year.

14. **CASUALTY LOSS:** If any part of the Property is damaged or destroyed by fire or other casualty after the effective date of this contract, Seller shall restore the Property to its previous condition as soon as reasonably possible, but in any event by the Closing Date. If Seller fails to do so due to factors beyond Seller's control, Buyer may (a) terminate this contract and the earnest money will be refunded to Buyer (b) extend the time for performance up to 15 days and the Closing Date will be extended as necessary or (c) accept the Property in its damaged condition with an assignment of insurance proceeds, if permitted by Seller's insurance carrier, and receive credit from Seller at closing in the amount of the deductible under the insurance policy. Seller's obligations under this paragraph are independent of any other obligations of Seller under this contract.

15. **DEFAULT:** If Buyer fails to comply with this contract, Buyer will be in default, and Seller may (a) enforce specific performance, seek such other relief as may be provided by law, or both, or (b) terminate this contract and receive the earnest money as liquidated damages, thereby releasing both parties from this contract. If Seller fails to comply with this contract, Seller will be in default and Buyer may (a) enforce specific performance, seek such other relief as may be provided by law, or both, or (b) terminate this contract and receive the earnest money, thereby releasing both parties from this contract.

16. **MEDIATION:** It is the policy of the State of Texas to encourage resolution of disputes through alternative dispute resolution procedures such as mediation. Any dispute between Seller and Buyer related to this contract which is not resolved through informal discussion will be submitted to a mutually acceptable mediation service or provider. The parties to the mediation shall bear the mediation costs equally. This paragraph does not preclude a party from seeking equitable relief from a court of competent jurisdiction.

17. **ATTORNEY'S FEES:** A Buyer, Seller, Listing Broker, Other Broker, or escrow agent who prevails in any legal proceeding related to this contract is entitled to recover reasonable attorney's fees and all costs of such proceeding.

18. **ESCROW:**
A. ESCROW: The escrow agent is not (i) a party to this contract and does not have liability for the performance or nonperformance of any party to this contract, (ii) liable for interest on the earnest money and (iii) liable for the loss of any earnest money caused by the failure of any financial institution in which the earnest money has been deposited unless the financial institution is acting as escrow agent.

B. EXPENSES: At closing, the earnest money must be applied first to any cash down payment, then to Buyer's Expenses and any excess refunded to Buyer. If no closing occurs, escrow agent may: (i) require a written release of liability of the escrow agent from all parties, (ii) require payment of unpaid expenses incurred on behalf of a party, and (iii) only deduct from the earnest money the amount of unpaid expenses incurred on behalf of the party receiving the earnest money.

C. DEMAND: Upon termination of this contract, either party or the escrow agent may send a release of earnest money to each party and the parties shall execute counterparts of the release and deliver same to the escrow agent. If either party fails to execute the release, either party may make a written demand to the escrow agent for the earnest money. If only one party makes written demand for the earnest money, escrow agent shall promptly provide a copy of the demand to the other party. If escrow agent does not receive written objection to the demand from the other party within 15 days, escrow agent may disburse the earnest money to the party making demand reduced by the amount of unpaid expenses incurred on behalf of the party receiving the earnest money and escrow agent may pay the same to the creditors. If escrow agent complies with the provisions of this paragraph, each party hereby releases escrow agent from all adverse claims related to the disbursal of the earnest money.

Contract Concerning _____ 51398 Tartar Ave. _____ Page 7 of 9   11-2-2015
(Address of Property)

D. DAMAGES: Any party who wrongfully fails or refuses to sign a release acceptable to the escrow agent within 7 days of receipt of the request will be liable to the other party for (i) damages; (ii) the earnest money; (iii) reasonable attorney's fees; and (iv) all costs of suit.

E. NOTICES: Escrow agent's notices will be effective when sent in compliance with Paragraph 21. Notice of objection to the demand will be deemed effective upon receipt by escrow agent.

19. **REPRESENTATIONS:** All covenants, representations and warranties in this contract survive closing. If any representation of Seller in this contract is untrue on the Closing Date, Seller will be in default. Unless expressly prohibited by written agreement, Seller may continue to show the Property and receive, negotiate and accept back up offers.

20. **FEDERAL TAX REQUIREMENTS:** If Seller is a "foreign person," as defined by applicable law, or if Seller fails to deliver an affidavit to Buyer that Seller is not a "foreign person," then Buyer shall withhold from the sales proceeds an amount sufficient to comply with applicable tax law and deliver the same to the Internal Revenue Service together with appropriate tax forms. Internal Revenue Service regulations require filing written reports if currency in excess of specified amounts is received in the transaction.

21. **NOTICES:** All notices from one party to the other must be in writing and are effective when mailed to, hand-delivered at, or transmitted by fax or electronic transmission as follows:

To Buyer at:	PO Box 1300	**To Seller at:**	51398 Tartar Ave
	Miguel, Texas 78010		Big Town, Texas 78231
Phone:	(830) 770-1984	Phone:	( )
Fax:	( ) same	Fax:	( )
E-mail:	blizenginvestments@xyz.com	E-mail:	contact lawyer for all correspondence

22. **AGREEMENT OF PARTIES:** This contract contains the entire agreement of the parties and cannot be changed except by their written agreement. Addenda which are a part of this contract are (Check all applicable boxes):

☑ Third Party Financing Addendum

☐ Seller Financing Addendum

☐ Addendum for Property Subject to Mandatory Membership in a Property Owners Association

☐ Buyer's Temporary Residential Lease

☐ Loan Assumption Addendum

☐ Addendum for Sale of Other Property by Buyer

☐ Addendum for Reservation of Oil, Gas and Other Minerals

☐ Addendum for "Back-Up" Contract

☐ Addendum for Coastal Area Property

☐ Environmental Assessment, Threatened or Endangered Species and Wetlands Addendum

☐ Seller's Temporary Residential Lease

☐ Short Sale Addendum

☐ Addendum for Property Located Seaward of the Gulf Intracoastal Waterway

☐ Addendum for Seller's Disclosure of Information on Lead-based Paint and Lead-based Paint Hazards as Required by Federal Law

☐ Addendum for Property in a Propane Gas System Service Area

☑ Other (list): Non Realty Items

Initialed for identification by Buyer_____ _____ and Seller _____ _____   TREC NO. 20-13

Contract Concerning _____ 51398 Tartar Ave. _____ Page 8 of 9   11-2-2015
(Address of Property)

23. TERMINATION OPTION: For nominal consideration, the receipt of which is hereby acknowledged by Seller, and Buyer's agreement to pay Seller $_____ 1,000 (Option Fee) within 3 days after the effective date of this contract, Seller grants Buyer the unrestricted right to terminate this contract by giving notice of termination to Seller within ____10____ days after the effective date of this contract (Option Period). Notices under this paragraph must be given by 5:00 p.m. (local time where the Property is located) by the date specified. If no dollar amount is stated as the Option Fee or if Buyer fails to pay the Option Fee to Seller within the time prescribed, this paragraph will not be a part of this contract and Buyer shall not have the unrestricted right to terminate this contract. If Buyer gives notice of termination within the time prescribed, the Option Fee will not be refunded; however, any earnest money will be refunded to Buyer. The Option Fee ☑will ☐will not be credited to the Sales Price at closing. **Time is of the essence for this paragraph and strict compliance with the time for performance is required.**

24. CONSULT AN ATTORNEY BEFORE SIGNING: TREC rules prohibit real estate license holders from giving legal advice. READ THIS CONTRACT CAREFULLY.

Buyer's
Attorney is: None

Seller's
Attorney is: G.E. Mack

32893 N. Ash Big Town, Texas 78231

Phone: (   ) _____   Phone: (214) 114-1994

Fax: (   ) _____   Fax: (   ) _____

E-mail: _____   E-mail: sumnow@hotspot.org

EXECUTED the _____day of _____, 20____ (EFFECTIVE DATE).
(BROKER: FILL IN THE DATE OF FINAL ACCEPTANCE.)

_____ Buyer

_____ Seller

_____ Buyer

_____ Seller

TREC NO. 20-13

Contract Concerning	51398 Tartar Ave.	Page 9 of 9 11-2-2015
	(Address of Property)	

BROKER INFORMATION
(Print name(s) only. Do not sign)

Linda Talbot Realty	XXXXXXX	Robert Vela	XXXXXXX
Other Broker Firm	License No.	Listing Broker Firm	License No.

represents   ☑ Buyer only as Buyer's agent   represents   ☐ Seller and Buyer as an intermediary
　　　　　　　☐ Seller as Listing Broker's subagent　　　　　　　　 ☑ Seller only as Seller's agent

Connie McKeag	YYYYYYY		
Associate's Name	License No.	Listing Associate's Name	License No.

Linda Talbot	see above		
Licensed Supervisor of Associate	License No.	Licensed Supervisor of Listing Associate	License No.

1103 Mission Trails	972-602-1954	1951 Frio Town Trail	
Other Broker's Address	Fax	Listing Broker's Office Address	Fax

Big Town	TX	78231	Big Town	Texas	78213
City	State	Zip	City	State	Zip

talbotsells@topdrawer.org		newboss@hotstuff.org	210-818-2014
Associate's Email Address	Phone	Listing Associate's Email Address	Phone

Selling Associate's Name	License No.

Licensed Supervisor of Selling Associate	License No.

Selling Associate's Office Address	Fax

City	State	Zip

Selling Associate's Email Address	Phone

Listing Broker has agreed to pay Other Broker____2.5%____of the total sales price when the Listing Broker's fee is received. Escrow agent is authorized and directed to pay other Broker from Listing Broker's fee at closing.

OPTION FEE RECEIPT

Receipt of $_____1,000_____ (Option Fee) in the form of _____check_____ is acknowledged.

_____	_____
Seller or Listing Broker	Date

CONTRACT AND EARNEST MONEY RECEIPT

Receipt of ☐Contract and ☐$_____Earnest Money in the form of _____
is acknowledged.

Escrow Agent: _____   Date: _____

By: _____
　　　　　　　　　　　　　　　　　　　　　 _____
_____   Email Address
Address　　　　　　　　　　　　　　　　　　　　　　　　 Phone: (____)_____

_____   Fax: (____)_____
City　　　　　　　　State　　　　　　　Zip

PROMULGATED BY THE TEXAS REAL ESTATE COMMISSION (TREC)   12-05-11

ADDENDUM FOR
RELEASE OF LIABILITY ON ASSUMED LOAN
AND/OR RESTORATION OF SELLER'S VA ENTITLEMENT

TO CONTRACT CONCERNING THE PROPERTY AT

1948 Avenida del Toro
(Address of Property)

☐ **A. RELEASE OF SELLER'S LIABILITY ON LOAN TO BE ASSUMED:**

Within _____5_____ days after the effective date of this contract Seller and Buyer shall apply for release of Seller's liability from (a) any conventional lender, (b) VA and any lender whose loan has been guaranteed by VA, or (c) FHA and any lender whose loan has been insured by FHA. Seller and Buyer shall furnish all required information and documents. If any release of liability has not been approved by the Closing Date: (check one box only)

☑ (1) This contract will terminate and the earnest money will be refunded to Buyer.

☐ (2) Failure to obtain release approval will not delay closing.

☐ **B. RESTORATION OF SELLER'S ENTITLEMENT FOR VA LOAN:**

Within _____30_____ days after the effective date of this contract Seller and Buyer shall apply for restoration of Seller's VA entitlement and shall furnish all information and documents required by VA. If restoration has not been approved by the Closing Date: (check one box only)

☑ (1) This contract will terminate and the earnest money will be refunded to Buyer.

☐ (2) Failure to obtain restoration approval will not delay closing.

NOTICE: VA will not restore Seller's VA entitlement unless Buyer: (a) is a veteran, (b) has sufficient unused VA entitlement and (c) is otherwise qualified. If Seller desires restoration of VA entitlement, paragraphs A and B should be used.

Seller shall pay the cost of securing the release and restoration.

Seller's deed will contain any loan assumption clause required by FHA, VA or any lender.

_____   _____
Buyer   Seller

_____   _____
Buyer   Seller

PROMULGATED BY THE TEXAS REAL ESTATE COMMISSION (TREC)
11-2-2015
ONE TO FOUR FAMILY RESIDENTIAL CONTRACT (RESALE)

NOTICE: Not For Use For Condominium Transactions

1. PARTIES: The parties to this contract are _Berle T. Barnett and wife Barbara S. Barnett_
(Seller) and _Elmer W. Lindsey and wife Helen Elizabeth Lindsey_ (Buyer).
Seller agrees to sell and convey to Buyer and Buyer agrees to buy from Seller the Property defined below.

2. PROPERTY: The land, improvements and accessories are collectively referred to as the "Property".

- A. LAND: Lot _14_ Block _11_, _Avenida del Sol_
  Addition, City of _Walkertown_, County of _Propserous_,
  Texas, known as _1948 Avenida del Toro 78007_
  (address/zip code), or as described on attached exhibit.
- B. IMPROVEMENTS: The house, garage and all other fixtures and improvements attached to the above-described real property, including without limitation, the following **permanently installed and built-in items,** if any: all equipment and appliances, valances, screens, shutters, awnings, wall-to-wall carpeting, mirrors, ceiling fans, attic fans, mail boxes, television antennas, mounts and brackets for televisions and speakers, heating and air-conditioning units, security and fire detection equipment, wiring, plumbing and lighting fixtures, chandeliers, water softener system, kitchen equipment, garage door openers, cleaning equipment, shrubbery, landscaping, outdoor cooking equipment, and all other property owned by Seller and attached to the above described real property.
- C. ACCESSORIES: The following described related accessories, if any: window air conditioning units, stove, fireplace screens, curtains and rods, blinds, window shades, draperies and rods, door keys, mailbox keys, above ground pool, swimming pool equipment and maintenance accessories, artificial fireplace logs, and controls for: (i) garage doors, (ii) entry gates, and (iii) other improvements and accessories.
- D. EXCLUSIONS: The following improvements and accessories will be retained by Seller and must be removed prior to delivery of possession: _none_.

3. SALES PRICE:

- A. Cash portion of Sales Price payable by Buyer at closing .... $_____100,000_
- B. Sum of all financing described in the attached: ☐ Third Party Financing Addendum,
  ☑ Loan Assumption Addendum, ☐ Seller Financing Addendum .... $_____69,000_
- C. Sales Price (Sum of A and B) .... $_____169,000_

4. LICENSE HOLDER DISCLOSURE: Texas law requires a real estate license holder who is a party to a transaction or acting on behalf of a spouse, parent, child, business entity in which the license holder owns more than 10%, or a trust for which the license holder acts as a trustee or of which the license holder or the license holder's spouse, parent or child is a beneficiary, to notify the other party in writing before entering into a contract of sale. Disclose if applicable:_____

5. EARNEST MONEY: Upon execution of this contract by all parties, Buyer shall deposit $_10,000_ as earnest money with _Pam Jason_, as escrow agent, at _Jodaro Title Company 15022 Red Robin Walkertown, Texas 78007_ (address). Buyer shall deposit additional earnest money of $_____None_ with escrow agent within __0__ days after the effective date of this contract. If Buyer fails to deposit the earnest money as required by this contract, Buyer will be in default.

6. TITLE POLICY AND SURVEY:

- A. TITLE POLICY: Seller shall furnish to Buyer at ☑ Seller's ☐ Buyer's expense an owner policy of title insurance (Title Policy) issued by _Jodaro Title Company_ (Title Company) in the amount of the Sales Price, dated at or after closing, insuring Buyer against loss under the provisions of the Title Policy, subject to the promulgated exclusions (including existing building and zoning ordinances) and the following exceptions:
  (1) Restrictive covenants common to the platted subdivision in which the Property is located.
  (2) The standard printed exception for standby fees, taxes and assessments.
  (3) Liens created as part of the financing described in Paragraph 3.
  (4) Utility easements created by the dedication deed or plat of the subdivision in which the Property is located.

Initialed for identification by Buyer_____ _____ and Seller _____ _____   TREC NO. 20-13

Contract Concerning _____ 1948 Avenida del Toro _____ Page 2 of 9   11-2-2015
(Address of Property)

(5) Reservations or exceptions otherwise permitted by this contract or as may be approved by Buyer in writing.

(6) The standard printed exception as to marital rights.

(7) The standard printed exception as to waters, tidelands, beaches, streams, and related matters.

(8) The standard printed exception as to discrepancies, conflicts, shortages in area or boundary lines, encroachments or protrusions, or overlapping improvements: ☑(i) will not be amended or deleted from the title policy; or ☐(ii) will be amended to read, "shortages in area" at the expense of ☐Buyer ☐Seller.

B. COMMITMENT: Within 20 days after the Title Company receives a copy of this contract, Seller shall furnish to Buyer a commitment for title insurance (Commitment) and, at Buyer's expense, legible copies of restrictive covenants and documents evidencing exceptions in the Commitment (Exception Documents) other than the standard printed exceptions. Seller authorizes the Title Company to deliver the Commitment and Exception Documents to Buyer at Buyer's address shown in Paragraph 21. If the Commitment and Exception Documents are not delivered to Buyer within the specified time, the time for delivery will be automatically extended up to 15 days or 3 days before the Closing Date, whichever is earlier. If, due to factors beyond Seller's control, the Commitment and Exception Documents are not delivered within the time required, Buyer may terminate this contract and the earnest money will be refunded to Buyer.

C. SURVEY: The survey must be made by a registered professional land surveyor acceptable to the Title Company and Buyer's lender(s). (Check one box only)

☐(1) Within _____ days after the effective date of this contract, Seller shall furnish to Buyer and Title Company Seller's existing survey of the Property and a Residential Real Property Affidavit promulgated by the Texas Department of Insurance (T-47 Affidavit). **If Seller fails to furnish the existing survey or affidavit within the time prescribed, Buyer shall obtain a new survey at Seller's expense no later than 3 days prior to Closing Date.** If the existing survey or affidavit is not acceptable to Title Company or Buyer's lender(s), Buyer shall obtain a new survey at ☐Seller's ☐Buyer's expense no later than 3 days prior to Closing Date.

☐(2) Within _____ days after the effective date of this contract, Buyer shall obtain a new survey at Buyer's expense. Buyer is deemed to receive the survey on the date of actual receipt or the date specified in this paragraph, whichever is earlier.

☑(3) Within ___10___ days after the effective date of this contract, Seller, at Seller's expense shall furnish a new survey to Buyer.

D. OBJECTIONS: Buyer may object in writing to defects, exceptions, or encumbrances to title: disclosed on the survey other than items 6A(1) through (7) above; disclosed in the Commitment other than items 6A(1) through (8) above; or which prohibit the following use or activity: _None_____.
Buyer must object the earlier of (i) the Closing Date or (ii) ___10___ days after Buyer receives the Commitment, Exception Documents, and the survey. Buyer's failure to object within the time allowed will constitute a waiver of Buyer's right to object; except that the requirements in Schedule C of the Commitment are not waived by Buyer. Provided Seller is not obligated to incur any expense, Seller shall cure the timely objections of Buyer or any third party lender within 15 days after Seller receives the objections and the Closing Date will be extended as necessary. If objections are not cured within such 15 day period, this contract will terminate and the earnest money will be refunded to Buyer unless Buyer waives the objections.

E. TITLE NOTICES:

(1) ABSTRACT OR TITLE POLICY: Broker advises Buyer to have an abstract of title covering the Property examined by an attorney of Buyer's selection, or Buyer should be furnished with or obtain a Title Policy. If a Title Policy is furnished, the Commitment should be promptly reviewed by an attorney of Buyer's choice due to the time limitations on Buyer's right to object.

(2) MEMBERSHIP IN PROPERTY OWNERS ASSOCIATION(S): The Property ☐is ☑is not subject to mandatory membership in a property owners association(s). If the Property is subject to mandatory membership in a property owners association(s), Seller notifies Buyer under §5.012, Texas Property Code, that, as a purchaser of property in the residential community identified in Paragraph 2A in which the Property is located, you are obligated to be a member of the property owners association(s). Restrictive covenants governing the use and occupancy of the Property and all dedicatory instruments governing the establishment, maintenance, or operation of this residential community have been or will be recorded in the Real Property Records of the county in which the Property is located. Copies of the restrictive covenants and dedicatory instruments may be obtained from the county clerk. **You are obligated to pay assessments to the property owners association(s). The amount of the assessments is subject to**

Initialed for identification by Buyer_____ _____ and Seller _____ _____   TREC NO. 20-13

Contract Concerning _____ 1948 Avenida del Toro _____ Page 3 of 9   11-2-2015
(Address of Property)

change. Your failure to pay the assessments could result in enforcement of the association's lien on and the foreclosure of the Property.
Section 207.003, Property Code, entitles an owner to receive copies of any document that governs the establishment, maintenance, or operation of a subdivision, including, but not limited to, restrictions, bylaws, rules and regulations, and a resale certificate from a property owners' association. A resale certificate contains information including, but not limited to, statements specifying the amount and frequency of regular assessments and the style and cause number of lawsuits to which the property owners' association is a party, other than lawsuits relating to unpaid ad valorem taxes of an individual member of the association. These documents must be made available to you by the property owners' association or the association's agent on your request.
If Buyer is concerned about these matters, the TREC promulgated Addendum for Property Subject to Mandatory Membership in a Property Owners Association(s) should be used.

(3) STATUTORY TAX DISTRICTS: If the Property is situated in a utility or other statutorily created district providing water, sewer, drainage, or flood control facilities and services, Chapter 49, Texas Water Code, requires Seller to deliver and Buyer to sign the statutory notice relating to the tax rate, bonded indebtedness, or standby fee of the district prior to final execution of this contract.

(4) TIDE WATERS: If the Property abuts the tidally influenced waters of the state, §33.135, Texas Natural Resources Code, requires a notice regarding coastal area property to be included in the contract. An addendum containing the notice promulgated by TREC or required by the parties must be used.

(5) ANNEXATION: If the Property is located outside the limits of a municipality, Seller notifies Buyer under §5.011, Texas Property Code, that the Property may now or later be included in the extraterritorial jurisdiction of a municipality and may now or later be subject to annexation by the municipality. Each municipality maintains a map that depicts its boundaries and extraterritorial jurisdiction. To determine if the Property is located within a municipality's extraterritorial jurisdiction or is likely to be located within a municipality's extraterritorial jurisdiction, contact all municipalities located in the general proximity of the Property for further information.

(6) PROPERTY LOCATED IN A CERTIFICATED SERVICE AREA OF A UTILITY SERVICE PROVIDER: Notice required by §13.257, Water Code: The real property, described in Paragraph 2, that you are about to purchase may be located in a certificated water or sewer service area, which is authorized by law to provide water or sewer service to the properties in the certificated area. If your property is located in a certificated area there may be special costs or charges that you will be required to pay before you can receive water or sewer service. There may be a period required to construct lines or other facilities necessary to provide water or sewer service to your property. You are advised to determine if the property is in a certificated area and contact the utility service provider to determine the cost that you will be required to pay and the period, if any, that is required to provide water or sewer service to your property. The undersigned Buyer hereby acknowledges receipt of the foregoing notice at or before the execution of a binding contract for the purchase of the real property described in Paragraph 2 or at closing of purchase of the real property.

(7) PUBLIC IMPROVEMENT DISTRICTS: If the Property is in a public improvement district, §5.014, Property Code, requires Seller to notify Buyer as follows: As a purchaser of this parcel of real property you are obligated to pay an assessment to a municipality or county for an improvement project undertaken by a public improvement district under Chapter 372, Local Government Code. The assessment may be due annually or in periodic installments. More information concerning the amount of the assessment and the due dates of that assessment may be obtained from the municipality or county levying the assessment. The amount of the assessments is subject to change. Your failure to pay the assessments could result in a lien on and the foreclosure of your property.

(8) TRANSFER FEES: If the Property is subject to a private transfer fee obligation, §5.205, Property Code, requires Seller to notify Buyer as follows: The private transfer fee obligation may be governed by Chapter 5, Subchapter G of the Texas Property Code.

(9) PROPANE GAS SYSTEM SERVICE AREA: If the Property is located in a propane gas system service area owned by a distribution system retailer, Seller must give Buyer written notice as required by §141.010, Texas Utilities Code. An addendum containing the notice approved by TREC or required by the parties should be used.

(10) NOTICE OF WATER LEVEL FLUCTUATIONS: If the Property adjoins an impoundment of water, including a reservoir or lake, constructed and maintained under Chapter 11, Water Code, that has a storage capacity of at least 5,000 acre-feet at the impoundment's normal operating level, Seller hereby notifies Buyer: "The water level of the impoundment of water adjoining the Property fluctuates for various reasons, including as

Initialed for identification by Buyer_____ _____ and Seller _____ _____   TREC NO. 20-13

Contract Concerning _____1948 Avenida del Toro_____ Page 4 of 9   11-2-2015
(Address of Property)

a result of: (1) an entity lawfully exercising its right to use the water stored in the impoundment; or (2) drought or flood conditions."

7.PROPERTY CONDITION:

A. ACCESS, INSPECTIONS AND UTILITIES: Seller shall permit Buyer and Buyer's agents access to the Property at reasonable times. Buyer may have the Property inspected by inspectors selected by Buyer and licensed by TREC or otherwise permitted by law to make inspections. Any hydrostatic testing must be separately authorized by Seller in writing. Seller at Seller's expense shall immediately cause existing utilities to be turned on and shall keep the utilities on during the time this contract is in effect.

B. SELLER'S DISCLOSURE NOTICE PURSUANT TO §5.008, TEXAS PROPERTY CODE (Notice): (Check one box only)

☑ (1) Buyer has received the Notice.

❑ (2) Buyer has not received the Notice. Within _____ days after the effective date of this contract, Seller shall deliver the Notice to Buyer. If Buyer does not receive the Notice, Buyer may terminate this contract at any time prior to the closing and the earnest money will be refunded to Buyer. If Seller delivers the Notice, Buyer may terminate this contract for any reason within 7 days after Buyer receives the Notice or prior to the closing, whichever first occurs, and the earnest money will be refunded to Buyer.

❑ (3)The Seller is not required to furnish the notice under the Texas Property Code.

C. SELLER'S DISCLOSURE OF LEAD-BASED PAINT AND LEAD-BASED PAINT HAZARDS is required by Federal law for a residential dwelling constructed prior to 1978.

D. ACCEPTANCE OF PROPERTY CONDITION: "As Is" means the present condition of the Property with any and all defects and without warranty except for the warranties of title and the warranties in this contract. Buyer's agreement to accept the Property As Is under Paragraph 7D(1) or (2) does not preclude Buyer from inspecting the Property under Paragraph 7A, from negotiating repairs or treatments in a subsequent amendment, or from terminating this contract during the Option Period, if any.
(Check one box only)

☑ (1) Buyer accepts the Property As Is.

❑ (2) Buyer accepts the Property As Is provided Seller, at Seller's expense, shall complete the following specific repairs and treatments: _____.
_____.
(Do not insert general phrases, such as "subject to inspections" that do not identify specific repairs and treatments.)

E. LENDER REQUIRED REPAIRS AND TREATMENTS: Unless otherwise agreed in writing, neither party is obligated to pay for lender required repairs, which includes treatment for wood destroying insects. If the parties do not agree to pay for the lender required repairs or treatments, this contract will terminate and the earnest money will be refunded to Buyer. If the cost of lender required repairs and treatments exceeds 5% of the Sales Price, Buyer may terminate this contract and the earnest money will be refunded to Buyer.

F. COMPLETION OF REPAIRS AND TREATMENTS: Unless otherwise agreed in writing: (i) Seller shall complete all agreed repairs and treatments prior to the Closing Date; and (ii) all required permits must be obtained, and repairs and treatments must be performed by persons who are licensed to provide such repairs or treatments or, if no license is required by law, are commercially engaged in the trade of providing such repairs or treatments. At Buyer's election, any transferable warranties received by Seller with respect to the repairs and treatments will be transferred to Buyer at Buyer's expense. If Seller fails to complete any agreed repairs and treatments prior to the Closing Date, Buyer may exercise remedies under Paragraph 15 or extend the Closing Date up to 5 days if necessary for Seller to complete the repairs and treatments.

G. ENVIRONMENTAL MATTERS: Buyer is advised that the presence of wetlands, toxic substances, including asbestos and wastes or other environmental hazards, or the presence of a threatened or endangered species or its habitat may affect Buyer's intended use of the Property. If Buyer is concerned about these matters, an addendum promulgated by TREC or required by the parties should be used.

H. RESIDENTIAL SERVICE CONTRACTS: Buyer may purchase a residential service contract from a residential service company licensed by TREC. If Buyer purchases a residential service contract, Seller shall reimburse Buyer at closing for the cost of the residential service contract in an amount not exceeding $_____None__. Buyer should review any residential service contract for the scope of coverage, exclusions and limitations. **The purchase of a residential service contract is optional. Similar coverage may be purchased from various companies authorized to do business in Texas.**

8.BROKERS' FEES: All obligations of the parties for payment of brokers' fees are contained in separate written agreements.

Initialed for identification by Buyer_____ _____ and Seller _____ _____   TREC NO. 20-13

Contract Concerning _____ 1948 Avenida del Toro _____ Page 5 of 9   11-2-2015
(Address of Property)

9. CLOSING:

A. The closing of the sale will be on or before _____ Septermber 9 _____, 20 _15_, or within 7 days after objections made under Paragraph 6D have been cured or waived, whichever date is later (Closing Date). If either party fails to close the sale by the Closing Date, the non-defaulting party may exercise the remedies contained in Paragraph 15.

B. At closing:

(1) Seller shall execute and deliver a general warranty deed conveying title to the Property to Buyer and showing no additional exceptions to those permitted in Paragraph 6 and furnish tax statements or certificates showing no delinquent taxes on the Property.

(2) Buyer shall pay the Sales Price in good funds acceptable to the escrow agent.

(3) Seller and Buyer shall execute and deliver any notices, statements, certificates, affidavits, releases, loan documents and other documents reasonably required for the closing of the sale and the issuance of the Title Policy.

(4) There will be no liens, assessments, or security interests against the Property which will not be satisfied out of the sales proceeds unless securing the payment of any loans assumed by Buyer and assumed loans will not be in default.

(5) If the Property is subject to a residential lease, Seller shall transfer security deposits (as defined under §92.102, Property Code), if any, to Buyer. In such an event, Buyer shall deliver to the tenant a signed statement acknowledging that the Buyer has acquired the Property and is responsible for the return of the security deposit, and specifying the exact dollar amount of the security deposit.

10. POSSESSION:

A. Buyer's Possession: Seller shall deliver to Buyer possession of the Property in its present or required condition, ordinary wear and tear excepted: ☑upon closing and funding ☐according to a temporary residential lease form promulgated by TREC or other written lease required by the parties. Any possession by Buyer prior to closing or by Seller after closing which is not authorized by a written lease will establish a tenancy at sufferance relationship between the parties. **Consult your insurance agent prior to change of ownership and possession because insurance coverage may be limited or terminated. The absence of a written lease or appropriate insurance coverage may expose the parties to economic loss.**

B. Leases:

(1) After the Effective Date, Seller may not execute any lease (including but not limited to mineral leases) or convey any interest in the Property without Buyer's written consent.

(2) If the Property is subject to any lease to which Seller is a party, Seller shall deliver to Buyer copies of the lease(s) and any move-in condition form signed by the tenant within 7 days after the Effective Date of the contract.

11. SPECIAL PROVISIONS: (Insert only factual statements and business details applicable to the sale. TREC rules prohibit license holders from adding factual statements or business details for which a contract addendum, lease or other form has been promulgated by TREC for mandatory use.)

Sale is conditional upon Buyer's ability to assume existing VA loan in the amount of $69,000. Sellers attorney to review and approve any documents associated with this sale prior to Sellers signing.

12. SETTLEMENT AND OTHER EXPENSES:

A. The following expenses must be paid at or prior to closing:

(1) Expenses payable by Seller (Seller's Expenses):

(a) Releases of existing liens, including prepayment penalties and recording fees; release of Seller's loan liability; tax statements or certificates; preparation of deed; one-half of escrow fee; and other expenses payable by Seller under this contract.

(b) Seller shall also pay an amount not to exceed $_____ None to be applied in the following order: Buyer's Expenses which Buyer is prohibited from paying by FHA, VA, Texas Veterans Land Board or other governmental loan programs, and then to other Buyer's Expenses as allowed by the lender.

(2) Expenses payable by Buyer (Buyer's Expenses): Appraisal fees; loan application fees; origination charges; credit reports; preparation of loan documents; interest on the notes from date of disbursement to one month prior to dates of first monthly payments; recording fees; copies of easements and restrictions; loan title policy with endorsements required by lender; loan-related inspection fees; photos; amortization schedules; one-half of escrow fee; all prepaid items, including required premiums for flood and hazard insurance, reserve deposits for insurance, ad valorem taxes and special governmental assessments; final compliance inspection; courier fee; repair inspection; underwriting fee; wire transfer fee; expenses incident to any loan; Private

Initialed for identification by Buyer_____ _____ and Seller _____ _____   TREC NO. 20-13

Mortgage Insurance Premium (PMI), VA Loan Funding Fee, or FHA Mortgage Insurance Premium (MIP) as required by the lender; and other expenses payable by Buyer under this contract.

B. If any expense exceeds an amount expressly stated in this contract for such expense to be paid by a party, that party may terminate this contract unless the other party agrees to pay such excess. Buyer may not pay charges and fees expressly prohibited by FHA, VA, Texas Veterans Land Board or other governmental loan program regulations.

13. **PRORATIONS:** Taxes for the current year, interest, maintenance fees, assessments, dues and rents will be prorated through the Closing Date. The tax proration may be calculated taking into consideration any change in exemptions that will affect the current year's taxes. If taxes for the current year vary from the amount prorated at closing, the parties shall adjust the prorations when tax statements for the current year are available. If taxes are not paid at or prior to closing, Buyer shall pay taxes for the current year.

14. **CASUALTY LOSS:** If any part of the Property is damaged or destroyed by fire or other casualty after the effective date of this contract, Seller shall restore the Property to its previous condition as soon as reasonably possible, but in any event by the Closing Date. If Seller fails to do so due to factors beyond Seller's control, Buyer may (a) terminate this contract and the earnest money will be refunded to Buyer (b) extend the time for performance up to 15 days and the Closing Date will be extended as necessary or (c) accept the Property in its damaged condition with an assignment of insurance proceeds, if permitted by Seller's insurance carrier, and receive credit from Seller at closing in the amount of the deductible under the insurance policy. Seller's obligations under this paragraph are independent of any other obligations of Seller under this contract.

15. **DEFAULT:** If Buyer fails to comply with this contract, Buyer will be in default, and Seller may (a) enforce specific performance, seek such other relief as may be provided by law, or both, or (b) terminate this contract and receive the earnest money as liquidated damages, thereby releasing both parties from this contract. If Seller fails to comply with this contract, Seller will be in default and Buyer may (a) enforce specific performance, seek such other relief as may be provided by law, or both, or (b) terminate this contract and receive the earnest money, thereby releasing both parties from this contract.

16. **MEDIATION:** It is the policy of the State of Texas to encourage resolution of disputes through alternative dispute resolution procedures such as mediation. Any dispute between Seller and Buyer related to this contract which is not resolved through informal discussion will be submitted to a mutually acceptable mediation service or provider. The parties to the mediation shall bear the mediation costs equally. This paragraph does not preclude a party from seeking equitable relief from a court of competent jurisdiction.

17. **ATTORNEY'S FEES:** A Buyer, Seller, Listing Broker, Other Broker, or escrow agent who prevails in any legal proceeding related to this contract is entitled to recover reasonable attorney's fees and all costs of such proceeding.

18. **ESCROW:**
A. ESCROW: The escrow agent is not (i) a party to this contract and does not have liability for the performance or nonperformance of any party to this contract, (ii) liable for interest on the earnest money and (iii) liable for the loss of any earnest money caused by the failure of any financial institution in which the earnest money has been deposited unless the financial institution is acting as escrow agent.

B. EXPENSES: At closing, the earnest money must be applied first to any cash down payment, then to Buyer's Expenses and any excess refunded to Buyer. If no closing occurs, escrow agent may: (i) require a written release of liability of the escrow agent from all parties, (ii) require payment of unpaid expenses incurred on behalf of a party, and (iii) only deduct from the earnest money the amount of unpaid expenses incurred on behalf of the party receiving the earnest money.

C. DEMAND: Upon termination of this contract, either party or the escrow agent may send a release of earnest money to each party and the parties shall execute counterparts of the release and deliver same to the escrow agent. If either party fails to execute the release, either party may make a written demand to the escrow agent for the earnest money. If only one party makes written demand for the earnest money, escrow agent shall promptly provide a copy of the demand to the other party. If escrow agent does not receive written objection to the demand from the other party within 15 days, escrow agent may disburse the earnest money to the party making demand reduced by the amount of unpaid expenses incurred on behalf of the party receiving the earnest money and escrow agent may pay the same to the creditors. If escrow agent complies with the provisions of this paragraph, each party hereby releases escrow agent from all adverse claims related to the disbursal of the earnest money.

Initialed for identification by Buyer_____ _____ and Seller _____ _____   TREC NO. 20-13

Contract Concerning _____ 1948 Avenida del Toro _____ Page 7 of 9   11-2-2015
(Address of Property)

D. DAMAGES: Any party who wrongfully fails or refuses to sign a release acceptable to the escrow agent within 7 days of receipt of the request will be liable to the other party for (i) damages; (ii) the earnest money; (iii) reasonable attorney's fees; and (iv) all costs of suit.

E. NOTICES: Escrow agent's notices will be effective when sent in compliance with Paragraph 21. Notice of objection to the demand will be deemed effective upon receipt by escrow agent.

19. **REPRESENTATIONS:** All covenants, representations and warranties in this contract survive closing. If any representation of Seller in this contract is untrue on the Closing Date, Seller will be in default. Unless expressly prohibited by written agreement, Seller may continue to show the Property and receive, negotiate and accept back up offers.

20. **FEDERAL TAX REQUIREMENTS:** If Seller is a "foreign person," as defined by applicable law, or if Seller fails to deliver an affidavit to Buyer that Seller is not a "foreign person," then Buyer shall withhold from the sales proceeds an amount sufficient to comply with applicable tax law and deliver the same to the Internal Revenue Service together with appropriate tax forms. Internal Revenue Service regulations require filing written reports if currency in excess of specified amounts is received in the transaction.

21. **NOTICES:** All notices from one party to the other must be in writing and are effective when mailed to, hand-delivered at, or transmitted by fax or electronic transmission as follows:

To Buyer at:	4242 Lighthouse Way	**To Seller at:**	1948 Avenida del Toro
	Walkertown, Texas 78007		Walkertown, Texas 78007
Phone:	(555) 393-0270	Phone:	(555) 393-0654
Fax:	( ) None	Fax:	( ) Same as above
E-mail:	None	E-mail:	LTCBB@southsan.com

22. **AGREEMENT OF PARTIES:** This contract contains the entire agreement of the parties and cannot be changed except by their written agreement. Addenda which are a part of this contract are (Check all applicable boxes):

❑ Third Party Financing Addendum

❑ Seller Financing Addendum

❑ Addendum for Property Subject to Mandatory Membership in a Property Owners Association

❑ Buyer's Temporary Residential Lease

❑ Loan Assumption Addendum

❑ Addendum for Sale of Other Property by Buyer

❑ Addendum for Reservation of Oil, Gas and Other Minerals

❑ Addendum for "Back-Up" Contract

❑ Addendum for Coastal Area Property

❑ Environmental Assessment, Threatened or Endangered Species and Wetlands Addendum

❑ Seller's Temporary Residential Lease

❑ Short Sale Addendum

❑ Addendum for Property Located Seaward of the Gulf Intracoastal Waterway

❑ Addendum for Seller's Disclosure of Information on Lead-based Paint and Lead-based Paint Hazards as Required by Federal Law

❑ Addendum for Property in a Propane Gas System Service Area

☑ Other (list): Release of Liability on Assumed Loan
_____

Initialed for identification by Buyer_____ _____ and Seller _____ _____   TREC NO. 20-13

Contract Concerning _____ 1948 Avenida del Toro _____ Page 8 of 9   11-2-2015
(Address of Property)

23. TERMINATION OPTION: For nominal consideration, the receipt of which is hereby acknowledged by Seller, and Buyer's agreement to pay Seller $_____ 500 (Option Fee) within 3 days after the effective date of this contract, Seller grants Buyer the unrestricted right to terminate this contract by giving notice of termination to Seller within ____15____ days after the effective date of this contract (Option Period). Notices under this paragraph must be given by 5:00 p.m. (local time where the Property is located) by the date specified. If no dollar amount is stated as the Option Fee or if Buyer fails to pay the Option Fee to Seller within the time prescribed, this paragraph will not be a part of this contract and Buyer shall not have the unrestricted right to terminate this contract. If Buyer gives notice of termination within the time prescribed, the Option Fee will not be refunded; however, any earnest money will be refunded to Buyer. The Option Fee ☑will ☐will not be credited to the Sales Price at closing. **Time is of the essence for this paragraph and strict compliance with the time for performance is required.**

24. CONSULT AN ATTORNEY BEFORE SIGNING: TREC rules prohibit real estate license holders from giving legal advice. READ THIS CONTRACT CAREFULLY.

Buyer's
Attorney is: Christene Stanley

PO Box 2309 Walkerstown, Texas 78007

Phone: (555) 223-2250

Fax: (   ) Same

E-mail: chris@stanleylaw.org

Seller's
Attorney is: Debra Crowther

Phone: (555) 393-1257

Fax: (   ) Same

E-mail: crowtherlaw@legal.org

**EXECUTED the _____day of _____, 20____ (EFFECTIVE DATE).
(BROKER: FILL IN THE DATE OF FINAL ACCEPTANCE.)**

_____
Buyer

_____
Seller

_____
Buyer

_____
Seller

The form of this contract has been approved by the Texas Real Estate Commission. TREC forms are intended for use only by trained real estate license holders. No representation is made as to the legal validity or adequacy of any provision in any specific transactions. It is not intended for complex transactions. Texas Real Estate Commission, P.O. Box 12188, Austin, TX 78711-2188, (512) 936-3000 (http://www.trec.texas.gov) TREC NO. 20-13. This form replaces TREC NO. 20-12.

TREC NO. 20-13

Contract Concerning _____ 1948 Avenida del Toro _____ Page 9 of 9   11-2-2015
(Address of Property)

BROKER INFORMATION
(Print name(s) only. Do not sign)

CB Anderson Realty   XXXXXXX   None
Other Broker Firm   License No.   Listing Broker Firm   License No.

represents ☑ Buyer only as Buyer's agent   represents ☐ Seller and Buyer as an intermediary
            ☐ Seller as Listing Broker's subagent   ☐ Seller only as Seller's agent

Betty Anderson   XXXXXXX
Associate's Name   License No.   Listing Associate's Name   License No.

Licensed Supervisor of Associate   License No.   Licensed Supervisor of Listing Associate   License No.

303 Langford Blvd. Suite 144
Other Broker's Address   Fax   Listing Broker's Office Address   Fax

Smallerville   Texas   78281
City   State   Zip   City   State   Zip

betty@cbarealty.com   555-822-1756
Associate's Email Address   Phone   Listing Associate's Email Address   Phone

                                              Selling Associate's Name   License No.

                                              Licensed Supervisor of Selling Associate   License No.

                                              Selling Associate's Office Address   Fax

                                              City   State   Zip

                                              Selling Associate's Email Address   Phone

Listing Broker has agreed to pay Other Broker_____N/A_____of the total sales price when the Listing Broker's fee is received. Escrow agent is authorized and directed to pay other Broker from Listing Broker's fee at closing.

OPTION FEE RECEIPT

Receipt of $_____500____ (Option Fee) in the form of _____Cashiers Check_____ is acknowledged.

_____   _____
Seller or Listing Broker   Date

CONTRACT AND EARNEST MONEY RECEIPT

Receipt of ☐Contract and ☐$_____Earnest Money in the form of _____
is acknowledged.

Escrow Agent: _____   Date: _____

By: _____
                                    Email Address
_____   Phone: (____)_____
Address
_____   Fax: (____)_____
City   State   Zip

as liquidated damages in the event of default as addressed in the identified remedies listed in paragraph 15, and is not necessary to bind the contract. There is no set rule for what amount the earnest money must be.

2. When must earnest money be deposited with an escrow agent?

   TREC Rule 535.146 (a)(b) requires that earnest money be deposited with the escrow agent selected by the parties no later than the close of the second business day after the date the broker receives it.

3. Who should deliver the earnest money to the escrow agent?

   The buyer's agent or buyer should deliver the earnest money to the escrow agent named in paragraph 5 of the contract. The only exception occurs when the principals agree that a deposit may be delayed and a different time is expressly defined in paragraph 11 of the contract [Rule 535.146 (a)(b)(3)].

4. What is an option fee?

   The option fee is a nominal amount which allows the buyer the unrestricted right to terminate the contract by giving notice of termination to the seller within a predetermined number of days after the effective date of the contract ("Option Period"). The typical option fee is $10 per day for the length of the option period.

5. When must the option fee be delivered to the seller?

   Paragraph 23 of the contract says that the buyer's option fee will be delivered to the seller within three calendar days of the effective date of the contract. If it is delivered to an agent at the listing broker's office, legally it has been delivered to the seller.

6. What is a title policy?

   A title policy is title insurance that indemnifies the buyer from financial loss in the event of title failure. Providing title insurance is the best way for the seller to show evidence of clear title.

LESSONS TO LEARN ANSWER

Becky has a few options. Since she is still within her option period, she can cancel the contract and receive her earnest money back. She can present her inspection to the seller's agent and request that the plumbing be fixed as a condition of closing. Or she can pay to have the plumbing fixed herself and proceed with the contract.

CHAPTER 5

CASE STUDY/WORKSHOP

1. Using the One to Four Family Residential (Resale) Contract, where are the seller's expenses found? The buyer?

   Seller: Paragraph 12A(1)

   Buyer: Paragraph 12A(2)

2. According to paragraph 23, the option money is to be delivered to whom?

   The seller

3. If the option money is not delivered to the proper party within the proper time frame, what is the status of the contract?

   If the option money is not delivered to the proper party within the proper time frame, the contract is still valid, however, paragraph 23 is NOT a part of the contract, and the buyer will not have the unrestricted right to terminate the contract.

4. A property closes on February 2. The buyer and seller agreed to a 10-day Seller's Temporary Residential Lease. On February 15, the seller is still in the home. What, if any, remedies does the buyer have?

   The landlord (buyer) may charge the tenant (seller) a predetermined daily rate as damages during the period of any possession after the termination date, in addition to any other remedies to which the landlord is entitled by law.

5. What happens if the buyer fails to pay the option fee to the seller within the required time period? How many days does the buyer have to give the option money to the seller?

   The buyer must deliver the option fee within three calendar days. If the fee is not received within the required time period, the contract is still valid; however, paragraph 23 is NOT a part of the contract, and the buyer will not have the unrestricted right to terminate the contract.

6. A property appraises for $200,000 and, prior to closing, sustains $14,000 worth of fire damage. The seller refuses to pay for the repairs. Does the buyer have to cover the expense of the repairs? Why or why not?

   According to paragraph 14:

   - The buyer may terminate the contract and receive their earnest money,

- The buyer may also extend the time for performance up to 15 days, and the closing date will be extended as necessary, or

- Accept the property in its currently damaged condition with an assignment of insurance proceeds and receive a credit from the seller at closing in the amount of the deductible under the insurance policy.

The seller is responsible for the property up until the closing date.

LESSONS TO LEARN

Steven and Barry have a couple of options: Steven can ask Barry to agree to execute a Seller's Temporary Lease for his 7 day stay after closing. Or Barry can agree to a 7 day extension of the closing date using the Amendment Form.

CHAPTER 6

CASE STUDY/WORKSHOP

1. Which contracts discuss rollback taxes?

   Both of the New Home Contracts, the Unimproved Property Contract, and the Farm and Ranch Contract discuss rollback taxes.

2. What happens when paragraph 6G(8) of the Farm and Ranch Contract informs the consumer that the property is subject to a private transfer fee?

   The seller must notify the buyer as follows: The private transfer fee obligation may be governed by Chapter 5, Subchapter G of the Texas Property Code. The contract is considered notice to the buyer.

3. Which TREC promulgated contract form gives disclosure about the type of insulation in the property?

   Both of the New Home Contracts.

4. Which TREC promulgated contract form excludes a survey provision?

   The Residential Condominium Contract (Resale) excludes a survey provision.

5. Where does the seller provide disclosure on the Unimproved Property Contract?

The seller provides disclosure on the Unimproved Property Contract in Paragraph 7E.

6. How many contract forms does TREC promulgate?

There are 6 promulgated contracts.

LESSONS TO LEARN

If the home is newly constructed, the builder may use his or her own contract form. Jerry is in compliance with TREC.

CHAPTER 7

CASE STUDY/WORKSHOP

1. Who must use the Consumer Information Form?

The TREC Consumer Information Form (TREC Form1-1) must be prominently displayed in the office of every licensed broker and inspector in Texas.

2. Who must complete the Subdivision Information, Including Resale Certificate for Property Subject to Mandatory Membership in a Property Owners' Association form?

The form is filled out by the representative of the homeowners' association, not the licensee. Typically, a fee is assessed for filling out the form.

3. If the Back-Up Contract is negotiated with an option period of seven days, with an original effective date of March 3, and an amended effective date of March 14, when does the option period end?

March 21 at 11:59 p.m.

Paragraph D of the Addendum for Back-Up Contract states that if the back-up buyer has an unrestricted right to terminate the Back-Up Contract, the time for giving notice of termination begins on the effective date of the Back-Up Contract. The notice continues after the amended effective date for the number of days agreed to in paragraph 23 of the contract. It ends upon the expiration of the buyer's unrestricted right to terminate the Back-Up Contract.

4. What form would a buyer use if he wants to make an offer contingent upon the seller agreeing to allow him to move in two weeks prior to closing?

   Buyer's Temporary Residential Lease

5. What addendum must be used if the seller is going to carry a second lien for a portion of her equity?

   Seller Financing Addendum

6. What addendum must be used if the property was built prior to 1978?

   Lead-Based Paint Addendum

LESSONS TO LEARN

Yes. The buyer has all of the rights and privileges that the contract offers. The option period will not start until the primary contract is terminated.

CHAPTER 8

REVIEW AND DISCUSSION

1. How is fraud different than puffing and misrepresentation?

   In fraud, there is an intent to deceive. While puffing is making something sound very good. Sometimes this is called "sales talk". And in misrepresentation, a mistake, although not on purpose, was made.

2. What are the Pick 7 protected classes?

   Race, religion, color, national origin, sex, familial status, disability.

3. Is it the licensee's responsibility to inquire or inform people about a structural problem with a property that caused an injury or death?

   Yes.

4. Same question as above, but this time regarding the passing of an occupant due to natural causes within the building.

   No.

5. What are the two situations wherein a licensee can safely guide people to or away from certain areas?

   Personal preference and financial capacity.

6. How is the act of commission different from the act of omission?

Commission means someone did something, while omission means failed to do something.

LESSONS TO LEARN

Edie Huff is a widower that you attend church with. She has come to you with a question regarding a solicitation from another real estate company. The person contacting her had spoken of "changes in the neighborhood" regarding a more diverse group of homeowners acquiring property close to her. Edie has lived in her home nearly 40 years and did not understand the statement. When asked for a clarification, the licensee commented that "it was not too late to sell before any more changes occurred." Edie wants to know what the person is talking about and how she should respond. What is your advice to her?

We recommend you not immediately jump up and down and "call the other license out" for attempts at blockbusting or panic selling. It may be the "changes" are of a commercial nature for the area, or some other logical demographic adjustment. You may want to discuss with Ms. Huff if she is still happy to live in the area and what her future plans to move, if any, might be. You can offer to discuss values by doing an up-to-date CMA for her. If that is not your area, you may want to find out what changes are happening by seeking a competent practitioner knowledgeable with that specific marketplace. A final suggestion is that with Ms. Huff's permission, you might want to discuss with the caller what was attempting to be communicated with the call.

CHAPTER 9

PROMULGATED BY THE TEXAS REAL ESTATE COMMISSION (TREC)

12-05-11

EQUAL HOUSING OPPORTUNITY

ADDENDUM FOR
SALE OF OTHER PROPERTY BY BUYER

TO CONTRACT CONCERNING THE PROPERTY AT

1300 San Pedro, Bigfoot, Texas 78000

(Address of Property)

A. The contract is contingent upon Buyer's **receipt of the proceeds** from the sale of Buyer's property at _____3131 Reville Blvd., Gusgus, TX 78400_____ (Address) on or before _____March 7_____, 20___16____ (the Contingency). If the Contingency is not satisfied or waived by Buyer by the above date, the contract will terminate automatically and the earnest money will be refunded to Buyer.

NOTICE: The date inserted in this Paragraph should be no later than the Closing Date specified in Paragraph 9 of the contract.

B. If Seller accepts a written offer to sell the Property, Seller shall notify Buyer (1) of such acceptance **AND** (2) that Seller requires Buyer to waive the Contingency. Buyer must waive the Contingency on or before the _____10_____ day after Seller's notice to Buyer; otherwise the contract will terminate automatically and the earnest money will be refunded to Buyer.

C. Buyer may waive the Contingency only by notifying Seller of the waiver and depositing $10,000 after closing of 3131 Reville with escrow agent as additional earnest money. All notices and waivers must be in writing and are effective when delivered in accordance with the contract.

D. If Buyer waives the Contingency and fails to close and fund solely due to Buyer's non-receipt of proceeds from Buyer's property described in Paragraph A above, Buyer will be in default. If such default occurs, Seller may exercise the remedies specified in Paragraph 15 of the contract.

E. For purposes of this Addendum time is of the essence; strict compliance with the times for performance stated herein is required.

_____   _____
Buyer   Seller

_____   _____
Buyer   Seller

Source: © 2015 OnCourse Learning

TREC No. 10-6

PROMULGATED BY THE TEXAS REAL ESTATE COMMISSION (TREC)
ONE TO FOUR FAMILY RESIDENTIAL CONTRACT (RESALE)
NOTICE: Not For Use For Condominium Transactions

4-28-2014

1. **PARTIES:** The parties to this contract are <u>Robert Zeigler and wife Mary</u>
(Seller) and <u>Stewart Rogers and wife Theresa</u>
(Buyer). Seller agrees to sell and convey to Buyer and Buyer agrees to buy from Seller the Property defined below.

2. **PROPERTY:** The land, improvements and accessories are collectively referred to as the "Property".
   A. LAND: Lot <u>12</u> Block <u>34</u>, <u>Hardy Oaks</u>
      Addition, City of <u>Bigfoot</u>, County of <u>Prosperous</u>,
      Texas, known as <u>1300 San Pedro</u>
      (address/zip code), or as described on attached exhibit.
   B. IMPROVEMENTS: The house, garage and all other fixtures and improvements attached to the above-described real property, including without limitation, the following **permanently installed and built-in items,** if any: all equipment and appliances, valances, screens, shutters, awnings, wall-to-wall carpeting, mirrors, ceiling fans, attic fans, mail boxes, television antennas, mounts and brackets for televisions and speakers, heating and air-conditioning units, security and fire detection equipment, wiring, plumbing and lighting fixtures, chandeliers, water softener system, kitchen equipment, garage door openers, cleaning equipment, shrubbery, landscaping, outdoor cooking equipment, and all other property owned by Seller and attached to the above described real property.
   C. ACCESSORIES: The following described related accessories, if any: window air conditioning units, stove, fireplace screens, curtains and rods, blinds, window shades, draperies and rods, door keys, mailbox keys, above ground pool, swimming pool equipment and maintenance accessories, artificial fireplace logs, and controls for: (i) garage doors, (ii) entry gates, and (iii) other improvements and accessories.
   D. EXCLUSIONS: The following improvements and accessories will be retained by Seller and must be removed prior to delivery of possession:<u>None</u>

3. **SALES PRICE:**
   A. Cash portion of Sales Price payable by Buyer at closing .... $ <u>75,000</u>
   B. Sum of all financing described below (excluding any loan funding
      fee or mortgage insurance premium) .... $ <u>290,000</u>
   C. Sales Price (Sum of A and B)... $ <u>365,000</u>

4. **FINANCING (Not for use with reverse mortgage financing):** The portion of Sales Price not payable in cash will be paid as follows: (Check applicable boxes below)
   ☒ A.THIRD PARTY FINANCING: One or more third party mortgage loans in the total amount of
      $ <u>290,000</u> (excluding any loan funding fee or mortgage insurance premium).
      (1) Property Approval: If the Property does not satisfy the lenders' underwriting requirements for the loan(s) (including, but not limited to appraisal, insurability and lender required repairs), Buyer may terminate this contract by giving notice to Seller prior to closing and the earnest money will be refunded to Buyer.
      (2) Credit Approval: (Check one box only)
         ☒ (a) This contract is subject to Buyer being approved for the financing described in the attached Third Party Financing Addendum for Credit Approval.
         ☐ (b) This contract is not subject to Buyer being approved for financing and does not involve FHA or VA financing.
   ☐ B. ASSUMPTION: The assumption of the unpaid principal balance of one or more promissory notes described in the attached TREC Loan Assumption Addendum.
   ☐ C. SELLER FINANCING: A promissory note from Buyer to Seller of $_____, secured by vendor's and deed of trust liens, and containing the terms and conditions described in the attached TREC Seller Financing Addendum. If an owner policy of title insurance is furnished, Buyer shall furnish Seller with a mortgagee policy of title insurance.

Initialed for identification by Buyer_____ _____and Seller _____ _____   TREC NO. 20-12

Contract Concerning 1300 San Pedro, Bigfoot, TX _____Page 2 of 9   4-28-2014
                                                       (Address of Property)

5. **EARNEST MONEY:** Upon execution of this contract by all parties, Buyer shall deposit $ _10,000_ as earnest money with Hoyhak Title Co., as escrow agent, at 1665 GarDon Blvd., Bigfoot, TX. Buyer shall deposit additional earnest money of $ _10,000_ with escrow agent within _30_ days after the sale of their existing home. If Buyer fails to deposit the earnest money as required by this contract, Buyer will be in default.

6. **TITLE POLICY AND SURVEY:**
   A. TITLE POLICY: Seller shall furnish to Buyer at ☒ Seller's ☐ Buyer's expense an owner policy of title insurance (Title Policy) issued by Hoyhak Title Co. in the amount of the Sales Price, dated at or after closing, insuring Buyer against loss under the provisions of the Title Policy, subject to the promulgated exclusions (including existing building and zoning ordinances) and the following exceptions:
      (1) Restrictive covenants common to the platted subdivision in which the Property is located.
      (2) The standard printed exception for standby fees, taxes and assessments.
      (3) Liens created as part of the financing described in Paragraph 4.
      (4) Utility easements created by the dedication deed or plat of the subdivision in which the Property is located.
      (5) Reservations or exceptions otherwise permitted by this contract or as may be approved by Buyer in writing.
      (6) The standard printed exception as to marital rights.
      (7) The standard printed exception as to waters, tidelands, beaches, streams, and related matters.
      (8) The standard printed exception as to discrepancies, conflicts, shortages in area or boundary lines, encroachments or protrusions, or overlapping improvements: ☐(i) will not be amended or deleted from the title policy; ☐(ii) will be amended to read, "shortages in area" at the expense of ☐Buyer ☒Seller.
   B. COMMITMENT: Within 20 days after the Title Company receives a copy of this contract, Seller shall furnish to Buyer a commitment for title insurance (Commitment) and, at Buyer's expense, legible copies of restrictive covenants and documents evidencing exceptions in the Commitment (Exception Documents) other than the standard printed exceptions. Seller authorizes the Title Company to deliver the Commitment and Exception Documents to Buyer at Buyer's address shown In Paragraph 21. If the Commitment and Exception Documents are not delivered to Buyer within the specified time, the time for delivery will be automatically extended up to 15 days or 3 days before the Closing Date, whichever is earlier. If, due to factors beyond Seller's control, the Commitment and Exception Documents are not delivered within the time required, Buyer may terminate this contract and the earnest money will be refunded to Buyer.
   C. SURVEY: The survey must be made by a registered professional land surveyor acceptable to the Title Company and Buyer's lender(s). (Check one box only)
   ☒ (1) Within _5_ days after the effective date of this contract, Seller shall furnish to Buyer and Title Company Seller's existing survey of the Property and a Residential Real Property Affidavit promulgated by the Texas Department of Insurance (T-47 Affidavit). **If Seller fails to furnish the existing survey or affidavit within the time prescribed, Buyer shall obtain a new survey at Seller's expense no later than 3 days prior to Closing Date.** If the existing survey or affidavit is not acceptable to Title Company or Buyer's lender(s), Buyer shall obtain a new survey at ☐Seller's ☒Buyer's expense no later than 3 days prior to Closing Date.
   ☐(2) Within _____days after the effective date of this contract, Buyer shall obtain a new survey at Buyer's expense. Buyer is deemed to receive the survey on the date of actual receipt or the date specified in this paragraph, whichever is earlier.
   ☐(3) Within _____ days after the effective date of this contract, Seller, at Seller's expense shall furnish a new survey to Buyer.
   D. OBJECTIONS: Buyer may object in writing to defects, exceptions, or encumbrances to title: disclosed on the survey other than items 6A(1) through (7) above; disclosed in the Commitment other than items 6A(1) through (8) above; or which prohibit the following use or activity: _N/A_____
   _____.
   Buyer must object the earlier of (i) the Closing Date or (ii) _____days after Buyer receives the Commitment, Exception Documents, and the survey. Buyer's failure to object within the time allowed will constitute a waiver of Buyer's right to object; except that the requirements in Schedule C of the Commitment are not waived by Buyer. Provided Seller is not obligated to incur any expense, Seller shall cure the timely objections of Buyer or any third party lender

Initialed for identification by Buyer_____ _____and Seller _____ _____   TREC NO. 20-12

Contract Concerning 1300 San Pedro, Bigfoot, TX _____ Page 3 of 9   4-28-2014
                          (Address of Property)

within 15 days after Seller receives the objections and the Closing Date will be extended as necessary. If objections are not cured within such 15 day period, this contract will terminate and the earnest money will be refunded to Buyer unless Buyer waives the objections.

E. TITLE NOTICES:

(1) ABSTRACT OR TITLE POLICY: Broker advises Buyer to have an abstract of title covering the Property examined by an attorney of Buyer's selection, or Buyer should be furnished with or obtain a Title Policy. If a Title Policy is furnished, the Commitment should be promptly reviewed by an attorney of Buyer's choice due to the time limitations on Buyer's right to object.

(2) MEMBERSHIP IN PROPERTY OWNERS ASSOCIATION(S): The Property ☒is ☐is not subject to mandatory membership in a property owners association(s). If the Property is subject to mandatory membership in a property owners association(s), Seller notifies Buyer under §5.012, Texas Property Code, that, as a purchaser of property in the residential community identified in Paragraph 2A in which the Property is located, you are obligated to be a member of the property owners association(s). Restrictive covenants governing the use and occupancy of the Property and all dedicatory instruments governing the establishment, maintenance, or operation of this residential community have been or will be recorded in the Real Property Records of the county in which the Property is located. Copies of the restrictive covenants and dedicatory instruments may be obtained from the county clerk. **You are obligated to pay assessments to the property owners association(s). The amount of the assessments is subject to change. Your failure to pay the assessments could result in enforcement of the association's lien on and the foreclosure of the Property.** Section 207.003, Property Code, entitles an owner to receive copies of any document that governs the establishment, maintenance, or operation of a subdivision, including, but not limited to, restrictions, bylaws, rules and regulations, and a resale certificate from a property owners' association. A resale certificate contains information including, but not limited to, statements specifying the amount and frequency of regular assessments and the style and cause number of lawsuits to which the property owners' association is a party, other than lawsuits relating to unpaid ad valorem taxes of an individual member of the association. These documents must be made available to you by the property owners' association or the association's agent on your request. **If Buyer is concerned about these matters, the TREC promulgated Addendum for Property Subject to Mandatory Membership in a Property Owners Association(s) should be used.**

(3) STATUTORY TAX DISTRICTS: If the Property is situated in a utility or other statutorily created district providing water, sewer, drainage, or flood control facilities and services, Chapter 49, Texas Water Code, requires Seller to deliver and Buyer to sign the statutory notice relating to the tax rate, bonded indebtedness, or standby fee of the district prior to final execution of this contract.

(4) TIDE WATERS: If the Property abuts the tidally influenced waters of the state, §33.135, Texas Natural Resources Code, requires a notice regarding coastal area property to be included in the contract. An addendum containing the notice promulgated by TREC or required by the parties must be used.

(5) ANNEXATION: If the Property is located outside the limits of a municipality, Seller notifies Buyer under §5.011, Texas Property Code, that the Property may now or later be included in the extraterritorial jurisdiction of a municipality and may now or later be subject to annexation by the municipality. Each municipality maintains a map that depicts its boundaries and extraterritorial jurisdiction. To determine if the Property is located within a municipality's extraterritorial jurisdiction or is likely to be located within a municipality's extraterritorial jurisdiction, contact all municipalities located in the general proximity of the Property for further information.

(6) PROPERTY LOCATED IN A CERTIFICATED SERVICE AREA OF A UTILITY SERVICE PROVIDER: Notice required by §13.257, Water Code: The real property, described in Paragraph 2, that you are about to purchase may be located in a certificated water or sewer service area, which is authorized by law to provide water or sewer service to the properties in the certificated area. If your property is located in a certificated area there may be special costs or charges that you will be required to pay before you can receive water or sewer service. There may be a period required to construct lines or other facilities necessary to provide water or sewer service to your property. You are advised to determine if the property is in a certificated area and contact the utility service provider to determine the cost that you will be required to pay and the period, if any, that is required to provide water or sewer service to your property. The undersigned Buyer hereby acknowledges receipt of the foregoing notice at or before the execution of a binding contract for the purchase of the real property described in Paragraph 2 or at closing of purchase of the real property.

Initialed for identification by Buyer_____ _____and Seller _____ _____   TREC NO. 20-12

Contract Concerning **1300 San Pedro, Bigfoot, TX** _____ Page 4 of 9   4-28-2014
(Address of Property)

(7) PUBLIC IMPROVEMENT DISTRICTS: If the Property is in a public improvement district, §5.014, Property Code, requires Seller to notify Buyer as follows: As a purchaser of this parcel of real property you are obligated to pay an assessment to a municipality or county for an improvement project undertaken by a public improvement district under Chapter 372, Local Government Code. The assessment may be due annually or in periodic installments. More information concerning the amount of the assessment and the due dates of that assessment may be obtained from the municipality or county levying the assessment. The amount of the assessments is subject to change. Your failure to pay the assessments could result in a lien on and the foreclosure of your property.

(8) TRANSFER FEES: If the Property is subject to a private transfer fee obligation, §5.205, Property Code, requires Seller to notify Buyer as follows: The private transfer fee obligation may be governed by Chapter 5, Subchapter G of the Texas Property Code.

(9) PROPANE GAS SYSTEM SERVICE AREA: If the Property is located in a propane gas system service area owned by a distribution system retailer, Seller must give Buyer written notice as required by §141.010, Texas Utilities Code. An addendum containing the notice approved by TREC or required by the parties should be used.

7. **PROPERTY CONDITION:**

A. ACCESS, INSPECTIONS AND UTILITIES: Seller shall permit Buyer and Buyer's agents access to the Property at reasonable times. Buyer may have the Property inspected by inspectors selected by Buyer and licensed by TREC or otherwise permitted by law to make inspections. Seller at Seller's expense shall immediately cause existing utilities to be turned on and shall keep the utilities on during the time this contract is in effect.

B. SELLER'S DISCLOSURE NOTICE PURSUANT TO §5.008, TEXAS PROPERTY CODE (Notice): (Check one box only)

☒ (1) Buyer has received the Notice.

☐ (2) Buyer has not received the Notice. Within _____ days after the effective date of this contract, Seller shall deliver the Notice to Buyer. If Buyer does not receive the Notice, Buyer may terminate this contract at any time prior to the closing and the earnest money will be refunded to Buyer. If Seller delivers the Notice, Buyer may terminate this contract for any reason within 7 days after Buyer receives the Notice or prior to the closing, whichever first occurs, and the earnest money will be refunded to Buyer.

☐ (3) The Seller is not required to furnish the notice under the Texas Property Code.

C. SELLER'S DISCLOSURE OF LEAD-BASED PAINT AND LEAD-BASED PAINT HAZARDS is required by Federal law for a residential dwelling constructed prior to 1978.

D. ACCEPTANCE OF PROPERTY CONDITION: "As Is" means the present condition of the Property with any and all defects and without warranty except for the warranties of title and the warranties in this contract. Buyer's agreement to accept the Property As Is under Paragraph 7D(1) or (2) does not preclude Buyer from inspecting the Property under Paragraph 7A, from negotiating repairs or treatments in a subsequent amendment, or from terminating this contract during the Option Period, if any. (Check one box only)

☐ (1) Buyer accepts the Property As Is.

☒ (2) Buyer accepts the Property As Is provided Seller, at Seller's expense, shall complete the following specific repairs and treatments: _____ Roof repair is needed _____
_____.
(Do not insert general phrases, such as "subject to inspections" that do not identify specific repairs and treatments.)

E. LENDER REQUIRED REPAIRS AND TREATMENTS: Unless otherwise agreed in writing, neither party is obligated to pay for lender required repairs, which includes treatment for wood destroying insects. If the parties do not agree to pay for the lender required repairs or treatments, this contract will terminate and the earnest money will be refunded to Buyer. If the cost of lender required repairs and treatments exceeds 5% of the Sales Price, Buyer may terminate this contract and the earnest money will be refunded to Buyer.

F. COMPLETION OF REPAIRS AND TREATMENTS: Unless otherwise agreed in writing: (i) Seller shall complete all agreed repairs and treatments prior to the Closing Date; and (ii) all required permits must be obtained, and repairs and treatments must be performed by persons who are licensed to provide such repairs or treatments or, if no license is required by law, are commercially engaged in the trade of providing such repairs or treatments. At Buyer's election, any transferable warranties received by Seller with respect to the repairs and treatments will be transferred to Buyer at Buyer's expense. If Seller fails to complete any agreed repairs and treatments prior to the Closing Date, Buyer may exercise remedies under Paragraph 15 or extend the Closing Date up to 5 days if necessary for Seller to complete the repairs and treatments.

G. ENVIRONMENTAL MATTERS: Buyer is advised that the presence of wetlands, toxic substances, including asbestos and wastes or other environmental hazards, or the presence of a threatened or endangered species or its habitat may affect Buyer's intended use of the

Initialed for identification by Buyer_____ _____and Seller _____ _____   TREC NO. 20-12

Contract Concerning 1300 San Pedro, Bigfoot, TX _____ Page 5 of 9 4-28-2014
(Address of Property)

Property. If Buyer is concerned about these matters, an addendum promulgated by TREC or required by the parties should be used.

H. RESIDENTIAL SERVICE CONTRACTS: Buyer may purchase a residential service contract from a residential service company licensed by TREC. If Buyer purchases a residential service contract, Seller shall reimburse Buyer at closing for the cost of the residential service contract in an amount not exceeding $ __N/A__ . Buyer should review any residential service contract for the scope of coverage, exclusions and limitations. **The purchase of a residential service contract is optional. Similar coverage may be purchased from various companies authorized to do business in Texas.**

8. **BROKERS' FEES:** All obligations of the parties for payment of brokers' fees are contained in separate written agreements.

9. **CLOSING:**
   A. The closing of the sale will be on or before _____ 60 days _____, 20____, or within 7 days after objections made under Paragraph 6D have been cured or waived, whichever date is later (Closing Date). If either party fails to close the sale by the Closing Date, the non-defaulting party may exercise the remedies contained in Paragraph 15.
   B. At closing:
      (1) Seller shall execute and deliver a general warranty deed conveying title to the Property to Buyer and showing no additional exceptions to those permitted in Paragraph 6 and furnish tax statements or certificates showing no delinquent taxes on the Property.
      (2) Buyer shall pay the Sales Price in good funds acceptable to the escrow agent.
      (3) Seller and Buyer shall execute and deliver any notices, statements, certificates, affidavits, releases, loan documents and other documents reasonably required for the closing of the sale and the issuance of the Title Policy.
      (4) There will be no liens, assessments, or security interests against the Property which will not be satisfied out of the sales proceeds unless securing the payment of any loans assumed by Buyer and assumed loans will not be in default.
      (5) If the Property is subject to a residential lease, Seller shall transfer security deposits (as defined under §92.102, Property Code), if any, to Buyer. In such an event, Buyer shall deliver to the tenant a signed statement acknowledging that the Buyer has received the security deposit and is responsible for the return of the security deposit, and specifying the exact dollar amount of the security deposit.

10. **POSSESSION:**
    A Buyer's Possession: Seller shall deliver to Buyer possession of the Property in its present or required condition, ordinary wear and tear excepted: ☒ upon closing and funding ☐ according to a temporary residential lease form promulgated by TREC or other written lease required by the parties. Any possession by Buyer prior to closing or by Seller after closing which is not authorized by a written lease will establish a tenancy at sufferance relationship between the parties. **Consult your insurance agent prior to change of ownership and possession because insurance coverage may be limited or terminated. The absence of a written lease or appropriate insurance coverage may expose the parties to economic loss.**
    B. Leases:
       (1) After the Effective Date, Seller may not execute any lease (including but not limited to mineral leases) or convey any interest in the Property without Buyer's written consent.
       (2) If the Property is subject to any lease to which Seller is a party, Seller shall deliver to Buyer copies of the lease(s) and any move-in condition form signed by the tenant within 7 days after the Effective Date of the contract.

11. **SPECIAL PROVISIONS:** (Insert only factual statements and business details applicable to the sale. TREC rules prohibit licensees from adding factual statements or business details for which a contract addendum, lease or other form has been promulgated by TREC for mandatory use.) **See Exhibit "A" of personal property to stay.**

12. **SETTLEMENT AND OTHER EXPENSES:**
    A. The following expenses must be paid at or prior to closing:
       (1) Expenses payable by Seller (Seller's Expenses):
          (a) Releases of existing liens, including prepayment penalties and recording fees; release of Seller's loan liability; tax statements or certificates; preparation of deed; one-half of escrow fee; and other expenses payable by Seller under this contract.
          (b) Seller shall also pay an amount not to exceed $_____ to be applied in the

Initialed for identification by Buyer_____ _____and Seller _____ _____   TREC NO. 20-12

Contract Concerning _1300 San Pedro, Bigfoot, TX_____ Page 6 of 9   4-28-2014
(Address of Property)

    following order: Buyer's Expenses which Buyer is prohibited from paying by FHA, VA, Texas Veterans Land Board or other governmental loan programs, and then to other Buyer's Expenses as allowed by the lender.

(2) Expenses payable by Buyer (Buyer's Expenses): Appraisal fees; loan application fees; adjusted origination charges; credit reports; preparation of loan documents; interest on the notes from date of disbursement to one month prior to dates of first monthly payments; recording fees; copies of easements and restrictions; loan title policy with endorsements required by lender; loan-related inspection fees; photos; amortization schedules; one-half of escrow fee; all prepaid items, including required premiums for flood and hazard insurance, reserve deposits for insurance, ad valorem taxes and special governmental assessments; final compliance inspection; courier fee; repair inspection; underwriting fee; wire transfer fee; expenses incident to any loan; Private Mortgage Insurance Premium (PMI), VA Loan Funding Fee, or FHA Mortgage Insurance Premium (MIP) as required by the lender; and other expenses payable by Buyer under this contract.

B. If any expense exceeds an amount expressly stated in this contract for such expense to be paid by a party, that party may terminate this contract unless the other party agrees to pay such excess. Buyer may not pay charges and fees expressly prohibited by FHA, VA, Texas Veterans Land Board or other governmental loan program regulations.

13. **PRORATIONS:** Taxes for the current year, interest, maintenance fees, assessments, dues and rents will be prorated through the Closing Date. The tax proration may be calculated taking into consideration any change in exemptions that will affect the current year's taxes. If taxes for the current year vary from the amount prorated at closing, the parties shall adjust the prorations when tax statements for the current year are available. If taxes are not paid at or prior to closing, Buyer shall pay taxes for the current year.

14. **CASUALTY LOSS:** If any part of the Property is damaged or destroyed by fire or other casualty after the effective date of this contract, Seller shall restore the Property to its previous condition as soon as reasonably possible, but in any event by the Closing Date. If Seller fails to do so due to factors beyond Seller's control, Buyer may (a) terminate this contract and the earnest money will be refunded to Buyer (b) extend the time for performance up to 15 days and the Closing Date will be extended as necessary or (c) accept the Property in its damaged condition with an assignment of insurance proceeds and receive credit from Seller at closing in the amount of the deductible under the insurance policy. Seller's obligations under this paragraph are independent of any other obligations of Seller under this contract.

15. **DEFAULT:** If Buyer fails to comply with this contract, Buyer will be in default, and Seller may (a) enforce specific performance, seek such other relief as may be provided by law, or both, or (b) terminate this contract and receive the earnest money as liquidated damages, thereby releasing both parties from this contract. If Seller fails to comply with this contract, Seller will be in default and Buyer may (a) enforce specific performance, seek such other relief as may be provided by law, or both, or (b) terminate this contract and receive the earnest money, thereby releasing both parties from this contract.

16. **MEDIATION:** It is the policy of the State of Texas to encourage resolution of disputes through alternative dispute resolution procedures such as mediation. Any dispute between Seller and Buyer related to this contract which is not resolved through informal discussion will be submitted to a mutually acceptable mediation service or provider. The parties to the mediation shall bear the mediation costs equally. This paragraph does not preclude a party from seeking equitable relief from a court of competent jurisdiction.

17. **ATTORNEY'S FEES:** A Buyer, Seller, Listing Broker, Other Broker, or escrow agent who prevails in any legal proceeding related to this contract is entitled to recover reasonable attorney's fees and all costs of such proceeding.

18. **ESCROW:**

A. ESCROW: The escrow agent is not (i) a party to this contract and does not have liability for the performance or nonperformance of any party to this contract, (ii) liable for interest on the earnest money and (iii) liable for the loss of any earnest money caused by the failure of any financial institution in which the earnest money has been deposited unless the financial institution is acting as escrow agent.

B. EXPENSES: At closing, the earnest money must be applied first to any cash down payment, then to Buyer's Expenses and any excess refunded to Buyer. If no closing occurs, escrow agent may: (i) require a written release of liability of the escrow agent from all parties, (ii) require payment of unpaid expenses incurred on behalf of a party, and (iii) only deduct from the earnest money the amount of unpaid expenses incurred on behalf of the party receiving the earnest money.

C. DEMAND: Upon termination of this contract, either party or the escrow agent may send a release of earnest money to each party and the parties shall execute counterparts of

Initialed for identification by Buyer_____ _____and Seller _____ _____   TREC NO. 20-12

Contract Concerning __1300 San Pedro, Bigfoot, TX_____Page 7 of 9   4-28-2014
(Address of Property)

the release and deliver same to the escrow agent. If either party fails to execute the release, either party may make a written demand to the escrow agent for the earnest money. If only one party makes written demand for the earnest money, escrow agent shall promptly provide a copy of the demand to the other party. If escrow agent does not receive written objection to the demand from the other party within 15 days, escrow agent may disburse the earnest money to the party making demand reduced by the amount of unpaid expenses incurred on behalf of the party receiving the earnest money and escrow agent may pay the same to the creditors. If escrow agent complies with the provisions of this paragraph, each party hereby releases escrow agent from all adverse claims related to the disbursal of the earnest money.

   D. DAMAGES: Any party who wrongfully fails or refuses to sign a release acceptable to the escrow agent within 7 days of receipt of the request will be liable to the other party for liquidated damages in an amount equal to the sum of: (i) three times the amount of the earnest money; (ii) the earnest money; (iii) reasonable attorney's fees; and (iv) all costs of suit.

   E. NOTICES: Escrow agent's notices will be effective when sent in compliance with Paragraph 21. Notice of objection to the demand will be deemed effective upon receipt by escrow agent.

19. REPRESENTATIONS: All covenants, representations and warranties in this contract survive closing. If any representation of Seller in this contract is untrue on the Closing Date, Seller will be in default. Unless expressly prohibited by written agreement, Seller may continue to show the Property and receive, negotiate and accept back up offers.

20. FEDERAL TAX REQUIREMENTS: If Seller is a "foreign person," as defined by applicable law, or if Seller fails to deliver an affidavit to Buyer that Seller is not a "foreign person," then Buyer shall withhold from the sales proceeds an amount sufficient to comply with applicable tax law and deliver the same to the Internal Revenue Service together with appropriate tax forms. Internal Revenue Service regulations require filing written reports if currency in excess of specified amounts is received in the transaction.

21. NOTICES: All notices from one party to the other must be in writing and are effective when mailed to, hand-delivered at, or transmitted by facsimile or electronic transmission as follows:

To Buyer at: **PO Box 12048**_____   **To Seller at:** **1300 San Pedro**_____
Gusgus, TX 78400   Bigfoot, TX 78000

Telephone: (281) 492-6391_____   Telephone: (555-222-9999)_____

Facsimile: Same_____   Facsimile: N/A_____

E-mail: oilpro@drilling.net_____   Email: prez@gogettum.com_____

22. AGREEMENT OF PARTIES: This contract contains the entire agreement of the parties and cannot be changed except by their written agreement. Addenda which are a part of this contract are (Check all applicable boxes):

☒ Third Party Financing Addendum for Credit Approval	☐ Environmental Assessment, Threatened or Endangered Species and Wetlands Addendum
☐ Seller Financing Addendum	☐ Seller's Temporary Residential Lease
☒ Addendum for Property Subject to Mandatory Membership in a Property Owners Association	☐ Short Sale Addendum
☐ Buyer's Temporary Residential Lease	☐ Addendum for Property Located Seaward of the Gulf Intracoastal Waterway
☐ Loan Assumption Addendum	☒ Addendum for Seller's Disclosure of Information on Lead-based Paint and Lead-based Paint Hazards as Required by Federal Law
☒ Addendum for Sale of Other Property by Buyer	
☐ Addendum for Reservation of Oil, Gas and Other Minerals	☐ Addendum for Property in a Propane Gas System Service Area
☐ Addendum for "Back-Up" Contract	☐ Other (list): _____
☐ Addendum for Coastal Area Property	_____

Initialed for identification by Buyer_____ _____and Seller _____ _____   TREC NO. 20-12

Contract Concerning 1300 San Pedro, Bigfoot, TX   Page 8 of 9   4-28-2014
                                    (Address of Property)

23. TERMINATION OPTION: For nominal consideration, the receipt of which is hereby acknowledged by Seller, and Buyer's agreement to pay Seller $ 1,000 _____ (Option Fee) within 3 days after the effective date of this contract, Seller grants Buyer the unrestricted right to terminate this contract by giving notice of termination to Seller within ___10___ days after the effective date of this contract (Option Period). If no dollar amount is stated as the Option Fee or if Buyer fails to pay the Option Fee to Seller within the time prescribed, this paragraph will not be a part of this contract and Buyer shall not have the unrestricted right to terminate this contract. If Buyer gives notice of termination within the time prescribed, the Option Fee will not be refunded; however, any earnest money will be refunded to Buyer. The Option Fee ☐will ☐will not be credited to the Sales Price at closing. **Time is of the essence for this paragraph and strict compliance with the time for performance is required.**

24. CONSULT AN ATTORNEY BEFORE SIGNING: TREC rules prohibit real estate licensees from giving legal advice. READ THIS CONTRACT CAREFULLY.

Buyer's
Attorney is: N/A _____

Seller's
Attorney is: Rouke Oeli _____

Telephone: ( ) _____

Telephone: (830) 222-0602 _____

Facsimile: ( ) _____

Facsimile: ( ) _____

E-mail: _____

E-mail: roukelaw@umail.com _____

**EXECUTED the _____ day of _____, 20____ (EFFECTIVE DATE).
(BROKER: FILL IN THE DATE OF FINAL ACCEPTANCE.)**

Buyer _____

Seller _____

Buyer _____

Seller _____

TREC NO. 20-12

Contract Concerning 1300 San Pedro, Bigfoot, TX   Page 9 of 9   4-28-2014
_____(Address of Property)_____

BROKER INFORMATION
(Print name(s) only. Do not sign)

Top Notch Realty	XXXXX	John Pursch, Realtors	XXXXX
Other Broker Firm	License No.	Listing Broker Firm	License No.

represents ☒ Buyer only as Buyer's agent   represents ☐ Seller and Buyer as an intermediary
☐ Seller as Listing Broker's subagent   ☒ Seller only as Seller's agent

Jackie Hernandez	409-815-6409	N/A	512-061-1951
Name Associate's Licensed Supervisor	Telephone	Name of Associate's Licensed Supervisor	Telephone

N/A

Associate's Name	Telephone	Listing Associate's Name	Telephone

1409 Gemini Circle   7551 Olymipa

Other Broker's Address   Facsimile   Listing Broker's Office Address   Facsimile

Gusgus, TX 78400   Bulverde Springs, TX 79123

City   State   Zip   City   State   Zip

Jackie@topnotch.com   sicem@hotshot.net

Associate's Email Address   Listing Associate's Email Address

Selling Associate's Name   Telephone

Name of Selling Associate's Licensed Supervisor   Telephone

Selling Associate's Office Address   Facsimile

City   State   Zip

Selling Associate's Email Address

Listing Broker has agreed to pay Other Broker___2 ½ %___of the total sales price when the Listing Broker's fee is received. Escrow agent is authorized and directed to pay other Broker from Listing Broker's fee at closing.

OPTION FEE RECEIPT

Receipt of $_____(Option Fee) in the form of _____is acknowledged.

Seller or Listing Broker   Date

CONTRACT AND EARNEST MONEY RECEIPT

Receipt of ☐Contract and ☐$_____Earnest Money in the form of _____ is acknowledged.

Escrow Agent: _____   Date: _____

By: _____
                    Email Address
_____   Telephone (___)_____
Address
_____   Facsimile: (___) _____
City   State   Zip

Source: © 2015 OnCourse Learning   TREC NO. 20-12

EQUAL HOUSING
OPPORTUNITY

PROMULGATED BY THE TEXAS REAL ESTATE COMMISSION (TREC)

THIRD PARTY FINANCING ADDENDUM

TO CONTRACT CONCERNING THE PROPERTY AT

1300 San Pedro Bigfoot, Texas 78000

(Street Address and City)

A. **TYPE OF FINANCING AND DUTY TO APPLY AND OBTAIN APPROVAL:** Buyer shall apply promptly for all financing described below and make every reasonable effort to obtain approval for the financing, including but not limited to furnishing all information and documents required by Buyer's lender. (Check applicable boxes):

☑ 1. Conventional Financing:

☑ (a) A first mortgage loan in the principal amount of $ _____ 290,000 (excluding any financed PMI premium), due in full in ___15___ year(s), with interest not to exceed __5__% per annum for the first ___15___ year(s) of the loan with Origination Charges as shown on Buyer's Loan Estimate for the loan not to exceed ____1____% of the loan.

☐ (b) A second mortgage loan in the principal amount of $_____ N/A (excluding any financed PMI premium), due in full in _____year(s), with interest not to exceed _____% per annum for the first _____year(s) of the loan with Origination Charges as shown on Buyer's Loan Estimate for the loan not to exceed _____% of the loan.

☐ 2. Texas Veterans Loan: A loan(s) from the Texas Veterans Land Board of $ _____ for a period in the total amount of _____years at the interest rate established by the Texas Veterans Land Board.

☐ 3. FHA Insured Financing: A Section _____ FHA insured loan of not less than $_____(excluding any financed MIP), amortizable monthly for not less than _____years, with interest not to exceed _____% per annum for the first _____year(s) of the loan with Origination Charges as shown on Buyer's Loan Estimate for the loan not to exceed _____ % of the loan.

☐ 4. VA Guaranteed Financing: A VA guaranteed loan of not less than $_____(excluding any financed Funding Fee), amortizable monthly for not less than_____years, with interest not to exceed_____% per annum for the first _____year(s) of the loan with Origination Charges as shown on Buyer's Loan Estimate for the loan not to exceed _____% of the loan.

☐ 5. USDA Guaranteed Financing: A USDA-guaranteed loan of not less than $ _____ (excluding any financed Funding Fee), amortizable monthly for not less than_____years, with interest not to exceed _____% per annum for the first _____year(s) of the loan with Origination Charges as shown on Buyer's Loan Estimate for the loan not to exceed _____% of the loan.

☐ 6. Reverse Mortgage Financing: A reverse mortgage loan (also known as a Home Equity Conversion Mortgage loan) in the original principal amount of $ _____ (excluding any financed PMI premium or other costs), with interest not to exceed _____% per annum for the first _____ year(s) of the loan with Origination Charges as shown on Buyer's Loan Estimate for the loan not to exceed _____% of the loan. The reverse mortgage loan ☐will ☐ will not be an FHA insured loan.

Initialed for identification by Buyer____ _____ and Seller_____ _____   TREC NO. 40-7
11-2-2015

Third Party Financing Addendum Concerning   Page 2 of 2

1300 San Pedro

(Address of Property)

B. APPROVAL OF FINANCING: Approval for the financing described above will be deemed to have been obtained when Buyer Approval and Property Approval are obtained.

1. <u>Buyer Approval</u>:

☑ This contract is subject to Buyer obtaining Buyer Approval. If Buyer cannot obtain Buyer Approval, Buyer may give written notice to Seller within ___30___ days after the effective date of this contract and this contract will terminate and the earnest money will be refunded to Buyer. If Buyer does not terminate the contract under this provision, the contract shall no longer be subject to the Buyer obtaining Buyer Approval. Buyer Approval will be deemed to have been obtained when (i) the terms of the loan(s) described above are available and (ii) lender determines that Buyer has satisfied all of lender's requirements related to Buyer's assets, income and credit history.

☐ This contract is not subject to Buyer obtaining Buyer Approval.

2. <u>Property Approval</u>: Property Approval will be deemed to have been obtained when the Property has satisfied lender's underwriting requirements for the loan, including but not limited to appraisal, insurability, and lender required repairs. If Property Approval is not obtained, Buyer may terminate this contract by giving notice to Seller before closing and the earnest money will be refunded to Buyer.

3. Time is of the essence for this paragraph and strict compliance with the time for performance is required.

C. SECURITY: Each note for the financing described above must be secured by vendor's and deed of trust liens.

D. FHA/VA REQUIRED PROVISION: If the financing described above involves FHA insured or VA financing, it is expressly agreed that, notwithstanding any other provision of this contract, the purchaser (Buyer) shall not be obligated to complete the purchase of the Property described herein or to incur any penalty by forfeiture of earnest money deposits or otherwise: (i) unless the Buyer has been given in accordance with HUD/FHA or VA requirements a written statement issued by the Federal Housing Commissioner, Department of Veterans Affairs, or a Direct Endorsement Lender setting forth the appraised value of the Property of not less than $_____N/A_ ; or (ii) if the contract purchase price or cost exceeds the reasonable value of the Property established by the Department of Veterans Affairs.

(1) The Buyer shall have the privilege and option of proceeding with consummation of the contract without regard to the amount of the appraised valuation or the reasonable value established by the Department of Veterans Affairs.

(2) If FHA financing is involved, the appraised valuation is arrived at to determine the maximum mortgage the Department of Housing and Urban Development will insure. HUD does not warrant the value or the condition of the Property. The Buyer should satisfy himself/herself that the price and the condition of the Property are acceptable.

(3) If VA financing is involved and if Buyer elects to complete the purchase at an amount in excess of the reasonable value established by the VA, Buyer shall pay such excess amount in cash from a source which Buyer agrees to disclose to the VA and which Buyer represents will not be from borrowed funds except as approved by VA. If VA reasonable value of the Property is less than the Sales Prices, Seller may reduce the Sales Price to an amount equal to the VA reasonable value and the sale will be closed at the lower Sales Price with proportionate adjustments to the down payment and the loan amount.

E. AUTHORIZATION TO RELEASE INFORMATION:

(1) Buyer authorizes Buyer's lender to furnish to Seller or Buyer or their representatives information relating to the status of the approval for the financing.

(2) Seller and Buyer authorize Buyer's lender, title company, and escrow agent to disclose and furnish a copy of the closing disclosures provided in relation to the closing of this sale to the parties' respective brokers and sales agents identified on the last page of the contract.

_____   _____
Buyer   Seller

_____   _____
Buyer   Seller

TREC NO. 40-7
11-2-2015

APPROVED BY THE TEXAS REAL ESTATE COMMISSION   10-10-11

ADDENDUM FOR SELLER'S DISCLOSURE OF INFORMATION ON LEAD-BASED PAINT AND LEAD-BASED PAINT HAZARDS AS REQUIRED BY FEDERAL LAW

CONCERNING THE PROPERTY AT 1300 San Pedro, Bigfoot, TX 7800 _____
(Street Address and City)

A. LEAD WARNING STATEMENT: "Every purchaser of any interest in residential real property on which a residential dwelling was built prior to 1978 is notified that such property may present exposure to lead from lead-based paint that may place young children at risk of developing lead poisoning. Lead poisoning in young children may produce permanent neurological damage, including learning disabilities, reduced intelligence quotient, behavioral problems, and impaired memory. Lead poisoning also poses a particular risk to pregnant women. The seller of any interest in residential real property is required to provide the buyer with any information on lead-based paint hazards from risk assessments or inspections in the seller's possession and notify the buyer of any known lead-based paint hazards. A risk assessment or inspection for possible lead-paint hazards is recommended prior to purchase."

NOTICE: Inspector must be properly certified as required by federal law.

B. SELLER'S DISCLOSURE:
1. PRESENCE OF LEAD-BASED PAINT AND/OR LEAD-BASED PAINT HAZARDS (check one box only):
   ❏ (a) Known lead-based paint and/or lead-based paint hazards are present in the Property (explain): _____
   _____ .
   ☒ (b) Seller has no actual knowledge of lead-based paint and/or lead-based paint hazards in the Property.
2. RECORDS AND REPORTS AVAILABLE TO SELLER (check one box only):
   ❏ (a) Seller has provided the purchaser with all available records and reports pertaining to lead-based paint and/or lead-based paint hazards in the Property (list documents):_____
   _____ .
   ☒ (b) Seller has no reports or records pertaining to lead-based paint and/or lead-based paint hazards in the Property.

C. BUYER'S RIGHTS (check one box only):
❏1. Buyer waives the opportunity to conduct a risk assessment or inspection of the Property for the presence of lead-based paint or lead-based paint hazards.
☒2. Within ten days after the effective date of this contract, Buyer may have the Property inspected by inspectors
   selected by Buyer. If lead-based paint or lead-based paint hazards are present, Buyer may terminate this contract by giving Seller written notice within 14 days after the effective date of this contract, and the earnest money will be refunded to Buyer.

D. BUYER'S ACKNOWLEDGMENT (check applicable boxes):
❏1. Buyer has received copies of all information listed above.
❏2. Buyer has received the pamphlet *Protect Your Family from Lead in Your Home*.

E. BROKERS' ACKNOWLEDGMENT: Brokers have informed Seller of Seller's obligations under 42 U.S.C. 4852d to: (a) provide Buyer with the federally approved pamphlet on lead poisoning prevention; (b) complete this addendum; (c) disclose any known lead-based paint and/or lead-based paint hazards in the Property; (d) deliver all records and reports to Buyer pertaining to lead-based paint and/or lead-based paint hazards in the Property; (e) provide Buyer a period of up to 10 days to have the Property inspected; and (f) retain a completed copy of this addendum for at least 3 years following the sale. Brokers are aware of their responsibility to ensure compliance.

F. CERTIFICATION OF ACCURACY: The following persons have reviewed the information above and certify, to the best of their knowledge, that the information they have provided is true and accurate.

_____   _____   _____   _____
Buyer   Date   Seller   Date

_____   _____   _____   _____
Buyer   Date   Seller   Date

_____   _____   _____   _____
Other Broker   Date   Listing Broker   Date

The form of this addendum has been approved by the Texas Real Estate Commission for use only with similarly approved or promulgated forms of contracts. Such approval relates to this contract form only. TREC forms are intended for use only by trained real estate licensees. No representation is made as to the legal validity or adequacy of any provision in any specific transactions. It is not suitable for complex transactions. Texas Real Estate Commission, P.O. Box 12188, Austin, TX 78711-2188, 512-936-3000 (http://www.trec.texas.gov)

TREC NO. OP-L

PROMULGATED BY THE TEXAS REAL ESTATE COMMISSION (TREC) 11-2-2015
FARM AND RANCH CONTRACT

1. PARTIES: The parties to this contract are <u>Debbie Rodriguez, a single person</u>
(Seller) and <u>Corban Walker and Christopher John</u> (Buyer). Seller agrees to
sell and convey to Buyer and Buyer agrees to buy from Seller the Property defined below.

2. PROPERTY: The land, improvements, accessories and crops except for the exclusions and reservations, are collectively referred to as the "Property".

  A. LAND: The land situated in the County of <u>Prosperous</u>, Texas, described as follows: <u>720 acres out of Abstract 731, BS&M Survey No.6151, Meets and Bounds attached to contra</u>

  or as described on attached exhibit, also known as _____
(address/zip code), together with all rights, privileges, and appurtenances pertaining thereto, including but not limited to: water rights, claims, permits, strips and gores, easements, and cooperative or association memberships.

  B. IMPROVEMENTS:
    (1) FARM and RANCH IMPROVEMENTS: The following **permanently installed and built-in items**, if any: windmills, tanks, barns, pens, fences, gates, sheds, outbuildings, and corrals.
    (2) RESIDENTIAL IMPROVEMENTS: The house, garage, and all other fixtures and improvements attached to the above-described real property, including without limitation, the following **permanently installed and built-in items**, if any: all equipment and appliances, valances, screens, shutters, awnings, wall-to-wall carpeting, mirrors, ceiling fans, attic fans, mail boxes, television antennas, mounts and brackets for televisions and speakers, heating and air-conditioning units, security and fire detection equipment, wiring, plumbing and lighting fixtures, chandeliers, water softener system, kitchen equipment, garage door openers, cleaning equipment, shrubbery, landscaping, outdoor cooking equipment, and all other property owned by Seller and attached to the above described real property.

  C. ACCESSORIES:
    (1) FARM AND RANCH ACCESSORIES: The following described related accessories: (check boxes of conveyed accessories) ☐ portable buildings ☐ hunting blinds ☐ game feeders ☐ livestock feeders and troughs ☐ irrigation equipment ☐ fuel tanks ☑ submersible pumps ☑ pressure tanks ☐ corrals ☐ gates ☐ chutes ☐ other:_____
    (2) RESIDENTIAL ACCESSORIES: The following described related accessories, if any: window air conditioning units, stove, fireplace screens, curtains and rods, blinds, window shades, draperies and rods, door keys, mailbox keys, above ground pool, swimming pool equipment and maintenance accessories, artificial fireplace logs, and controls for: (i) garages, (ii) entry gates, and (iii) other improvements and accessories.
  D. CROPS: Unless otherwise agreed in writing, Seller has the right to harvest all growing crops until delivery of possession of the Property.
  E. EXCLUSIONS: The following improvements, accessories, and crops will be retained by Seller and must be removed prior to delivery of possession: <u>None</u>.
  F. RESERVATIONS: Any reservation for oil, gas, or other minerals, water, timber, or other interests is made in accordance with an attached addendum or Special Provisions.

3. SALES PRICE:
  A. Cash portion of Sales Price payable by Buyer at closing....................$<u>1,980,000</u>
  B. Sum of all financing described in the attached: ☐ Third Party Financing Addendum, ☐ Loan Assumption Addendum, ☐ Seller Financing Addendum ...$<u>0</u>
  C. Sales Price (Sum of A and B) ....$<u>1,980,000</u>
  D. The Sales Price ☐ will ☑ will not be adjusted based on the survey required by Paragraph 6C. If the Sales Price is adjusted, the Sales Price will be calculated on the basis of $ <u>N/A</u> per acre. If the Sales Price is adjusted by more than 10%, either party may terminate this contract by providing written notice to the other party within <u>N/A</u> days after the terminating party receives the survey. If neither party terminates this contract or if the variance is 10% or less, the adjustment will be made to the amount in ☐ 3A ☐ 3B ☐ proportionately to 3A and 3B.

4. LICENSE HOLDER DISCLOSURE: Texas Law requires a real estate license holder who is a party to a transaction or acting on behalf of a spouse, parent, child, business entity in which the license holder owns more than 10%, or a trust for which the license holder acts as trustee or of which the license holder or the license holder's spouse, parent or child is a beneficiary, to notify the other party in writing before entering into a contract of sale. Disclose if applicable:_____
<u>N/A but disclosure is still made that Seller is sister of the Listing Broker.</u>

5. EARNEST MONEY: Upon execution of this contract by all parties, Buyer shall deposit $<u>80,000</u> as earnest money with, <u>Sindon Title Company</u>
as escrow agent, at <u>1939 Miguel Ave. Whitestone, Tx 78123</u>
(address). Buyer shall deposit additional earnest money of $_____<u>N/A</u> with escrow agent within <u>N/A</u> days after the effective date of this contract. If Buyer fails to deposit the earnest money as required by this contract, Buyer will be in default.

Initialed for identification by Buyer_____ _____ and Seller _____ _____ TREC NO. 25-11

Contract Concerning _____720 acres Properous Co. Texas_____ Page 2 of 10   11-2-2015
(Address of Property)

6. TITLE POLICY AND SURVEY:

A. TITLE POLICY: Seller shall furnish to Buyer at ☑Seller's ☐Buyer's expense an owner policy of title insurance (Title Policy) issued by: Sindon Title Company _____ (Title Company) in the amount of the Sales Price, dated at or after closing, insuring Buyer against loss under the provisions of the Title Policy, subject to the promulgated exclusions (including existing building and zoning ordinances) and the following exceptions:

(1) The standard printed exception for standby fees, taxes and assessments.
(2) Liens created as part of the financing described in Paragraph 3.
(3) Reservations or exceptions otherwise permitted by this contract or as may be approved by Buyer in writing.
(4) The standard printed exception as to marital rights.
(5) The standard printed exception as to waters, tidelands, beaches, streams, and related matters.
(6) The standard printed exception as to discrepancies, conflicts, shortages in area or boundary lines, encroachments or protrusions, or overlapping improvements: ☑ (i) will not be amended or deleted from the title policy; or ☐(ii) will be amended to read, "shortages in area" at the expense of ☐Buyer ☐Seller.

B. COMMITMENT: Within 20 days after the Title Company receives a copy of this contract, Seller shall furnish to Buyer a commitment for title insurance (Commitment) and, at Buyer's expense, legible copies of restrictive covenants and documents evidencing exceptions in the Commitment (Exception Documents) other than the standard printed exceptions. Seller authorizes the Title Company to deliver the Commitment and Exception Documents to Buyer at Buyer's address shown in Paragraph 21. If the Commitment and Exception Documents are not delivered to Buyer within the specified time, the time for delivery will be automatically extended up to 15 days or 3 days before the Closing Date, whichever is earlier. If, due to factors beyond Seller's control, the Commitment and Exception Documents are not delivered within the time required, Buyer may terminate this contract and the earnest money will be refunded to Buyer.

C. SURVEY: The survey must be made by a registered professional land surveyor acceptable to the Title Company and Buyer's lender(s). (Check one box only):
☑ (1) Within __5__ days after the effective date of this contract, Seller shall furnish to Buyer and Title Company Seller's existing survey of the Property and a Residential Real Property Affidavit promulgated by the Texas Department of Insurance (T-47 Affidavit). **If Seller fails to furnish the existing survey or affidavit within the time prescribed, Buyer shall obtain a new survey at Seller's expense no later than 3 days prior to Closing Date.** The existing survey ☐ will ☑ will not be recertified to a date subsequent to the effective date of this contract at the expense of ☐ Buyer ☐ Seller. If the existing survey is not approved by the Title Company or Buyer's lender(s), a new survey will be obtained at the expense of ☐ Buyer ☐ Seller no later than 3 days prior to Closing Date.
☐ (2) Within _____ days after the effective date of this contract, Buyer shall obtain a new survey at Buyer's expense. Buyer is deemed to receive the survey on the date of actual receipt or the date specified in this paragraph, whichever is earlier.
☐ (3) Within _____ days after the effective date of this contract, Seller, at Seller's expense shall furnish a new survey to Buyer.
☐ (4) No survey is required.

D. OBJECTIONS: Buyer may object in writing to (i) defects, exceptions, or encumbrances to title disclosed on the survey other than items 6A(1) through (5) above; or disclosed in the Commitment other than items 6A(1) through (6) above; (ii) any portion of the Property lying in a special flood hazard area (Zone V or A) as shown on the current Federal Emergency Management Agency map; or (iii) any exceptions which prohibit the following use or activity: N/A _____.

Buyer must object the earlier of (i) the Closing Date or (ii) __N/A__ days after Buyer receives the Commitment, Exception Documents, and the survey. Buyer's failure to object within the time allowed will constitute a waiver of Buyer's right to object; except that the requirements in Schedule C of the Commitment are not waived by Buyer. Provided Seller is not obligated to incur any expense, Seller shall cure the timely objections of Buyer or any third party lender within 15 days after Seller receives the objections and the Closing Date will be extended as necessary. If objections are not cured within such 15 day period, this contract will terminate and the earnest money will be refunded to Buyer unless Buyer waives the objections.

E. EXCEPTION DOCUMENTS: Prior to the execution of the contract, Seller has provided Buyer with copies of the Exception Documents listed below or on the attached exhibit. Matters reflected in the Exception Documents listed below or on the attached exhibit will be permitted exceptions in the Title Policy and will not be a basis for objection to title:

Document	Date	Recording Reference
Easement for Properous Electric Coop.		Deed Records Co. Clerk Offic

Initialed for identification by Buyer_____ _____ and Seller _____ _____   TREC NO. 25-11

Contract Concerning _____ 720 acres Properous Co. Texas _____ Page 3 of 10   11-2-2015
(Address of Property)

F. SURFACE LEASES: Prior to the execution of the contract, Seller has provided Buyer with copies of written leases and given notice of oral leases (Leases) listed below or on the attached exhibit. The following Leases will be permitted exceptions in the Title Policy and will not be a basis for objection to title: None

G. TITLE NOTICES:
(1) ABSTRACT OR TITLE POLICY: Broker advises Buyer to have an abstract of title covering the Property examined by an attorney of Buyer's selection, or Buyer should be furnished with or obtain a Title Policy. If a Title Policy is furnished, the Commitment should be promptly reviewed by an attorney of Buyer's choice due to the time limitations on Buyer's right to object.
(2) STATUTORY TAX DISTRICTS: If the Property is situated in a utility or other statutorily created district providing water, sewer, drainage, or flood control facilities and services, Chapter 49, Texas Water Code, requires Seller to deliver and Buyer to sign the statutory notice relating to the tax rate, bonded indebtedness, or standby fee of the district prior to final execution of this contract.
(3) TIDE WATERS: If the Property abuts the tidally influenced waters of the state, §33.135, Texas Natural Resources Code, requires a notice regarding coastal area property to be included in the contract. An addendum containing the notice promulgated by TREC or required by the parties must be used.
(4) ANNEXATION: If the Property is located outside the limits of a municipality, Seller notifies Buyer under §5.011, Texas Property Code, that the Property may now or later be included in the extraterritorial jurisdiction of a municipality and may now or later be subject to annexation by the municipality. Each municipality maintains a map that depicts its boundaries and extraterritorial jurisdiction. To determine if the Property is located within a municipality's extraterritorial jurisdiction or is likely to be located within a municipality's extraterritorial jurisdiction, contact all municipalities located in the general proximity of the Property for further information.
(5) PROPERTY LOCATED IN A CERTIFICATED SERVICE AREA OF A UTILITY SERVICE PROVIDER: Notice required by §13.257, Water Code: The real property, described in Paragraph 2, that you are about to purchase may be located in a certificated water or sewer service area, which is authorized by law to provide water or sewer service to the properties in the certificated area. If your property is located in a certificated area there may be special costs or charges that you will be required to pay before you can receive water or sewer service. There may be a period required to construct lines or other facilities necessary to provide water or sewer service to your property. You are advised to determine if the property is in a certificated area and contact the utility service provider to determine the cost that you will be required to pay and the period, if any, that is required to provide water or sewer service to your property. The undersigned Buyer hereby acknowledges receipt of the foregoing notice at or before the execution of a binding contract for the purchase of the real property described in Paragraph 2 or at closing of purchase of the real property.
(6) PUBLIC IMPROVEMENT DISTRICTS: If the Property is in a public improvement district, §5.014, Property Code, requires Seller to notify Buyer as follows: As a purchaser of this parcel of real property you are obligated to pay an assessment to a municipality or county for an improvement project undertaken by a public improvement district under Chapter 372, Local Government Code. The assessment may be due annually or in periodic installments. More information concerning the amount of the assessment and the due dates of that assessment may be obtained from the municipality or county levying the assessment. The amount of the assessments is subject to change. Your failure to pay the assessments could result in a lien on and the foreclosure of your property.
(7) TEXAS AGRICULTURAL DEVELOPMENT DISTRICT: The Property ☐ is ☐ is not located in a Texas Agricultural Development District. For additional information contact the Texas Department of Agriculture
(8) TRANSFER FEES: If the Property is subject to a private transfer fee obligation, §5.205, Property Code, requires Seller to notify Buyer as follows: The private transfer fee obligation may be governed by Chapter 5, Subchapter G of the Texas Property Code.
(9) PROPANE GAS SYSTEM SERVICE AREA: If the Property is located in a propane gas system service area owned by a distribution system retailer, Seller must give Buyer written notice as required by §141.010, Texas Utilities Code. An addendum containing the notice approved by TREC or required by the parties should be used.
(10) NOTICE OF WATER LEVEL FLUCTUATIONS: If the Property adjoins an impoundment of water, including a reservoir or lake, constructed and maintained under Chapter 11, Water Code, that has a storage capacity of at least 5,000 acre-feet at the impoundment's normal operating level, Seller hereby notifies Buyer: "The water level of the impoundment of water adjoining the Property fluctuates for various reasons, including as a result of: (1) an entity lawfully exercising its right to use the water stored in the impoundment; or (2) drought or flood conditions."

Initialed for identification by Buyer_____ _____ and Seller _____ _____   TREC NO. 25-11

7. PROPERTY CONDITION:

A. ACCESS, INSPECTIONS AND UTILITIES: Seller shall permit Buyer and Buyer's agents access to the Property at reasonable times. Buyer may have the Property inspected by inspectors selected by Buyer and licensed by TREC or otherwise permitted by law to make inspections. Any hydrostatic testing must be separately authorized by Seller in writing. Seller at Seller's expense shall immediately cause existing utilities to be turned on and shall keep the utilities on during the time this contract is in effect .
NOTICE: Buyer should determine the availability of utilities to the Property suitable to satisfy Buyer's needs.

B. SELLER'S DISCLOSURE NOTICE PURSUANT TO §5.008, TEXAS PROPERTY CODE (Notice):
(Check one box only)
☐ (1) Buyer has received the Notice
☐ (2) Buyer has not received the Notice. Within _____ days after the effective date of this contract, Seller shall deliver the Notice to Buyer. If Buyer does not receive the Notice, Buyer may terminate this contract at any time prior to the closing and the earnest money will be refunded to Buyer. If Seller delivers the Notice, Buyer may terminate this contract for any reason within 7 days after Buyer receives the Notice or prior to the closing, whichever first occurs, and the earnest money will be refunded to Buyer.
☑ (3) The Texas Property Code does not require this Seller to furnish the Notice.

C. SELLER'S DISCLOSURE OF LEAD-BASED PAINT AND LEAD-BASED PAINT HAZARDS is required by Federal law for a residential dwelling constructed prior to 1978.

D. ACCEPTANCE OF PROPERTY CONDITION: "As Is" means the present condition of the Property with any and all defects and without warranty except for the warranties of title and the warranties in this contract. Buyer's agreement to accept the Property As Is under Paragraph 7D (1) or (2) does not preclude Buyer from inspecting the Property under Paragraph 7A, from negotiating repairs or treatments in a subsequent amendment, or from terminating this contract during the Option Period, if any.
(Check one box only)
☐ (1) Buyer accepts the Property As Is.
☑ (2) Buyer accepts the Property As Is provided Seller, at Seller's expense, shall complete the following specific repairs and treatments: water well to be in working condition at time of closing.
.
(Do not insert general phrases, such as "subject to inspections," that do not identify specific repairs and treatments.)

E. COMPLETION OF REPAIRS: Unless otherwise agreed in writing: (i) Seller shall complete all agreed repairs and treatments prior to the Closing Date; and (ii) all required permits must be obtained, and repairs and treatments must be performed by persons who are licensed to provide such repairs or treatments or, if no license is required by law, are commercially engaged in the trade of providing such repairs or treatments. At Buyer's election, any transferable warranties received by Seller with respect to the repairs will be transferred to Buyer at Buyer's expense. If Seller fails to complete any agreed repairs prior to the Closing Date, Buyer may exercise remedies under Paragraph 15 or extend the Closing Date up to 5 days if necessary for Seller to complete repairs.

F. LENDER REQUIRED REPAIRS AND TREATMENTS: Unless otherwise agreed in writing, neither party is obligated to pay for lender required repairs, which includes treatment for wood destroying insects. If the parties do not agree to pay for the lender required repairs or treatments, this contract will terminate and the earnest money will be refunded to Buyer. If the cost of lender required repairs and treatments exceeds 5% of the Sales Price, Buyer may terminate this contract and the earnest money will be refunded to Buyer.

G. ENVIRONMENTAL MATTERS: Buyer is advised that the presence of wetlands, toxic substances, including asbestos and wastes or other environmental hazards, or the presence of a threatened or endangered species or its habitat may affect Buyer's intended use of the Property. If Buyer is concerned about these matters, an addendum promulgated by TREC or required by the parties should be used.

H. SELLER'S DISCLOSURES: Except as otherwise disclosed in this contract, Seller has no knowledge of the following:
(1) any flooding of the Property which has had a material adverse effect on the use of the Property;
(2) any pending or threatened litigation, condemnation, or special assessment affecting the Property;
(3) any environmental hazards that materially and adversely affect the Property;
(4) any dumpsite, landfill, or underground tanks or containers now or previously located on the Property;
(5) any wetlands, as defined by federal or state law or regulation, affecting the Property; or
(6) any threatened or endangered species or their habitat affecting the Property.

I. RESIDENTIAL SERVICE CONTRACTS: Buyer may purchase a residential service contract from a residential service company licensed by TREC. If Buyer purchases a residential service contract, Seller shall reimburse Buyer at closing for the cost of the residential service contract in an amount not exceeding $_____ N/A. Buyer should review any residential service contract

Initialed for identification by Buyer_____ _____ and Seller _____ _____   TREC NO. 25-11

for the scope of coverage, exclusions and limitations. **The purchase of a residential service contract is optional. Similar coverage may be purchased from various companies authorized to do business in Texas.**

J. GOVERNMENT PROGRAMS: The Property is subject to the government programs listed below or on the attached exhibit: None_____.
Seller shall provide Buyer with copies of all governmental program agreements. Any allocation or proration of payment under governmental programs is made by separate agreement between the parties which will survive closing.

8. BROKERS' FEES: All obligations of the parties for payment of brokers' fees are contained in separate written agreements.

9. CLOSING:

A. The closing of the sale will be on or before _____ August 22, 20 15___, or within 7 days after objections made under Paragraph 6D have been cured or waived, whichever date is later (Closing Date). If either party fails to close the sale by the Closing Date, the non-defaulting party may exercise the remedies contained in Paragraph 15.

B. At closing:

(1) Seller shall execute and deliver a general warranty deed conveying title to the Property to Buyer and showing no additional exceptions to those permitted in Paragraph 6, an assignment of Leases, and furnish tax statements or certificates showing no delinquent taxes on the Property.

(2) Buyer shall pay the Sales Price in good funds acceptable to the escrow agent.

(3) Seller and Buyer shall execute and deliver any notices, statements, certificates, affidavits, releases, loan documents and other documents reasonably required for the closing of the sale and the issuance of the Title Policy.

(4) There will be no liens, assessments, or security interests against the Property which will not be satisfied out of the sales proceeds unless securing the payment of any loans assumed by Buyer and assumed loans will not be in default.

(5) If the Property is subject to a residential lease, Seller shall transfer security deposits (as defined under §92.102, Property Code), if any, to Buyer. In such an event, Buyer shall deliver to the tenant a signed statement acknowledging that the Buyer has acquired the Property and is responsible for the return of the security deposit, and specifying the exact dollar amount of the security deposit.

10. POSSESSION:

A. Buyer's Possession: Seller shall deliver to Buyer possession of the Property in its present or required condition, ordinary wear and tear excepted: ☑ upon closing and funding ☐ according to a temporary residential lease form promulgated by TREC or other written lease required by the parties. Any possession by Buyer prior to closing or by Seller after closing which is not authorized by a written lease will establish a tenancy at sufferance relationship between the parties. **Consult your insurance agent prior to change of ownership and possession because insurance coverage may be limited or terminated. The absence of a written lease or appropriate insurance coverage may expose the parties to economic loss.**

B. Leases:

(1) After the Effective Date, Seller may not execute any lease (including but not limited to mineral leases) or convey any interest in the Property without Buyer's written consent.

(2) If the Property is subject to any lease to which Seller is a party, Seller shall deliver to Buyer copies of the lease(s) and any move-in condition form signed by the tenant within 7 days after the Effective Date of the contract.

11. SPECIAL PROVISIONS: (Insert only factual statements and business details applicable to the sale. TREC rules prohibit license holders from adding factual statements or business details for which a contract addendum or other form has been promulgated by TREC for mandatory use.)

None.

12. SETTLEMENT AND OTHER EXPENSES:

A. The following expenses must be paid at or prior to closing:
  (1) Expenses payable by Seller (Seller's Expenses):
    (a) Releases of existing liens, including prepayment penalties and recording fees; release of Seller's loan liability; tax statements or certificates; preparation of deed; one-half of escrow fee; and other expenses payable by Seller under this contract.
    (b) Seller shall also pay an amount not to exceed $ _____ None to be applied in the following order: Buyer's Expenses which Buyer is prohibited from paying by FHA, VA, Texas Veterans Land Board or other governmental loan programs, and then to other Buyer's Expenses as allowed by the lender.
  (2) Expenses payable by Buyer (Buyer's Expenses) Appraisal fees; loan application fees; origination charges; credit reports; preparation of loan documents; interest on the notes from date of disbursement to one month prior to dates of first monthly payments; recording fees; copies of easements and restrictions; loan title policy with endorsements required by lender; loan-related inspection fees; photos; amortization schedules; one-half of escrow fee; all prepaid items, including required premiums for flood and hazard insurance, reserve deposits for insurance, ad valorem taxes and special governmental assessments; final compliance inspection; courier fee; repair inspection; underwriting fee; wire transfer fee; expenses incident to any loan; Private Mortgage Insurance Premium (PMI), VA Loan Funding Fee, or FHA Mortgage Insurance Premium (MIP) as required by the lender; and other expenses payable by Buyer under this contract.
B. If any expense exceeds an amount expressly stated in this contract for such expense to be paid by a party, that party may terminate this contract unless the other party agrees to pay such excess. Buyer may not pay charges and fees expressly prohibited by FHA, VA, Texas Veterans Land Board or other governmental loan program regulations.

13. PRORATIONS AND ROLLBACK TAXES:

A. PRORATIONS: Taxes for the current year, interest, maintenance fees, assessments, dues and rents will be prorated through the Closing Date. The tax proration may be calculated taking into consideration any change in exemptions that will affect the current year's taxes. If taxes for the current year vary from the amount prorated at closing, the parties shall adjust the prorations when tax statements for the current year are available. If taxes are not paid at or prior to closing, Buyer shall pay taxes for the current year. Rentals which are unknown at time of closing will be prorated between Buyer and Seller when they become known.
B. ROLLBACK TAXES: If this sale or Buyer's use of the Property after closing results in the assessment of additional taxes, penalties or interest (Assessments) for periods prior to closing, the Assessments will be the obligation of Buyer. If Assessments are imposed because of Seller's use or change in use of the Property prior to closing, the Assessments will be the obligation of Seller. Obligations imposed by this paragraph will survive closing.

14. CASUALTY LOSS:
If any part of the Property is damaged or destroyed by fire or other casualty after the effective date of this contract, Seller shall restore the Property to its previous condition as soon as reasonably possible, but in any event by the Closing Date. If Seller fails to do so due to factors beyond Seller's control, Buyer may (a) terminate this contract and the earnest money will be refunded to Buyer, (b) extend the time for performance up to 15 days and the Closing Date will be extended as necessary or (c) accept the Property in its damaged condition with an assignment of insurance proceeds, if permitted by Seller's insurance carrier, and receive credit from Seller at closing in the amount of the deductible under the insurance policy. Seller's obligations under this paragraph are independent of any other obligations of Seller under this contract.

15. DEFAULT:
If Buyer fails to comply with this contract, Buyer will be in default, and Seller may (a) enforce specific performance, seek such other relief as may be provided by law, or both, or (b) terminate this contract and receive the earnest money as liquidated damages, thereby releasing both parties from this contract. If Seller fails to comply with this contract for any other reason, Seller will be in default and Buyer may (a) enforce specific performance, seek such other relief as may be provided by law, or both, or (b) terminate this contract and receive the earnest money, thereby releasing both parties from this contract.

16. MEDIATION:
It is the policy of the State of Texas to encourage resolution of disputes through alternative dispute resolution procedures such as mediation. Any dispute between Seller and Buyer related to this contract which is not resolved through informal discussion will be submitted to a mutually acceptable mediation service or provider. The parties to the mediation shall bear the mediation costs equally. This paragraph does not preclude a party from seeking equitable relief from a court of competent jurisdiction.

17. ATTORNEY'S FEES:
A Buyer, Seller, Listing Broker, Other Broker, or escrow agent who prevails in any legal proceeding related to this contract is entitled to recover reasonable attorney's fees and all costs of such proceeding.

18.ESCROW:

A. ESCROW: The escrow agent is not (i) a party to this contract and does not have liability for the performance or nonperformance of any party to this contract, (ii) liable for interest on the earnest money and (iii) liable for the loss of any earnest money caused by the failure of any financial institution in which the earnest money has been deposited unless the financial institution is acting as escrow agent.

B. EXPENSES: At closing, the earnest money must be applied first to any cash down payment, then to Buyer's Expenses and any excess refunded to Buyer. If no closing occurs, escrow agent may: (i) require a written release of liability of the escrow agent from all parties, (ii) require payment of unpaid expenses incurred on behalf of a party, and (iii) only deduct from the earnest money the amount of unpaid expenses incurred on behalf of the party receiving the earnest money.

C. DEMAND: Upon termination of this contract, either party or the escrow agent may send a release of earnest money to each party and the parties shall execute counterparts of the release and deliver same to the escrow agent. If either party fails to execute the release, either party may make a written demand to the escrow agent for the earnest money. If only one party makes written demand for the earnest money, escrow agent shall promptly provide a copy of the demand to the other party. If escrow agent does not receive written objection to the demand from the other party within 15 days, escrow agent may disburse the earnest money to the party making demand reduced by the amount of unpaid expenses incurred on behalf of the party receiving the earnest money and escrow agent may pay the same to the creditors. If escrow agent complies with the provisions of this paragraph, each party hereby releases escrow agent from all adverse claims related to the disbursal of the earnest money.

D. DAMAGES: Any party who wrongfully fails or refuses to sign a release acceptable to the escrow agent within 7 days of receipt of the request will be liable to the other party for (i) damages; (ii) the earnest money; (iii) reasonable attorney's fees; and (iv) all costs of suit.

E. NOTICES: Escrow agent's notices will be effective when sent in compliance with Paragraph 21. Notice of objection to the demand will be deemed effective upon receipt by escrow agent.

19.REPRESENTATIONS: All covenants, representations and warranties in this contract survive closing. If any representation of Seller in this contract is untrue on the Closing Date, Seller will be in default. Unless expressly prohibited by written agreement, Seller may continue to show the Property and receive, negotiate and accept back up offers.

20.FEDERAL TAX REQUIREMENTS: If Seller is a "foreign person," as defined by applicable law, or if Seller fails to deliver an affidavit to Buyer that Seller is not a "foreign person," then Buyer shall withhold from the sales proceeds an amount sufficient to comply with applicable tax law and deliver the same to the Internal Revenue Service together with appropriate tax forms. Internal Revenue Service regulations require filing written reports if currency in excess of specified amounts is received in the transaction.

21.NOTICES: All notices from one party to the other must be in writing and are effective when mailed to, hand-delivered at, or transmitted by fax or electronic transmission as follows:

To Buyer	**To Seller**
at: 82214 August Lane	at: 2070 Bonita Blvd.
Whitestone, Texas 78213	Whitestone, Texas 78213
Phone: (409) 513-1998	Phone: (409) 846-0513
Fax: ( ) same as above	Fax: ( )None
E-mail: cwalker@bigguy.net	E-mail: debbier@grtc.com

Initialed for identification by Buyer_____ _____ and Seller _____ _____   TREC NO. 25-11

Contract Concerning _____ Page 8 of 10   11-2-2015
(Address of Property)

22. AGREEMENT OF PARTIES: This contract contains the entire agreement of the parties and cannot be changed except by their written agreement. Addenda which are a part of this contract are (check all applicable boxes):

☐ Third Party Financing Addendum

☐ Seller Financing Addendum

☐ Addendum for Property Subject to Mandatory Membership in a Property Owners Association

☐ Buyer's Temporary Residential Lease

☐ Loan Assumption Addendum

☐ Addendum for Sale of Other Property by Buyer

☐ Addendum for "Back-Up" Contract

☐ Addendum for Coastal Area Property

☑ Environmental Assessment, Threatened or Endangered Species and Wetlands Addendum

☐ Seller's Temporary Residential Lease

☐ Short Sale Addendum

☐ Addendum for Property Located Seaward of the Gulf Intracoastal Waterway

☐ Addendum for Seller's Disclosure of Information on Lead-based Paint and Lead-based Paint Hazards as Required by Federal Law

☐ Addendum for Property in a Propane Gas System Service Area

☑ Other (list): Addendum for Oil, gas and Other Mine

23. TERMINATION OPTION: For nominal consideration, the receipt of which is hereby acknowledged by Seller, and Buyer's agreement to pay Seller $_____ 500 (Option Fee) within 3 days after the effective date of this contract, Seller grants Buyer the unrestricted right to terminate this contract by giving notice of termination to Seller within ___30___ days after the effective date of this contract (Option Period). Notices under this paragraph must be given by 5:00 p.m. (local time where the Property is located) by the date specified. If no dollar amount is stated as the Option Fee or if Buyer fails to pay the Option Fee to Seller within the time prescribed, this paragraph will not be a part of this contract and Buyer shall not have the unrestricted right to terminate this contract. If Buyer gives notice of termination within the time prescribed, the Option Fee will not be refunded; however, any earnest money will be refunded to Buyer. The Option Fee ☑will ☐will not be credited to the Sales Price at closing. **Time is of the essence for this paragraph and strict compliance with the time for performance is required.**

24. CONSULT AN ATTORNEY BEFORE SIGNING: TREC rules prohibit real estate license holders from giving legal advice. READ THIS CONTRACT CAREFULLY.

Buyer's
Attorney is: N/A _____

Phone: (___) _____

Fax: (___) _____

E-mail: _____

Seller's
Attorney is: N/A _____

Phone: (___) _____

Fax: (___) _____

E-mail: _____

EXECUTED the _____ day of _____, 20____ (EFFECTIVE DATE).
(BROKER: FILL IN THE DATE OF FINAL ACCEPTANCE.)

_____
Buyer

_____
Buyer

_____
Seller

_____
Seller

The form of this contract has been approved by the Texas Real Estate Commission. TREC forms are intended for use only by trained real estate. No representation is made as to the legal validity or adequacy of any provision in any specific transactions. It is not intended for complex transactions. Texas Real Estate Commission, P.O. Box 12188, Austin, TX 78711-2188, (512) 936-3000 (http://www.trec.texas.gov) TREC NO. 25-11. This form replaces TREC NO. 25-10.

TREC NO. 25-11

Contract Concerning _____Page 9 of 10   11-2-2015
(Address of Property)

RATIFICATION OF FEE

Listing Broker has agreed to pay Other Broker_____N/A_____ of the total Sales Price when Listing Broker's fee is received. Escrow Agent is authorized and directed to pay Other Broker from Listing Broker's fee at closing.

Other Broker: Listing Broker:

By: _____   By: _____

BROKER INFORMATION AND AGREEMENT FOR PAYMENT OF BROKERS' FEES

		Rene Rodriguez	XXXXXX
Other Broker	License No.	Listing or Principal Broker	License No.
		N/A	
Associate's Name	License No.	Listing Associate's Name	License No.
Licensed Supervisor of Associate	License No.	Licensed Supervisor of Listing Associate	License No.
		218 N. Ash	
Other Broker's Office Address		Listing Broker's Office Address	
		Whitestone Texas 78213	
City State Zip		City State Zip	
		210-814-0328 same	
Phone Fax		Phone Fax	
		rene@ranch.sales.com	
Associate's Email Address		Listing Associate's Email Address	

represents ☐ Buyer only as Buyer's agent
☐ Seller as Listing Broker's subagent

Selling Associate   License No.

Licensed Supervisor of Selling Associate   License No.

Selling Associate's Office Address   Fax

City   State   Zip

Selling Associate's Email Address   Phone

represents ☑ Seller only
☐ Buyer only
☐ Seller and Buyer as an intermediary

Upon closing of the sale by Seller to Buyer of the Property described in the contract to which this fee agreement is attached: (a) ☐Seller ☐ Buyer will pay Listing/Principal Broker ☐a cash fee of $_____ NONE or ☐ _____% of the total Sales Price; and (b) ☐Seller ☐ Buyer will pay Other Broker ☐a cash fee of $_____ or ☐ _____% of the total Sales Price. Seller/Buyer authorizes and directs Escrow Agent to pay the brokers from the proceeds at closing.

Brokers' fees are negotiable. Brokers' fees or the sharing of fees between brokers are not fixed, controlled, recommended, suggested or maintained by the Texas Real Estate Commission.

_____   _____
Seller   Buyer

_____   _____
Seller   Buyer
Do not sign if there is a separate written agreement for payment of Brokers' fees.

TREC NO. 25-11

Contract Concerning _____ Page 10 of 10   11-2-2015
(Address of Property)

OPTION FEE RECEIPT

Receipt of $_____500__ (Option Fee) in the form of _personal check # 1819_____ is acknowledged.

_____   _____
Seller or Listing Broker   Date

CONTRACT AND EARNEST MONEY RECEIPT

Receipt of ☐Contract and ☐$_____ Earnest Money in the form of _____
is acknowledged.
Escrow Agent: _____   Date: _____

By: _____   _____
_____   Email Address
Address   Phone: (_____) _____
_____   Fax: (_____) _____
City   State   Zip

PROMULGATED BY THE TEXAS REAL ESTATE COMMISSION (TREC)   12-05-11

ENVIRONMENTAL ASSESSMENT, THREATENED OR ENDANGERED SPECIES, AND WETLANDS ADDENDUM

TO CONTRACT CONCERNING THE PROPERTY AT

720 acres Prosperous Co., Texas
(Address of Property)

☒ A. ENVIRONMENTAL ASSESSMENT: Buyer, at Buyer's expense, may obtain an environmental assessment report prepared by an environmental specialist.

B. THREATENED OR ENDANGERED SPECIES: Buyer, at Buyer's expense, may obtain a report from a natural resources professional to determine if there are any threatened or endangered species or their habitats as defined by the Texas Parks and Wildlife Department or the U.S. Fish and Wildlife Service.

C. WETLANDS: Buyer, at Buyer's expense, may obtain a report from an environmental specialist to determine if there are wetlands, as defined by federal or state law or regulation.

Within __20__ days after the effective date of the contract, Buyer may terminate the contract by furnishing Seller a copy of any report noted above that adversely affects the use of the Property and a notice of termination of the contract. Upon termination, the earnest money will be refunded to Buyer.

_____   _____
Buyer   Seller

_____   _____
Buyer   Seller

PROMULGATED BY THE TEXAS REAL ESTATE COMMISSION (TREC)   12-05-11

ADDENDUM FOR RESERVATION OF OIL, GAS, AND OTHER MINERALS

ADDENDUM TO CONTRACT CONCERNING THE PROPERTY AT

720 Acres Prosperous Co.
(Street Address and City)

NOTICE: For use only if Seller reserves all or a portion of the Mineral Estate.

A. "Mineral Estate" means all oil, gas, and other minerals in or under the Property, any royalty under any existing or future lease covering any part of the Property, surface rights (including rights of ingress and egress), production and drilling rights, lease payments, and all related benefits.

B. The Mineral Estate owned by Seller, if any, will be conveyed unless reserved as follows (check one box only):

   ☐ (1) Seller reserves all of the Mineral Estate owned by Seller.

   ☒ (2) Seller reserves an undivided _____25_____% interest in the Mineral Estate owned by Seller. *NOTE: If Seller does not own all of the Mineral Estate, Seller reserves only this percentage of Seller's interest.*

C. Seller ☐ waives ☐ does not waive Seller's surface rights (including rights of ingress and egress). *NOTE: Any waiver of surface rights by Seller does not affect any surface rights that may be held by others.*

D. If B(2) applies, Seller shall, on or before the Closing Date, provide Buyer contact information known to Seller for any existing lessee.

If either party is concerned about the legal rights or impact of the above provisions, that party is advised to consult an attorney BEFORE signing.

TREC rules prohibit real estate licensees from giving legal advice.

_____   _____
Buyer   Seller

_____   _____
Buyer   Seller

PROMULGATED BY THE TEXAS REAL ESTATE COMMISSION (TREC)   11-2-2015

UNIMPROVED PROPERTY CONTRACT
NOTICE: Not For Use For Condominium Transactions

1. **PARTIES:** The parties to this contract are Bobby D. Mackey, Kara B. Jones, Dena R. Smith   (Seller) and Danny Harrington and Lovell Harrington (son and mother)   (Buyer).   Seller agrees to sell and convey to Buyer and Buyer agrees to buy from Seller the Property defined below.

2. **PROPERTY:** Lot 17 , Block 4   , Wildwood Estate subdivision   Addition, City of Gulf Coast , County of Prosperous   , Texas, known as 1849 Wagon Wheel 77070   (address/zip code), or as described on attached exhibit together with all rights, privileges and appurtenances pertaining thereto, including but not limited to: water rights, claims, permits, strips and gores, easements, and cooperative or association memberships (the Property).

3. **SALES PRICE:**
    A. Cash portion of Sales Price payable by Buyer at closing ....$_____20,000
    B. Sum of all financing described in the attached: ☐ Third Party Financing Addendum,
        ☐ Loan Assumption Addendum, ☐ Seller Financing Addendum.............$_____70,000
    C. Sales Price (Sum of A and B) ....$_____90,000

4. **LICENSE HOLDER DISCLOSURE:** Texas law requires a real estate license holder who is a party to a transaction or acting on behalf of a spouse, parent, child, business entity in which the license holder owns more than 10%, or a trust for which the license holder acts as trustee or of which the license holder or the license holder's spouse, parent or child is a beneficiary, to notify the other party in writing before entering into a contract of sale. Disclose if applicable:_____ .

5. **EARNEST MONEY:** Upon execution of contract by all parties, Buyer shall deposit $_____2500 as earnest money with De Robertis Title Comapny   , as escrow agent, at 1987 Miguel, Gulf Coast, Texas 77077   (address). Buyer shall deposit additional earnest money of $_____N/A with escrow agent within 0 days after the effective date of this contract. If Buyer fails to deposit the earnest money as required by this contract, Buyer will be in default.

6. **TITLE POLICY AND SURVEY:**
    A. TITLE POLICY: Seller shall furnish to Buyer at ☑Seller's ☐Buyer's expense an owner's policy of title insurance (Title Policy) issued by De Robertis Title Company (Title Company) in the amount of the Sales Price, dated at or after closing, insuring Buyer against loss under the provisions of the Title Policy, subject to the promulgated exclusions (including existing building and zoning ordinances) and the following exceptions:
        (1) Restrictive covenants common to the platted subdivision in which the Property is located.
        (2) The standard printed exception for standby fees, taxes and assessments.
        (3) Liens created as part of the financing described in Paragraph 3.
        (4) Utility easements created by the dedication deed or plat of the subdivision in which the Property is located.
        (5) Reservations or exceptions otherwise permitted by this contract or as may be approved by Buyer in writing.
        (6) The standard printed exception as to marital rights.
        (7) The standard printed exception as to waters, tidelands, beaches, streams, and related matters.
        (8) The standard printed exception as to discrepancies, conflicts, shortages in area or boundary lines, encroachments or protrusions, or overlapping improvements: ☑ (i) will not be amended or deleted from the title policy; or ☐(ii) will be amended to read, "shortages in area" at the expense of ☐Buyer ☐Seller.
    B. COMMITMENT: Within 20 days after the Title Company receives a copy of this contract, Seller shall furnish to Buyer a commitment for title insurance (Commitment) and, at Buyer's expense, legible copies of restrictive covenants and documents evidencing exceptions in the Commitment (Exception Documents) other than the standard printed exceptions. Seller authorizes the Title Company to deliver the Commitment and Exception Documents to Buyer at Buyer's address shown in Paragraph 21. If the Commitment and Exception Documents are not delivered to Buyer within the specified time, the time for delivery will be automatically extended up to 15 days or 3 days before the Closing Date, whichever is earlier. If, due to factors beyond Seller's control, the Commitment and Exception Documents are not delivered within the time required, Buyer may terminate this contract and the earnest money will be refunded to Buyer.
    C. SURVEY: The survey must be made by a registered professional land surveyor acceptable to the Title Company and Buyer's lender(s). (Check one box only)
    ☐ (1) Within _____ days after the effective date of this contract, Seller shall furnish to Buyer and Title Company Seller's existing survey of the Property and a Residential Real Property

Contract Concerning _____ 1849 Wagon Wheel _____ Page 2 of 8 11-2-2015
                                            (Address of Property)

Affidavit promulgated by the Texas Department of Insurance (T-47 Affidavit). **If Seller fails to furnish the existing survey or affidavit within the time prescribed, Buyer shall obtain a new survey at Seller's expense no later than 3 days prior to Closing Date.** If the existing survey or affidavit is not acceptable to Title Company or Buyer's lender(s), Buyer shall obtain a new survey at ☐ Seller's ☐Buyer's expense no later than 3 days prior to Closing Date.

☐ (2) Within _____ days after the effective date of this contract, Buyer shall obtain a new survey at Buyer's expense. Buyer is deemed to receive the survey on the date of actual receipt or the date specified in this paragraph, whichever is earlier.

☑ (3) Within __40__ days after the effective date of this contract, Seller, at Seller's expense shall furnish a new survey to Buyer.

D. OBJECTIONS: Buyer may object in writing to (i) defects, exceptions, or encumbrances to title: disclosed on the survey other than items 6A(1) through (7) above; or disclosed on the Commitment other than items 6A(1) through (8) above; (ii) any portion of the Property lying in a special flood hazard area (Zone V or A) as shown on the current Federal Emergency Management Agency map; or (iii) any exceptions which prohibit the following use or activity: No restriction to build a residence on the subject property. _____.
Buyer must object the earlier of (i) the Closing Date or (ii) __15__ days after Buyer receives the Commitment, Exception Documents, and the survey. Buyer's failure to object within the time allowed will constitute a waiver of Buyer's right to object; except that the requirements in Schedule C of the Commitment are not waived. Provided Seller is not obligated to incur any expense, Seller shall cure the timely objections of Buyer or any third party lender within 15 days after Seller receives the objections and the Closing Date will be extended as necessary. If objections are not cured within such 15 day period, this contract will terminate and the earnest money will be refunded to Buyer unless Buyer waives the objections.

E. TITLE NOTICES:
(1) ABSTRACT OR TITLE POLICY: Broker advises Buyer to have an abstract of title covering the Property examined by an attorney of Buyer's selection, or Buyer should be furnished with or obtain a Title Policy. If a Title Policy is furnished, the Commitment should be promptly reviewed by an attorney of Buyer's choice due to the time limitations on Buyer's right to object.

(2) MEMBERSHIP IN PROPERTY OWNERS ASSOCIATION(S): The Property ☐is ☐is not subject to mandatory membership in a property owners association(s). If the Property is subject to mandatory membership in a property owners association(s), Seller notifies Buyer under §5.012, Texas Property Code, that, as a purchaser of property in the residential community identified in Paragraph 2 in which the Property is located, you are obligated to be a member of the property owners association(s). Restrictive covenants governing the use and occupancy of the Property and all dedicatory instruments governing the establishment, maintenance, and operation of this residential community have been or will be recorded in the Real Property Records of the county in which the Property is located. Copies of the restrictive covenants and dedicatory instruments may be obtained from the county clerk. **You are obligated to pay assessments to the property owners association(s). The amount of the assessments is subject to change. Your failure to pay the assessments could result in enforcement of the association's lien on and the foreclosure of the Property.**
Section 207.003, Property Code, entitles an owner to receive copies of any document that governs the establishment, maintenance, or operation of a subdivision, including, but not limited to, restrictions, bylaws, rules and regulations, and a resale certificate from a property owners' association. A resale certificate contains information including, but not limited to, statements specifying the amount and frequency of regular assessments and the style and cause number of lawsuits to which the property owners' association is a party, other than lawsuits relating to unpaid ad valorem taxes of an individual member of the association. These documents must be made available to you by the property owners' association or the association's agent on your request.
If Buyer is concerned about these matters, the TREC promulgated Addendum for Property Subject to Mandatory Membership in a Property Owners Association should be used.

(3) STATUTORY TAX DISTRICTS: If the Property is situated in a utility or other statutorily created district providing water, sewer, drainage, or flood control facilities and services, Chapter 49, Texas Water Code, requires Seller to deliver and Buyer to sign the statutory notice relating to the tax rate, bonded indebtedness, or standby fee of the district prior to final execution of this contract.

(4) TIDE WATERS: If the Property abuts the tidally influenced waters of the state, §33.135, Texas Natural Resources Code, requires a notice regarding coastal area property to be included in the contract. An addendum containing the notice promulgated by TREC or required by the parties must be used.

(5) ANNEXATION: If the Property is located outside the limits of a municipality, Seller notifies Buyer under §5.011, Texas Property Code, that the Property may now or later be included in

Initialed for identification by Buyer_____ _____ and Seller _____ _____   TREC NO. 9-12

the extraterritorial jurisdiction of a municipality and may now or later be subject to annexation by the municipality. Each municipality maintains a map that depicts its boundaries and extraterritorial jurisdiction. To determine if the Property is located within a municipality's extraterritorial jurisdiction or is likely to be located within a municipality's extraterritorial jurisdiction, contact all municipalities located in the general proximity of the Property for further information.

(6) PROPERTY LOCATED IN A CERTIFICATED SERVICE AREA OF A UTILITY SERVICE PROVIDER: Notice required by §13.257, Water Code: The real property, described in Paragraph 2, that you are about to purchase may be located in a certificated water or sewer service area, which is authorized by law to provide water or sewer service to the properties in the certificated area. If your property is located in a certificated area there may be special costs or charges that you will be required to pay before you can receive water or sewer service. There may be a period required to construct lines or other facilities necessary to provide water or sewer service to your property. You are advised to determine if the property is in a certificated area and contact the utility service provider to determine the cost that you will be required to pay and the period, if any, that is required to provide water or sewer service to your property. The undersigned Buyer hereby acknowledges receipt of the foregoing notice at or before the execution of a binding contract for the purchase of the real property described in Paragraph 2 or at closing of purchase of the real property.

(7) PUBLIC IMPROVEMENT DISTRICTS: If the Property is in a public improvement district, §5.014, Property Code, requires Seller to notify Buyer as follows: As a purchaser of this parcel of real property you are obligated to pay an assessment to a municipality or county for an improvement project undertaken by a public improvement district under Chapter 372, Local Government Code. The assessment may be due annually or in periodic installments. More information concerning the amount of the assessment and the due dates of that assessment may be obtained from the municipality or county levying the assessment. The amount of the assessments is subject to change. Your failure to pay the assessments could result in a lien on and the foreclosure of your property.

(8) TEXAS AGRICULTURAL DEVELOPMENT DISTRICT: The Property ❑ is ❑ is not located in a Texas Agricultural Development District. For additional information, contact the Texas Department of Agriculture.

(9) TRANSFER FEES: If the Property is subject to a private transfer fee obligation, §5.205, Property Code requires Seller to notify Buyer as follows: The private transfer fee obligation may be governed by Chapter 5, Subchapter G of the Texas Property Code.

(10) PROPANE GAS SYSTEM SERVICE AREA: If the Property is located in a propane gas system service area owned by a distribution system retailer, Seller must give Buyer written notice as required by §141.010, Texas Utilities Code. An addendum containing the notice approved by TREC or required by the parties should be used.

(11) NOTICE OF WATER LEVEL FLUCTUATIONS: If the Property adjoins an impoundment of water, including a reservoir or lake, constructed and maintained under Chapter 11, Water Code, that has a storage capacity of at least 5,000 acre-feet at the impoundment's normal operating level, Seller hereby notifies Buyer: "The water level of the impoundment of water adjoining the Property fluctuates for various reasons, including as a result of: (1) an entity lawfully exercising its right to use the water stored in the impoundment; or (2) drought or flood conditions."

7. PROPERTY CONDITION:
A. ACCESS, INSPECTIONS AND UTILITIES: Seller shall permit Buyer and Buyer's agents access to the Property at reasonable times. Buyer may have the Property inspected by inspectors selected by Buyer and licensed by TREC or otherwise permitted by law to make inspections. Seller at Seller's expense shall immediately cause existing utilities to be turned on and shall keep the utilities on during the time this contract is in effect.
NOTICE: Buyer should determine the availability of utilities to the Property suitable to satisfy Buyer's needs.
B. ACCEPTANCE OF PROPERTY CONDITION: "As Is" means the present condition of the Property with any and all defects and without warranty except for the warranties of title and the warranties in this contract. Buyer's agreement to accept the Property As Is under Paragraph 7B (1) or (2) does not preclude Buyer from inspecting the Property under Paragraph 7A, from negotiating repairs or treatments in a subsequent amendment, or from terminating this contract during the Option Period, if any.
(Check one box only)
☑ (1) Buyer accepts the Property As Is.
❑ (2) Buyer accepts the Property As Is provided Seller, at Seller's expense, shall complete the following specific repairs and treatments: _____.

(Do not insert general phrases, such as "subject to inspections" that do not identify specific repairs and treatments.)
C. COMPLETION OF REPAIRS: Unless otherwise agreed in writing: (i) Seller shall complete all agreed repairs and treatments prior to the Closing Date; and (ii) all required permits must be obtained, and repairs and treatments must be performed by persons who are licensed to

Initialed for identification by Buyer_____ _____ and Seller _____ _____   TREC NO. 9–12

Contract Concerning _____ 1849 Wagon Wheel _____ Page 4 of 8 11-2-2015
(Address of Property)

provide such repairs or treatments or, if no license is required by law, are commercially engaged in the trade of providing such repairs or treatments. At Buyer's election, any transferable warranties received by Seller with respect to the repairs and treatments will be transferred to Buyer at Buyer's expense. If Seller fails to complete any agreed repairs and treatments prior to the Closing Date, Buyer may exercise remedies under Paragraph 15 or extend the Closing Date up to 5 days, if necessary, for Seller to complete repairs and treatments.

D. ENVIRONMENTAL MATTERS: Buyer is advised that the presence of wetlands, toxic substances, including asbestos and wastes or other environmental hazards, or the presence of a threatened or endangered species or its habitat may affect Buyer's intended use of the Property. If Buyer is concerned about these matters, an addendum promulgated by TREC or required by the parties should be used.

E. SELLER'S DISCLOSURES: Except as otherwise disclosed in this contract, Seller has no knowledge of the following:
   (1) any flooding of the Property which has had a material adverse effect on the use of the Property;
   (2) any pending or threatened litigation, condemnation, or special assessment affecting the Property;
   (3) any environmental hazards that materially and adversely affect the Property;
   (4) any dumpsite, landfill, or underground tanks or containers now or previously located on the Property;
   (5) any wetlands, as defined by federal or state law or regulation, affecting the Property; or
   (6) any threatened or endangered species or their habitat affecting the Property.

8. **BROKERS' FEES:** All obligations of the parties for payment of brokers' fees are contained in separate written agreements.

9. **CLOSING:**
   A. The closing of the sale will be on or before _____ 60 days of effective date , 20_____, or within 7 days after objections made under Paragraph 6D have been cured or waived, whichever date is later (Closing Date). If either party fails to close the sale by the Closing Date, the non-defaulting party may exercise the remedies contained in Paragraph 15.
   B. At closing:
      (1) Seller shall execute and deliver a general warranty deed conveying title to the Property to Buyer and showing no additional exceptions to those permitted in Paragraph 6 and furnish tax statements or certificates showing no delinquent taxes on the Property.
      (2) Buyer shall pay the Sales Price in good funds acceptable to the escrow agent.
      (3) Seller and Buyer shall execute and deliver any notices, statements, certificates, affidavits, releases, loan documents and other documents reasonably required for the closing of the sale and the issuance of the Title Policy.
      (4) There will be no liens, assessments, or security interests against the Property which will not be satisfied out of the sales proceeds unless securing the payment of any loans assumed by Buyer and assumed loans will not be in default.

10. **POSSESSION:**
    A. Buyer's Possession: Seller shall deliver to Buyer possession of the Property in its present or required condition upon closing and funding.
    B. Leases:
       (1) After the Effective Date, Seller may not execute any lease (including but not limited to mineral leases) or convey any interest in the Property without Buyer's written consent.
       (2) If the Property is subject to any lease to which Seller is a party, Seller shall deliver to Buyer copies of the lease(s) and any move-in condition form signed by the tenant within 7 days after the Effective Date of the contract.

11. **SPECIAL PROVISIONS:** (Insert only factual statements and business details applicable to the sale. TREC rules prohibit license holders from adding factual statements or business details for which a contract addendum or other form has been promulgated by TREC for mandatory use.)

   None

12. **SETTLEMENT AND OTHER EXPENSES:**
    A. The following expenses must be paid at or prior to closing:
       (1) Expenses payable by Seller (Seller's Expenses):
          (a) Releases of existing liens, including prepayment penalties and recording fees; release of Seller's loan liability; tax statements or certificates; preparation of deed; one-half of escrow fee; and other expenses payable by Seller under this contract.
          (b) Seller shall also pay an amount not to exceed $ _____ None to be applied in the following order: Buyer's Expenses which Buyer is prohibited from paying by FHA, VA, Texas Veterans Land Board or other governmental loan programs, and then to other Buyer's Expenses as allowed by the lender.

Initialed for identification by Buyer_____ _____ and Seller _____ _____   TREC NO. 9–12

Contract Concerning _____ 1849 Wagon Wheel _____ Page 5 of 8 11-2-2015
(Address of Property)

(2) Expenses payable by Buyer (Buyer's Expenses): Appraisal fees; loan application fees; origination charges; credit reports; preparation of loan documents; interest on the notes from date of disbursement to one month prior to dates of first monthly payments; recording fees; copies of easements and restrictions; loan title policy with endorsements required by lender; loan-related inspection fees; photos; amortization schedules; one-half of escrow fee; all prepaid items, including required premiums for flood and hazard insurance, reserve deposits for insurance, ad valorem taxes and special governmental assessments; final compliance inspection; courier fee; repair inspection; underwriting fee; wire transfer fee; expenses incident to any loan; Private Mortgage Insurance Premium (PMI), VA Loan Funding Fee, or FHA Mortgage Insurance Premium (MIP) as required by the lender; and other expenses payable by Buyer under this contract.

B. If any expense exceeds an amount expressly stated in this contract for such expense to be paid by a party, that party may terminate this contract unless the other party agrees to pay such excess. Buyer may not pay charges and fees expressly prohibited by FHA, VA, Texas Veterans Land Board or other governmental loan program regulations.

13. **PRORATIONS AND ROLLBACK TAXES:**
A. PRORATIONS: Taxes for the current year, interest, maintenance fees, assessments, dues and rents will be prorated through the Closing Date. The tax proration may be calculated taking into consideration any change in exemptions that will affect the current year's taxes. If taxes for the current year vary from the amount prorated at closing, the parties shall adjust the prorations when tax statements for the current year are available. If taxes are not paid at or prior to closing, Buyer shall pay taxes for the current year.

B. ROLLBACK TAXES: If this sale or Buyer's use of the Property after closing results in the assessment of additional taxes, penalties or interest (Assessments) for periods prior to closing, the Assessments will be the obligation of Buyer. If Assessments are imposed because of Seller's use or change in use of the Property prior to closing, the Assessments will be the obligation of Seller. Obligations imposed by this paragraph will survive closing.

14. **CASUALTY LOSS:** If any part of the Property is damaged or destroyed by fire or other casualty after the effective date of this contract, Seller shall restore the Property to its previous condition as soon as reasonably possible, but in any event by the Closing Date. If Seller fails to do so due to factors beyond Seller's control, Buyer may (a) terminate this contract and the earnest money will be refunded to Buyer (b) extend the time for performance up to 15 days and the Closing Date will be extended as necessary or (c) accept the Property in its damaged condition with an assignment of insurance proceeds, if permitted by Seller's insurance carrier, and receive credit from Seller at closing in the amount of the deductible under the insurance policy. Seller's obligations under this paragraph are independent of any other obligations of Seller under this contract.

15. **DEFAULT:** If Buyer fails to comply with this contract, Buyer will be in default, and Seller may (a) enforce specific performance, seek such other relief as may be provided by law, or both, or (b) terminate this contract and receive the earnest money as liquidated damages, thereby releasing both parties from this contract. If Seller fails to comply with this contract, Seller will be in default and Buyer may (a) enforce specific performance, seek such other relief as may be provided by law, or both, or (b) terminate this contract and receive the earnest money, thereby releasing both parties from this contract.

16. **MEDIATION:** It is the policy of the State of Texas to encourage resolution of disputes through alternative dispute resolution procedures such as mediation. Any dispute between Seller and Buyer related to this contract which is not resolved through informal discussion will be submitted to a mutually acceptable mediation service or provider. The parties to the mediation shall bear the mediation costs equally. This paragraph does not preclude a party from seeking equitable relief from a court of competent jurisdiction.

17. **ATTORNEY'S FEES:** A Buyer, Seller, Listing Broker, Other Broker, or escrow agent who prevails in any legal proceeding related to this contract is entitled to recover reasonable attorney's fees and all costs of such proceeding.

18. **ESCROW:**
A. ESCROW: The escrow agent is not (i) a party to this contract and does not have liability for the performance or nonperformance of any party to this contract, (ii) liable for interest on the earnest money and (iii) liable for the loss of any earnest money caused by the failure of any financial institution in which the earnest money has been deposited unless the financial institution is acting as escrow agent.

B. EXPENSES: At closing, the earnest money must be applied first to any cash down payment, then to Buyer's Expenses and any excess refunded to Buyer. If no closing occurs, escrow agent may: (i) require a written release of liability of the escrow agent from all parties, (ii) require payment of unpaid expenses incurred on behalf of a party, and (iii) only deduct from the earnest money the amount of unpaid expenses incurred on behalf of the party receiving the earnest money.

C. DEMAND: Upon termination of this contract, either party or the escrow agent may send a release of earnest money to each party and the parties shall execute counterparts of the release and deliver same to the escrow agent. If either party fails to execute the release, either party may make a written demand to the escrow agent for the earnest money. If only one party makes written demand for the earnest money, escrow agent shall promptly provide

Initialed for identification by Buyer_____ _____ and Seller _____ _____   TREC NO. 9-12

Contract Concerning _____ 1849 Wagon Wheel _____ Page 6 of 8 11-2-2015
(Address of Property)

a copy of the demand to the other party. If escrow agent does not receive written objection to the demand from the other party within 15 days, escrow agent may disburse the earnest money to the party making demand reduced by the amount of unpaid expenses incurred on behalf of the party receiving the earnest money and escrow agent may pay the same to the creditors. If escrow agent complies with the provisions of this paragraph, each party hereby releases escrow agent from all adverse claims related to the disbursal of the earnest money.

   D. DAMAGES: Any party who wrongfully fails or refuses to sign a release acceptable to the escrow agent within 7 days of receipt of the request will be liable to the other party for (i) damages; (ii) the earnest money; (iii) reasonable attorney's fees; and (iv) all costs of suit.

   E. NOTICES: Escrow agent's notices will be effective when sent in compliance with Paragraph 21. Notice of objection to the demand will be deemed effective upon receipt by escrow agent.

19. REPRESENTATIONS: All covenants, representations and warranties in this contract survive closing. If any representation of Seller in this contract is untrue on the Closing Date, Seller will b e in default. Unless expressly prohibited by written agreement, Seller may continue to show the Property and receive, negotiate and accept back up offers.

20. FEDERAL TAX REQUIREMENTS: If Seller is a "foreign person," as defined by applicable law, or if Seller fails to deliver an affidavit to Buyer that Seller is not a "foreign person," then Buyer shall withhold from the sales proceeds an amount sufficient to comply with applicable tax law and deliver the same to the Internal Revenue Service together with appropriate tax forms. Internal Revenue Service regulations require filing written reports if currency in excess of specified amounts is received in the transaction.

21. NOTICES: All notices from one party to the other must be in writing and are effective when mailed to, hand-delivered at, or transmitted by fax or electronic transmission as follows:

To Buyer at:	32894 Jodaro Street	**To Seller at:**	PO Bos 2250
	Frio Town, Texas 78301		Roger Mills, Texas 70980
Phone:	(555) 928-3131	Phone:	(555) 917-7022
Fax:	( ) same	Fax:	( ) same
E-mail:	dlh@farming.net	E-mail:	wildbob@nail,net

22. AGREEMENT OF PARTIES: This contract contains the entire agreement of the parties and cannot be changed except by their written agreement. Addenda which are a part of this contract are (check all applicable boxes):

☐ Third Party Financing Addendum

☑ Seller Financing Addendum

☐ Addendum for Property Subject to Mandatory Membership in a Property Owners Association

☐ Buyer's Temporary Residential Lease

☐ Seller's Temporary Residential Lease

☐ Addendum for Reservation of Oil, Gas and Other Minerals

☐ Addendum for "Back-Up" Contract

☑ Addendum for Coastal Area Property

☐ Environmental Assessment, Threatened or Endangered Species and Wetlands Addendum

☑ Addendum for Property Located Seaward of the Gulf Intracoastal Waterway

☐ Addendum for Sale of Other Property by Buyer

☐ Addendum for Property in a Propane Gas System Service Area

☐ Other (list): _____

Initialed for identification by Buyer_____ _____ and Seller _____ _____   TREC NO. 9–12

Contract Concerning _____ 1849 Wagon Wheel _____ Page 7 of 8 11-2-2015
(Address of Property)

23. **TERMINATION OPTION:** For nominal consideration, the receipt of which is hereby acknowledged by Seller, and Buyer's agreement to pay Seller $_____ 250 (Option Fee) within 3 days after the effective date of this contract, Seller grants Buyer the unrestricted right to terminate this contract by giving notice of termination to Seller within ___10___ days after the effective date of this contract (Option Period). Notices under this paragraph must be given by 5:00 p.m. (local time where the Property is located) by the date specified. If no dollar amount is stated as the Option Fee or if Buyer fails to pay the Option Fee to Seller within the time prescribed, this paragraph will not be a part of this contract and Buyer shall not have the unrestricted right to terminate this contract. If Buyer gives notice of termination within the time prescribed, the Option Fee will not be refunded; however, any earnest money will be refunded to Buyer. The Option Fee ☐will ☐will not be credited to the Sales Price at closing. **Time is of the essence for this paragraph and strict compliance with the time for performance is required.**

24. **CONSULT AN ATTORNEY BEFORE SIGNING:** TREC rules prohibit real estate license holders from giving legal advice. READ THIS CONTRACT CAREFULLY.

Buyer's
Attorney is: Roberta Young

Seller's
Attorney is: Clint Saylers

Phone: (555) 270-2250

Phone: (555) 257-7008

Fax: (555) 222-0223

Fax: (555) 257-3006

E-mail: ryoung@millstonelaw.org

E-mail: clint@saylerlaw.com

EXECUTED the _____day of _____, 20_____ (EFFECTIVE DATE).
(BROKER: FILL IN THE DATE OF FINAL ACCEPTANCE.)

Buyer

Seller

Buyer

Seller

Contract Concerning _____ 1849 Wagon Wheel _____ Page 8 of 8 11-2-2015
(Address of Property)

BROKER INFORMATION
(Print name(s) only. Do not sign)

NONE		MCW Realty	XXXXXXX
Other Broker Firm	License No.	Listing Broker Firm	License No.

represents   ❑ Buyer only as Buyer's agent   represents   ❑ Seller and Buyer as an intermediary
           ❑ Seller as Listing Broker's subagent   ☑ Seller only as Seller's agent

		Carolyn Weathersby	555-822-1957
Associate's Name	License No.	Listing Associate's Name	License No.
		N/A	
Licensed Supervisor of Associate	License No.	Licensed Supervisor of Listing Associate	License No.
		1413 Vista View	
Other Broker's Address	Fax	Listing Broker's Office Address	Fax
		Roger Mills, Texas 70980	
City	State	Zip	City State Zip
		Carolyn@mcwrealty.org	
Associate's Email Address	Phone	Listing Associate's Email Address	Phone
		Selling Associate's Name	License No.
		Licensed Supervisor of Selling Associate	License No.
		Selling Associate's Office Address	Fax
		City State Zip	
		Selling Associate's Email Address	Phone

Listing Broker has agreed to pay Other Broker_____N/A_____ of the total sales price when the Listing Broker's fee is received. Escrow agent is authorized and directed to pay other Broker from Listing Broker's fee at closing.

OPTION FEE RECEIPT

Receipt of $_____250 (Option Fee) in the form of _Money Order_____ is acknowledged.

_____ _____
Seller or Listing Broker   Date

CONTRACT AND EARNEST MONEY RECEIPT

Receipt of   ❑Contract and ❑$_____ Earnest Money in the form of _____
is acknowledged.
Escrow Agent: _____   Date: _____

By: _____
                                             Email Address
_____   Phone: (_____) _____
Address
_____   Fax: (_____) _____
City   State   Zip

PROMULGATED BY THE TEXAS REAL ESTATE COMMISSION (TREC)

12-05-11

ADDENDUM FOR COASTAL
AREA PROPERTY
(SECTION 33.135, TEXAS NATURAL RESOURCES CODE)

TO CONTRACT CONCERNING THE PROPERTY AT

1849 Wagon Wheel Drive, Gulf Coast, TX 77077
_____
(Address of Property)

NOTICE REGARDING COASTAL AREA PROPERTY

1. The real property described in and subject to this contract adjoins and shares a common boundary with the tidally influenced submerged lands of the state. The boundary is subject to change and can be determined accurately only by a survey on the ground made by a licensed state land surveyor in accordance with the original grant from the sovereign. The owner of the property described in this contract may gain or lose portions of the tract because of changes in the boundary.

2. The seller, transferor, or grantor has no knowledge of any prior fill as it relates to the property described in and subject to this contract except:_____none_____
_____
_____.

3. State law prohibits the use, encumbrance, construction, or placing of any structure in, on, or over state-owned submerged lands below the applicable tide line, without proper permission.

4. The purchaser or grantee is hereby advised to seek the advice of an attorney or other qualified person as to the legal nature and effect of the facts set forth in this notice on the property described in and subject to this contract. Information regarding the location of the applicable tide line as to the property described in and subject to this contract may be obtained from the surveying division of the General Land Office in Austin.

_____   _____
Buyer   Seller

_____   _____
Buyer   Seller

PROMULGATED BY THE TEXAS REAL ESTATE COMMISSION (TREC)   11-2-2015

EQUAL HOUSING
OPPORTUNITY

SELLER FINANCING ADDENDUM
TO CONTRACT CONCERNING THE PROPERTY AT

1849 Wagon Wheel Gulf Coast, Texas
(Address of Property)

A. CREDIT DOCUMENTATION. To establish Buyer's creditworthiness, Buyer shall deliver to Seller within ___10___ days after the effective date of this contract, ☑ credit report ❑ verification of employment, including salary ☑ verification of funds on deposit in financial institutions ❑ current financial statement and ❑ _____ _____. Buyer hereby authorizes any credit reporting agency to furnish copies of Buyer's credit reports to Seller at Buyer's sole expense.

B. BUYER'S CREDIT APPROVAL. If the credit documentation described in Paragraph A is not delivered within the specified time, Seller may terminate this contract by notice to Buyer within 7 days after expiration of the time for delivery, and the earnest money will be paid to Seller. If the credit documentation is timely delivered, and Seller determines in Seller's sole discretion that Buyer's credit is unacceptable, Seller may terminate this contract by notice to Buyer within 7 days after expiration of the time for delivery and the earnest money will be refunded to Buyer. If Seller does not terminate this contract, Seller will be deemed to have approved Buyer's creditworthiness.

C. PROMISSORY NOTE. The promissory note in the amount of $_____70,000_ (Note), included in Paragraph 3B of the contract payable by Buyer to the order of Seller will bear interest at the rate of __5__% per annum and be payable at the place designated by Seller. Buyer may prepay the Note in whole or in part at any time without penalty. Any prepayments are to be applied to the payment of the installments of principal last maturing and interest will immediately cease on the prepaid principal. The Note will contain a provision for payment of a late fee of 5% of any installment not paid within 10 days of the due date. Matured unpaid amounts will bear interest at the rate of 1½% per month or at the highest lawful rate, whichever is less. The Note will be payable as follows:

❑ (1) In one payment due _____ after the date of the Note with interest payable ❑ at maturity ❑ monthly ❑ quarterly. (check one box only)

☑ (2) In monthly installments of $ _____1,321_ ☑ including interest ❑plus interest (check one box only) beginning _____30 days_____ after the date of the Note and continuing monthly thereafter for_____59_____ months when the balance of the Note will be due and payable.

❑ (3) Interest only in monthly installments for the first _____ month(s) and thereafter in installments of $_____ ❑ including interest ❑ plus interest (check one box only) beginning _____ after the date of the Note and continuing monthly thereafter for_____ months when the balance of the Note will be due and payable.

D. DEED OF TRUST. The deed of trust securing the Note will provide for the following:

(1) PROPERTY TRANSFERS: (check one box only)

❑ (a) Consent Not Required: The Property may be sold, conveyed or leased without the consent of Seller, provided any subsequent buyer assumes the Note.

☑ (b) Consent Required: If all or any part of the Property is sold, conveyed, leased for a period longer than 3 years, leased with an option to purchase, or otherwise sold (including any contract for deed), without Seller's prior written consent, which consent may be withheld in Seller's sole discretion, Seller may declare the balance of the Note

Initialed for identification by Buyer_____ and Seller_____   TREC NO. 26-7

Seller Financing Addendum Concerning   Page 2 of 2   11-2-2015

_____1849 Wagon Wheel_____
(Address of Property)

to be immediately due and payable. The creation of a subordinate lien, any conveyance under threat or order of condemnation, any deed solely between buyers, or the passage of title by reason of the death of a buyer or by operation of law will not entitle Seller to exercise the remedies provided in this paragraph.

NOTE: *Under (a) or (b), Buyer's liability to pay the Note will continue unless Buyer obtains a release of liability from Seller.*

(2) TAX AND INSURANCE ESCROW: (check one box only)

☑ (a) Escrow Not Required: Buyer shall furnish Seller, before each year's ad valorem taxes become delinquent, evidence that all ad valorem taxes on the Property have been paid. Buyer shall annually furnish Seller evidence of paid-up casualty insurance naming Seller as a mortgagee loss payee.

☐ (b) Escrow Required: With each installment Buyer shall deposit in escrow with Seller a pro rata part of the estimated annual ad valorem taxes and casualty insurance premiums for the Property. Buyer shall pay any deficiency within 30 days after notice from Seller. Buyer's failure to pay the deficiency will be a default under the deed of trust. Buyer is not required to deposit any escrow payments for taxes and insurance that are deposited with a superior lienholder. The casualty insurance must name Seller as a mortgagee loss payee.

(3) PRIOR LIENS: Any default under any lien superior to the lien securing the Note will be a default under the deed of trust securing the Note.

_____   _____
Buyer   Seller

_____   _____
Buyer   Seller

PROMULGATED BY THE TEXAS REAL ESTATE COMMISSION (TREC)

11-2-2015

NOTICE: Not For Use Where Seller Owns Fee Simple Title To Land Beneath Unit

RESIDENTIAL CONDOMINIUM CONTRACT (RESALE)

1. **PARTIES:** The parties to this contract are P.K. Parker, as single person (Seller) and John A Price and wife Cynthia C. (Buyer). Seller agrees to sell and convey to Buyer and Buyer agrees to buy from Seller the Property defined below.

2. **PROPERTY AND CONDOMINIUM DOCUMENTS:**

   A. The Condominium Unit, improvements and accessories described below are collectively referred to as the "Property".

      (1) CONDOMINIUM UNIT: Unit 1 , in Building 7 , of Fancy Place Condominiums , a condominium project, located at 831 Upper Crust Blvd.

      (address/zip code), City of Silk Stocking ,County of 78711

      Texas, described in the Condominium Declaration and Plat and any amendments thereto of record in said County; together with such Unit's undivided interest in the Common Elements designated by the Declaration, including those areas reserved as Limited Common Elements appurtenant to the Unit and such other rights to use the Common Elements which have been specifically assigned to the Unit in any other manner. Parking areas assigned to the Unit are: NoneNone .

      (2) IMPROVEMENTS: All fixtures and improvements attached to the above described real property including without limitation, the following **permanently installed and built-in items**, if any: all equipment and appliances, valances, screens, shutters, awnings, wall-to-wall carpeting, mirrors, ceiling fans, attic fans, mail boxes, television antennas, mounts and brackets for televisions and speakers, heating and air conditioning units, security and fire detection equipment, wiring, plumbing and lighting fixtures, chandeliers, shrubbery, landscaping, outdoor cooking equipment, and all other property owned by Seller and attached to the above described Condominium Unit.

      (3) ACCESSORIES: The following described related accessories, if any: window air conditioning units, stove, fireplace screens, curtains and rods, blinds, window shades, draperies and rods, door keys, mailbox keys, above ground pool, swimming pool equipment and maintenance accessories, artificial fireplace logs, and controls for: (i) garage doors, (ii) entry gates, and (iii) other improvements and accessories.

      (4) EXCLUSIONS: The following improvements and accessories will be retained by Seller and must be removed prior to delivery of possession: None .

   B. The Declaration, Bylaws and any Rules of the Association are called "Documents". (Check one box only):

      ☐ (1) Buyer has received a copy of the Documents. Buyer is advised to read the Documents before signing the contract.

      ☑ (2) Buyer has not received a copy of the Documents. Seller shall deliver the Documents to Buyer within 15 days after the effective date of the contract. Buyer may cancel the contract before the sixth day after Buyer receives the Documents by hand-delivering or mailing written notice of cancellation to Seller by certified United States mail, return receipt requested. If Buyer cancels the contract pursuant to this paragraph, the contract will terminate and the earnest money will be refunded to Buyer.

   C. The Resale Certificate from the condominium owners association (the Association) is called the "Certificate". The Certificate must be in a form promulgated by TREC or required by the parties. The Certificate must have been prepared no more than 3 months before the date it is delivered to Buyer and must contain at a minimum the information required by Section 82.157, Texas Property Code.
   (Check one box only):

      ☐ (1) Buyer has received the Certificate.

      ☑ (2) Buyer has not received the Certificate. Seller shall deliver the Certificate to Buyer within 10 days after the effective date of the contract. Buyer may cancel the contract before the sixth day after the date Buyer receives the Certificate by hand-delivering or mailing written notice of cancellation to Seller by certified United States mail, return receipt requested. If Buyer cancels the contract pursuant to this paragraph, the contract will terminate and the earnest money will be refunded to Buyer.

      ☐ (3) Buyer has received Seller's affidavit that Seller requested information from the Association concerning its financial condition as required by the Texas Property Code, and that the Association did not provide a Certificate or information required in the Certificate. Buyer and Seller agree to waive the requirement to furnish the Certificate.

   D. If the Documents reveal that the Property is subject to a right of refusal under which the Association or a member of the Association may purchase the Property, the effective date shall be amended to the date that Buyer receives a copy of the Association's certification that: (i) Seller has complied with the requirements under the right of refusal; and (ii) all persons who may exercise the right of refusal have not exercised or have waived the right to buy the Property. If Buyer does not receive the Association's certification within _____ days after the effective date or if the right of refusal is exercised, this contract shall terminate and the earnest money shall be refunded to Buyer.

Initialed for identification by Buyer_____ _____ and Seller _____ _____

TREC NO. 30-12

Contract Concerning _____ 831 Upper Crust Blvd. _____ Page 2 of 8   11-2-2015
(Address of Property)

3. SALES PRICE:
  A. Cash portion of Sales Price payable by Buyer at closing.................. $_____ 151,000
  B. Sum of all financing described in the attached: ❏   Third Party Financing Addendum,
      ❏   Loan Assumption Addendum, ❏   Seller Financing Addendum ... $_____ 0
  C. Sales Price (Sum of A and B).. $_____ 151,000

4. LICENSE HOLDER DISCLOSURE: Texas law requires a real estate license holder who is a party to a transaction or acting on behalf of a spouse, parent, child, business entity in which the license holder owns more than 10%, or a trust for which the license holder acts as trustee or of which the license holder or the license holder's spouse, parent or child is a beneficiary, to notify the other party in writing before entering into a contract of sale. Disclose if applicable: N/A
_____.

5. EARNEST MONEY: Upon execution of this contract by all parties, Buyer shall deposit $ _____ as earnest money with Calvert Title Company _____, as escrow agent, at 82214 Princess Pass   Silk Stocking, Texas 78711 _____(address). Buyer shall deposit additional earnest money of $_____ N/A with escrow agent within ___0___ days after the effective date of this contract. If Buyer fails to deposit the earnest money as required by this contract, Buyer will be in default.

6. TITLE POLICY:
  A. TITLE POLICY: Seller shall furnish to Buyer at ☑Seller's ❏Buyer's expense an owner policy of title insurance (Title Policy) issued by Calvert Title Company _____(Title   Company) in the amount of the Sales Price, dated at or after closing, insuring Buyer against loss under the provisions of the Title Policy, subject to the promulgated exclusions (including existing building and zoning ordinances) and the following exceptions:
    (1) Restrictive covenants common to the platted subdivision in which the Property is located.
    (2) The standard printed exception for standby fees, taxes and assessments.
    (3) Liens created as part of the financing described in Paragraph 3.
    (4) Terms and provisions of the Documents including the assessments and platted easements.
    (5) Reservations or exceptions otherwise permitted by this contract or as may be approved by Buyer in writing.
    (6) The standard printed exception as to marital rights.
    (7) The standard printed exception as to waters, tidelands, beaches, streams, and related matters.
    (8) The standard printed exception as to discrepancies, conflicts, shortages in area or boundary lines, encroachments or protrusions, or overlapping improvements.
  B. COMMITMENT: Within 20 days after the Title Company receives a copy of this contract, Seller shall furnish to Buyer a commitment for title insurance (Commitment) and, at Buyer's expense, legible copies of restrictive covenants and documents evidencing exceptions in the Commitment (Exception Documents) other than the standard printed exceptions. Seller authorizes the Title Company to deliver the Commitment and Exception Documents to Buyer at Buyer's address shown in Paragraph 21. If the Commitment and Exception Documents are not delivered to Buyer within the specified time, the time for delivery will be automatically extended up to 15 days or 3 days before the Closing Date, whichever is earlier. If, due to factors beyond Seller's control, the Commitment and Exception Documents are not delivered within the time required, Buyer may terminate this contract and the earnest money will be refunded to Buyer.
  C. OBJECTIONS: Buyer may object in writing to defects, exceptions, or encumbrances to title: disclosed in the Commitment other than items 6A(1) through (8) above; or which prohibit the following use or activity: None _____.

  Buyer must object the earlier of (i) the Closing Date or (ii)   15   days after Buyer receives the Commitment and Exception Documents. Buyer's failure to object within   the   time allowed will constitute a waiver of Buyer's right to object; except that the requirements in Schedule C of the Commitment are not waived by Buyer. Provided Seller is not obligated to incur any expense, Seller shall cure the timely objections of Buyer or any third party lender within 15 days after Seller receives the objections and the Closing Date will be extended as necessary. If objections are not cured within such 15 day period, this contract will terminate and the earnest money will be refunded to Buyer unless Buyer waives the objections.
  D. TITLE NOTICES:
    (1) ABSTRACT OR TITLE POLICY: Broker advises Buyer to have an abstract of title covering the Property examined by an attorney of Buyer's selection, or Buyer should be furnished with or obtain a Title Policy. If a Title Policy is furnished, the Commitment should be promptly reviewed by an attorney of Buyer's choice due to the time limitations on Buyer's right to object.
    (2) STATUTORY TAX DISTRICTS: If the Property is situated in a utility or other statutorily created district providing water, sewer, drainage, or flood control facilities and services, Chapter 49, Texas Water Code, requires Seller to deliver and Buyer to sign the statutory notice relating to the tax rate, bonded indebtedness, or standby fee of the district prior to final execution of this contract.

Initialed for identification by Buyer_____ _____ and Seller _____ _____   TREC NO. 30-12

Contract Concerning_____ 831 Silk Stocking Blvd. _____Page 3 of 8 11-2-2015
(Address of Property)

(3) **TIDE WATERS:** If the Property abuts the tidally influenced waters of the state, §33.135, Texas Natural Resources Code, requires a notice regarding coastal area property to be included in the contract. An addendum containing the notice promulgated by TREC or required by the parties must be used.

(4) **ANNEXATION:** If the Property is located outside the limits of a municipality, Seller notifies Buyer under §5.011, Texas Property Code, that the Property may now or later be included in the extraterritorial jurisdiction of a municipality and may now or later be subject to annexation by the municipality. Each municipality maintains a map that depicts its boundaries and extraterritorial jurisdiction. To determine if the Property is located within a municipality's extraterritorial jurisdiction or is likely to be located within a municipality's extraterritorial jurisdiction, contact all municipalities located in the general proximity of the Property for further information.

(5) **PROPERTY LOCATED IN A CERTIFICATED SERVICE AREA OF A UTILITY SERVICE PROVIDER:** Notice required by §13.257, Water Code: The real property, described in Paragraph 2, that you are about to purchase may be located in a certificated water or sewer service area, which is authorized by law to provide water or sewer service to the properties in the certificated area. If your property is located in a certificated area there may be special costs or charges that you will be required to pay before you can receive water or sewer service. There may be a period required to construct lines or other facilities necessary to provide water or sewer service to your property. You are advised to determine if the property is in a certificated area and contact the utility service provider to determine the cost that you will be required to pay and the period, if any, that is required to provide water or sewer service to your property. The undersigned Buyer hereby acknowledges receipt of the foregoing notice at or before the execution of a binding contract for the purchase of the real property described in Paragraph 2 or at closing of purchase of the real property.

(6) **TRANSFER FEES:** If the Property is subject to a private transfer fee obligation, §5.205, Property Code, requires Seller to notify Buyer as follows: The private transfer fee obligation may be governed by Chapter 5, Subchapter G of the Texas Property Code.

(7) **PROPANE GAS SYSTEM SERVICE AREA:** If the Property is located in a propane gas system service area owned by a distribution system retailer, Seller must give Buyer written notice as required by §141.010, Texas Utilities Code. An addendum containing the notice approved by TREC or required by the parties should be used.

(8) **NOTICE OF WATER LEVEL FLUCTUATIONS:** If the Property adjoins an impoundment of water, including a reservoir or lake, constructed and maintained under Chapter 11, Water Code, that has a storage capacity of at least 5,000 acre-feet at the impoundment's normal operating level, Seller hereby notifies Buyer: "The water level of the impoundment of water adjoining the Property fluctuates for various reasons, including as a result of: (1) an entity lawfully exercising its right to use the water stored in the impoundment; or (2) drought or flood conditions."

7. PROPERTY CONDITION:
A. **ACCESS, INSPECTIONS AND UTILITIES:** Seller shall permit Buyer and Buyer's agents access to the Property at reasonable times. Buyer may have the Property inspected by inspectors selected by Buyer and licensed by TREC or otherwise permitted by law to make inspections. Any hydrostatic testing must be separately authorized by Seller in writing. Seller at Seller's expense shall immediately cause existing utilities to be turned on and shall keep the utilities on during the time this contract is in effect .
B. **SELLER'S DISCLOSURE NOTICE PURSUANT TO §5.008, TEXAS PROPERTY CODE (Notice):** (Check one box only)
☑ (1) Buyer has received the Notice.
☐ (2) Buyer has not received the Notice. Within _____ days after the effective date of this contract, Seller shall deliver the Notice to Buyer. If Buyer does not receive the Notice, Buyer may terminate this contract at any time prior to the closing and the earnest money will be refunded to Buyer. If Seller delivers the Notice, Buyer may terminate this contract for any reason within 7 days after Buyer receives the Notice or prior to the closing, whichever first occurs, and the earnest money will be refunded to Buyer.
☐ (3) The Texas Property Code does not require this Seller to furnish the Notice.
C. **SELLER'S DISCLOSURE OF LEAD-BASED PAINT AND LEAD-BASED PAINT HAZARDS** is required by Federal law for a residential dwelling constructed prior to 1978.
D. **ACCEPTANCE OF PROPERTY CONDITION:** "As Is" means the present condition of the Property with any and all defects and without warranty except for the warranties of title and the warranties in this contract. Buyer's agreement to accept the Property As Is under Paragraph 7D(1) or (2) does not preclude Buyer from inspecting the Property under Paragraph 7A, from negotiating repairs or treatments in a subsequent amendment, or from terminating this contract during the Option Period, if any.
(Check one box only)
☑ (1) Buyer accepts the Property As Is.
☐ (2) Buyer accepts the Property As Is provided Seller, at Seller's expense, shall complete the following specific repairs and treatments:_____.
(Do not insert general phrases, such as "subject to inspections," that do not identify specific repairs and treatments.)
E. **LENDER REQUIRED REPAIRS AND TREATMENTS:** Unless otherwise agreed in writing, neither party is obligated to pay for lender required repairs, which includes treatment for wood

Initialed for identification by Buyer_____ _____ and Seller _____ _____   TREC NO. 30-12

Contract Concerning _____ 831 Silk Stocking Blvd. _____ Page 4 of 8   11-2-2015
(Address of Property)

destroying insects. If the parties do not agree to pay for the lender required repairs or treatments, this contract will terminate and the earnest money will be refunded to Buyer. If the cost of lender required repairs and treatments exceeds 5% of the Sales Price, Buyer may terminate this contract and the earnest money will be refunded to Buyer.

F. **COMPLETION OF REPAIRS AND TREATMENTS:** Unless otherwise agreed in writing: (i) Seller shall complete all agreed repairs and treatments prior to the Closing Date; and (ii) all required permits must be obtained, and repairs and treatments must be performed by persons who are licensed to provide such repairs or treatments or, if no license is required by law, are commercially engaged in the trade of providing such repairs or treatments. At Buyer's election, any transferable warranties received by Seller with respect to the repairs and treatments will be transferred to Buyer at Buyer's expense. If Seller fails to complete any agreed repairs and treatments prior to the Closing Date, Buyer may exercise remedies under Paragraph 15 or extend the Closing Date up to 5 days if necessary for Seller to complete repairs and treatments.

G. **ENVIRONMENTAL MATTERS:** Buyer is advised that the presence of wetlands, toxic substances, including asbestos and wastes or other environmental hazards or the presence of a threatened or endangered species or its habitat may affect Buyer's intended use of the Property. If Buyer is concerned about these matters, an addendum promulgated by TREC or required by the parties should be used.

H. **RESIDENTIAL SERVICE CONTRACTS:** Buyer may purchase a residential service contract from a residential service company licensed by TREC. If Buyer purchases a residential service contract, Seller shall reimburse Buyer at closing for the cost of the residential service contract in an amount not exceeding $_____ None . Buyer should review any residential service contract for the scope of coverage, exclusions and limitations. **The purchase of a residential service contract is optional. Similar coverage may be purchased from various companies authorized to do business in Texas.**

8. **BROKERS' FEES:** All obligations of the parties for payment of brokers' fees are contained in separate written agreements.

9. **CLOSING:**

A. The closing of the sale will be on or before _____ November 1 , 20 15 , or within 7 days after objections to matters disclosed in the Commitment have been cured, whichever date is later (Closing Date). If either party fails to close the sale by the Closing Date, the non-defaulting party may exercise the remedies contained in Paragraph 15.

B.   At closing:

(1) Seller shall execute and deliver a general warranty deed conveying title to the Property to Buyer and showing no additional exceptions to those permitted in Paragraph 6 and furnish tax statements or certificates showing no delinquent taxes on the Property.

(2) Buyer shall pay the Sales Price in good funds acceptable to the escrow agent.

(3) Seller and Buyer shall execute and deliver any notices, statements, certificates, affidavits, releases, loan documents and other documents reasonably required for the closing of the sale and the issuance of the Title Policy.

(4) There will be no liens, assessments, or security interests against the Property which will not be satisfied out of the sales proceeds unless securing the payment of any loans assumed by Buyer and assumed loans will not be in default.

(5) If the Property is subject to a residential lease, Seller shall transfer security deposits (as defined under §92.102, Property Code), if any, to Buyer. In such an event, Buyer shall deliver to the tenant a signed statement acknowledging that the Buyer has acquired the Property and is responsible for the return of the security deposit, and specifying the exact dollar amount of the security deposit.

10. **POSSESSION:**

A. Buyers Possession: Seller shall deliver to Buyer possession of the Property in its present or required condition, ordinary wear and tear excepted: ☑ upon closing and funding ☐ according to a temporary residential lease form promulgated by TREC or other written lease required by the parties. Any possession by Buyer prior to closing or by Seller after closing which is not authorized by a written lease will establish a tenancy at sufferance relationship between the parties. **Consult your insurance agent prior to change of ownership and possession because insurance coverage may be limited or terminated. The absence of a written lease or appropriate insurance coverage may expose the parties to economic loss.**

B. Leases:

(1) After the Effective Date, Seller may not execute any lease (including but not limited to mineral leases) or convey any interest in the Property without Buyer's written consent.

(2) If the Property is subject to any lease to which Seller is a party, Seller shall deliver to Buyer copies of the lease(s) and any move-in condition form signed by the tenant within 7 days after the Effective Date of the contract.

11. **SPECIAL PROVISIONS:** (Insert only factual statements and business details applicable to the sale. TREC rules prohibit license holders from adding factual statements or business details for which a contract addendum, lease or other form has been promulgated by TREC for mandatory use.)

See Backup Contract Addendum.

Initialed for identification by Buyer_____ _____ and Seller _____ _____   TREC NO. 30-12

Contract Concerning _____ 831 Silk Stocking Blvd. _____ Page 5 of 8 11-2-2015
(Address of Property)

12.SETTLEMENT AND OTHER EXPENSES:
A. The following expenses must be paid at or prior to closing:
(1) Expenses payable by Seller (Seller's Expenses):
(a) Releases of existing liens, including prepayment penalties and recording fees; lender, FHA, or VA completion requirements; tax statements or certificates; preparation of deed; one-half of escrow fee; and other expenses payable by Seller under this contract.
(b) Seller shall also pay an amount not to exceed $_____None_____ to be applied in the following order: Buyer's Expenses which Buyer is prohibited from paying by FHA, VA, Texas Veterans Land Board or other governmental loan programs, and then to other Buyer's Expenses as allowed by the lender.
(2) Expenses payable by Buyer (Buyer's Expenses): Appraisal fees; loan application fees; origination charges; credit reports; preparation of loan documents; interest on the notes from date of disbursement to one month prior to dates of first monthly payments; recording fees; copies of easements and restrictions; loan title policy with endorsements required by lender; loan-related inspection fees; photos; amortization schedules; one-half of escrow fee; all prepaid items, including required premiums for flood and hazard insurance, reserve deposits for insurance, ad valorem taxes and special governmental assessments; final compliance inspection; courier fee; repair inspection; underwriting fee; wire transfer fee; expenses incident to any loan; Private Mortgage Insurance Premium (PMI), VA Loan Funding Fee, or FHA Mortgage Insurance Premium (MIP) as required by the lender; and other expenses payable by Buyer under this contract.
(3) Except as provided by 12(A)(4) below, Buyer shall pay any and all Association fees or other charges resulting from the transfer of the Property not to exceed $ All fees paid by Buyer and Seller shall pay any excess.
(4) Buyer shall pay any deposits for reserves required at closing by the Association.
B. If any expense exceeds an amount expressly stated in this contract for such expense to be paid by a party, that party may terminate this contract unless the other party agrees to pay such excess. Buyer may not pay charges and fees expressly prohibited by FHA, VA, Texas Veterans Land Board or other governmental loan program regulations.

13. PRORATIONS: Taxes for the current year, interest, maintenance fees, regular condominium assessments, dues and rents will be prorated through the Closing Date. The tax proration may be calculated taking into consideration any change in exemptions that will affect the current year's taxes. If taxes for the current year vary from the amount prorated at closing, the parties shall adjust the prorations when tax statements for the current year are available. If taxes are not paid at or prior to closing, Buyer shall pay taxes for the current year. Cash reserves from regular condominium assessments for deferred maintenance or capital improvements established by the Association will not be credited to Seller. Any special condominium assessment due and unpaid at closing will be the obligation of Seller.

14. CASUALTY LOSS: If any part of the Unit which Seller is solely obligated to maintain and repair under the terms of the Declaration is damaged or destroyed by fire or other casualty, Seller shall restore the same to its previous condition as soon as reasonably possible, but in any event by the Closing Date. If Seller fails to do so due to factors beyond Seller's control, Buyer may (a) terminate this contract and the earnest money will be refunded to Buyer, (b) extend the time for performance up to 15 days and the Closing Date will be extended as necessary or (c) accept the Property in its damaged condition with an assignment of insurance proceeds, if permitted by Seller's insurance carrier, and receive credit from Seller at closing in the amount of the deductible under the insurance policy. If any part of the Common Elements or Limited Common Elements appurtenant to the Unit is damaged or destroyed by fire or other casualty loss, Buyer will have 7 days from receipt of notice of such casualty loss within which to notify Seller in writing that the contract will be terminated unless Buyer receives written confirmation from the Association that the damaged condition will be restored to its previous condition within a reasonable time at no cost to Buyer. Unless Buyer gives such notice within such time, Buyer will be deemed to have accepted the Property without confirmation of such restoration. Seller will have 7 days from the date of receipt of Buyer's notice within which to cause to be delivered to Buyer such confirmation. If written confirmation is not delivered to Buyer as required above, Buyer may terminate this contract and the earnest money will be refunded to Buyer. Seller's obligations under this paragraph are independent of any other obligations of Seller under this contract.

15. DEFAULT: If Buyer fails to comply with this contract, Buyer will be in default, and Seller may (a) enforce specific performance, seek such other relief as may be provided by law, or both, or (b) terminate this contract and receive the earnest money as liquidated damages, thereby releasing both parties from this contract. If Seller fails to comply with this contract for any other reason, Seller will be in default and Buyer may (a) enforce specific performance, seek such other relief as may be provided by law, or both, or (b) terminate this contract and receive the earnest money, thereby releasing both parties from this contract.

16. MEDIATION: It is the policy of the State of Texas to encourage resolution of disputes through alternative dispute resolution procedures such as mediation. Any dispute between Seller and Buyer related to this contract which is not resolved through informal discussion will be submitted to a mutually acceptable mediation service or provider. The parties to the mediation shall bear the mediation costs equally. This paragraph does not preclude a party from seeking equitable relief from a court of competent jurisdiction.

17. ATTORNEY'S FEES: A Buyer, Seller, Listing Broker, Other Broker, or escrow agent who prevails in any legal proceeding related to this contract is entitled to recover reasonable attorney's fees and all costs of such proceeding.

Initialed for identification by Buyer_____ _____ and Seller _____ _____   TREC NO. 30-12

Contract Concerning_____ 831 Silk Stocking Blvd. _____Page 6 of 8   11-2-2015
(Address of Property)

18. ESCROW:
  A. ESCROW: The escrow agent is not (i) a party to this contract and does not have liability for the performance or nonperformance of any party to this contract, (ii) liable for interest on the earnest money and (iii) liable for the loss of any earnest money caused by the failure of any financial institution in which the earnest money has been deposited unless the financial institution is acting as escrow agent.
  B. EXPENSES: At closing, the earnest money must be applied first to any cash down payment, then to Buyer's Expenses and any excess refunded to Buyer. If no closing occurs, escrow agent may: (i) require a written release of liability of the escrow agent from all parties, (ii) require payment of unpaid expenses incurred on behalf of a party, and (iii) only deduct from the earnest money the amount of unpaid expenses incurred on behalf of the party receiving the earnest money.
  C. DEMAND: Upon termination of this contract, either party or the escrow agent may send a release of earnest money to each party and the parties shall execute counterparts of the release and deliver same to the escrow agent. If either party fails to execute the release, either party may make a written demand to the escrow agent for the earnest money. If only one party makes written demand for the earnest money, escrow agent shall promptly provide a copy of the demand to the other party. If escrow agent does not receive written objection to the demand from the other party within 15 days, escrow agent may disburse the earnest money to the party making demand reduced by the amount of unpaid expenses incurred on behalf of the party receiving the earnest money and escrow agent may pay the same to the creditors. If escrow agent complies with the provisions of this paragraph, each party hereby releases escrow agent from all adverse claims related to the disbursal of the earnest money.
  D. DAMAGES: Any party who wrongfully fails or refuses to sign a release acceptable to the escrow agent within 7 days of receipt of the request will be liable to the other party for (i) damages; (ii) the earnest money; (iii) reasonable attorney's fees; and (iv) all costs of suit.
  E. NOTICES: Escrow agent's notices will be effective when sent in compliance with Paragraph 21. Notice of objection to the demand will be deemed effective upon receipt by escrow agent.
19. REPRESENTATIONS: All covenants, representations and warranties in this contract survive closing. If any representation of Seller in this contract is untrue on the Closing Date, Seller will be in default. Unless expressly prohibited by written agreement, Seller may continue to show the Property and receive, negotiate and accept back up offers.
20. FEDERAL TAX REQUIREMENTS: If Seller is a "foreign person," as defined by applicable law, or if Seller fails to deliver an affidavit to Buyer that Seller is not a "foreign person," then Buyer shall withhold from the sales proceeds an amount sufficient to comply with applicable tax law and deliver the same to the Internal Revenue Service together with appropriate tax forms. Internal Revenue Service regulations require filing written reports if currency in excess of specified amounts is received in the transaction.
21. NOTICES: All notices from one party to the other must be in writing and are effective when mailed to, hand-delivered at, or transmitted by fax or electronic transmission as follows:

To Buyer at: 11814 Landon James Park	**To Seller** at: 831 Upper Crust Blvd.
Silk Stocking, Texas 78711	Silk Stocking, Texas 78711
Phone: (555) 118-1953	Phone: (555) 061-1991
Fax: ( ) same as above	Fax: ( ) same as above
E-mail: JC Price @ itsus.com	E-mail: pparker@luna.net

22. AGREEMENT OF PARTIES: This contract contains the entire agreement of the parties and cannot be changed except by their written agreement. Addenda which are a part of this contract are (check all applicable boxes):

- ☐ Third Party Financing Addendum
- ☐ Loan Assumption Addendum
- ☐ Buyer's Temporary Residential Lease
- ☐ Seller's Temporary Residential Lease
- ☐ Addendum for Sale of Other Property by Buyer
- ☑ Addendum for "Back-Up" Contract
- ☐ Seller Financing Addendum
- ☐ Addendum for Coastal Area Property
- ☐ Short Sale Addendum
- ☐ Addendum for Seller's Disclosure of Information on Lead-based Paint and Lead-based Paint Hazards as Required by Federal Law

- ☐ Environmental Assessment, Threatened or Endangered Species and Wetlands Addendum
- ☐ Addendum for Property Located Seaward of the Gulf Intracoastal Waterway
- ☐ Addendum for Release of Liability on Assumption of FHA, VA, or Conventional Loan Restoration of Seller's Entitlement for VA Guaranteed Loan
- ☐ Addendum for Property in a Propane Gas System Service Area
- ☑ Other (list): Condo. Resale Certificate _____

Contract Concerning_____ 831 Silk Stocking Blvd. _____Page 7 of 8 11-2-2015
(Address of Property)

23. TERMINATION OPTION: For nominal consideration, the receipt of which is hereby acknowledged by Seller, and Buyer's agreement to pay Seller $_____100 (Option Fee) within 3 days after the effective date of this contract, Seller grants Buyer the unrestricted right to terminate this contract by giving notice of termination to Seller within _____5_____ days after the effective date of this contract (Option Period). Notices under this paragraph must be given by 5:00 p.m. (local time where the Property is located) by the date specified. If no dollar amount is stated as the Option Fee or if Buyer fails to pay the Option Fee to Seller within the time prescribed, this paragraph will not be a part of this contract and Buyer shall not have the unrestricted right to terminate this contract. If Buyer gives notice of termination within the time prescribed, the Option Fee will not be refunded; however, any earnest money will be refunded to Buyer. The Option Fee ❑will ❑will not be credited to the Sales Price at closing. **Time is of the essence for this paragraph and strict compliance with the time for performance is required.**

24. CONSULT AN ATTORNEY BEFORE SIGNING: TREC rules prohibit real estate license holders from giving legal advice. READ THIS CONTRACT CAREFULLY.

Buyer's
Attorney is: N/A _____

Seller's
Attorney is: N/A _____

Phone: (   ) _____

Fax: (   ) _____

E-mail: _____

Phone: (   ) _____

Fax: (   ) _____

E-mail: _____

EXECUTED the _____day of _____, 20_____ (EFFECTIVE DATE).
(BROKER: FILL IN THE DATE OF FINAL ACCEPTANCE.)

Buyer _____

Seller _____

Buyer _____

Seller _____

The form of this contract has been approved by the Texas Real Estate Commission. TREC forms are intended for use only by trained real estate license holders. No representation is made as to the legal validity or adequacy of any provision in any specific transactions. It is not intended for complex transactions. Texas Real Estate Commission, P.O. Box 12188, Austin, TX 78711-2188, (512) 936-3000 (http://www.trec.texas.gov) TREC NO. 30-12. This form replaces TREC NO. 30-11.

Initialed for identification by Buyer_____ _____ and Seller _____ _____   TREC NO. 30-12

Contract Concerning _____ 831 Upper Crust Blvd. _____ Page 8 of 8 11-2-2015
(Address of Property)

BROKER INFORMATION
(Print name(s) only. Do not sign)

Use Your Own Info here.

_____   _____
Other Broker Firm   License No.   Listing Broker Firm   License No.

represents ☐ Buyer only as Buyer's agent   represents ☐ Seller and Buyer as an intermediary
☐ Seller as Listing Broker's subagent   ☐ Seller only as Seller's agent

_____   _____
Associate's Name   License No.   Listing Associate's Name   License No.

_____   _____
Licensed Supervisor of Associate   License No.   Licensed Supervisor of Listing Associate   License No.

_____   _____
Other Broker's Address   Fax   Listing Broker's Office Address   Fax

_____   _____
City   State   Zip   City   State   Zip

_____   _____
Associate's Email Address   Phone   Listing Associate's Email Address   Phone

_____
Selling Associate's Name   License No.

_____
Licensed Supervisor of Selling Associate   License No.

_____
Selling Associate's Office Address   Fax

_____
City   State   Zip

_____
Selling Associate's Email Address   Phone

Listing Broker has agreed to pay Other Broker_____of the total sales price when the Listing Broker's fee is received. Escrow agent is authorized and directed to pay other Broker from Listing Broker's fee at closing.

OPTION FEE RECEIPT

Receipt of $_____100_____ (Option Fee) in the form of _Personal Check # 1215_ is acknowledged.

_____   _____
Seller or Listing Broker   Date

CONTRACT AND EARNEST MONEY RECEIPT

Receipt of ☐Contract and ☐$_____ Earnest Money in the form of _____
is acknowledged.
Escrow Agent: _____   Date: _____

By: _____
                                                    _____
                                                    Email Address

_____   Phone: (_____) _____
Address

_____   Fax: (_____) _____
City   State   Zip

Initialed for identification by Buyer_____ _____ and Seller _____ _____   TREC NO. 30-12

PROMULGATED BY THE TEXAS REAL ESTATE COMMISSION (TREC)   8-17-2015

CONDOMINIUM RESALE CERTIFICATE
(Section 82.157, Texas Property Code)

Condominium Certificate concerning Condominium Unit _____, in Building _____, of _____
_____,a condominium project, located at _____
_____(Address), City of _____,
County of _____, Texas, on behalf of the condominium owners' association
(the Association) by the Association's governing body (the Board).

A. The Declaration ☐does ☐does not contain a right of first refusal or other restraint that restricts
   the right to transfer the Unit. If a right of first refusal or other restraint exists, see Section
   _____of the Declaration.

B. The periodic common expense assessment for the Unit is $_____ per _____.

C. There ☐ is ☐is not a common expense or special assessment due and unpaid by the Seller to the
   Association. The total unpaid amount is $_____ and is for _____.

D. Other amounts ☐are ☐are not payable by Seller to the Association. The total unpaid amount is
   $_____and is for _____.

E. Capital expenditures approved by the Association for the next 12 months are $_____.

F. Reserves for capital expenditures are $_____;of this amount $_____
   has been designated for_____.

G. The current operating budget and balance sheet of the Association is attached.

H. The amount of unsatisfied judgments against the Association is $ _____.

I. There ☐are ☐are not any suits pending against the Association. The nature of the suits is
   _____.

J. The Association ☐does ☐does not provide insurance coverage for the benefit of unit owners as per
   the attached summary from the Association's insurance agent.

K. The Board ☐has ☐has no knowledge of alterations or improvements to the Unit or to the limited
   common elements assigned to the Unit or any portion of the project that violate any provision of the
   Declaration, by-laws or rules of the Association. Known violations are:_____
   _____.

L. The Board ☐has ☐has not received notice from a governmental authority concerning violations
   of health or building codes with respect to the Unit, the limited common elements assigned to the
   Unit, or any other portion of the condominium project. Notices received are: _____
   _____.

M. The remaining term of any leasehold estate that affects the condominium is _____
   and the provisions governing an extension or a renewal of the lease are: _____
   _____
   _____.

N. The Association's managing agent is _____
                                                         (Name of Agent)

_____
                              (Mailing Address)

_____   _____
            (Phone)   (Fax)

_____
                              (E-mail Address)

TREC NO. 32-4

Condominium Resale Certificate Concerning	Page 2 of 2

_____
(Address of Property)

O. Association fees resulting from the transfer of the unit described above:

Description	Paid To	Amount
_____	_____	_____
_____	_____	_____
_____	_____	_____

P. Required contribution, if any, to the capital reserves account $_____.

REQUIRED ATTACHMENTS:
1. Operating Budget
2. Insurance Summary
3. Balance Sheet

NOTICE: The Certificate must be prepared no more than three months before the date it is delivered to Buyer.

_____
Name of Association

By: _____

Name: _____

Title: _____

Date:_____

Mailing Address: _____

E-mail: _____

This form has been approved by the Texas Real Estate Commission for use with similarly approved or promulgated contract forms. Such approval relates to this form only. TREC forms are intended for use only by trained real estate license holders. No representation is made as to the legal validity or adequacy of any provision in any specific transactions. It is not suitable for complex transactions. Texas Real Estate Commission, P.O. Box 12188, Austin, TX 78711-2188, 512-936-3000 (http://www.trec.texas.gov) TREC No. 32-4. This form replaces TREC No. 32-3.

EQUAL HOUSING
OPPORTUNITY

PROMULGATED BY THE TEXAS REAL ESTATE COMMISSION (TREC)   12-05-11

ADDENDUM FOR
"BACK-UP" CONTRACT

TO CONTRACT CONCERNING THE PROPERTY AT

Unit 1 Bld. 7, 831 Upper Crust Blvd., Silk Stocking, TX 78711
(Address of Property)

A. The contract to which this Addendum is attached (the Back-Up Contract) is binding upon execution by the parties, and the earnest money and any Option Fee must be paid as provided in the Back-Up Contract. The Back-Up Contract is contingent upon the termination of a previous contract (the First Contract) dated _____June 3_____, 20__15____, for the sale of Property. Except as provided by this Addendum, neither party is required to perform under the Back-Up Contract while it is contingent upon the termination of the First Contract.

B. If the First Contract does not terminate on or before _November 1_____, 20__15____, the Back-Up Contract terminates and the earnest money will be refunded to Buyer. Seller must notify Buyer immediately of the termination of the First Contract. For purposes of performance, the effective date of the Back-Up Contract changes to the date Buyer receives notice of termination of the First Contract (Amended Effective Date).

C. An amendment or modification of the First Contract will not terminate the First Contract.

D. If Buyer has the unrestricted right to terminate the Back-Up Contract, the time for giving notice of termination begins on the effective date of the Back-Up Contract, continues after the Amended Effective Date and ends upon the expiration of Buyer's unrestricted right to terminate the Back-Up Contract.

E. For purposes of this Addendum, time is of the essence. Strict compliance with the times for performance stated herein is required.

_____   _____
Buyer   Seller

_____   _____
Buyer   Seller

This form has been approved by the Texas Real Estate Commission for use with similarly approved or promulgated contract forms. Such approval relates to this form only. TREC forms are intended for use only by trained real estate licensees. No representation is made as to the legal validity or adequacy of any provision in any specific transactions. It is not suitable for complex transactions. Texas Real Estate Commission, P.O. Box 12188, Austin, TX 78711-2188, 512-936-3000 (http://www.trec.texas.gov) TREC No. 11-7. This form replaces TREC No. 11-6.

INDEX